A Touch of Sleeve

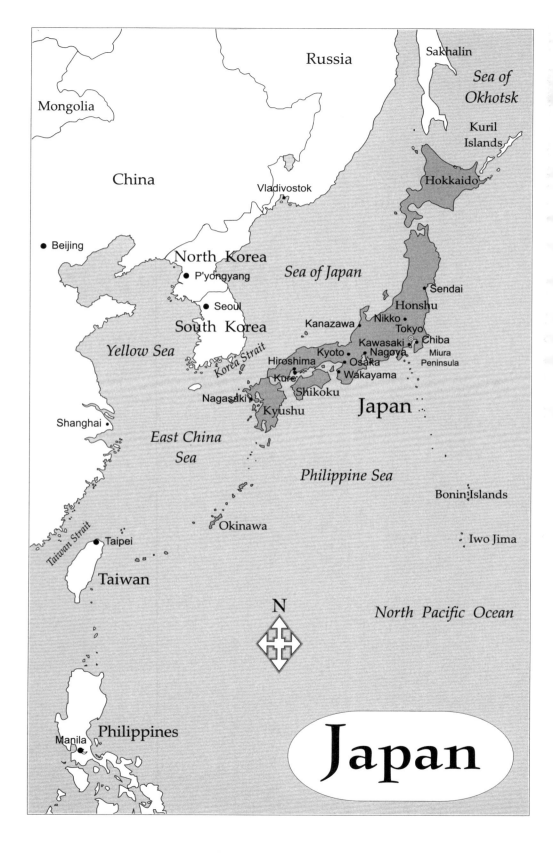

A Touch of Sleeve

Hisashi's Story

SUSAN BELL

Longacre Press

This book is dedicated to Hisashi

This book is copyright. Apart from any fair dealing for the purpose of private study, research, criticism or review, as permitted under the Copyright Act, no part may be reproduced by any process without prior permission of Longacre Press and the author.

Susan Bell asserts her moral right to be identified as the author of this work.

© Susan Bell

ISBN 978 1 877361 79 1

A catalogue record for this book is available from the National Library of New Zealand.

First published by Longacre Press, 2007
30 Moray Place, Dunedin, New Zealand.

Photographs are from the Furuya family collection unless otherwise credited. The poem by Jitsuzen on pages 59 and 60 were originally translated by Hisashi, and the version shown here is written by Emma Neale

Book and cover design by Christine Buess
Printed by Astra Print, Wellington, New Zealand

www.longacre.co.nz

CONTENTS

Map of Japan 2

Notes for the Reader 6

The Rise of Japan 7

Prologue 13

Hisashi's Family Tree 20

PART ONE: *Giri* to the Ages 21

PART TWO: *Giri* to the World 101

    Map of the Pacific Ocean 178

PART THREE: *Giri* to the Emperor 179

PART FOUR: *Giri* to His Name 259

PART FIVE: *Giri* Metamorphosed 413

    Epilogue 445

    Glossary 475

    Bibliography 481

    Acknowledgements 485

Notes for the Reader

A Touch of Sleeve: Hisashi's Story is written in chronological order, with dates shown according to the Western calendar. To help establish context, significant world events have been included in the footnotes. Every effort has been made to be accurate as regards dates and events.

The Japanese count a child's age from conception, so at birth, a child is one-year-old. However, ages in this book are in Western form.

Japanese words have been used when appropriate, including those commonly known, such as *kimono* and *tatami*, honorifics, and place names. The first time a Japanese word is used it is followed by its English meaning in brackets. A glossary of Japanese words is included on page 475.

Plurals do not exist in the Japanese language, for example *kimono* is used for the singular one *kimono*, as well as the plural many *kimono*.

Some names in the book have been changed, but those of Hisashi and his extended family have not. For the most part, names are written in the Western fashion with family name following the given name, however in Part Four they are written in Japanese style with a suffix attached to the proper name, such as Furuya-*san*, Yoshio-*kun*, and Yanagida-*shi*. The glossary explains the circumstances of their use.

In traditional Japan, including the period when Hisashi grew up, 'silence was preferred over eloquence'. To speak directly and frankly was considered rude. Relying on intuition and non-verbal communication, feelings were expressed in a restrained and indirect fashion, thus proverbs were popular. While they embody a general truth, proverbs are sufficiently vague so that their interpretation is up to the individual and will cause offence to no one. Japanese proverbs are used as chapter headings throughout the book.

CHRONOLOGY

The Rise of Japan

AEONS AGO GODDESS *Amaterasu-Omikami* sent her grandson Ninigi to rule over Japan – his descendents the first mortals to inhabit the land

660 B.C. First Emperor of Japan is enthroned

Kofun Period (A.D. 300–710)*

The rise of the Yamato dynasty; Buddhism and Confucianism arrive

Nara Period (710–794)

Adoption of all things Chinese, with Buddhism used officially to authorise the system of central government established in the capital of Nara

Heian Period (794–1185)

The age of the Imperial Court and the formation of private estates

794   Imperial capital established in *Heian* (present day Kyoto)

Kamakura Period (1185–1333)

Samurai seize political power from the Emperor. Buddhism is all-powerful

1192   First *shogun* establishes a military government in Kamakura

Muromachi Period (1333–1568)

Despite almost continuous civil war the arts flourish

1543   First Westerners, the Portuguese, arrive

Azuchi-momoyama Period (1568–1600)

After even more battles in the end the nation is unified

1583   **Hisashi's ancestor Bunzaemon goes into battle**

---

* Era Names: Prior to 1868, Japanese history was divided into periods named according to the location of the seat of power, however, following the *Meiji* Revolution, each era was identified by the name given to that particular Emperor's reign.

• 7

Edo Period (1600–1868)

Isolated from the world, suppressed under the caste system and reliant on a rice economy, a period of relative peace fosters urban growth; Edo the seat of power

1603	Ieyasu Tokugawa founds the Tokugawa *shogunate*
1620	**Hisashi's ancestor Sakuzaemon travels to Edo**
1639	Policy of National Seclusion fully enforced
1848	**Hisashi's paternal grandfather Hajime is born**
1851	**Hisashi's maternal grandfather Jitsuzen is born**
1853	Commodore Perry and his *kuro fune* sail into Edo Bay
1856	**Hisashi's paternal grandmother Tatsuko is born**
1861	**Jitsuzen enters the priesthood**

Meiji Period (1868–1912)

Restoration of Imperial Rule revives Shintoism and disestablishes Buddhism, Japan transformed into a modern Westernised industrial society

1867	The *Meiji* Revolution overthrows *shogunal* rule
	Edo renamed Tokyo and becomes the new capital
1871	Caste system abolished
1876	**Hisashi's maternal grandmother Umeko is born**
1880	**Hajime marries Tatsuko**
1884	**Their son, Hisashi's father, Jinjiro, is born**
1893	**Jitsuzen visits America**
	Tatsuko dies
1894/95	Japan wins Sino–Japanese war
1895	**Jitsuzen marries Umeko**
1896	**Their daughter, Hisashi's mother, Ryoko, is born**
1902	**Jinjiro migrates to America**
1904/05	Japan wins Russo–Japanese War
1909	**Hajime dies**
1910	Annexation of Korea

Taisho Period (1912–1926)
Educated urban middle class emerge along with budding democracy, the latter soon squashed

1914/18	Japan sides with Britain in World War I
1914/19	**Jinjiro serves on the navy's flagship *Mikasa***
1914	**Jinjiro marries Ryoko**
1920	**Their son, Hisashi, is born at the Kure Naval Base**
1922	**The Furuya family move to Tokyo**
	Hisashi's sister Eiko is born
1923	Tokyo earthquake
	Jitsuzen dies
1925	Peace Preservation Law restricts speech and assembly
	The Furuya family buy their own house

Showa Period (1926–1989)
Ultranationalist militarists seize power and embark on a campaign to expand the Japanese Empire through war. Post-defeat, under Allied Occupation, the country is democratised and undergoes unparalleled economic growth

1926	**Hisashi's brother Yoh is born**
	Hisashi starts primary school
1930	Great Depression hits Japan
	Yoh dies
	Hisashi's sister Yayoi is born
1931	Manchurian Incident
1932	Prime Minister Inukai assassinated
	Hisashi enters middle school
1933	Withdrawal from the League of Nations
1936	Abrogation of naval treaties signed with the West
	Unsuccessful coup d'etat staged by young military officers
1937	Outbreak of war with China
	Nanking massacre

1938	National Mobilisation Law prepares nation for all-out war
1939	**Hisashi enters high school**
	Britain and France declare war on Germany
1940	Advance into South East Asia
	Rationing begins
	Tripartite Pact signed with Germany and Italy
1941	ABCD Encirclement – trade embargo, imposed on Japan
	Attack on Pearl Harbour and outbreak of the Pacific War
	European and Pacific Wars merge as World War II
1942	Battle of Midway
	Hisashi enters university
1943	Withdrawal from Guadalcanal
1944	Saipan falls
	Hisashi graduates from university and joins the navy
1945	US 'carpet' raids begin on the Japanese mainland
	Iwo Jima and Okinawa fall
	Germany surrenders in Europe
	Atomic bombs dropped on Hiroshima and Nagasaki
	Occupation begins
1946	**Jinjiro dies**
1950	**Hisashi starts work at Standard Vacuum**
1950/53	Korean War
1952	Occupation ends
1964	Summer Olympic Games held in Tokyo
1973	Worldwide oil crisis
	Ryoko dies

Heisei Period (1989–)

The bubble economy collapses, resulting in a severe recession and post-war systems are reformed

1989	**Hisashi and Yayoi migrate to New Zealand**
1999	**Yayoi dies**
	Hisashi shifts to his townhouse in the retirement village

THE WORLD HAS BEEN PLUNGED into a dreadful darkness. Amaterasu-Omikami, the Heavenly-Shining-Sun-Goddess, has withdrawn her resplendent beauty. In his latest tantrum, her brother-husband Takehaya-Susanowo, the Valiant-Impetuous-Storm-God, has caused towering thunderclouds, rotating winds and torrential rain, which have destroyed the divisions of her sacred rice paddies. Deafening claps of thunder and fiery forks of lightning are spewing from his mouth. Frightened, Amaterasu shuts herself in the 'Cave of the High Plain of Heaven' and no one can persuade her to come out. Susanowo, banished to the Netherworld, slays an eight-headed dragon, pulling from its tail a sacred iron sword.

In the blackness there is no birth, no growth, no order, just darkness, misery, and mayhem. Evil spirits run wild. Strange noises fill the air. An aeon passes.

In desperation, the gods light a bonfire and make an enormous commotion. Curious, Amaterasu ventures to the entrance of the cave, immediately attracted by a glittering string of jewels and a burnished bronze mirror that have been hung on a tree. As she tries the necklace on, the gods quickly close up the cave. Looking into the mirror, Amaterasu sees the reflection of her ancestors, reminding her that she is a member of the same Yamato clan as all the other gods. They are not her enemy, not even Susanowo. Donning the necklace makes her conscious of her status and wealth.

The sun shines again. Warmth, harmony and order return.

Beneath the 'High Plain of Heaven', in a tranquil turquoise sea, lie the islands of *Nippon* (Japan), the first solid land in the universe. Amaterasu sends her grandson, Ninigi, to rule over *Nippon*.*

---

* Nippon means the source of the sun.

Descending in his carriage of clouds, the heavenly grandchild takes with him some grains of rice and the insignia of imperial power: Amaterasu's necklace and mirror, and Susanowo's sword. Equipped with wealth, weapons and pedigree, he is destined to rule the world. Stepping from his carriage onto a mountain top, Ninigi feels the earth beneath his feet. Above him, blending with the dazzling yellow sun, the cerulean heaven stretches to infinity.

Time passes on the beautiful earth. The heavenly grandchild rules wisely in the land created by his heavenly forebears. He marries Sengen, the Goddess-of-Flowering-Trees, who inhabits the sacred Mount Fuji. Their first descendants are mortals. Jimmu Tennou, their great grandson, is the first Emperor of *Nippon*, enthroned in 660 B.C.*

All Emperors of *Nippon* are descendants of Amaterasau. Thus all Emperors of *Nippon* are 'living gods'. Accordingly, it is natural and inevitable that the world should fall under *Nipponese* rule.

---

* In India Gotama the Buddha gives his first sermon in 528 B.C. In China Confucius begins teaching in 520 B.C.

Prologue

Kuchi akete harawata miseru kawazu kana
Behold the frog who opens his mouth
to display his whole inside

THERE IS A SAYING IN JAPAN about a frog that opens its mouth to display its inside. By exposing its inside, the frog brings great shame upon itself.

Perhaps this saying is one reason little is known in the Western world about Japan and how its citizens fared following the 1941 attack on Pearl Harbour and the consequent occupation by foreign troops after the fighting stopped. However, one old man does not care about exposing his 'inner self' to public view. He has things he wants to say and, by chance, he wanted to say them to me.

In doing so he made himself vulnerable, allowing me to see the twists and turns of fortune's wheel; the contrasts of light and shade that occurred throughout his life. This is the story of a man who unconditionally entrusted me with his story, gifting me the benefit of his wisdom. Until he met me, Hisashi had never revealed his thoughts to anyone.

I did not set out to write this book. It just evolved from listening to Hisashi talk – he kept me enthralled, and I was unable to let go until I had pieced together his story. People always want to know how we met, and why he lives so far from Japan: in Dunedin, New Zealand. For a Japanese of Hisashi's generation, it was most unusual for him to choose to migrate. He says he is 'out of specification' and does not fit the stereotype of his peers.

Yayoi and Hisashi Furuya have long been part of my extended

family, and we have never seen our relationship as unusual. I met them in 1991, two years after they moved to Dunedin. Soon after their arrival they opened a souvenir shop. At that time I worked for a tertiary institution, coordinating groups of Japanese students who came for short-term study tours. As part of the programme we offered discount shopping so I approached the Furuyas to see if they would advertise in our promotional booklet. When I met them, I had assumed they were husband and wife, though they were in fact brother and sister, both single. And although they were older than my parents, I still had a sense that somehow they would become an important part of my life.

Hisashi has a fondness for proverbs: it's not unusual for him to quote one in conversation. He even has one to describe our meeting. '*Sode suriaumo tashono en*', which means 'When our sleeves touch it is karma'. He explains: 'You may think your sleeve touching with that of an unknown person passing by is a minor occurrence, but it is not. Even a chance meeting is due to karma in a previous life. During a lifetime you meet few of the world's vast population, so someone you do meet has been thrown in your way by chance.' Our friendship was inevitable. But little did I know my own background had been preparing me for it.

Until I met Hisashi and Yayoi, my perception of Japan relied on stereotypes. To me it was a mysterious, exotic land, where *geisha* (practitioners of the arts) served tea, *samurai* (warriors) strutted, priests whispered in prayer, and cherry blossom fell like confetti. At primary school I had absorbed such memorable images and, as a young girl, had fallen in love with the myth. I still have a project on Japan I did at school. Hisashi was intrigued to read it and thinks my encounter with Japan as a child was yet another 'touch of sleeve'. He says my experience remained unconsciously in my mind, and from that small seed my interest in Japanese culture grew.

But modern Japan presents a startlingly different picture. As the home of my Toshiba laptop and Pentax camera, and numerous makes of cars, Japan is easily viewed through a separate but still stereotypical lens. Juggling ancient stone lanterns with neon signs, an embroidered *kimono* (Japanese gown) with cutting-edge fashion, tolling temple bells with the din of modern industry, exquisitely presented dishes of *sashimi* (raw seafood) with plastic displays of fast foods, the serenity of meditation with the brutality of its soldiers in World War II, Japan presents facets of itself both bewildering and disconcerting.

For ten years I travelled overseas for work, visiting Japan many times. But it was not until starting our research for this book that I began to appreciate its complexities. Initially the Tokyo I saw was far from that of my schoolgirl imaginings. However, as I looked more carefully, I discovered a different city existed. I love to travel, as did my great-grandfather. In 1922 he took my 19-year-old grandmother around Asia on a Japanese cruise ship, my grandmother falling hopelessly in love with the young Japanese Purser. I have a letter he wrote to her. Maybe this prior 'touch of sleeve' lent a hand in fostering the empathy that drew me to the Furuyas.

Sadly, Yayoi died in July 1999, in Dunedin, just before her seventieth birthday. Hisashi was 79. Afterwards he gave me a beautiful grey coat that belonged to his mother.

I love my grey coat. Made of cashmere, it is sensuously soft, lined with silver-grey silk, and secured inside with silk ties. It has deep, broad sleeves, a high roll collar, wraps over in the front and fastens with three self-covered buttons, enfolding me snugly. Unmistakably a blend of East and West, its simple line, the fall of the sleeves, the drop of the collar, and the drape of the back, reflect the cut and swathe of a *kimono*. But it also has Western style, is functional and the epitome of modern chic.

I am certain there is no other coat like it in the world. I know it makes me look good. But there is much more to my coat that captures my imagination, inspired as it was by centuries of Japanese design. Its immaculate condition belies its age and history. When I unwrapped it, it had been folded away for 30 years. My coat represents the past and present. Here I am today, a tall, fair-skinned Western career woman wearing a coat tailored 70 years ago for Ryoko Furuya, a short, honey-skinned Japanese matron. It reaches my knees; for Ryoko it was ankle length.

Ryoko had purchased her coat in 1934 from a seamstress who had set up her own business after being discharged from her job in a Tokyo department store. In the ultra-nationalistic Japanese society of the time, such department stores had been forced to discontinue the sale of Western clothing. The grey coat survived the war. Buried alongside other household items, it escaped the air raids, and was kept rather than sold to buy food during the long period of postwar hardship. It was not until 14 years later that Ryoko wore it again, and then only on special occasions.

My beautiful coat carries a story of 70 eventful years, beginning with the hopes and dreams of the seamstress who demonstrated her skill in its tailoring. Being able to afford such a high-quality garment affirmed Ryoko's status in society. It was folded away during the long years of adversity during and after World War II, and this simply served to enhance her pleasure when she eventually wore it again. Today it hangs in my wardrobe. Would the seamstress approve of me wearing it? Would Ryoko?

This coat has crossed two cultures and generations, worn by two different women, but perfectly suiting us both. My grey cashmere coat makes me feel special, connecting me to the past and to the history of Japan, as well as to the Furuya family. It gives me hope for the future, showing friendships can cross cultures even between nationalities that 60 years earlier were enemies. I treasure this coat and feel privileged that it is mine.

This story centres on Hisashi. But to understand him and his perspective, I needed to fit his family into an historical context, learning about Buddhism, the family system, the Meiji Revolution, and the dichotomy of the Japanese character. As we traced the Furuya family history, I slowly began to build the story of their lives. Set against events preceding, during, and following World War II, this saga gives a picture of the times within which Hisashi grew up, and which shaped the man he is today.

His facial expression portrays a man who is mild, upright and wise. However, he is also unassuming and, whenever I mention his wisdom, he tells me not to exaggerate. He is insatiably curious, widely read, with a vast general knowledge, and able to hold a discussion on just about any topic. I was intrigued when one of the first questions he ever asked me was whether my mother had sung lullabies to me as a child.

My understanding and knowledge of Hisashi and Japan have unfolded like a Japanese garden. When he felt I was ready, Hisashi would reveal the next concept, the next example, according to the notion that things should be discovered slowly, one by one, giving me time to appreciate fully what I was learning.

He is pleased with my progress, and says he has taught me all he can. His birthday gift to me in 2005 meant I had reached the level he had hoped I would achieve: an English copy of *I am a Cat*, written by Soseki Natsume and published in 1905. A stray cat observes human nature. Through its eyes, Natsume comments on the social upheaval of the Meiji era; the biting words would have been unacceptable if he had written them as himself. A hundred years later, I am Hisashi's cat. Through my eyes his observations and commentary are more palatable than if he wrote them himself.

However, even with everything I have learned, I would never presume to think I fully know Hisashi or Japan. As a Westerner I can never completely understand. Likewise, Hisashi will continue to be bemused, sometimes confused, by the way we Westerners think and act.

I am not an historian. The story told here is Hisashi's interpretation of events, both at the time, and in hindsight. So the reader can experience the settings and share the emotions of the people whose lives we have pieced together, I have imagined and described scenarios, to try to convey life at the time. Sometimes the pace is fast and traumatic, other times slow and calm, reflecting the duality of the Japanese personality. Initially I focussed on ensuring my voice did not intrude. However, in reality, my questions with their Western slant have shaped the story into something other than what Hisashi would have written himself. As he says, his story has been written 'through my blue eyes'.

Part One

Giri to the Ages

Ko wa oya wo utsusu kagami
As the old birds sing, so the young ones twitter

Starting with his ancestors, Hisashi begins his story. I hope that learning about their lives, interwoven with the history of the day, brings you closer to appreciating what it means to be Japanese. Hisashi's story is the story of Japan. The story of Japan is Hisashi's story.

Picture a *samurai* honing his swordsmanship. Picture a Buddhist priest studying classical literature. Both pictures could be Hisashi. His ancient lineage on both sides of his family is *samurai* caste, and more recently his maternal grandfather was a highly ranked priest. However, while Hisashi only narrowly escaped becoming a priest, there was no chance of him becoming a *samurai*. The classical warrior caste disappeared 50 years before he was born. Nevertheless, those traits are inherent in his character, echoing the mystique of old Japan.

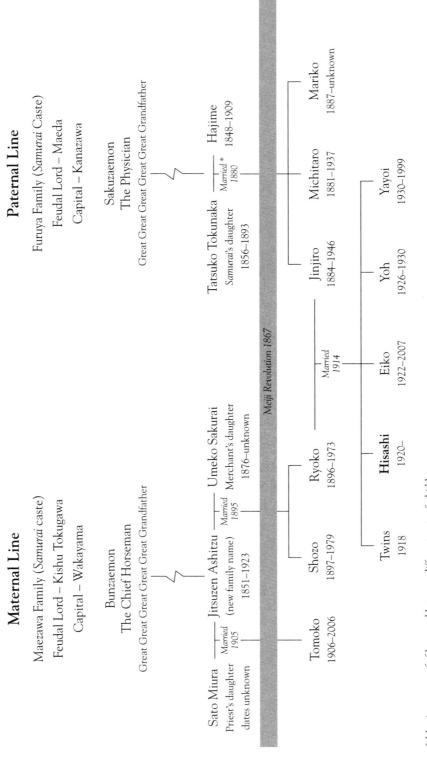

Chapter 1

The Way of the Samurai

Shinimono gurui
Leaping into the jaws of death without hesitation

SAMURAI WERE BORN, not made, and personified the ideal of the Japanese race.

It is 1583,* the year of the sheep. The sun shimmers on the grass. Some distance apart two bands of warriors wait. Encased in leather, lacquer and metal link, two sword handles protruding from their girdles, their heads hidden behind horned helmets, they are a terrifying sight. Thus garbed they will fight to the death, never surrendering, never being taken prisoner, dying when it is right to die.

One – Bunzaemon – breaks from their ranks. Astride his sweating steed, he brings his mount to a halt midway. He is calm. Single-mindedly he zeroes in on one man, marking his worthy prey. Every fibre of his being is focussed on winning, his opponent as prepared as him. He shouts his challenge.

Galloping straight for each other, the combatants collide, leaping to the ground, drawing long, lethal swords. Like a hawk, Bunzaemon swoops. Hit first, hit hard. Without wavering, he strikes, catching his opponent before he has assumed his fighting stance. Blades flash in the sun, the air fills with the clang of metal and guttural cries.

---
* Colombus discovers the American continent in 1498.

Bunzaemon strikes to kill. Suddenly it is over and a warrior lies still. With a slash, Bunzaemon cuts off his victim's head. Beneath his helmet, Bunzaemon's face is serene, his honour intact. The battle proper begins.

Bunzaemon valued honour above all else, demanding perfection on and off the battlefield. Cowardice, failure or surrender would have meant the loss of his honour. Preferring death to dishonour, he would have committed *seppuku* (suicide by piercing the abdomen)* ritually disembowelling himself. Only an honourable suicide would clear his name. He was a man instilled with *gishi* (rectitude), judged 'a jewel that shone brightest'.

Bunzaemon Maezawa was Hisashi's maternal great-great-great-great-great-grandfather. Possessed of an honoured family name, Bunzaemon was born into a family of retainers in the powerful Kishu Tokugawa fiefdom in Wakayama, his hereditary status that of chief horseman, caring for his lord's favourite steed. His status was fixed.

From a young age, often in pain, he had been trained for battle, his mind and body programmed, imbuing him with stamina and daring. His parents would scold him and call him a coward if he cried, making him go without food. By exercise and example, he had been taught to endure and behave correctly. He had to brave the dark alone and to meet strangers in unfamiliar places. In winter he had to walk to school with bare feet. Sometimes he had to stay awake all night, taking his turn to read aloud. Thus he was inured against hunger, fear, cold and lack of sleep. He learned polite behaviour and speech, how to serve others, how to read and write, and even the correct way to walk down the street. He learned to fire a bow and arrow, ride, wrestle and swim, but foremost was the art of the sword, which he practised daily for hours.

By the time Bunzaemon was 15 he was a fully fledged warrior,

---

* *Seppuku* was the exclusive right of nobles and *samurai*.

easily identified by his dress and his hair styled in a topknot. Required to wear two swords, one long and one short, he dusted and polished them daily, wearing them sheathed, tucked through his *obi* (*kimono* sash). For his rite of passage he beheaded six convicts. Yet there was another side to the life of a *samurai*. Bunzaemon wrote poetry, hosted the tea ceremony, arranged flowers, and gazed at the beauty of the moon, maple leaves, and cherry blossom.

> On the day of the battle, Bunzaemon wakes before dawn. After bathing in cold water, he cuts his nails and shaves his forehead. He then oils his hair, gathers it into a queue and doubles it back over his crown, tying it where it doubles and cutting off the end. As is customary he saves a few strands, enclosing them in rice paper for his wife. As a warrior, he knows he is destined to die young and the routine of his scrupulous grooming hardens his resolve to die in battle.
>
> He sits cross-legged for two hours before the family altar. Beside the altar, in a sturdy vase, a bough of cherry blossom inspires a feeling of affinity, reminding him of the transience of his own life. Falling to the ground, still in their prime, the fragile blooms come and go quickly. Like all *samurai*, Bunzaemon regards dying in his prime as a thing of great pride and beauty. He reports to his ancestors that he is going into battle, resolved to die. He requests their permission to lose his life in protecting his lord and his earthly family, asking also that the Buddha favours his family after his death. Finally, he meditates on his inevitable death, imagining himself slashed by his opponent's sword, falling to the ground, blood gushing from a gaping wound in his chest. His mind at peace, he is reconciled to his inevitable death.
>
> He dresses in his best silk under-jacket and pantaloons,* their design, fabric, colour and number of stitches consistent with his importance. Stored with resinous balls of incense, the fabric contains

---

* There were 216 rules that spelt out permissible caste dress. Only the ruling class dressed in silk *kimono*. Commoners wore cotton, though wealthy farmers and merchants overcame the rule by lining their *kimono* with embroidered silks.

the lingering scent of sandalwood.* His black linked armour made of small iron plates is arranged neatly over the top, his master's *mon* (crest) inscribed on a banner across his back. In his pantaloons pocket he puts three copper coins to pay his ferry fare across the mythical *River Sanzu* to the Buddhist Styx.

He is ready, prepared and willing to die for his lord, his mind and body honed to perfection. He picks up his sword and his metal helmet. As he walks through his gate he considers himself already dead.

The *samurai* ideals of behaviour were derived from Shinto (the indigenous religion), Confucianism (Chinese philosophy), and Buddhism (a widespread Asian religion). Despite the passage of centuries and changes in political and personal lives, the *samurai* code continued to permeate society and was still, unconsciously perhaps, part of Hisashi's upbringing, shaping his character and spiritual outlook on life. He inherited not only Bunzaemon's genes, but his attitude to life, his stoicism, loyalty and integrity, his appreciation of all things beautiful, and his preparedness for death.

Shinto, which means 'The Way of the Gods', endowed Bunzaemon with nationalistic beliefs in the divine importance of the Emperor and of Japan. Followers venerated the forces of nature, and recognised ancestors and heroes as protective gods called *kami*. There were great deities such as Amaterasu and Susanowo, and lesser gods who dwelled in stones, streams, trees, houses and stars. *Kami* were the source of good fortune, as well as providing protection from the cruelties of life.

Confucianism required that Bunzaemon put his lord first, before family or friends. Though not a religion, Confucianism had been absorbed into Buddhist philosophy when it arrived in Japan, and

---

* Smell was important and, like everything else, there were perfumes per class: sandalwood and musk for the elite, cedar or camphor for lower classes. For those who could not afford to store their clothes with balls of incense, it was common for both sexes to carry a tiny bag containing lesser perfumes in the sleeve of their *kimono*, or attached to their *obi*. These released a pleasing perfume as they moved.

provided a set of moral codes on which to form the basis of a social and political hierarchy.

From Buddhism, Bunzaemon learned that life was temporary, which gave him a no-nonsense reason to face death with composure. Dying a death of honour, giving his life for others, had for him greater value than his own life. Buddhism recognised that men have always been and always will be destined to fight and kill each other, the weak the victims of the strong. He accepted the inevitability of suffering, recognising his powerlessness against it. But by detaching himself from worldly desires, and disciplining his mind without thought of himself, he was liberated from suffering.

Before the arrival of Buddhism,* there was only Shinto, an undemanding practice with no official theology or holy books. Easily accepted, partly because its dissimilarity to Shinto represented little threat, and partly because it was immediately modified, Buddhism was simply added to existing rituals and customs.

Buddhism was founded by a particular person, while Shinto had evolved from the beliefs of the original inhabitants, who had embraced Shamanism from northern Europe, Siberia and Alaska. Shinto focussed on daily life; Buddhism prepared for the afterlife. Shinto had an infinite number of gods; Buddhism had one god, Buddha. Shinto believers worshipped in shrines; Buddhist believers worshipped in temples. Often shrines and temples stood side by side, the shrine protecting the Buddha.

So the rhythm of people's lives was dictated to by a mixture of Shinto, Confucianism and Buddhism: their diverse beliefs and rites co-existing in harmony, though Buddhism was all powerful. Japanese society was based on the principle of mutual dependence, essentially a moral code espousing reciprocal obligations, with antagonistic feelings and individual rivalry suppressed for the sake of harmony.

---

* From India, through China and Korea, Buddhism reached Japan in the mid sixth century; though it had absorbed so many other philosophies before its arrival it had changed radically from the original version.

The concepts of *on* and *giri* arrived with Buddhism and Confucianism.* Throughout his life, with every interaction and association, Bunzaemon passively received *on* (a hierarchy of obligations), rendering him endlessly indebted: to the *shogun* (literally the 'barbarian-subduing Great General') and his *daimyo* (lord); to his parents and teachers; and to his ancestors. The instant his obligation became onerous, *giri* stopped him from shirking. Giri (right reason, implying the obligation to repay *on*) was huge and debts were repaid in accordance with the favour received.

There was his '*giri* to the world', including his Kishu Tokugawa *daimyo*, his extended family, and for gifts or loans he was given; and his '*giri* to the Maezawa family name', such as clearing his reputation or taking revenge after an insult, as well as observing all 'respect behaviour', living within his 'proper station', and curbing his emotions. Most importantly, 'to know *giri*' meant having selflessly to devote himself to his *daimyo*, to whom he owed everything. In repaying his *giri*, Bunzaemon was even prepared to sacrifice his life. If he failed in his *giri*, his *haji* (shame) would be unbearable.

Gimu required the full, unconditional repayment of every debt: his duty to *shogun* Toyotomi Hideyoshi, the law, and Japan; his duty to his parents and ancestors; and his duty to his work – even when it was to his own disadvantage. Neither should he forget his benevolence and charity to others.

These forces began with Hisashi's ancestors, and continue to influence and affect his behaviour to this day.

---

* The 'Schematic Table of Japanese Obligations and their Reciprocals' is shown on p116 of *The Chrysanthemum and the Sword* by Ruth Benedict.

Chapter 2

Warrior, Farmer, Craftsman, Merchant

Kirisute-gomen
Cut, throw away, pardon

JAPANESE SOCIETY REMAINED UNCHANGED for a thousand years. Even with cosmetic changes, the traditional way of thinking was still very much part of Hisashi's way of thinking and, as the teacher, he knew that, for me to understand him, I needed to understand the social structures into which he had been born.

Modelled on the Confucian belief that a stable and happy society relied on order and hierarchy, Japan had been ruled by Emperors in direct succession from Her-Heavenly-Highness Amaterasu-Omikami. However, by the twelfth century the imperial family had become so weak they could not control crime, so rich landholders recruited their own armies of *samurai*, meaning 'one who serves'. Ongoing civil wars enveloped the country for centuries, the first *shogun* seizing power in 1192 and establishing a *bakufu* or *shogunate* (military government), with the Emperor a figurehead confined within his court of hereditary nobles.* Underpinned by fatalism, survival depended on an unchanging social order, with society divided into four castes.

Everyone knew their 'proper place', and there was no movement

---

* Around that time: the Magna Carta was issued by King John of England in 1215; the Incas settled at Cuzco in 1250; and Venetian Marco Polo set out on his journey to the court of the Mongol Emperor Kublai Khan in 1271.

between castes. First, came the *samurai* caste including the *shogun* and 600 *daimyo* who controlled large fiefdoms. Important positions and territories went to the 'Inside Lords', a *shogun*'s most loyal supporters. Some clans collapsed; others expanded. The *daimyo* built castles to show their strength and to defend themselves. Towns grew up around the castles, with the *samurai* at the core, and artisans and merchants settling on the outskirts. The *samurai* tradition flourished, and 400 years later Bunzaemon still followed the old ways.

Next were the farmers who, at 80 per cent of the population, were important for the food they grew and the economic power their rice crops gave each fiefdom.* Then came the artisans, who made useful goods; with merchants, considered parasites for enriching themselves off another's toil, they occupied bottom place.

Forcing everyone into villages, the *daimyo* established control over the agricultural world. Leasing land to a limited few,** they received over half the rice harvest in taxes, though much of that was paid to the *shogun*. Each village served a particular industry, with its own temple and school of Buddhism for the particular caste. Births, marriages and deaths had to be registered at the temple; thus the government could determine the rice revenue from each fiefdom. This record keeping also meant priests were of high status. Not ranked within the caste system, they were protected and used by the government to administer the census.† Below the recognised castes were the *hinin* (non-humans): beggars, prostitutes, fugitives and itinerant entertainers. Below them again, were the *eta* (full of filth), including torturers, executioners and corpse handlers, slaughterers of animals, skinners, tanners and leather workers.

Each *shogun* ruled as he liked. However, his power depended on

---

* Rice was ever-present: for the wealthy, served daily in bowls and turned into fiery wine; for hired workers, as rice cakes at New Year. The *samurai*'s stipend was calculated in rice.

** Rice plots ranged in size from a fraction of an acre to 4 or 5 acres (16–20 hectares).

† Self-supporting, the temples generated income from the paddy fields allotted them, and from public donations demanded for the performance of official duties.

the loyalty of his *samurai*, so he treated them well. The imperial sword of Japan had been pulled from the tail of the dragon by Susanowo, thus the sword was sacred, only permitted for nobles and *samurai* who enjoyed the right of *kirisute-gomen* (cut, throw away, pardon).

Every social interaction indicated status. Every corner of life was constrained by laws regulating where people lived: the size, design and structure of their homes; and even the size and style of storage chests, lanterns and children's toys. Clothing, too, proclaimed importance, allowing people to interact appropriately. How and to whom one spoke was stipulated and it was forbidden to speak directly to a superior. A wise man spoke vaguely, proverbs in abundance – a subtle statement considered more polite than a frank explanation. To whom and how much one bowed was stipulated.

Restrictions were huge, but they created order and security. People could trust a dependable world, though ruthless punishments were meted out by magistrates to those who strayed. Primary communities were collectives of 40 homes, within which each family member was answerable to the head of the family, the individual household answerable to groups of households, and all the households answerable to the community headman. A misdemeanour of any member brought down punishment on the whole community. Smaller five-family associations, *gonin-gumi*, were directly responsible for each other: one household being responsible for its actions to the two families on either side, as well as the two families opposite.

In the mid sixteenth century, Japan's world had expanded rapidly with the arrival first of the Portuguese and Spanish, then the Dutch and English, who brought new religions and technology like clocks and guns. For a time the *gaijin* (foreigners) had been tolerated; then quarrels arose between them. Each would warn the Japanese that the other was not to be trusted. Concerned about its increasing influence, the government suspected Christianity was a cloak for those wanting to colonise Japan. The fear that the Christian belief in one God was weakening their authority, meant isolation seemed the only way to prevent colonisation. The then government embarked on a campaign to protect the nation from foreign influence, in particular missionaries, and in 1614 Christianity was outlawed, with most *gaijin* driven from the country. Only a handful remained under strict supervision and limited to specific areas.

In 1603, Ieyasu Tokugawa had come to power, his dynasty dominating the next two-and-a-half centuries in comparative peace. However, people's freedom was even more restricted. The government forbade movement between territories, and between *daimyo*, the thinking being that, if people could move freely, it would be easier to rebel. Economic power relied on labour and rice production, a *daimyo*'s crucial source of income. If workers left it would cause a labour shortage, which would affect production, the *daimyo*'s wealth, and ultimately the government's power.

All foreign vessels, except those from Holland, China and Korea, were forbidden entry into Japanese waters. Foreign books were banned. It was a capital offence to build a boat larger than 90 tons. Overseas trade and travel was forbidden on pain of death. Japan remained isolated from the rest of the world for some 240 years.

In the bourgeoning urban society, fewer than two million of the country's 30 million people were *samurai*, and the *samurai* indulged in unrestrained tyranny. Warriors without a war to fight, they were forced to live in castle towns, unable to change career or caste. The model *samurai* now aspired to the Confucian ideal of man as both warrior and scholar. Many became bureaucrats, the remaining 260 *daimyo* having greater need for educated administrators than warriors. But with insufficient work for them all, many *samurai* spent their time looking for entertainment or trouble, and falling into debt through luxurious living. Hisashi claims the Tokugawa regime cunningly destabilised the strength of its subordinates to prevent rebellion, ensuring the obedience of the *daimyo* by keeping them financially strapped.

Kyoto,* home of the Emperor, was still the capital, but from 1603 the seat of power was in Edo, modern day Tokyo. *Daimyo* were required to reside in Edo every alternate year. They could then return to their fiefdom, but their families stayed in Edo – in effect hostages. The cost of maintaining two households, and the expensive, time-consuming processions to and from Edo, meant *daimyo* had neither the time nor the funds to be a serious threat to the regime. It was the same for the *samurai*, who on fixed salaries were tied to their hereditary *daimyo*.

Bunzaemon would spend much of every year apart from his family, who were cloistered in Edo. It was the same for Sakuzaemon Furuya, Hisashi's paternal great-great-great-great-great-grandfather, a *samurai* born into a family of learned physicians in hereditary service to their *daimyo*, Maeda.

---

* Kyoto, with a population of nearly 400 000, was built to model the Chinese Tang dynasty capital, contemporary Xian; in its centre was the palace, where successive Emperors lived in secluded helplessness.

Chapter 3

The Flowering of Edo

Sankin kotai
Hostages in a gilded cage

The slow moving, 400-strong entourage enters the outer gates of Edo at Shinagawa. In 1620,* it is a long and arduous trip from Kanazawa on the west coast to Edo on the east, and Sakuzaemon is tired.

TWELVE DAYS TO KYOTO by way of a second class *kaido* (highway), then another 30 days along the 600-kilometre Tokaido.† Like all major *kaido*, the Tokaido was served by post-stations with inns, teahouses, restaurants, stalls and unlicensed brothels. Rugged and mountainous, Japan stretched from the cold northeast to the semitropical southwest. Summers were very hot, the Pacific winds bringing high temperatures and humidity. By contrast, winters were very cold, with winds from the Asian mainland blowing snow across much of the country. Travelling through the wild countryside was dangerous and intentionally inconvenient. With numerous rivers, the Tokugawa government forced the use of water transportation. But building bridges over rivers that interrupted trunk roads was prohibited. The poor roads, lack of bridges, and numerous checkpoints controlled movement, making it impossible for *daimyo* armies to move in secret to attack the *shogun*. But still, traffic was dense.

---

* The same year, the Pilgrim Fathers sail for America.
† The Tokaido is the Edo to Kyoto highway.

Along narrow zigzagging paths littered with stones, over tortuous mountain terrain, across fragile bridges straddling yawning gullies and rushing streams, through valleys, forests, and marshlands, past villages, castles, temples, and shrines, *daimyo* Maeda's mandatory escort, banners aloft with his *mon*, proceeds along the Tokaido bound for Edo. Large sections of the *kaido* are flanked with tall, thickly planted cedar, forming windbreaks and making it difficult for travellers to go astray.

At the overnight post-station at Kawasaki beside the Tama-*gawa* (*gawa* means river) the exhausted travellers eat, rest and hire new porters and horses. Many buy new straw sandals. Now on this their final day, they set out. With no bridge over the Tama, they cross according to their status; in litters, on the shoulders of porters, or wading through the waist-deep water.

Back on land, grunting rhythmically and jogging with their stiff-legged gait, Maeda's porters carry him shoulder high in a *palanquin* (portable litter). Immediately behind are a dozen *samurai* on horseback, then several officials and priests in screened oxen-drawn carts, followed by 130 marching men, 100 servants and 200 hired porters: the requisite group considered no threat to the government.

Maeda's physician, Sakuzaemon Furuya, rides directly behind the *palanquin*. Like the other mounted men, he wears a divided skirt and a *kimono*-shaped jacket with padded shoulders, but unlike them his hair is cropped short, the style setting his profession apart. Dressed in blues, browns and greys the sea of men march behind him. The foot soldiers wear leggings, their breeches caught up at the knee, their half-coats characteristically lifted at the back by their swords.

Ahead of the procession, pilgrims head for a shrine. A peasant leads an ox. A woman carries a bundle of branches on her head. A *hinin* hauls his cart. 'Down, down!' shout the procession leaders. The commoners prostrate themselves on the side of the *kaido*. Without fear of reprisal, a foot soldier breaks rank, unsheathes his new sword and slashes the *hinin* to death.

Entering the Edo boundary, Maeda's entourage stops at the Shinagawagate, where customs officials check their travel documents, and search for females, farmers, muskets and merchant invoices. Spies keep the *shogun* well informed of a *daimyo*'s activities and expenses.

A man caught evading the barrier has just been decapitated, his head skewered on a stake; his now shaven-headed female companion is up for sale.

Edo, literally 'river town', was ideally located at the confluence of the three principal rivers: Edo-*gawa*, Sumida-*gawa* and Tama-*gawa*. Once a humble village, its population had grown to nearly a million by 1620. Three hundred years later the footprint of Edo would still be seen in Hisashi's boyhood Tokyo. But back in 1620…

The city was an impregnable stronghold: bordered to the west by mountains, to the east by the Pacific Ocean, to the south by the Tama-*gawa*, and to the northeast by the Edo-*gawa*. While the open sea provided easy access for supplies, the marshy tidal flats could not be built on. So channels had been dug, rivers diverted and hills reduced, with the excavated earth having been dumped into the lagoon, turning the waterfront into an efficient network of interconnecting canals and docklands. Reclamation had transformed the city. At its centre was Edo castle, guarded by a complex system of moats; immense stone ramparts sloped into the water at such angles that they were impossible to scale.

Carefully planned, the city radiated around the castle, land allocated according to caste and deliberately separated into different worlds. Substantial buildings clung to the hillsides. On the flat, an ocean of tiled roofs of smaller wooden structures were tightly packed in a maze of narrow alleys. Encircling the outer city, shrines and temples provided spiritual protection. A complex labyrinth of blind alleys, bridgeless waterways and narrow lanes that turned at right angles kept out unwanted visitors. Each enclave had only one gate opening onto a public road and watchtowers commanded a view over the neighbourhood. Where the five main *kaido* cut the outer circle of Edo, such as at Shinagawa, even bigger gates secured the boundary.

From Shinagawa the procession crosses the narrow strip of coastland to Takanawa. Fishing fleets are bringing home the daily catch, many boats already anchored in Edo Bay. Keeping to the *Tokaido*, the city's central conduit, they flow northwards. To the left Mount Fuji floats above the city; then there is Edo castle outlined against the skyline. On the hills behind the castle was *Yamanote* (Uptown), where the sprawling estates of the elite, including Bunzaemon's *daimyo*, form a bulwark on the western boundary. The *shogun*'s other most trusted supporters live in mansions in *Marunouchi* (meaning within the castle walls), which buffers the castle from the commoners.

Maeda's men press on through the thriving commercial centre that is concentrated on reclaimed land far from the palace. Past the *Ginza* (*gin* meaning silver and *za* place) site of the *shogun*'s mint; past the wholesalers, merchants and moneylenders congregating nearby. Teeming with life, busy streets burst with shops, outstretched eaves providing relief from the sun. As the procession progresses the street clears before it, one and all prostrate as Maeda's men pass.

Sakuzaemon looks around pleased this is not his address. The shopkeepers live in two-storied, heavily slatted, wooden row-houses. Raised ground floors share walls with neighbours on both sides, the shops opening onto the street, with living quarters behind and above. Like all double-storied structures, the top stories have low ceilings. Looking out from the windows, the commoners have no choice but to stoop as a superior passes by. With fire a constant danger, water tubs and stacks of buckets are positioned at intervals of every few shops; watchtowers every ten blocks. But here and there, charred buildings mark a recent blaze.

Merchandise spills into the narrow streets, on shelves and trays, in barrels, baskets and boxes. Beauty, order and colour are captured in every display. Everything is sold that can be sold: pottery, knives, chopsticks, straw baskets, cages for birds, cages for insects, pipes, rice paper, fans, *kimono*, freshly-cut flowers, amulets, incense and funeral stones. Rice, millet, noodles and tea are piled in heaps. *Sake* (rice wine) barrels protected with straw are stacked and stored. Squares of *tofu* (a curd made from mashed soya beans), steamed cakes, and slabs of sweetened bean jelly are presented for inspection. Silverfish slap in buckets, their scales gleaming in the sun.

Here also are mountains of red-skinned sweet potatoes, white potatoes, ears of corn, soybeans and young snow peas, Chinese cabbage, purple *nasu* (eggplant), and bulbous onions; bundles of carrots, white *daikon* (radish), shoots of *negi* (spring onion), bracken, flowering ferns, and broad-leaved burdock. On woven platters fancifully shaped dried mushrooms nestle next to strips of dried gourd, black sheets of dried kelp and green sheets of dried *nori* (seaweed). Lush mounds of fragrant fruit beckon, with summer oranges stacked next to plump peaches, yellow loquats, *yuzu* (Chinese lemons), bunches of dusty-sheened grapes and curvaceous watermelons.

In the oppressive heat, the cloying scent of incense from a nearby shrine clashes with the pungent odour of dried bonito, sea eel and sardines, dried salted plums, grilled quail, and the sweet, syrupy aroma of pickles marinating in vinegar, soy sauce and sugar.

As the procession passes, the bustle resumes, inhabitants jostling for space. Chattering servants and housewives press and prod the produce. Straw-hatted farmers lug laden carts. Porters and street vendors manoeuvre cumbersome poles. White faced *geisha* hurry to appointments. Perfumed *samurai* saunter and strut. Priests, jugglers, jesters, tumblers and musicians collect alms. A curtained ox-drawn cart struggles through the throng, a long embroidered sleeve dangling from under its screen.

Coming to the northern fringes the procession swarms over the arched, red bridge. Sakuzaemon, impassively passing the decapitated heads at its southern end, is glad he is nearly home. Spanning the creek branching off the Sumida-*gawa*, *Nihom-bashi* (*Nippon* Bridge, *bashi* meaning bridge) is the hub of the five main *kaido*. Distances in Japan are measured from a bronze marker in the middle of the bridge.

The riverside is alive with fishmongers, storehouses and timber yards, boats laden with goods, and men angling from the bank. To the right, Sakuzaemon glimpses *Shitamachi* (literally Downtown), the low-lying landfill developed for utilities, trades, and entertainment. Here nearly 75 per cent of the population is jammed into 20 per cent of the land, the people deliberately grouped by their profession into *machii* (enclaves) to facilitate control.

Tucked away in their studios, potters pound lumps of clay. Basket-makers split bamboo into elastic wisps. Swordsmiths forge the sharpest blades. Their hands remembering the spaces between, comb-makers cut wooden teeth. Weavers with grooves in their fingernails separate the weave and tighten the weft. Coopers construct buckets. Blacksmiths beat metal into horseshoes, stonemasons carve lanterns and lacquerers lacquer trays with varnish tapped from the lac tree.

The incessant babble of voices merges into the melee of sounds: wheels creaking, hammering, the clang of iron striking iron, the kattan-kotton, kattan-kotton of wooden looms, the karan-koron, karan-koron of *geta* (wooden sandals with high supports). But Sakuzaemon ignores it all, anticipating *Shitamachi*'s pleasures to come, remembering his previous visit: days and nights strolling along the tree-lined banks of the Sumida-*gawa*, or drifting on its clean waters; picnicking under the cherry blossom; singing, drinking and floating in the world of hedonism. Maeda and his entourage keep moving, through Ueno, renowned for its temples, shrines and parks, finally heading towards the mansion in Hongo, its double-doored red gate a most welcome sight.

Shitamachi* was a self-contained city within the city, where, escaping the hierarchy and regimentation of everyday life, Edoites delighted in pleasure, men and women living for the moment in the 'evanescent floating world'. Squalor and poverty did exist, but the *samurai* and *chonin* (tradesmen, craftsmen and merchants) lived luxuriously, many of the low *chonin* class having become the new rich.

The following evening, Sakuzaemon and a friend went to Yoshiwara, 'the world of flowers and willow'. By day, shrouded in secrecy, dark tightly slatted façades concealed a private world of luxury, while beauties, shyly shielded beneath paper parasols, promenaded beneath the cherry trees. By evening, behind reed screens, they entertained the elite.

> Joining the throng, the two men enter through the large gate, their *palanquin* and swords prohibited, and their servants dismissed. Glittering with lanterns, the streets are lined with elegant double-storey teahouses, houses of assignation and cherry trees. Looking like painted dolls, fashionably gowned *geisha* parade to work, stepping along (karan-koron, karan-koron) on high platform *geta*, exposing their dainty feet in white *tabi* (socks). Red lips smile from painted white faces; their black hair is looped and stiffened, anchored with hairpins and combs, and adorned with quivering, tinkling ornaments.
>
> Windows and doors clatter open, sliding along their grooves. From behind upper-storey blinds, accompanied by *shamisen* (a three-stringed instrument shaped like a banjo), haunting voices drift out. On the ground floor, screened by wooden grills, lower-graded *geisha* flirt with passersby. Upstairs, Sakuzaemon is immediately engrossed with a charming, cultivated companion. Entertained with coquettish jokes, music, song and dance, he sits back and relaxes. While bending to pour *sake*, his companion reveals a tantalising glimpse of the nape of a painted neck.

According to Hisashi, life in Japan virtually stood still, untainted by outside influences, for another two centuries. Nevertheless, internal forces were fomenting. By 1800, its population having grown to over

---

* *Shitamachi* comprises the *machii* Kanda, Ueno, Asakusa, Yoshiwara and Kiba.

a million, Edo was said to be the biggest city in the world. But social order had been turned on its head, the government no longer able to repress the despised merchant caste in the new money economy. With *samurai* stipends still paid in rice, and rice production out of step with the rising standard of living, the *samurai* were increasingly impoverished. *Daimyo*, unable to pay their *samurai*, increased taxes on farmers, with many farmers now in dire poverty.

Uprisings increased. Academic appreciation for Confucianism escalated. Horrified by the increasing poverty and declining moral standards, and aroused by the scholars, a group of *samurai* and merchants lobbied for the restoration of imperial rule and the revival of the indigenous Shinto. In parallel, pressure from the West mounted. Foreign ships passed the headlands more frequently. In 1837, an American vessel carrying shipwrecked Japanese sailors sailed into Edo Bay, only to be driven off by cannon fire. The distinctive red, white and blue flag with its stars and stripes was seen again on other ships.

Then, in July 1853, the US [United States of America] made its most menacing move, the ultimate trigger that would change the course of Japanese history and the future and make-up of Hisashi's family lineage.

Chapter 4

Cracks Appear

Sonno-joi
Revere the Emperor, repel the barbarians

Appearing on the horizon, through the haze of a summer's day, the four black steam-powered frigates look to the Japanese like enormous smoking dragons. Causing great consternation, the kuro-fune (Black Ships) steam determinedly into forbidden waters. Commodore Matthew Perry of the US navy watches as the city grows closer. In a box wrapped in scarlet cloth, a letter written on vellum from the President to the Emperor emphasises American strength and makes it clear America is serious. Shipwrecked US sailors are to be treated more kindly. American ships are to be allowed to replenish coal and supplies. Japan is to open more ports to foreign trade.

Threading their way through the busy harbour, the *kuro-fune* drop anchor in the middle of Edo Bay. Temple bells warn of disaster, while the people pray to the gods to send a *kamikaze* (divine wind) to blow the monsters away.

PERRY WAS ORDERED to take his ships to Nagasaki, the only port open to foreigners. He refused. Up till now the government had disregarded demands to reopen Japan, but this was different. Aware of the threat behind American requests, they were mindful of China's defeat in the 1842 Opium War. The Japanese must either end their isolation or fight, though they knew resistance was ultimately futile. Japan had no coastal guns and no fleet, and the preparedness of the samurai was questionable. So the Japanese government acceded to American demands.

Other countries followed and Japan raised its bamboo barrier. A series of unfavourable trade agreements, giving the foreigners more and more rights, as signed. Tokugawa opponents condemned the government for failing to protect Japan from the *gaijin* and, in 1868, supported by the rebels, the Emperor seized power from the *shogun* who had ruled Japan for 700 years. The reign of the new Emperor was named the Meiji era (the 'Illumined reign'), though the 16-year-old Emperor, nominally restored to power, remained a puppet of the revolutionary government.

Chapter 5

Released From Worldly Thoughts

Sendan wa futaba yori kanbashi
Sandalwood is fragrant even in seed leaf
(Talent displays itself even in childhood)

INTO SUCH CONFUSION, Jitsuzen Maezawa, Hisashi's maternal grandfather and a descendant of Bunzaemon was born in 1851, 17 years before the Meiji Revolution. One of nine children, Jitsuzen, along with all his siblings, was adopted out, his parents unable to feed them. And so the family line was terminated.

Previously, a *samurai* family without an heir would have been disconnected from the fiefdom, and the hereditary stipend discontinued. Thus adoption of a fellow warrior's son occurred often, benefiting younger sons as well as families without sons. Now as class barriers crumbled, many *samurai* sold their status, or married into the *chonin* class. As the *chonin* grew richer, they too used adoption to maintain a prosperous business; by adopting the son of a *samurai*, they also bought his status.

Jitsuzen was adopted into a high-ranked Buddhist temple near his home town of Wakayama, south of Osaka. Fate decreed he be brought up within the shelter of a temple, rather than being adopted by merchants like his brothers or subjected to the brutal world of his *samurai* lineage.

Buddhism is woven into every aspect of Japanese life, and it is hard to think of Japan without thinking of Buddhism. Different schools of thought, each with their own rituals and lore limited to specific *sutra*,* developed and readjusted according to caste. But the one Buddha was universal, the embodiment of perfect wisdom and compassion.†

Jitsuzen entered the *Tendai* School. Literally *Tendai* means 'supporting heaven's base', and the school acted as guardian for the imperial family. Even though the country was controlled by the *shogun*, the Emperor still commanded enormous respect.

> The young boy walks silently towards the massive two-storey gate. Its doors are open, on either side a giant statue guarding the temple from evil. He looks warily at their ferocious faces. Turning hesitantly, he takes one last look at his father striding away. Hearing a polite cough, he turns to face the shaven-headed, black-robed youth beckoning him onwards.

The *hondo* (main hall) with its gently curled, tiled roof was supported by sturdy red columns. Nearby, a cavernous bronze bell hung from an open pavilion, a hefty beam suspended horizontally, poised to strike; to its left, a five-tiered pagoda. Behind the *hondo* were halls for secondary Buddhas and *bodhisattva* (Buddhas-to-be), scripture and treasure houses and, in the quietest corner, halls for study and meditation. Living quarters were to the side, adjacent to the burial ground.

For Jitsuzen, every day of every year began very early.

> One monk rises earlier. Slowly he walks through the monastery, beating a wooden bell, chanting as he goes, the sound breaking the stillness of the pre-dawn hour.
>
> The dozen trainees sleep in one large room. Like all dwellings,

---

* Texts derived from the Buddha and other enlightened beings.
† Original Buddhist philosophy theorised about the soul and life after death. Over time this changed until most schools of thought prayed for prosperity and assistance in the material world. The *samurai* and Emperor's family, however, continued to focus beyond this life. The *samurai* was always thinking about death; having few grievances in this existence, the Emperor and his family need only worry about their next life.

the dormitory is up off the ground, well-suited to the hot, humid summers, but not the chilly winters. Hearing the bell, the trainees get up quickly and roll up their *futon*,* dress, and then wash outside in rainwater. Eleven-year-old Jitsuzen is glad of his thicker garb, but still he shivers. He is cold, having already been up twice and required to douse himself with icy water. The bronze bell echoes in the blackness, pealing far and wide, bidding everyone to the *hondo*; not just the hundred priests and acolytes, but every living creature is called forth to hear the words of the Buddha.

Lanterns illuminate the path to the *hondo*, its outer chamber dimly lit with candles. Overhead, defined by massive beams, the vaulted ceiling rises steeply. Seated barefoot on the wooden floor, Jitsuzen faces the inner sanctuary, his baggy trousers and jacket comfortable for sitting cross-legged.

The altar, crowded with religious relics and offerings of food and flowers, shimmers through a haze of smouldering incense. Candles burn in brass candelabra, flickering flames revealing the dais and highlighting items of gold. Seated benignly in their midst, the serene face and form of the immense bronze Buddha smiles over them all: alongside are smaller images of *bodhisattvas*.

Fragrant fumes of cedar waft from the censers. Silent, influential, the spiralling smoke transports prayers to the deities, purifies the living, protects against evil, and offers tributes to the souls of the dead. Inhaling, immersed in the atmosphere, Jitsuzen feels at peace, inspired to follow his path. He joins the chanting as louder and louder, in rhythm to the beat of a metal drum, their voices rise in unison, filling the hall.

Gate gate paragate
Form is nothingness

---

* Traditional Japanese beds are quilted mattresses called *futon*, which are rolled out on the floor at night, and put away in a cupboard during the day.

Parasamgate omn sraha
Nothingness is form

After chanting, each priest went to his duty. Early every morning and again in the evening, Jitsuzen joined the older trainees to spend hours in formal *zazen* (sitting in religious contemplation).

> The meditation hall is dark and draughty, and the acolytes sit cross-legged facing the windowless wall. All that is heard is the sound of their breathing, and the whispering breeze in the trees outside.
>
> Just as the *sugi* (Japanese cedar) reaches for the sun, Jitsuzen straightens his spine. He relaxes his shoulders, his arms drooping like sodden leaves. He inclines his head ever so slightly, his lips gently closed. He rests his hands in his lap, the fingers of his right hand facing up, resting on the fingers of his left, thumb tips gently touching. He closes his eyes and focusses on his breathing. His body in neutral, his mind at rest, he ponders over his first ever *koan*:* 'What is *mu* (nothingness)?' Jitsuzen has held this *koan* in his mind for months as it whittles away at his logical mind. Eventually his concentration should overload, causing his rational thinking to collapse and provoking a breakthrough. Enlightenment will be triggered suddenly, his mind freed from its restraints.
>
> He sits in the silence. He is tired and, not having eaten since midday the previous day, hungry. He is bored. He wants to scratch. Yet again he asks himself: What is *mu*? Does it exist? His Master wants an answer, but it is nonsense. There is no answer. Behind him, the barefooted trainer moves soundlessly backwards and forwards across the room. Jitsuzen starts to daydream. He starts to think about breakfast. He tries to drag himself back to the *koan*, but too late.

---

* Used as a tool in meditation, a *koan* is a non-rational conundrum coined by an ancient master: 'conceive the sound of one hand clapping', 'yearn for one's mother before conception'. There is no single, correct answer. In itself, the answer is irrelevant; rather it is the process by which the *koan* is understood that is important, as it opens the mind 'to a new way of seeing'.

Thwack, he is whacked soundly on his right shoulder with the sword-like 'encouraging' stick. As it should, the shock galvanises him and his mind rattles on.

Time and again, the Master refused Jitsuzen's latest response. Often the Master tried to confuse Jitsuzen, while other times he ignored him, or shouted, or smacked him on the knuckles. Once he tripped up Jitsuzen as he left. But the Master would know when the answer was grasped, and then there would be another *koan* to crack.

For an aspirant priest like Jitsuzen, life revolved around study; his training was tough, rigorous and challenging. As well as the *koan* there was much to memorise. The *Sanskrit* (sacred Indian script) and classical Chinese texts were the well of wisdom and knowledge, and like the *sutra*, he needed to know them by heart. He also did chores, and learned chanting, calligraphy, and how to live harmoniously with his roommates, entrusting his life to Buddha.

For the boy, there seemed to be no change, his training continuing day after day, season after season. But for Buddhism, momentous changes were occurring. With the demise of the *shogunate*, the fortunes of the temples reversed. The Tokugawa regime had protected temples over shrines, so the new Meiji government took the opposite stance and slowly the power of Buddhism disintegrated. The new power was wealth, raising the merchant class into superior position, with many *samurai* compelled to become clerks or teachers, or to learn trades.

Moving from Kyoto to Edo, the Emperor took up residence in the *shogunal* palace. Edo, renamed Tokyo (meaning 'Eastern capital'), became the new imperial capital.* Fiefdoms were requisitioned and re-established as 47 *prefectures*, which became the new units of local administration. The *daimyo*'s buildings were turned into government offices, or given to the military. Farmers could buy and sell their land.

Every individual became equal by law; even *hinin*. While the dress

---

* By 1900, Tokyo's population had swelled to two million.

of caste was outlawed, police, postmen, civil servants, soldiers and students had to wear Western uniforms, an obvious and easy way to encourage the adoption of Western methods and manners, while still allowing others to interact appropriately. Everyone was entitled to a basic education, and universities were established. Up until this time, family names and genealogies had been the prerogative of the upper classes; commoners had been known only by their personal name and a prefix indicating their trade or fiefdom. With an increasing population, and a larger government structure, family lines now needed to be identified more precisely, thus a radically different Western approach was adopted. Registration offices were transferred from local temples to local government and, in 1875, family names became compulsory.

But with reorganisation comes upheaval, and the Japanese people were being asked to make drastic changes. Disarmed and pensioned off, the *samurai* took it badly, staging a series of minor revolts. To immobilise them, and to secure Japan's external autonomy, compulsory military service was introduced. A national army was conscripted from the general populace, an army answerable to the Emperor, not the government.

Chapter 6

Ascending Dragon

Ja wa sun ni shite, hito o nomu
A snake, even when an inch long, attempts to swallow a man
(The greatness of a man can be seen even in childhood)

IN 1865, 14-YEAR-OLD JITSUZEN took his monastic vows. He received his *kesa*, the mantle worn on special occasions, at the ordination ceremony. He also changed his family name to Ashitzu, beginning a new family line.

The *kesa* was made from scraps of donated cloth, sewn together with specific stitches into a patchwork, organised in odd numbers of columns and surrounded by a border.* The more columns there were, the higher the rank. Wearing his new, ankle-length robe, the *kesa* draped over his left shoulder, Jitsuzen was now a fully ordained member of the *Tendai* community. Three years later came the Meiji Revolution.

Even as a boy, Jitsuzen had attracted the attention of senior priests. Temple records state he was 'bestowed with a clear head', marking him out as an original thinker. At 20, having been promoted and transferred to Tokyo, he associated with people he would never have met in Wakayama, and it was a stimulating time in the capital as the new regime made its mark and a new society evolved. There were new-style politicians; newly rich merchants, financiers and industrialists; and a new intelligentsia class of novelists, poets, publishers and

---

* The centre column symbolises the Buddha, the two flanking squares his attendants. The four corner squares within the border represent the four cardinal directions.

Western-style doctors. Opportunities abounded. Jitsuzen had a head for business and, as he was responsible for the temple's fund-raising, he soon established a valuable network.

Over the centuries, conscious of their heritage, wealth and political power, *Tendai* priests had become complacent, caught up in the prevailing hedonism of society and corrupted by good living. Close behind the *kuro-fune* and foreign traders, Protestant missionaries had arrived, once again attacking Buddhism for its worship of idols. Under threat, *Tendai* needed politically astute managers, like Jitsuzen. By age 29, independent and articulate, and knowing how to utilise his powerful connections, Jitsuzen had already initiated new systems and promotional activities to raise funds and increase numbers of followers. He was promoted on to the Supreme Assembly of *Tendai*, based at Hiei-zan Enryaku-*ji* (*ji* means temple) in Kyoto, the Headquarters of *Tendai* and the pinnacle of Buddhist academia.

The ancient city of Kyoto was landlocked by mountains. Highest of all was Hiei, the Mount of Wisdom, its thick, primeval forest hiding the seat of *Tendai*. Centuries old, the temple was established in the pre-*shogun* days when the Emperor held power. Perched on the hillside, it stood watch, protecting Kyoto and the imperial family from evil spirits. Important strategically, it was positioned in the middle of the narrowest neck of Japan, equidistant from the Pacific Ocean and the Japan Sea. The whole mountain was the temple called Hiei-zan Enryaku-*ji*. Known by its more popular name, Eizan-*ji*, it was one of the biggest temples in Japan, housing more than a thousand priests but, by its very location, excluding people at large.

Jitsuzen influenced numerous major developments in contemporary Buddhist thinking. While in Tokyo, he had followed the progress of the first newspaper, the *Yokohama Mainichi Shinbun* (1871). Recognising the opportunities it gave for promotion, he decided something similar would benefit Buddhism, and launched the first monthly religious bulletin, *Shimei Yoka*, after arriving in Kyoto.

The priests worked day and night, laboriously compiling and

editing articles and sermons written by 'men of profound learning'. The bulletin had to be easy to read for everyone so, except for poetry, texts written in classical Chinese had to be translated into Japanese.

Jitsuzen's ideas were bold and thought-provoking. Spurred by the teachings of American Protestantism, a religious revolution was taking place. Chaos reigned within and between different schools, and Jitsuzen wrote many commentaries on the place of Buddhism. He and several other high-ranking priests endeavoured to protect Buddhism against the Protestants, encouraging worshippers to save their religion, and other Buddhist schools to fight against Christianity. With Japan's literacy rate comparable to much of Western Europe, the bulletin was an effective medium, being accessible to everyone.

The Japanese had always been tolerant with regard to religion, following Shinto, Buddhism and Confucianism. One reason Christianity seemed so strange to them was that both the religion and its followers were intolerant; Christians considered their beliefs the only correct ones. To the Japanese, Christianity, despite its strangeness, was a belief that could be added to their own beliefs.

Jitsuzen's bulletin also generated income for the temple from donations, as well as furthering Jitsuzen's reputation in political circles. Throughout his career he wrote profusely, not just for the bulletins, but also books on the religious history of Japan, as well as revisions of Buddhist texts. In 1886, he was assigned Chief Priest of Kimi-In Temple within the Eizan compound, one of the top positions. But, given the rigidity of the temple's promotional structure, this was as far as he could go in *Tendai*. After his long years of study and hard work, this was a severe disappointment to him.

Chapter 7
Shaking the Foundations

Wako dojin
Tempering the light (of intelligence) and
mingling with the dust (of the world)
(Don't be aloof from the world, mingle with everyone)

IN 1893, JITSUZEN AND THREE COLLEAGUES attended The World's First Parliament of Religions held in Chicago in connection with the World Fair. From Tokyo via Hawaii to Seattle by steamship, then overland by train to Chicago, the four priests crossed the American continent.* Jitsuzen had been on a train before, though had travelled short distances only. This American railway was a feat of engineering, the likes of which he had never imagined: a single line of metal track spanning nearly 3 000 kilometres. Intensely interested, he absorbed every detail.

> They head east across the vast, untamed land. Spewing filthy smoke, the train chugs laboriously upwards from the Californian valley. As hills change to mountains, curves become sharper and more frequent, and speed slackens – up and up the perilous slopes of the snow-capped Sierras. Wooden trestles a kilometre wide and hundreds of metres tall, bridge deep canyons. Dark tunnels penetrate granite mountains. After 50 bridges and 14 tunnels, Jitsuzen stops counting. Jerking and

---
* Completed 24 years earlier, the transcontinental Great Northern Railway meant it took only a week to cross the country. The Trans-Siberian Railway commenced in 1891, and the Suez Canal had opened in 1869.

> jolting, grinding and groaning, with ear-splitting screeches, the train edges upwards. Nervous, but exhilarated, he is relieved as finally they reach the top – 2 500 metres up, surrounded by snow.
>
> Swiftly descending into the Great Basin of Nevada, they continue eastwards. With a clear run to the salt flats of Utah, the train gathers momentum. Clattering relentlessly, glistening rails vanish beneath spinning wheels. Full steam ahead, spitting sparks, they hurtle across the western plains, the track stretching from horizon to horizon. The heat-shimmering desert is wider and more beautiful than he had imagined, staggering in its scale and unexpected beauty. Then, they are up and over the majestic Rocky Mountains.
>
> Down they speed to the Great Plains of Nebraska, an immense inland sea of rippling grass, scorched by the summer sun and dotted with grazing beasts. Pounding over hundreds of kilometres of dusty track, the big blue sky and rolling endless prairie stretch out beyond the skyline, beyond his vision, beyond his imagination. Then yet another vista: he gazes out at dense, brooding woodlands, streams and fertile valleys, until finally they reach Chicago.

At times, almost unable to comprehend the magnitude and diversity of the US, Jitsuzen was overwhelmed. It seemed to offer extraordinary excess in both nature and opportunity: a 'splendid, materialistic civilisation on a big scale', a country in which huge numbers of people lived the life available only to the elite in Japan.

> Soon after arriving in Chicago, Jitsuzen takes a walk. He watches, fascinated, as the Wells Street Bridge swings out over the Chicago River, a tugboat billowing steam as it pulls a heavily laden barge through the gap. He has stepped into a weird and exciting new world. Men wearing high silk hats, stiff collars and long-tailed coats walk beside women in bonnets and long, full gowns, tight at the waist. He is outraged to see a gentleman hold a woman's arm as they cross the street. In Japan, women walk behind men and touching a female in public is considered crude.

Chicago's World Fair was a magnificent exhibition of classic architecture from ancient Rome and Paris, and even featured a replica Japanese house; with bamboo artisans demonstrating basket-making. In association with the fair, the World's Parliament of Religions assembled on 11 August.

The distinguished international speakers assembled for a photograph: Anglican, Episcopalian, Lutheran, Presbyterian, Catholic, Baptist, Buddhist, Methodist, Pentecostal, Protestant, Orthodox Jew, Quaker, Hindu and Sikh. Brilliantly robed, shaven-headed Jitsuzen stood out among the dog collars, skull caps, mitres and turbans, and mainly dark-suited, bearded or mustachioed clergy.

> From the tips of his white *tabi* and black leather *zori* (sandals) to the hems of his immaculate, white pantaloons and yellow silk robe, the slightly built priest is an exotic, mysterious figure as he stands at the podium. Around his waist, attached by a strap over his left shoulder, his *kesa* glows vermilion, circular gold embroidered mandala* gleaming under the lights. Through an English interpreter, his lecture on 'Mahayanist Buddhism' begins: 'I will explain the highest human enlightenment, Buddha, according to the order of its five attitudes'.

Jitsuzen's visit to America had far-reaching consequences, modifying his view of the world and his attitude to other religious beliefs. He wrote, 'It instilled in me the strong belief that I lack knowledge of world affairs'. Never before had he seen such ornate houses, colourful gardens and tall church steeples. He was amazed at the world's first skyscraper and the glass-fronted shops. In particular, he could not understand why anyone would drink milk or eat butchered cattle. Drinking something produced by animals was considered unclean and, until recently, eating beef had been against the law in Japan.

To Jitsuzen, American houses, with their rooms divided by solid walls, seemed more complicated than necessary. Japanese houses had

---

* A *mandala* is symbolic of the universe.

no solid internal walls, and structural beams were left exposed. It also seemed extravagant to have separate rooms for eating, sitting and sleeping, and odd for parents to sleep separately from their children. Fluid space had always been part of Japanese life, sliding screens and hanging fabric defining space and accommodating changes in activity, weather and numbers of people. But Jitsuzen definitely preferred shiny glass windows to translucent paper.

The four priests were staying in a new hotel. Its Western grandeur, with arched leaded windows, sumptuous furnishings and imposing furniture, seemed ostentatious, though Jitsuzen liked the feel and warmth of the woollen carpets on his bare feet. When he first saw the flush toilet in his room he was completely bemused, not having the slightest idea what it was for. And it felt strange to sleep on a bed. All his life he had slept on a thin *futon* on the *tatami* (aromatic matting edged with fabric) with a wooden headrest, or bag of grain, for a pillow. The softness of the mattress and feather pillow was excessive, so he slept on the floor. Accustomed to sitting on the floor, he also found sitting on a chair uncomfortable.

It was strange travelling in the hotel's elevator. It was so fast, and he was not sure he liked the sensation, but it was such an intriguing phenomenon. People on different floors could be pushing buttons at the same time. Some would want to go up. Some would want to go down. But the car remembered to stop at all the right floors.

And equality was real. There was no obvious dress or behaviour proclaiming the status of important officials, making them hard to identify. A man and his host shook hands in greeting. They did not bow. He soon got used to men and women walking together, though witnessing couples dancing astounded him.

He was curious about everything and would have liked to have stayed longer. He took back to Japan a vast body of information, his report overflowing with wonder at the plenitude of life. Japan seemed far behind. However, observing the power of print media had confirmed his belief that his own publication had been a good idea.

Chapter 8

Descending Dragon

Hi kurete, michi toshi
Even at sunset the way is long
(Even in the final years, one has much to do)

WHILE THE WORLD OUTSIDE had been developing, Japan had been left far behind, knowing nothing of railways, factories, telegraph, steam-power, or electricity. Few Japanese would have known of the French* and American revolutions,† or that the Industrial Revolution had taken place, or that Victoria was Queen of England. Now the new government welcomed everything from the US and Europe: art, education, military strategy, medical techniques, and even religion. And to Jitsuzen it appeared they encouraged the Protestant attack on Buddhism. Shinto seemed to escape criticism, as it was not seen as such a threat: Shinto gods were not worshipped in human form like the Buddha.

He commented in the bulletin that changes made to a nearby temple, unused through lack of supporters, symbolised the shifting times. After the revolution, it was turned into a Christian church; but it had recently been converted into a girl's school, a reflection of government policy to improve education for females.

Jitsuzen's visit to America provoked him to switch from *Tendai*

---

* The storming of the Bastille was in 1789.
† The American War of Independence occurred between 1775 and 1783; the American Civil War between the north and south was fought between 1861 and 1865.

to Zen, his experience unsettling him at a time when he was already disillusioned with the lack of promotional opportunity in the *Tendai* School. However, coming as he did from a long line of *samurai*, maybe it is not surprising he found such appeal in the philosophy they so admired. Introduced from China in the late twelfth century, its qualities of discipline and concentration appealed to high-ranking *samurai*, and Zen temples thrived. Jitsuzen, attracted to its philosophy, 'sat at the feet of Dokuen' (a Zen priest famous for his efforts to protect Buddhism from non-believers), and was eventually ordained as a Zen priest.

Zen, which means meditation, concentrated on the original philosophy of Buddhism, praying for the afterlife. Different to other schools of thought, it found truth not in the scriptures or teachings, but in the experience of the mind and intuition, a supreme sixth sense enabling one 'to perceive soundless footsteps'. Characterised by its intense physical and mental effort, the school had a profound influence on a *samurai*'s approach to life, enabling him to teach himself to fight without fear of death. In Zen, a *samurai* found a belief in excellence on which to base the highest possible standards in fighting, living and dying, controlling events in his life through meditation. Meditation, along with the Zen arts of *ikebana* (flower arranging), the tea ceremony, poetry writing and calligraphy, were used to calm the self and develop inner strength and knowledge.

At that time in Japan, there were 17 different Buddhist schools of thought, including *Tendai* and Zen. Zen was split into two sects:* *Rinzai* for nobles and elite *samurai*, which concentrated on *koans*; and *Sodo* for warriors, which emphasised *zazen*. Jitsuzen's new position was Chief Abbot for *Rinzai* Zen,† whose headquarters were at Eigen-*ji* not far from Kyoto. From there, he administered 100 branch temples.

---

* A sect was an offshoot group subscribing to a different docrine within a particular school of thought.
† The position of Chief Abbot was not inherited. Second-tier priests elected their leader.

At age 54, this was an exceptional promotion in Japanese religious circles. However, given that Zen was smaller than *Tendai*, Jitsuzen saw it as a drop in status.

Eigen-*ji* lay cradled in the mountains, and was surrounded by lush deciduous forest. Semitropical bamboo mingled with maples and northern snow-country trees, oak, birch and elm, and in autumn the forest turned to flame.

Jitsuzen settled down to end his days at Eigen-*ji*. His appetite for study was still insatiable, and over the next 20 years he continued to publish, his voice of great influence with the government. Travelling extensively, he delivered lectures throughout Japan, Korea, Formosa (today's Taiwan) and Manchuria. However, he also loved writing poems, carrying at all times, in the sleeve of his robe, his favourite brush protected in a rice-stalk mat.* Increasingly his poems showed his disenchantment with the situation surrounding Buddhism. The traditional way of life was disappearing, and the role of priests was no longer valued. By 1920, their main functions were to maintain tomb-yards, and arrange funerals and weddings. Jitsuzen agonised over the trend, disappointed he could not prevent it.

> Returning to the temple the elderly priest is tired and feeling his age. From here it is only ten minutes to his quarters but, knowing he will soon be besieged with issues that have occurred in his absence, he has sent his entourage ahead. The autumnal setting suits his melancholy mood, but even now, deep in thought, he does not hesitate as he makes his way through the sparsely covered trees. Those unfamiliar with the steep, winding path would surely have lost their footing. But his feet pick their way with sureness among the stones and exposed tree roots.
>
> A light mist hovers over the compound. Maple leaves carpet the pathway to his room. As befits his importance, the room is situated

---

* Poetry writing had long been the preserve of the educated elite.

away from the other priests; still austere, but with its own garden where he can detach himself from the burden and responsibility of high office. Over the years as the seasons change he has been able to appreciate nature's show. Even in winter, the doors open wide, he sits and watches the falling snow, his heated stone against his chest.

Next day he sits in his room. Compared to the previous day, this clear, brisk morning invigorates him. Seated motionless on the *tatami* facing the open doors, his legs crossed, he relaxes. Sunlight filters through the remaining red and gold maple leaves. Beside an aged five-needled-pine, a stone basin nestles amid a tapestry of textures: a box tree, miniature bamboo, and rocks covered with moss. Small shrubs cast shadows, shrouding true shapes and colours. He sees the beauty in the fading hydrangea; and in the maple contrasted against a rock, the colours of the rock washed by the sun, the sun casting its shadow and changing in the shifting planes of light.

Inhaling the slightly spicy, musky scent of sandalwood wafting from the censer, and the sandalwood *tansu* (portable chest), he brings his body and mind into harmony. The priest can control his mind for hours, his garden an aid to attaining inner quiet. Every rock, stone, tree, leaf and droplet of water holds meaning: its shape, colour and texture indicating where it comes from, and where it will go. Every tangible thing reflects a common fate, destined to perish. Nature, the sound of the wind, even a group of stones can bring him comfort and inspiration. He empties his mind, focussing the rhythm of his breathing, and with his back perfectly upright, he hardly moves.

An hour later, Jitsuzen draws up his wooden desk and opens the writing box with its ink-stained drawers, placing his treasures methodically on the desk: to his right, the ink-stone, ink-stick, ink-pot, water-dropper, brush-rest, and wrist-rest; to his left, the brush-pot and brushes, paperweights and his seal – accessories carefully chosen and arranged to inspire him. He lays a thick cloth on the *tatami*, then slowly unfurls a fresh parchment over the top. To stop the *hanshi* (special use paper) from moving, he places two small rocks,

one at the top and one at the bottom. Patiently he rubs the ink-stick*
against the ink-stone, every so often lubricating the powder with a
droplet of water to create the densest black. Finally, he pours the
perfect ink into the ink-pot.

Kneeling before the *hanshi*, he unhurriedly reaches for his brush,
dipping it into the ink, just enough. Then, with his wrist elevated,
he breaks the pristine expanse with a bold upward slash. Swiftly and
surely his hand glides over the paper, characters frolicking across the
surface. There is no room for mistakes: each dash, dot, loop, stroke
and curve envisioned in advance; each character painted with a few
precise strokes. Varying the quantity of ink, a twist of his brush, a
subtle change of pressure, produces variations in tone and width,
conveying countless nuances. A loose whole-arm movement, the
laden brush held firmly near the top, renders bold black strokes,
sensuous and strong. Sharper accents or finer elongated marks require
a lighter consistency of ink, the brush held closer to its bristles. With
the brush nearly dry, delicate spidery lines graze the surface, capturing
a fleeting effect.

The scroll is a work of art, his repertoire of brush strokes, the
hallmark of a man of accomplishment.

> At the foot of the temple's hill
> I look up at the land of Eigen-*ji*
> as if into still water.

> My watching face,
> each bright, tear-like bead of dew,
> each gaudy bauble:
> they mirror each other
> as if difference hardly matters.

> Walking under the hill towards the temple
> I see trees are not in flower

---

* Ink came in sticks made from compressed charcoal mixed with resin.

and not a soul is on the path.

But, at long intervals,
birds release their cries,
over the path
under the hill
pressing me on
for an earlier return to Eigen-*ji*.

The temple always welcomes him. It is his haven where he can leave the world behind, ignoring the struggles overtaking religious circles in Japan.

Much of Jitsuzen's life went against tradition. He moved between castes, from *samurai* to priest. He was promoted through the ranks of the priesthood on merit, and he changed school, something not normally done. Archives filed on the Abbots of Zen record him as a 'man who combined erudition with action'. *Tendai* annals describe him as a 'tiger with wings'. Undoubtedly his talent, curiosity and openness to new ideas led to a life 'out of specification' with Japanese tradition.

In Hisashi's words, Jitsuzen was 'a strong weed defying removal'. Throughout his life he had believed that only a bold fighter with the strength of his convictions could stand up to adversity or disapproval. However, like a weed in the garden, there seemed to be no place for the likes of him in the new Japan.

The priest died in 1923, aged 72, disillusioned and regretful that nobody had listened to him. However, Jitsuzen was not only a priest, but also a husband and father. He had married Umeko Sakurai, the daughter of a rich Kyoto merchant, in 1895.

Chapter 9
A Hidden Flower

Danson-jo-hi
The dominance of men over women

UMEKO SAKURAI, Hisashi's maternal grandmother, was born in 1876, the youngest and eighth child of a merchant who lived on the outskirts of Kyoto at the foot of Mt Hiei near Eizan-*ji*. For two centuries her ancestors had held the monopoly on supplying the temple with its daily provisions. It was a most lucrative connection, but mutually beneficial, as the 'thank-money' paid to the temple amounted to a sizable income.

Merchant families like Umeko's were amassing fortunes. Acting as distributors for farmers, artisans and smaller merchants, they organised sales of goods to the temple, lent money in advance of harvest, and changed *samurai* stipends into cash. For every deal they charged a fee.

As warriors had their code, so too did merchants. Every exchange was important. Gonzaemon Sakurai was polite even to servants and children. He prepared his accounts daily. He repaid his *giri* to the temple, to his parents who had brought him up, and to his ancestors who had made the family prosperous. He worked assiduously, never wasting time or money.

Like all Japanese girls, whatever their station, his daughter centred her life on the home. While she led a luxurious life, she had little freedom, although she was probably better off than most other women. Noblewomen were no longer held as hostages of the *shogun*, but their lives were still far more restricted than Umeko's. Lower caste women might have had more independence, but only because they had to work.

The age-old formula for marriage was for girls to marry between 16 and 20 years, and men between 18 and 23 years. It was a mother's task to educate her daughter to be a hardworking, obedient wife.

As well as learning to cook, sew and wash clothes, feminine virtue and etiquette had been drummed into Umeko. She knew how to sit, stand, move with dignity, bow correctly, dress in good taste, and identify varieties of shellfish, tea and incense. As the daughter of a man of status, she had learned how to entertain family and clients, and had trained to sing, dance, compose poetry, play the *koto* (Japanese harp) and host the *cha-no-yu* (tea ceremony).*

As for every Japanese, *on* dictated Umeko's life and she was endlessly indebted. Even though she had no direct relationship with the Emperor, she had still received *on*. Under his umbrella Japan enjoyed a peaceful life, thus great thanks were due for his patronage and protection. Brought up in a safe environment, healthy, wealthy and educated, Umeko owed much to her parents – as she was continually reminded by relatives. She was indebted to her teachers for teaching her how to read and write, and how to behave according to the principles of *shushin* (moral training). Even when permitted to play with her cousins, she engendered *on*. And every spring and autumn she had to join with her family to give thanks officially to her ancestors for her privileged life.

As for everyone, *giri* stopped her from complaining and shirking her duties. It was her duty to her parents to help in daily life and to comply with their counsel, especially when it came time for her marriage. All through her life she had had to conform to the proprieties: her duty to maintain her 'proper place' in society; to become a sought-after bride;

---

* Tea was initially drunk by priests to help them stay awake during meditation, with the ritual raised to an art form in the late sixteenth century.

to cultivate her patience; and to suppress her emotions. She was a precious commodity, a hidden flower, a girl protected in a box 'not to be poisoned by other men before her marriage'. *Giri* was her constant companion. Virtuous and accomplished, she led a life of decorum and good taste.

Inspired by Zen, *cha-no-yu* trained the spirit while teaching social graces. For two centuries a male only preserve, women were now permitted to participate, Umeko having been trained by her father.

> Eighteen years old and beautiful, the young woman peers through a gap in the translucent paper window. From her upstairs bedroom, screened by the branches of a paulownia tree, Umeko observes the street. Under a red umbrella held aloft by a servant, Jitsuzen is passing by. In his mid-forties, dressed in bright robes as bespoke his importance, and surrounded by his retinue, he is a fascinating figure.

Jitsuzen came regularly to Umeko's parents' house to discuss the provision of supplies to the temple. When he visited, Umeko, as befitted her role, was required to serve tea or fruit.

The merchant's two-storey villa was enclosed behind high, earthen walls. It was a substantial home, for Gonzaemon was one of the richest men in the district and he occupied a prominent position. The house and land had been in the family for generations, and had expanded with the family's fortune. The house was always full of guests, for the most part, on business.

> Gonzaemon waits beside the gate-house to receive his esteemed guest who arrives punctually at 9.30. Jitsuzen is accompanied by his *otomo* (secretary). The merchant greets the priest, bowing low, acknowledging the priest's superior status and lowering his own.
>
> The garden greets the priest, the lustre of greenery pleasing to his eye. Set back, the house with its grey, shingled roof provides a graceful line and sense of stability, its overhanging eaves stretching several metres beyond the walls, extending the living space to the

veranda beneath. Taut, white paper, latticed windows and sliding doors contrast well with dark *sugi* uprights.

Following a quiet path between mature shrubs, the merchant leads the way to a gate in a walled enclosure. The one-roomed *cha-shitsu* (teahouse) stands alone in the *roji* (dew ground or the water sprinkled garden). A typical rustic *cha-shitsu*, its humble plaster walls, unfinished woodwork and thatched roof are in accordance with the principle of simplicity essential for the *cha-no-yu*.

Raked gravel, replicating flowing water, guides them in. A fresh green maple is lit from behind, its tender foliage swaying gently in the breeze; a lichen covered rock has been carefully placed to the side.* A pleasing sight of lofty conifers, bamboo and a tall triangular birch shadows a flourishing moss carpet. Broad hosta leaves contrast feathery fern fronds.

A stone water basin, complete with a bamboo dipper, its mouth appropriately facing left, nestles near the *cha-shitsu* door. By washing his hands and rinsing his mouth, Jitsuzen rids himself of the 'dust of the world', and purifies his mind and body. A bamboo pipe supplies a steady stream of water to the basin; beside it is an umbrella-shaped 'basin-attending lantern'. Two large rocks form the front steps. Pausing, they remove their *geta*, and place them facing back the way they have come. To keep the delicate *tatami* clean, they wear only their *tabi* inside.

As a show of humility, the three men drop to their knees to crawl through the low door,† their heads bowed, necks exposed; a reminder of *samurai* days when a suspicious host could behead his guest. Waiting inside with her mother, Umeko is anxious to make a good impression on the man she has seen from her window. With deep bows, they greet the priest. Umeko's black hair is pulled back

---

* In the sixteenth century armies looted prize rocks and stones from the gardens of the vanquished and sent them home wrapped in silk.
† The 'crawl door' is only 72 centimetres high.

with combs, her face and throat whitened,* her mouth rouged, and her eyebrows plucked into delicate arches.

Smelling faintly of musk, her *kimono*, worn left side over right, is in shades of blue and embroidered with spring flowers and birds. The long, swinging sleeves and the cream collar fitting snugly around her nape advertise her unmarried status. Tied tight and high on her waist, with an elaborate knot behind, her red *obi* is held firm with a pink cord, and her posture is such that the *obi* stays taut at all times.

Prior to the men's arrival, Umeko and her mother had washed and arranged the requisite utensils in the attached ante-room, and built up the fire in the tearoom, adding sandalwood incense.

The presence of *wabi* (the state of being quietly clear and calm) prevails. In readiness for the four-hour-long ceremony all is tranquil and calm. A fine scroll, on which the words '*kissa-hoo*'† have been written in vigorous script by a man of virtue, hangs in the *tokonoma* (alcove). Complementing the scroll, a bough of pink cherry blossom leans out to the side of a pottery vase, just as it appeared on the tree that morning. Showing his appreciation for his host's thoughtful preparations, Jitsuzen praises the scroll and vase. Other conversation is improper.

As honoured guest, he sits with his back to the *tokonoma*. Folding his legs, he rests on his heels, his big toes together. He savours the fragrance from the burning hearth. Intent on the ritual, he concentrates on Umeko's every action, and the simplicity of the occasion, relieved of weighty thoughts.

Umeko follows the 'proper practice'. With a silk cloth she slowly purifies the tea container and scoop, the feeling and folding of the cloth intensifying her concentration. Using the *hishaku* (wooden ladle) she ladles hot water into the *chawan* (tea bowl) to warm it, then rinses the fragile bamboo *chasen* (tea whisk). After emptying

---

* Face powder is made with a mixture of ground rice and white lead.

† *Kissa-hoo* signifies 'the spirit of thoughtfulness between giver and receiver'.

the water from the *chawan*, she dries it with a linen cloth. Jitsuzen following her movements admires the *chawan*'s glossy black glaze.

Sometimes Umeko's movements are smooth, at other times abrupt. Sometimes her movements are hurried, at other times slow, the differences creating the beauty of the occasion. Gonzaemon is pleased: his daughter has mastered the pursuit of the spirit of *ichigo ichie*,* treating the ritual with grave respect and their guest with deference and vigilant attention.

The room smells of charcoal, sandalwood and *igusa-rush*.† But another elusive fragrance ripens over time. As she bends over the fire, the smoke drifts through Umeko's brilliantined hair, the perfume of the pomade combining with her body odour.

With a slender bamboo *chashaku* (tea scoop), she takes three scoops of *matcha* (powdered green tea) from the tea container, placing the powder in the heated *chawan*; each scoop increases in quantity until she finally empties the contents of the container into the bowl. Slowly turning to face the kettle, she ladles enough boiling water into the *chawan* to form a paste; then, she adds more to bring it to a drinkable consistency. Holding the vessel steady with one hand, she whisks the *matcha* until foam appears, the colour of the pea-green brew enhanced by the *chawan*'s dark lustre.

Offering the tea first towards the Buddha, she then kneels before Jitsuzen, presenting the *chawan* on a red tray. Beside the *chawan* are a bamboo fork and a *wagashi*** shaped like a spring leaf and coloured green with *matcha*. Jitsuzen bows, unconsciously inhaling her fragrance. Taking the *chawan* with his right hand, he places it on the palm of his left, then, with his right, rotates it clockwise three times. Feeling the rough grooves formed by the potter's fingers, he senses the potter's spirit. The others watch as he takes a sip of tea, then a

---

* *Ichigo ichie* means making the occasion perfect, as it will never be repeated.
† *Igusa-rush* is grass from which *tatami* are woven.
** *Wagashi* is confectionery made from sweet bean paste.

mouthful of *wagashi*. The sweetness of the *wagashi* complements the acerbic taste of the *matcha*, its texture pleasing against his tongue.

Using his right hand, Jitsuzen wipes the *chawan* where his lips have touched, rotates it counterclockwise, and passes it to the *otomo*. After the *otomo* has taken a mouthful, he passes it to the merchant, who then passes it to his wife. After Umeko has taken her turn, she rinses the *chawan* and *chasen*, and wipes the *chashaku*, *hishaku* and tea jar. All items are then offered to the guests to examine more closely.

Jitsuzen compliments his host on the taste and appearance of the *wagashi*. He praises the beauty of the *chawan* and the quality of the *matcha*. No pains have been spared for his visit. And he is charmed by the young Umeko.

Before going to the house to discuss business over a light luncheon, the merchant conducts Jitsuzen on a tour of his garden. Enclosed by a meandering woodland walk, cedar, paulownia, *zelkova* and two-needled pine tower over camellia, azalea and rhododendrons.

Cool and fragrant, the garden is an understated picture of green. Surprises await Jitsuzen at each vista. Secluded areas provide refuge and solace. The pathway winds through a thicket of trees, then past a pond, its edges softened with reeds. A willow droops over a drift of irises splashing purple in a boggy hollow. Unexpectedly, in a grove of bamboo, they come upon a stone triad representing heaven, earth and man. A rustic crossing spans a mass of moss mimicking a stream.

In the shelter of the overhanging eaves, the men remove their *geta* and mount the wooden veranda step. There, as custom requires, the daughter of the house waits. Kneeling, head bowed, Umeko holds up a tray with three rolled wet towels. As Jitsuzen bends to take one, the sleeve of his robe brushes against the sleeve of her *kimono*.

Two weeks later, the priest came again on business. This time, on her father's instruction, only Umeko awaited his arrival at the teahouse.

Chapter 10

On Deeper than the Deepest Sea, Higher than the Highest Mountain

Chochin to tsurigane
A lantern and a bell
(The bride and groom are far apart in status)

ORIGINAL INDIAN BUDDHIST PHILOSOPHY forbade the marriage of priests as it would compromise their spiritual focus. However, the practice was adapted in Japan to fit the overriding importance of the family system and the hereditary male line. In turning a blind eye to a priest's 'common-law wife', succession was ensured. And, by housing his 'wife' outside the temple grounds, the priest could focus on his true calling. It was ambiguous, but everyone knew and accepted it. The Meiji Revolution allowed priests to marry, though it took decades for the practice to be sanctioned socially.

Gonzaemon decreed Umeko should marry Jitsuzen. It would consolidate his business alliance with the temple. His seven other children had all been married within the merchant caste, but Umeko was different, 'out of specification'. She had been adopted at birth, and Jitsuzen was of more suitable rank. The merchant's middleman approached the temple director to act for the priest.

Marriage was Umeko's only possible career. It was her duty to serve and obey three masters: her father, her husband and her sons. A daughter was a commodity to be traded, and she was rarely appreciated for her character or talent. A wife was seldom loved, and more often than not treated like a servant. Jitsuzen would have eventually married within the priestly caste, but now attracted as he was to Umeko, her father's offer was too good to refuse.

Umeko acknowledged the *on* she owed her parents. Kneeling, she placed her hands flat on the floor and keeping her buttocks down, lowered her forehead between her hands. Her *on* was much greater than usual. Not only had her parents found her a superior husband, but they continued to keep and protect her, giving her a house within their compound. As a high priest, Jitsuzen had to live at the temple, but visited his wife twice a week. In 1896, their daughter Ryoko was born; a year later their son Shozo.

Like all temples by the turn of the nineteenth century, the status of Eizan-*ji* began to fall and with it came a corresponding decline in Gonzaemon's business. Furthermore, with the family's monopolistic licence now forbidden, the merchant decided Umeko would divorce* Jitsuzen and marry someone richer. Induced financially, Jitsuzen sadly agreed. Gonzaemon directed that Umeko should keep their son Shozo and Jitsuzen their daughter Ryoko. Ryoko would be Hisashi's mother. Umeko and Ryoko never saw each other again. Another marriage to another priest was duly arranged for Umeko, but shortly afterwards she was forced to divorce yet again and marry someone else more promising. While there were no children with the second husband, she had two daughters with her third husband, also a priest.

Jitsuzen also remarried. His new wife, Sato, was a cleric from a middle-ranked priest family. He and several others had established schools nationwide for trainee priests, exclusive to family members

---

* Traditionally, it took just three set written lines for a husband to divorce his wife. He could divorce her simply by sending her back to her parents for such trivial reasons as poor health, infertility, even talkativeness. While a wife's adultery was punishable by death, this did not apply to husbands. A wife could initiate divorce only if her husband had committed a serious crime. Her only other escape from marriage was to take refuge in a temple.

of existing priests. Attending one of these schools, Sato met Jitsuzen and, after she graduated, they were married. They had one daughter Tomoko, born ten years after Ryoko. By this time the marriage of priests was socially approved, but Jitsuzen and Sato still lived separately, with Jitsuzen occasionally visiting her small temple. It was unusual for a female priest to be responsible for a temple, but with the disappearance of the *samurai* supporters after the revolution, there had been insufficient career prospects to attract a male priest. As there were no other options, Sato had been accepted.

Ryoko lived with her mother and grandparents for the first nine years of her life, leading a protected existence, never leaving the compound. She was a *shinso* (closeted maiden) brought up with the utmost care. After her parents' divorce, her father saw to it that she continued to be shielded from outside contact, but she never again knew a family atmosphere, or her mother's warmth. Sato wanted nothing to do with her and Jitsuzen visited only occasionally. Even when Ryoko went to school, her nanny delivered and collected her every day, so she had no opportunity to make friends. Protected from the stormy years of early twentieth century Japan, and living in isolated splendour in a villa attended by servants, she was ignorant of ordinary daily life, unaware of such household matters as how to supervise servants or budget for family expenses. But she knew no other way and had no reason to feel sorry for herself.

Chapter 11

The Young of a Frog is a Frog

Tsuki-matou-giri
Giri follows like a shadow

HAJIME, HISASHI'S PATERNAL GRANDFATHER, a descendant of Sakuzaemon, the physician, was born the eldest son of the Furuya family in 1848, 20 years before the Meiji Revolution. His ancestors had been retained as doctors for the Maeda family since the early sixteenth century. Although outside the caste system, doctors were ranked alongside *samurai* and, as heir, Hajime was educated to become his father's successor, with generations of secret knowledge, skills and instruments passed down from father to son. Be it doctor, warrior, farmer, artisan or merchant, in Japanese society no one argued with the rule that sons followed their fathers and grandfathers.

The Furuya family came from Kanazawa on the west coast of Honshu,* a wealthy and cultured fiefdom, the Maeda family so rich as to be self-sufficient.† A fertile region, Kanazawa was one of the largest and best rice-producing areas. Separated by the Alps, the west coast had a different culture and history to the east. People even looked different. Hajime would have had the single-lidded eyes inherited by his grandson Hisashi. Situated closer to the Korean Peninsula, with a

---

* Honshu is the main island of Japan.
† Wealth was measured by rice yield in *koku* (186 litres), the quantity eaten annually by a *samurai*. Maeda's fiefdom produced a million *koku* a year; 10 000 *koku* was the minimum to be a *daimyo*.

narrow strait for access, Buddhism and Korean culture blended in the west, whereas the culture and development of the east coast was more inclined towards Chinese culture.

Maeda's most important retainers lived nearest his castle, the size of their plot in proportion to their stipend. The Furuya family stipend of 1 000 *koku* meant that they lived on half an acre close to the castle. Most retainers were 'lower *samurai*', earning meagre stipends and living communally.

Hajime was proud of his occupation and family name and, in 1862 when he turned 14, he assumed manhood at a special ceremony blessed by his parents, relations and servants. He was then entitled to wear two swords. Having secured his hereditary stipend, all he wanted to do was devote his life to medicine. But his *on* was immeasurable and, while his inheritance gave him prestige and everything he could ask for, he was ambivalent, wanting to give thanks, but also resenting the burden. His every act made him eternally indebted to the *shogun* and to Maeda, to ten generations of ancestors who passed down his guaranteed stipend, skills and knowledge, and even to the herbalist who supplied his medicines. But, obediently, he accepted his burden.

Consequently his *giri* was enormous. It was his duty to the *shogun* to obey the law. It was his duty to follow the instructions of his *daimyo*, and to care for him and his family. It was his duty to his ancestors to maintain the family honour. It was his duty to repay his herbalist by providing free medical care to his children. It was his duty to his profession to be a conscientious, capable practitioner. But his greatest *giri* was to his father. It was his duty to assist his father in the family practice and to improve his own skills and knowledge. It was his duty to continue the family profession and manage his inheritance wisely. It was his duty to marry and have a son. It was his duty to observe all 'respect behaviour', live within his 'proper station' and curb his emotions.

Six years later, the *shogun* surrendered to the Imperial Court, the *daimyo* and *samurai* affiliated to his regime being deprived of their privileges. Many *daimyo* went bankrupt, unable to pay off their *samurai*. Fortunately for 20-year-old Hajime, his father received sufficient compensation to retire comfortably. And an unsuccessful attempt to gain a post in the new government did not set Hajime back. 'Out of specification' from his peers, he had his profession to fall back on, as well as a share of his father's compensation. This enabled him to explore his interest in Western medicine.

Hajime and his forebears had traditionally practised Chinese medicine, but few advances in treatment and knowledge had been made. Not being allowed to dissect human bodies, they were unaware that Chinese anatomical charts were less accurate than those that had reached Japan through the local Dutch community. As the popularity of Dutch studies grew, medicine progressed rapidly.

Hajime was wealthy enough to travel to Sakai on the east coast, one of the two ports that allowed Dutch trade. Increasing his *giri* even further, through Maeda's contacts, he met the local *daimyo*'s *otomo*, who introduced him to the Dutch-speaking Japanese doctor who was prepared to teach him Western medicine. Returning to thank the *otomo*, he was taken with his daughter Tatsuko, and it was Hajime himself who initiated the approach to the *nakodo* (middleman). In 1880, 32-year-old Hajime married 24-year-old Tatsuko. And Hajime's *giri* continued to grow.

Chapter 14

The Good Wife and Wise Mother

Ete ni ho o ageru
To hoist sails when the wind is favourable

LIKE UMEKO, TATSUKO HAD LIVED a pampered life. She had been trained to be a 'good wife and wise mother', and her status demanded many hours be set aside for personal grooming in order to achieve the perfect appearance required of a good wife. Every ten days, during an entire afternoon, Tatsuko's hair was restyled, her coiffure being her parent's pride, showing to all that they could afford the high cost of maintenance.

> The day before the wedding, an assistant arrives to prepare Tatsuko's hair for the master hairdresser. As her hair is never washed, it takes an hour of combing to remove the paste used to hold her hair in place. Tatsuko hates this stage. With her left hand grasping the hair near the roots, the hairdresser combs with her right, pressing heavily on Tatsuko's scalp. The pain is excruciating: she combs so ferociously, and pulls so tightly, Tatsuko worries her hair will fall out, and she will begin to go bald like her mother. The oak comb is strong,* gifted to her that day by her mother, who in turn received it from her mother

---

* Crafted by a master, the comb had taken ten years to make from cutting the tree to its final polish. For a family heirloom, the finest wood had to be used, smoke-dried and cured for years before a piece was cut.

just prior to her wedding day. This 'life-time comb' carries precious memories from a long line of women.

Eventually, the combing is finished and the master hairdresser arrives with the fresh *bintsuke abura*.* Thick and sticky, it requires another hour of pulling, teasing, twisting and winding, to pile her hair high in the extravagant *bunkin takashimada* (wedding style). How Tatsuko looks forward to her bath so she can soak away her headache.

Bathing was integral to Japanese life, a ritual, with a prescribed order for rinsing, washing and soaking. But only the wealthy had tubs at home; most people went to the *sento* (public bathhouse) where they bathed for a small fee, enjoying a gossip with the neighbours in the hot communal bath.

As usual her father bathed first, followed by her mother and two youngest sisters. Next was Tatsuko, then her other sisters, and lastly the servants. Everyone used the same water, retaining the heat between bathers by covering the tub with planks.

Before getting in, Tatsuko crouches on the tiled floor beside the wooden tub to wash herself. Her maid kneels behind, soaping her back, then, filling a small wooden bucket with hot water from the tub, rinses her off. Heaving a sigh of relief, her hair lifted up by the maid, Tatsuko lowers herself into the hot water, submerging her whole body. Leaning against the tub, her hair safe in the hands of her maid, she closes her eyes and embraces the heat. Water laps over the sides and the distinctive perfume of pomade permeates the balmy air, inducing a sensation of bliss, sultry and sensual. The bath is a haven of calm, encouraging her to linger. Luxuriating in the water, looking out at the lush greenery of the courtyard, she feels a frisson of excitement for the coming day.

---

* *Bintsuke abura* is a mixture of wax from the haze tree and camellia oil.

Afterwards she would sleep with a wooden concave box pillow that held her head firmly in place so she did not crush her coiffure.

Threatened by centuries of earthquakes, *taifu* (typhoons) and fire, the Japanese had learned to live lightly, in small homes with minimal furniture. Their mostly one-roomed houses were furnished by day with cushions and a low table.* In the evening, the table was moved aside and bedding brought out from storage. Tatsuko's home, like Umeko's, was different.

Within the curtain 'walls', the front half of the first floor had been set aside for the formal *tatami*-matted reception rooms, each room partitioned by *fusuma*.† The kitchen was at the rear, positioned to take advantage of the morning and evening light needed for food preparation. Family rooms and storage areas were up the narrow staircase on the second storey, while servants' quarters, storehouses and stables were out the back. An unpolished wooden *engawa* (corridor) wrapped around the exterior of the house, underneath the broad hovering roof. Outer *shoji** were protected by sliding, shutter-like panels that were partitioned in front at night or in bad weather.

> With the *fusuma* slid back, the reception rooms facing the garden become one. Pale walls and matting contrast with dark exposed beams. Shafts of sunlight fill the room with glowing light, and the newly laid *tatami* releases its pleasing perfume, its indigo edgings fitting perfectly.
>
> In the sparse room each detail assumes heightened significance.

---

* Houses were modular, built using fixed proportions, which enabled builders to work without intricate blueprints, and still to ensure overall harmony. The size of a room was measured by the number of *tatami*. The *tatami*, at roughly one by two metres, created a standardised scale that determined the size and shape of rooms, and placement of partitions, windows and doors. Freestanding staircase *tansu* provided storage and access if there was an upper storey.

† *Fusuma* are sliding screens covered with thick handmade paper.

** *Shoji* are wooden latticed screens paned with light-diffusing paper.

> Tatsuko's dowry *tansu* has been rolled to one corner, mother-of-pearl peonies glistening against the red-stained wood. In the opposite corner of the room, gold-leafed chrysanthemums flourish on a screen bordered with silk. In the *tokonoma* a white lily graces a sturdy red vase. Legless chairs with gold cushions have been placed at precise angles around low wooden tables; dinner will be served on individual, footed lacquer trays. Surveying the room, though it does not do to show other than a serene face, Tatsuko covers a smile with her hand.*

A large gathering had been invited for the extravagant evening wedding dinner. United to celebrate, they would eat, drink and philosophise.

> With much bowing, the guests arrive at last. Gone are the men's swords, *hakama* (pleated culotte skirts) and topknots; these have been replaced by stiff collars, Western suits and short hairstyles. Candlelight illuminates the room, picking up the magic of the golden screen, and the threads in the sumptuous gold and silver *obi* the women wear over their black silk *kimono*.

---

* When speaking to a superior it was also important to hold your hand in front of your mouth as it was considered rude to breathe on people.

Chapter 13

The Eyes of the World are Upon Us

Fukoku kyohei
Enrich the country, strengthen the military

HISASHI'S MATERNAL AND PATERNAL grandparents met and married as a result of drastic social change. Marriages between couples in different territories and of different *daimyo*, like that of Hajime and Tatsuko, were now possible; as were marriages between couples of different castes, like that of Jitsuzen, the *samurai* priest, and Umeko, the merchant's daughter. Jitsuzen and Umeko lived within the traditional order of Japan, while Hajime and Tatsuko were caught up in the new order. But those were not the only changes affecting their lives.

While the old conformist, hierarchical order had subsumed individual worth, it had provided cohesion, and with it a sense of security and national worth. As the 'bamboo curtain' lifted, the Japanese people realised Japan lagged behind much of the Western world. Desperate to catch up, the new government made enormous efforts to imitate the West; its slogan, *fukoku kyohei* (Enrich the country, strengthen the military) showed it was intent on reform and destroying all ties to the Tokugawa regime. At the same time, the 33 million citizens were expected to preserve their 'Japanese spirit'. But the two cultures were often so diverse they did not mix comfortably, and this policy of rapid modernisation led to uncertainty in everyday life, eroding traditional values and causing confusion and feelings of inferiority. People as individuals had little inner strength to fall back on. Their religion was like air, part of their lives providing a skeleton, but with no internal substance.

To judge their own worth, they had always looked outside themselves, making comparisons. And now the whole world seemed to be watching and waiting for them to make mistakes, such as happened with the 'Unequal trade treaties' signed after Commodore Perry's visit.* Even though the treaties were amended in 1894, the Japanese people never forgot the shame. The treaties had seemed to imply the Japanese were incapable of standing up for themselves to negotiate a fair arrangement, and their *haji* was intense.

Japan embarked on a period of frenetic and phenomenal growth. Western vessels quickly replaced Japanese sailing ships. Free trade developed with the outside world. Agriculture was modernised. Coal mines were opened. Roads were improved. A rail network expanded rapidly.† Post offices, banks, newspapers and insurance companies were established. The Western calendar, weights and measures were adopted. The *yen* (Japanese currency) and a whole new system of banking was introduced.**

The government was centralised on the Western model and ministers were allocated specific portfolios.†† In 1889, the Constitution of the Empire of Japan was adopted, opening the way to parliamentary government, though sovereignty remained vested in the Emperor and

---

* The unfair treaties were due for renewal in 1872. To show Japan was open to modernisation and worthy of international status, a group of leading politicians travelled to America and Europe. The mission was successful, and legal reforms modelled on the European system allowed the Japanese government to re-negotiate the treaties.

† The first train ran in 1872. The first gas lamps were lit in 1874. The first electric street-car ran in Kyoto in 1885. The first domestic electric light was switched on in Tokyo in 1886. The first automobile was imported in 1896.

** The new standardised system of currency, introduced in 1871, was modelled on the American system, with decimal denominations.

†† The new Meiji Government was an alliance between wealthy merchants and *samurai* administrators who had managed feudal monopolies. In the 1870s, dissatisfied *samurai* not represented in the new administration launched a movement for civil rights, forming the Liberal Party in 1881.

the government was administered by a predetermined hierarchy. In 1890, the first *Diet* (Japanese parliament) was opened.

New industries were set up with Western ideas and technology. With few natural resources, imports were vital, though exports were equally important to raise revenue for imports. Aiming to be the major supplier to the rest of Asia, Japan's only competitive weapon was to add value to imported raw materials using cheap labour. The government decided what new industries were needed, then financed and developed them, importing foreigners to advise and sending Japanese abroad to learn. Industrial growth shifted from textiles to heavy manufacturing, the key industries being arsenals, shipbuilding, ironworks and construction of the railways. Once established, the industries were sold to a preferred few, though the armaments industry remained in government hands.

People flocked to the cities for work. Some companies employed thousands of well-paid workers using the latest technology. But it was the medium-sized and smaller concerns that dominated the economy: those employing several hundred trained staff to manufacture specialised components for a final producer, and those who paid a pittance to a few low-skilled workers to process foods and crafts.

After more than ten centuries of power, Buddhism was disestablished; in its place came the revival of Shinto. The new government's version of history centred on Amaterasu as the creator of Japan, the Emperor her living manifestation, with the 1870 Imperial Rescript (official edict) detailing the relationship of Shinto to the State.* Descended from age eternal in unbroken succession, the Emperor was the supreme symbol of national unity. For the populace, the Emperor

---

* By the 1880s Shinto had been divided by law. Sectarian Shinto relied on worshippers for support, sectarian shrines emphasising the family and ancestor worship. State Shinto sought to perpetuate national loyalty and obedience by inculcating loyalty and obedience to the Emperor, followed by filial piety, and diligence in performing one's duties. Though declared non-religious in the hope of pleasing the West, it was regulated by the government and relied on 200 000 requisitioned shrines, whose ceremonies and festivals fostered devotion and undying allegiance to the Emperor.

reinforced the belief in Japanese superiority, and their divine right to rule the world.

Shogunal on was easily transferred to the Emperor and *Amaterasu*, to whom they now owed their safety and status. *Giri* and *on* had been tools used horizontally across the structure of society to maintain order, with the emphasis being on relationships between people at large. With State *Shinto*, the vertical relationship was all important, *giri* and *on* used to eliminate the influence of the Tokugawa and Buddhism, and to develop a modern nation while still controlling the people.

But as ideas of equality grew too popular, the government felt the need to rein in things Western, promoting instead values of patriotism, traditional obligations and *Bushido* (The Way of the Warrior).* Not wishing to become a colony of one of the expanding Western empires, Japan sought to create its own.

The highest indebtedness for the Japanese was an abiding duty to repay the Emperor for his favour, and even to die in war. Parents were urged to bring up their sons to be warriors, and their sons were needed in subsequent wars. Life stayed the same, showing nothing but a change of face.

Educational reform reinforced the ideology that was unified in the 1890 Imperial Rescript on Education. Issued in the Emperor's name, the revered text spelt out the morals of Emperor worship and filial piety. Japanese history and *shushin* enmeshed with State *Shinto* would give rise to the era of ultra-nationalism.

---

* The term *Bushido* was popularised in 1905 by the Imperial Nipponese Army apologist Dr Inazo Nitobein in his book *Bushido: The Soul of Japan*. He used the term to describe the traditional ideals of *samurai* conduct.

Chapter 14

Stepping Out

Shin-tenchi
Opening up a new world

IN 1884, HISASHI'S PATERNAL GRANDPARENTS moved to Tokyo. Hajime's dream of working in Western medicine was more likely to be realised in the new capital. As well, by moving away, Tatsuko would have less responsibility for her nine younger sisters, though she would not be freed from her *on*.

The first 12 years of their marriage were happy and productive. They had three children, two sons and a daughter. Their second son Jinjiro, Hisashi's father, was born in 1884. Hajime had found work easily as a senior manager in a company manufacturing Western pharmaceutical products. His ambition to be involved in research was realised in the development of Jin-tan, a mouthwash that can still be bought in Japan. Thus Hajime was well able to provide his family with an affluent standard of living. Their palatial home in a quiet, tree-lined street was situated on the hill in the up-scale suburb of Aoyama, southwest of the palace.

Soon after starting his new job, Hajime went to Yokohama to visit a comprador (Chinese agent) about importing a new American drug. Yokohama meaning 'side port' was the biggest port in Asia. Tokyo and Yokohama had been connected by telegraph since 1870, and rail since 1872, with the train jokingly called the *oka joki* (land steamer). Leaving early, Hajime could complete the trip in the one day: by rickshaw to Aoyama tram station, to Shim-*bashi* by tram, then travelling the 28 kilometres to Yokohama by *oka joki*.*

In 1858, Yokohama had been the first port open to foreign trade. Export revenue was urgently required to import much needed resources and the *shogun* had wanted the port developed quickly. The once struggling fishing village was now the second largest city in Japan. With its sheltered natural harbour, trade prospered due principally to the importing of raw cotton from India and the exporting of raw silk.

It was here in 'the city of silk', that most foreigners lived. Using cheap, imported Chinese labour the *gaijin* had laid the foundations of an entirely new settlement. Along the shoreline in Kannai, quarantine, customs, consuls, translators, and government offices were housed behind impressive Western edifices. Next door in Chukagai (Chinatown), narrow lanes crisscrossed willow-fringed creeks. Tightly sited, it was here that nearly 90 per cent of the population lived and worked. On the bluff above, in Yamate Heights, leading *gaijin* resided in handsome weatherboard homes.

As well as being the first port opened to foreigners and the first destination of the first-ever train, Yokohama was also the first place in Japan to publish a newspaper; to have a bakery, a photographic studio, a tennis club, a brewery, and Western-style horse racing; and to sell ice-cream.

> Talks go well and, after a quick courtesy call to the local government office, Hajime is free. He loves ice-cream and sets off to find some. In his *samurai*-style short *kimono*, *obi*, *hakama*, casual *haori* (jacket), Eton-style straw hat, *geta* and *tabi*, he is conspicuous among the otherwise European clientele. 'Ice-*clin*' is expensive, one scoop costing about half the average monthly wage.
>
> Satisfied, Hajime wanders back to the waterfront. On the horizon he can see the butterfly sails of an incoming junk. Closer in to shore,

---

* The world's first public railroad to employ steam power had opened in England in 1825.

foreign freight steamers rest alongside weatherworn Japanese windjammers and lofty-masted Chinese junks. Small bobbing sampans shuttle from ship to shore, dodged by lug-sailed fishing boats. Countless prows line the water's edge.

Entering Chukagai, Hajime revels in the rowdy merchant activity so different from Tokyo. Shops and stalls abound with exotic choices unavailable in the rest of Japan, with Chinese, Japanese and Indians peddling all sorts from imported foods and flashy gold jewellery to disposable rags. A herbalist is wedged between a second-hand clothing shop and a tailor, and upstairs a house of prostitution displays provocative washing suspended from a bamboo pole.

The air is heavy with unfamiliar smells, of chilli sizzling in a wok, ground shrimp, bloodied pork and the stench of the spiny durian.* Drawn to the aroma of *samosa* frying, Hajime waits hungrily as a hot triangular pastry is wrapped in a bamboo leaf and thrust into his hand. Next, served in a round bamboo basket, are steamed *dim sum* filled with minced shrimp, followed by freshly baked rice cakes – all washed down with a cup of Chinese tea. For Hajime, eating on the street is a unique and exotic culinary experience.

He is used to being among the Dutch from his days in Sakai, but he has never seen so many *gaijin* in one place: black hair, and blond, red and brown; short hair, long hair, shaven heads; a plaited queue swinging loose; a braid wound around the top of the head; short trimmed beards, bushy beards, long straggly beards; blue eyes and black. Voices bellow and haggle in Japanese, Chinese, Dutch, English, Russian and Hindu; people smile and nod their heads. They have things to do, many of which Hajime has never seen done in public before: a street barber trims a customer's beard, a fortune-teller stares at the hand of a pretty girl, an ear cleaner plies his trade, a sari-clad woman reclines on a chair. A bearded old man perambulates majestically through the throng, walking his caged canary.

---

* A durian is a Southeast Asian fruit containing a creamy pulp with an agreeable taste but a fetid smell.

His senses saturated, Hajime locates the herbalist who has been recommended to him. Brass canisters gleam in the small shadowy shop, glass-fronted cabinetry containing a pharmacopoeia of fossils, fungi, herbs, insects and seeds. Hajime removes his scarlet lacquered *inro* (a tiny storage box for holding medicines) that dangles from his *obi*. Into the top compartment goes Chinese yam to treat exhaustion, Ginseng root for dizzy spells, and in the bottom mulberry wood to lower his blood pressure.

Heading back to the railway station, he detours on to the new highway that runs along the seaside, parallel with the railroad and lined with new Western-style factories. Rickshaws pound the rough road recklessly bypassing drays loaded with coal. Hajime notices one heavily laden dray, the small horse struggling to haul its weight. He stops in disbelief as he recognises the poorly dressed driver. They were friends as boys. He wants to call out, but does not, afraid of hurting the man's pride. All the way home he ponders his fortunate position, his happy family and comfortable job.

At the weekends, Hajime liked to stroll with the family in the Ginza and enjoy an ice-cream at Fugetsudo, the cookie retailers, who were the first in Tokyo to sell the expensive treat.

In contrast to cosmopolitan Yokohama, Tokyo had taken on a Western look. Development still circled the palace, but busy urban centres were mushrooming outwards. The old *shogunal* castle, much of its grounds taken for redevelopment, had been replaced with a wooden structure. The newly built *Diet* and the Prime Minister's residence were up on the hill, not far from Aoyama, in neighbouring Nagatacho. East of the palace, adding valuable land to the heart of the city, even more of the shoreline had been reclaimed. Here the streets were paved with granite, the telegraph linked Japan to America and Europe and, as the sun set, electric lamps lit the way.

Building on the earlier Edo city map: starting from Shim-*bashi* where Hajime had caught the train to Yokohama, on the western side was Hibiya where the newly built Imperial Hotel provided luxurious surroundings for foreign entrepreneurs flocking to Japan; Hibiya merged into Yurakucho; Yurakucho into Marunouchi, long identified with power and prestige; and Marunouchi into Kasumi-ga-*seki*, then across the creek into the new Bunkyo Education Ward, location of the prestigious Tokyo Imperial University (commonly known as *Todai*).* Sited on the previous estate of the *daimyo* Maeda, it was where generations of wives and children of the Furuya family had lived with Maeda's family as hostages of the government. Apart from the splendid double-doored vermillion gate, which had been retained as the university's entrance, the area would be unrecognisable to Hajime's ancestor Sakuzaemon.

On the eastern side, starting from Shim-*bashi* was the Ginza, which stretched northwards into Nihom-*bashi*, formerly the hub of Shitamachi, and where prosperous wholesalers and moneylending businesses had evolved into banks, brokers and trading firms; into Kanda renowned for its bookshops and publishing houses, then Ueno-*eki* (railway station). Right of Ueno was Asakusa, also with its Shitamachi roots. Commercial focus had shifted into the Ginza, packed into a rectangular grid, known as 'Bricktown'. The government mint had relocated, but the name had stayed. Then, virtually destroyed by fire in 1872, the area had been remodelled.

> It is a hot Sunday in 1892. The day has a leisurely feel. After buying fresh bread from Kimuraya Bakery a few blocks before Nihom-*bashi*, the family can window-shop, drop into an exhibition, sip tea in an English-style tearoom, and eat pastries at a French-style café, or ice-cream at Fugetsudo.
>
> As always the Ginza is congested, but moving steadfastly through, two-horse teams tow boxcars along straight, shiny tracks, rickshaws, pedestrians, carts, and trams, competing for space. The metalled

---

* Tokyo Imperial University was founded by Imperial decree in 1877, followed 20 years later by Kyoto University, with five more universities established by 1939.

boulevard is flanked by concrete, red-brick, and granite buildings, embellished with wreaths and swags, bay windows, columns and elaborate door surrounds, trading names written boldly in black or gold calligraphy. Out of deference to the nearby palace, nothing is over eight floors in height. Dressed in their semi-best, the Furuya family stroll leisurely along the wide pavement, leafy willows offering welcome shade. Tatsuko, her generous proportions swathed in dark green silk is a commanding figure, obviously the wife of a well-to-do gentleman. Mariko is dressed likewise in a *kimono*, a pretty pink, suitable for a young girl. Tatsuko's menfolk, however, are dressed Western-style, Hajime in a tailor-made suit and derby hat, Michitaro and Jinjiro miniature versions of their father, fashion dictating over practicality, their suits uncomfortable in the summer heat.

It was here in the Ginza where the new breed indulged their whims, rarely venturing into the honeycomb of narrow, twisting back alleys. Just a couple of blocks away, cottage industries were prolific, families engaged in producing paper goods, *wagashi*, or fans. Cobblers made and repaired *geta*, nimble-fingered seamstresses mended or made over *kimono*. Locals shopped, gossiped and lingered over cups of tea.

Chapter 15

The World Tips

Tora wa shishite kawa o todome,
hito wa shishite na o nokosu
A tiger dies and leaves his skin;
a man dies and leaves his name

THERE WERE NUMEROUS BANKING FIRMS in Tokyo, from branches of major international houses to emerging local businesses. It was all the rage for ex-*samurai* with money to run a money lending business, which however, often failed, the trend incurring public ridicule. Hajime, too, dabbled in such a venture, losing not only his own money but that of other family members, which signalled the end of the good life for the Furuya family. Then less than a year later, in 1893, 37-year-old Tatsuko died, supposedly of a heart attack. Michitaro was 12 years old, Jinjiro 9 and Mariko 6.

Hajime was distraught. Ignoring the expectation that he marry again, he broke up the family, entering Michitaro in the Naval Academy, with Mariko being adopted by his brother. He kept Jinjiro with him and they continued to live in the family home for another eight years. But, with *otosan* (father) often away on business, it was a lonely life for the boy, who had only a servant for company. Then, in 1901, with his funds finally depleted, Hajime arranged for 17-year-old Jinjiro to be adopted, his new family sponsoring him to train as an accountant.

The Furuya family house was sold to pay creditors, and Hajime shifted to Kyoto where he was supported by his younger brother.

There he became involved with the organisation Ittoen,* whose members lived in the spirit of penitence, leading frugal lives in the service of others. Guilt-ridden and deeply ashamed, Hajime saw such a life as the ultimate penance, and a way to clear his reputation. His daily routine included begging for alms, and 'dipping-up night soils', his earnings donated to the poor.

Michitaro and Jinjiro were shattered he had chosen such a life, many years later discussing his actions. Why had he not remarried when *okasan* (mother) died and kept the family together? Why had he not continued his work as a doctor? Was *okasan*'s death part of the answer? They had never really believed it was heart failure as they had been told at the time. Had she actually committed suicide? They remembered *okasan* had encouraged her nine sisters and their husbands to invest in *otosan*'s money-lending business, then, suggested he lend most of the money to one of her friends. The resulting bad debt had never been recovered. Had *okasan* felt such loss of face that she had killed herself? They could understand how worried *otosan* would have been about the extent of his obligation to the other investors whose money he had lost, and also about the extent he was to blame for *okasan*'s death. But brought up under State Shinto with primary allegiance to the nation and only secondary allegiance to the family, the sons could never fully appreciate their father's unfathomable *haji*.

Hajime had believed he could protect his children and Tatsuko's sisters from ostracism, and retaliation by the other investors, by his drastic action. Despite his veneer of Western ways, at heart he was an old-fashioned *samurai* entrenched in the old horizontal *on*. His *haji* knew no bounds. Through his own fault he had brought dishonour to his family, betraying his father, his ancestors, his children, his wife and his in-laws, and in doing so he lost face with the world. He saw he had only two choices. But rather than choosing an honourable suicide, he attempted to attain Buddha-hood in exchange for relinquishing all

---
* Ittoen was founded by Tenko Nishida in 1904.

secular desires and ambitions. *Giri* still dogged his footsteps. He now had to behave within his new 'proper place', living the appropriate life, behaving himself within the confines of Ittoen, his *giri* to clear his reputation.

Hajime died alone in 1909, with nothing to call his own. In contrast, the once shabbily dressed dray driver sat at a splendid desk as president of the cement company to which he had once delivered coal. Part of a *zaibatsu* (financial clique),* his future was assured.

Having declared bankruptcy, Hajime had relinquished his responsibility as head of the line, irrevocably changing the course of his sons' lives. When Michitaro reached marriageable age, he had had to find a bride from a family 'out of specification' like his own. Hajime had called on Nun Shogetsu of Ittoen to choose a bride for Michitaro, and then adopt her. Nun Shogetsu a rich, retired *geisha* accordingly chose a young woman from the pleasure quarters.

Since first entering the Naval Academy, Michitaro had aspired to become an admiral, but adding his father's bankruptcy to his wife's background put an end to that. However, while his wife was a drawback for promotion in the navy, she was a plus for his retirement, when at age 50 he was appointed manager of the canteen at the Yokosuka Naval Base,† the base where he had been stationed most of his career. Albeit in a different area, thanks to his wife's influence, he acquired the status he had always wanted. Using her contacts, he was able to arrange every imaginable *geisha* spree desired by the officers. However, for Jinjiro, without the old certainties, life was confusing.

---

* Most large manufacturers emerged after the revolution: new government enterprises, including rail and shipping lines, shipyards, telephone and telegraph systems, and arsenals; independent firms manufacturing steel, paper, textiles, or glass, brewers, or sugar refineries. And then there were the *zaibatsu*, such as Mitsui, Sumitomo, Mitsubishi, and Yasuda. *Zaibatsu* were family owned, entrepreneurial conglomerates comprising interconnected businesses: a bank, an international trading house, a real estate firm, an insurance company, several manufacturers and a mining company. Generating their capital internally, they were autonomous and could protect themselves from the fluctuation of the capital market. Family control was exercised through a holding-company with interlocking directorships and the cross-holding of shares.

† The largest naval base in Japan.

At the beginning of the twentieth century, boys had opportunities that their fathers and grandfathers had never dreamed of, opportunities in engineering and business, as well as joining the new modern Japanese navy or army.* Jinjiro's step-parents were *narikin* ('pawns acting as big shots' or the new rich) with no children. His step-father ran an export–import business in Los Angeles, and Jinjiro was expected to immigrate to America and become his successor.

Having been protected all his life, even after his mother died, Jinjiro had never had the need to fight against hardship. He was used to a servant and did little for himself. He was a typical character among the well-to-do; gentle and compliant, somewhat naïve and sensitive, but earnest and sincere, and disliking confrontation. He much preferred spending his time reading poetry and classical literature. Put simply, Jinjiro did not have an adventurous or fighting spirit, and he was not the type to become a dedicated businessman. But trapped by *giri*, he was deeply indebted to his adoptive father. Added to this, he resented his own father's desertion, and his adoption and its social slur. A popular proverb surfaced regularly in his mind: *If you have three cups of rice bran never be an adopted husband.* In other words, even if you have few assets, have more pride than to sell yourself.

After only a few years in America, Jinjiro 'spun out'. His stepfather had broken the news that he had arranged a marriage for him and his bride would arrive shortly from Japan. Hearing this, Jinjiro disappeared, causing huge loss of face for the family. He was eventually found in Sacramento working as a labourer. His stepfather coaxed him repeatedly to return to Los Angeles, but Jinjiro would not budge. His upbringing had created a man 'out of specification'. Spoilt as a child, without a mother's influence in his formative teens, introverted, isolated from others, he had learned to please only himself, preferring to run from anything that made him feel uncomfortable.

---

* In 1903, Marie Curie discovers radium, and the Wright brothers achieve the first sustained flight in a power-driven aeroplane. In 1905, Albert Einstein announces his Theory of Relativity; and in 1914, the Panama Canal opens.

Chapter 16

The Next Generation

Kado-de
Get out of the gate
(Good luck starting a new life)

IN THE LATE NINETEENTH CENTURY, colonialism was at its peak in the Far East.* Worried that Britain, France, Germany and Russia would take advantage of the weakened Chinese Empire, including its tributary state of Korea, Japan wanted to secure the Korean Peninsula, which was less than 200 kilometres from Japan.

As a consequence of the Sino-Japanese War of 1894–95, China conceded Korea's independence, and gave Formosa and other islands to Japan. However, the Russians kept pushing towards Korea. In 1900, too close for comfort, they occupied Manchuria. Four years later, Japan demanded that Russia relinquish claims to Korea. Russia refused. Admiral Togo's surprise attack against the Russian fleet was steeped in *samurai* strategy and, in 1910, Korea was incorporated within the Japanese Empire.

When Commodore Perry had sailed his *kuro-fune* into Edo Bay in 1853, Japan had been a mediaeval nation. Within 50 years it had become a major, modern power, and Admiral Togo and the Japanese navy had destroyed the Russian fleet. The Japanese had absorbed and applied Western ideas in government, industry and military

---

* In 1900, the British Empire spanned a sixth of the world and, in 1902, the British won the Boer War in Southern Africa.

organisation with complete success. But, their rapid advance meant they were now a formidable competitor to Western manufacturers. Added to that, their victories against China and Russia fuelled fears of the inexplicable 'Yellow Peril' descending on the West.

Racism was rife on America's west coast to where Jinjiro (like many poor Japanese) had emigrated. 'Brown Asiatics Steal Brains of Whites', 'Japanese a Menace to American Women' screamed the 1905 headlines in the *San Francisco Chronicle*. In 1906, Japanese school children were segregated in San Francisco schools. The prospect of a Japanese attack on California was mooted in the media, movies and novels. Admiral Togo was urged to dispatch the Imperial Japanese fleet to put the Americans in their place. With the Russians defeated, America had become the main obstruction to the Japanese Empire.

At the onset of World War I,* Michitaro suggested that Jinjiro should return to Japan to join the Japanese navy. The navy required English speaking accountants and, having graduated top from the best accounting school in Japan, and now fluent in English, Jinjiro was duly appointed. As Chief Accountant aboard the navy's flagship *Mikasa*, which patrolled the Pacific Ocean, he regained his lost honour.

Around the time Jinjiro arrived back in Japan, Ryoko, Hisashi's mother, was about to graduate from school, and Jitsuzen was searching for a naval officer husband for her. Fully aware she was unprepared for the role of a wife, he wanted Ryoko married as soon as was decently possible. Marrying a young man in the military was not only something to be proud of, but Jitsuzen wanted his daughter to move beyond her cloistered environment where her only contact was with people who knew her story. As a modern, well-paid profession the navy would ensure Ryoko remained detached from the ordinary world and, in this new environment, she could start again without the stigma of her birth. Conscious of how 'out of specification' she was, he knew

---

* World War I begins in 1914, with peace declared in 1918. In 1917, Russia undergoes a Bolshevik coup.

it would only be possible for her to marry if he chose a man also 'out of specification'. Marriages between different castes and territories, though legal, were still uncommon so he wanted candidates from the same caste and territory.

Jitsuzen's younger sister acted as *nakodo*, preparing a list of prospects. The list was short, but by chance, Jinjiro's mother, Tatsuko, had originated from the same prefecture as Jitsuzen. Jitsuzen made his choice, and dialogue began with Michitaro who acted as *nakodo* for Jinjiro. Michitaro approved the match, pleased to have the famous priest's daughter as his brother's bride. She came with generous financial support from Jitsuzen and hearsay whispered she was a well-behaved girl. The couple did not meet until the actual wedding ceremony, though they exchanged photographs and written self-introductions.* Jinjiro was 30 years old, and Ryoko 18.

A discreet ceremony, paid for by Jitsuzen, was organised at the Officers' Club at Jinjiro's Naval Base in Kure near Hiroshima. An exclusive, outside 'cuisine cooker' arranged and provided everything, even the tableware and flowers. As was customary, a *kannushi* (Shinto priest) conducted the wedding rites.

> Accompanied by her hairdresser and *kimono* dresser, Ryoko arrives at the Officers Club by covered rickshaw. Her gold *obi* contrasts vividly against her black *kimono*, Jitsuzen's *mon* embroidered in the middle of the back. Her red painted lips and pencilled eyebrows are the only colour in a face covered with white chalky powder. Swept up in the ornate *bunkin takashimada* style, stiffened with resin, her black hair is adorned with ornaments that tinkle as she moves. Her white *tabi* peek from either side of the gold silk thongs of her black *zori*, and a fan hangs from her wrist.
>
> Adding a white bridal hood and a white robe over her *kimono*, with small steps, her head slightly inclined, Ryoko enters the room

---

* Traditionally, the couple are introduced by the *nakodo* at a formal meeting when betrothal gifts are exchanged between the two families.

escorted by Jitsuzen, her stepmother Sato, and her aunt. From the opposite direction in his white dress uniform, accompanied by Michitaro, their sister Mariko and her husband, Jinjiro walks towards her. Bowing, clapping and drinking sacred *sake* in front of a golden shrine, they exchange wedding rings and vows. Then standing at the dining room door, Jinjiro's senior officer accepts the guests' gifts of cash, each contained in an envelope secured with red and white silk threads.*

Gold-leafed chrysanthemums on a four-fold screen, another gift from Jitsuzen, provide a perfect backdrop for two handsome mahogany tables each set for ten with red placemats and napkins, crystal goblets, silver cutlery and lacquered *hashi* (chopsticks), in the centre a vase of white chrysanthemums with candles either side.

Following a prescribed order, numerous courses appear one after another. Lucky ingredients, beautifully arranged in odd numbers on receptacles chosen to complement the food are served to each guest. On such a hot evening, the navy's lemonade is offered along with *sake*, French claret, and a chilled hock. Hushed voices and the formality of the surroundings hang heavily over the guests and newly married couple.

Firstly, trimmed with an inedible red berry, boiled black beans swim in sweet syrup in a hexagonal bowl gilded with gold. Then, dressed with a stalk of green *shiso* (a herb) and looking well on a black triangular dish, three balls of mashed sweet potato sit alongside three sweetened chestnuts, but slightly apart to keep their aromas distinct. Ryoko sits in silence, all around her the conversation dominated by the men, sobering talk about the war.

For the main course the guests are treated to a succession of traditional wedding fare; taking pride of place, sea bream caught that very morning. Atop a *hosta* leaf on a cream rectangular plate, a whole

---

* The envelope is fastened with an auspicious bow, which is impossible to untie, symbolic of a marriage that will last forever, the contents removed by sliding the strands down.

seared fish, bright eyed and scales intact, is served per person. Placed cornerwise, its head is closer to the diner than its tail, and garnished with three marinated stems of ginger.

A whole boiled lobster is followed by *sashimi*, paper-thin, pink salmon and white sea bream frilled into rosettes and attached to a twig that sprouts from crushed ice, to the side a dish of soy sauce and grated *wasabi* (horseradish). Another wedding classic is the hotpot: the subtle fragrance of *yuzu* filling the air as the lid is lifted. In its rich base of fish stock with a hint of herbs, white fish meat and pink shrimp complement yellow circles of *yuzu* and the green of the herbs. Next, sitting on a rough square plate embellished with fiddle-fern heads, three minced turbo have been re-grilled in their shells.

As the evening advances, the diners relax, delighting in the thoughtful menu and its refined presentation. Other dishes include red and white tinted fish paste; chilled eggroll stuffed with eel; and *tempura*, crispy pieces of battered bream, prawn, mushroom, and shiso leaf.

After the main course, Ryoko disappears, re-emerging some 30 minutes later in a sumptuously embroidered red *kimono* with a heavily padded hem.

Soon after, pinkish boiled rice mixed with red beans arrives, accompanied by the requisite *tsukemono* (pickles). Then drinking from *chawan* of hot water smelling subtly of kelp, they rinse and refresh their mouths, before rounding off the meal with fresh fruits, their beauty unadorned: a slice of watermelon, a peeled and segmented peach and, to finish, a scoop of white ice-cream. Following dessert, Ryoko withdraws again, coming back in yet another lavish *kimono*, this time patterned with chrysanthemums and peonies, her status and wealth now obvious to all. Each *kimono* worn that night is one of a kind to be treasured as a family heirloom.

So began the marriage of Hisashi's parents. Jinjiro was satisfied he had the good wife he deserved, the daughter of a rich and famous man.

Ryoko was feeling lucky to have escaped her confinement to marry a naval officer, his profession the envy of all young girls.

After the wedding, Ryoko organised the obligatory 'return gifts' equivalent to half the value of the monetary offerings; boxes of red and white sugar cubes that were difficult to procure and much appreciated.

Part Two

Giri to the World

Hisashi is a boy of average height, slight but giving the impression of wiry strength. His close-cropped head lends the air of a scholar; the jutting cheekbones a look of refinement. His forehead is high, and he has a well-shaped nose with wide nostrils. His dark eyes are clear. From his father's Mongolian west coast origins, he inherits his single-lidded eyes. From his mother, he inherits the less common, light-coloured complexion of those from the east, originally from southern China. Pale in comparison to most, his colouring is a superficial handicap, people worrying about his health.

Chapter 17

The Birth of a Boy

Mitsugo no tamashii hyaku made
The soul of a three-year-old (stays) until a hundred

MARRIED IN THE EARLY DAYS of World War I, Jinjiro and Ryoko had set up home at the Kure Naval Base near Hiroshima. Throughout their first few years together, Jinjiro was away for extensive periods, firstly serving with the *Mikasa*, then spending a year in Europe after the war, helping recover Japan's share of reparation.* At the close of the war, most naval personnel had been dismissed but, because of his skills, Jinjiro was kept on.

Half a century had passed since the collapse of the Tokugawa regime. Although so much change had come about, some traditions remained. Every man and woman still had a duty to repay their *on* to their ancestors by maintaining the family line and bringing their own children up as they had been brought up. Every woman needed children, as motherhood bestowed status. Every man needed a son, for without an heir he was a failure.

In 1918, Ryoko had given birth to twin daughters, both of whom died days later in the cholera epidemic that swept the world. Everyone blamed her, saying it was due to careless nursing. From then on she ensured her standards of housekeeping were beyond reproach, her

---

* In World War I, Japan had sided with Britain, confining her energies to naval activity against German colonies: in the Pacific, the Mariana, Caroline and Marshall Islands and in China, capturing the German-controlled Shandong area, which gave a foothold on the continent, and strengthened her presence in Asia.

fixation for cleanliness renowned. Then, to the joy of Ryoko and Jinjiro, the much wanted son was born on 21 April 1920 in the year of the monkey.* The son was named Hisashi Furuya.

For the middle classes, home births were the norm. A midwife was usually supported by the husband's mother, in whose home the young couple would be living. Hisashi was born at the naval hospital. Custom prevailed that the wife's parents visited within the first week of the birth, bearing gifts and celebratory foods. Jinjiro and Ryoko celebrated Kure style, where such customs were disregarded. In the close-knit naval community, neighbours took on the role of family, giving gifts and much needed advice.

The first three days had been difficult as Ryoko waited for her 'true milk' to come, forbidden to feed Hisashi until then. Her tiny son had cried pitifully, prompting unwelcome memories of the twins; but soon she was able to feed on demand, and Ryoko began to enjoy her baby.

Jitsuzen, the only surviving grandparent, visited the family frequently over the years before his death. He stayed at a nearby temple as the house was too small for guests. In celebration of his grandson's birth, he commissioned a bi-fold screen with cranes and turtles painted in monochrome ink.

Though not believers, Ryoko and Jinjiro placed inherent faith in Shinto as a way of recognising their cultural identity. So, when Hisashi was 30 days old, they tied him to Ryoko's back and visited the shrine to report his birth to the gods, and to pray for his healthy growth: only after this visit could the boy be carried about safely in public.

For the first few months Hisashi's every whim was indulged, then his training began. At four months he was toilet trained and Ryoko dispensed with his diapers. Anticipating his needs, she held him over the toilet, whistling in an unvaried tone until he recognised its

---
* The Japanese count a child's age from conception, so at birth Hisashi is one-year-old. However, ages in the book will follow Western lines.

purpose. At eight months he was weaned; much earlier than the usual practice of continuing until the next child was born, but the women on the base were versed in contemporary childrearing practices. Traditionally, crawling was discouraged and walking prevented until a year old but, in keeping with the latest trend, Hisashi was taught to walk at nine months.

From the time he could understand, he was taught restraint. 'Respect rules' were rigorously drilled. *Otosan* was almighty. Hisashi learned to bow, *okasan* pushing his head down when greeting or leaving *otosan*'s presence.

At a year old, when he could hold out his arms, he went from sleeping on a *futon* beside *okasan* to sleeping in her arms. When his sister Eiko was born in January 1922, it was her turn to sleep next to *okasan*, and Hisashi slept with *otosan*. When he was two, *otosan* taught him to sit on the *tatami*, reprimanding him if he fidgeted or slumped. And the age-old teasing began: if Hisashi cried when he fell over, he was called a girl, or compared with another boy who did not cry. Once when he was naughty in front of *otosan*'s superior, *okasan* asked the officer to take him away. As the officer picked Hisashi up, she softened, as the small boy hysterically swore to be good.

Chapter 18

The Prodigal Returns

Korogaru ishi niwa koke ga haenu
Moss doesn't grow on a rolling stone

IN THE SPRING OF 1922, Jinjiro was transferred to Naval Headquarters in Tokyo, where the family moved to a rented house in the inner city. After an absence of nearly 20 years, Jinjiro had to be reacquainted with his home town. However, there were no friends and relatives waiting to welcome him. Apart from *niisan* ('elder brother' as he appropriately called Michitaro), who lived two hours away at the Yokosuka Naval Base, he had no immediate family nearby. His sister Mariko lived in Kyoto. His adoptive parents had retired to Yokohama. He had made few friends at college and his childhood family friends had disowned him.

Jinjiro found the city essentially the same, but the open spaces were disappearing as the city expanded. The jumble of mostly wooden structures was even more crowded together, with two-thirds now built on reclaimed land. Nearly 85 per cent of the four million inhabitants of the city lived in *Shitamachi*. The palace and temple roofs were still the tallest, though telephone and power wires now scored numerous lines across the sky. When he had left Tokyo there had been no rail connection between Shim-*bashi* and Ueno, now midway between them, was the red-brick Tokyo railway station. And, unlike America, passenger cars were uncommon.

The day before starting his new job Jinjiro took the tram to Shi-buya, the terminus for several lines, then changed lines for Hibiya, where many government buildings, including naval headquarters, were located. Nearby, behind high walls and thick foliage, the Emperor still lived unseen.

> Walking past naval HQ, he crosses Hibiya Park, exiting near the remodelled Imperial Hotel where the American architect, Frank Lloyd Wright's Mayan-style design is close to completion, and then on into the Ginza and Nihom-*bashi*. A number of *gaijin*, including small groups of tourists, are conspicuous in the procession of pedestrians.*
>
> Jinjiro has forgotten about the chaos. Electric trams bump noisily alongside deliverymen peddling bicycles towing trailers. Masses of bicycles add to the congestion; a number of commercial trucks dotted in their midst. There are fewer rickshaws, their presence not tolerated in the faster moving traffic. And there are far more people than he remembers, and they still persist in using the streets as footpaths.
>
> He recalls those happy Sunday boyhood outings strolling along the Ginza. Next to the Hattori Clock Tower (now Wako) his mother's favourite bakery, Kimuraya, has survived. South of the crossing, Kyukyodo, still sells traditional paper and calligraphy brushes. In Nihom-*bashi*, the old wooden bridge has been replaced with a stone and metal structure, but Fugetsudo is as it was 20 years earlier.

The age of urbanisation had evolved, and with it had come the rise of the educated, urban, middle-class '*sararii-man*', a minority of bureaucrats and managers, including Jinjiro.†

There were many different Japans. Those who lived on the west coast were different to those on the east coast. Those who lived upcountry had no idea how city dwellers lived. Those who lived in Tokyo did not understand life in Kyoto. Those who lived in semi-detached houses with gardens in suburbia were oblivious to those

---
* My grandmother, Constance, could have been one of those tourists.

† Derived from the English 'salaried man', it distinguished salaried white-collar workers from blue-collar waged workers.

who lived in hovels in teeming slums. Not everyone had benefited from the influx of modern conveniences. But for the families of the *zaibatsu*, the *narikin* and the middle class or intelligentsia, there was greater use of electricity and telephone. Access to public transport gave the opportunity for more leisure and social activities, such as Western-style dancing and watching American baseball, while the cinema provided glamour and escapism.

The Furuya family ate well. Jinjiro smoked and drank. Ryoko bought beautiful *kimono* for herself and Eiko. They also had a live-in maid. Knowing that she would be without the support of the wives on the base to help with two young children in Tokyo, Ryoko had demanded a servant. Servants were cheap and the household ran smoothly thanks to the maid, Matsu, the daughter of a poor farmer.*

The Furuya family could also afford train and tram fares. They bought newspapers, went to concerts and movies, and on outings to the countryside. On one occasion Jinjiro took Hisashi to *Shitamachi* to relive one of his own boyhood memories. Ryoko and Matsu stayed home with baby Eiko.

Since 1868, on the last Saturday of July, mid-summer *Hanabi-taikai* (firework exhibitions) had been held between rival factories in *Shitamachi*. Straddling the wide, slow-moving Sumida-*gawa* all the way to the mouth at Tokyo Bay, *Shitamachi*'s network of canals provided boat access to small factories, warehouses, markets and mills. Two-storied tenements with sliding doors stood cheek by jowl with bathhouses, teahouses, theatres, restaurants and inns. Under lattice windows, potted plants were cultivated with care, while outside each dwelling sat a bamboo bench on which to gossip, play chess, or pass the time of day. *Shitamachi* was like nowhere else in Japan. Small retailers mingled with actors, artisans, dancers, musicians and poets: theirs an earthy, jovial temperament, quarrelling over trifles,

---

* Many less fortunate girls were sold by their parents, and forced into prostitution or employed in the textile industry.

but with a prevailing sense of community. The public baths were their community hall and, in Asakusa, anchoring it all, was the seventh century Senso-ji.

> The river of people flowing to Senso-ji surge beneath the weathered 'Thunder Gate'* with its massive red, paper lantern. Locals and visitors, young and old, chattering and laughing, are carried along the narrow lane that is bedecked with lanterns. Fresh from their bath, many locals are dressed in *yukata* (light cotton summer *kimono*), with fathers leading wide-eyed children by the hand, and mothers with babies on their backs. In *happi* (loose informal jacket) and fitting trousers, boisterous groups of bachelors blend in. Posturing *sumo* wrestlers dressed in black stir the air with their fans, and *geisha* teeter along on platformed *geta*, whiffs of musk following in their wake. Hisashi carried on *otosan*'s shoulders looks around with wonder.
>
> Through the 'Treasure Gate', a steady cluster of visitors swarm around a colossal bronze bowl, poking smouldering sticks of incense into the mound of ash. With *otosan*'s help, Hisashi places his stick, the fumes fanning his face.
>
> Dusk is falling as they leave the temple and wend their way to Ryogoku-*bashi*.† There is no moon, and the lamp-lighter, stepladder on his shoulder, scurries between gas lamps. The cherry trees along the riverbank are lit with fanciful lanterns. Dozens of *yatai* (mobile, open-air stalls) sell *sushi*, noodles, sweets and *sake*, flowers and trinkets. *Otosan* buys Hisashi spun sugar on a stick for a treat.
>
> Spectators, packed into wooden compartments separated by ramps, stretch along the riverbank. Along the ramps food sellers reach customers and runners for the rich run to the *yatai*.
>
> Whizzing and whooshing, suddenly the air is filled with flashes

---

* The *'Thunder Gate'*, the temple's entrance gate, is flanked on the right by a statue of Fujin, the wind god, and on the left by Raijin, the thunder god, the massive lantern hanging beneath it, embossed with the character for thunder.

† Ryogoku-*bashi* is the first of the 11 bridges over the Sumida-*gawa*.

and bangs, and the smell of gunpowder. Ohhhhh! Ahhhhhh! From four boats anchored either side of the bridge, the rivals fire in five-minute volleys, separated by short musical breaks. Arrows and rockets dart across the sky. Stars explode into red, green, yellow, blue and white. Dragons breathe fire, Mount Fuji erupts, and Niagara Falls overflows. Palm trees flourish. Willows trail their tendrils in the river. Multi-hued peonies and chrysanthemums bloom briefly, vanishing with a pop. A glittering arc forms above the river, momentarily reflected in the dark, smooth waters of the Sumida-*gawa*, silhouetting the arched struts of Ryogoku-*bashi* and the concrete-lined river bank. The crowd, faces highlighted in the garish glow, shout their delight in a storm of clapping. Jinjiro smiles at his rapt young son, mouth open, eyes glued; he is too mesmerised to be scared.

Chapter 19

Fire is the Flower of Edo

Jishin, kaminari, kaji, oyaji
The things feared most in this world are
earthquakes, thunder, fires and fathers

IT HAS BEEN A VERY FINE SUMMER. The first day of September 1923 is balmy with not a cloud in the sky, and people are going about their normal activities. It is just before midday; pedestrians are crowding the pavements, while workers lunch in cubbyhole restaurants.

Three-year-old Hisashi is sitting on a cushion at the kitchen table looking at a book. His sister Eiko is taking a nap, Matsu having just modestly closed the baby girl's legs. Nearby *okasan* prepares lunch. *Otosan* is at work. All morning a strange stillness has filled the air. There is no wind. The trees and flowers are motionless. Hisashi senses the mounting oppressive mood and plays quietly.

Suddenly, the house creaks and groans, and a menacing roar rises from the bowels of the earth. The ground begins to shake violently. Hisashi topples over. There is a roaring in his head. He is too shocked to cry or speak. Ryoko and Matsu stagger, fighting to keep their balance. As if she is far away, he hears *okasan* telling him to get under the door frame.

Roof tiles fall with a crash. The glass in the kitchen window shatters. Plaster falls from the walls and the air fills with dust. Scrolls tumble from the walls. China smashes together on the *tatami*. Eiko is crying. Everything in the room is going round and round, things skidding across the floor. The *tansu* topples, but fortunately Matsu picks Eiko up seconds before it crashes to the spot where she has been lying.

The shaking and rumbling eventually stop and the earth stills, but it is a brief lull only. A second quake strikes, shuddering beneath their feet.

They hurry to get out of the house, Ryoko carrying Eiko, Matsu holding Hisashi's hand. Fire bells toll quickly and continuously. Joining their neighbours, they sit stunned on the side of the road. Their house has little damage, but down the street others have collapsed. Hisashi clings to Matsu. No one can believe what has happened, but at least they are safe, as hopefully is Jinjiro.

Jinjiro's office at naval headquarters in Hibiya is 4 kilometres away. Like other substantial buildings near the palace, built under the eye of European architects, it withstands the quake. But still the gigantic jolt lifts the building, sending Jinjiro and his assistant sprawling to the floor. Heaving and groaning, the walls sway back and forth. The light swings like a pendulum, flickers and goes out. Bookcases topple over.

Tokyo has been wrenched by an earthquake with a magnitude of 7.9 on the Richter Scale, one of the worst in its history. Massive dust clouds fill the air. Hillsides subside. Rocks and boulders block streams and rivers, changing their course. Waves, 10 metres high, wash wildly back and forth, destroying the harbour lagoon and leaving the sea bed exposed. Rail tracks lie twisted like snakes. Roads undulate like waves. Great brick buildings in the central city sink into the soft reclaimed subsoil. Wooden buildings fall like houses of cards. Bridges collapse, lamp posts snap and trees topple. Terrified people rush screaming into the streets, only to be crushed as buildings collapse.

But worse was to follow. Across the city cooking fires had been kindled ready to cook lunch. The quake hit, then what was left of the city turned into a blazing furnace. Trapped or injured, unable to escape the flames, thousands died on the spot.

Fire broke out in 134 different locations, a south wind fanning the flames. Many of these 'flowers of Edo', as they were nicknamed, were too much for the fire brigade, with only a third of the fires extinguished. The wooden warehouses and shops in the civic centre caught fire, but thanks to the network of canals, the fire brigade managed to staunch the flames. But in other areas fire fighters stood helplessly, their manpower, equipment and water inadequate against the ferocity of the flames.

Roads were impassable. Power lines dangled dangerously, so electricity was cut off. Telegraph poles snapped, so communications broke down. Water pipes shattered beneath the ground, so supply was interrupted. The exposed bed of the harbour was strewn with dead fish and seaweed, and it was feared diseases like cholera would spread. Latrines were being dug around the city, and waste, carcases and corpses were already being burned.

It was usually an hour's walk between home and office but on this day, Jinjiro, beside himself with worry about his family, took several hours to make the journey.

The city burned for three days and nights.

It had been a disaster waiting to happen. The wooden houses tightly packed in narrow alleys burned like cardboard boxes. The greatest damage and loss of life caused by the 'double punch' was in *Shitamachi* around the Sumida-*gawa*. A squall of flames sweeping upstream engulfed everything in its path. All the wooden bridges and boats were destroyed, but the biggest single disaster was at the army supply depot nearby. The depot had been turned into a shelter for the homeless, and by the late afternoon of the first day it was crammed with people. It also caught fire. Within minutes nearly 50 000 people burned to death. Only those standing next to the doors survived. Thousands more were killed at a temple when it burnt to the ground, transformed into another graveyard within minutes.

The Furuya family were safe and their home escaped serious damage. However, with the possibility of aftershocks, Jinjiro decided they would camp outside until things settled down. Hisashi remembers it as a thrilling experience, 'an unexpected adventure', as they spent several days camping with three other families in a bamboo grove near the house.*

Mosquito mesh suspended between stems of bamboo transformed the grove into a cocoon, made comfortable with kitchenware, furniture and bedding. The outside no longer seemed the frightening place it had been. And for years afterwards Ryoko loved to tell of the small boy who earnestly declared, 'Do not worry, Hisashi is here'.

Thankfully the earthquake hit during the day, and in summer. The weather remained fine and it was shady and pleasant in the bamboo bush. Tremors shook the ground for several more weeks, but after four days Jinjiro thought it safe to shift back into the house. He was more afraid of attack by looters than aftershocks.

Fired by racial prejudice, some alleged that many looters were Korean. It was also rumoured that Koreans had poisoned the water supply. In the midst of the panic, an estimated 6 000 Koreans were killed, the army and police reportedly goading vigilantes.† Tokyo was placed under martial law.

Towns and cities for miles around were gutted; in some areas hardly a building remained standing. The final death toll varies, some newspapers reporting as high as 500 000. Another 2.5 million people lost their homes.** Japanese houses were designed to rock gently in an earthquake. Held without nails, interlocking posts and beams support the structure, the walls non-loadbearing. But even so, more

---

* Bamboo is very strong, and can withstand an earthquake. Its roots bind the soil so the ground around it will not crack, and it also protects the deep wells used for drinking water.

† Following the annexation of Korea in 1910 and during World War I, Koreans had been drafted as cheap labour. They were distrusted and intensely hated.

** The newspaper reported only 13 500 and 6 500 homeless for Tokyo and Yokohama respectively, figures presumably excluding those who lost their homes but had somewhere else to go. Victims fled to relations living within a few hours' walk. Temples and shrines also provided temporary shelter. The Imperial Hotel, scheduled to reopen that very day, came through unscathed, and provided accommodation for hundreds of homeless.

than 70 per cent of Tokyo houses were destroyed, while Yokohama, close to the epicentre of the quake, was levelled.

Japan's geological instability means frequent tremors, though mostly they are too slight to notice. The giant catfish living under the sea bed is kept pinned under an enormous rock but, when it escapes and swings its tail, the ground trembles.

Chapter 20

The Sararii-man

Maihomushugi
My-home-ism
(Love of family life)

AFTER THE QUAKE, blueprints were drawn up to rebuild Tokyo, but insufficient funds reduced the grand reconstruction plan. Haphazard redevelopment began immediately and gradually the refugees returned to the city.

One radical consequence of the re-development was a new residential quarter designed for middle-class families. It was a test case for the first-ever suburb and included an entire community structure, complete with its own amenities. Each householder leased the land from the nearby temple, but owned their house. Given its modernity, it was considered a very prestigious place to live.

Typically in Japan three generations lived together. However, these houses were designed for the nuclear family, which was fundamental to the emerging middle-class lifestyle, and the driving force behind the new urban consumer society. The Furuya family was allocated one of the available 70 townhouses. For Jinjiro and Ryoko, already used to living as a nuclear family, their new living arrangements were perfect. 'Out of specification' with the traditional way of life, they adapted easily to their new environment.

Considerable thought had been given to the nature of services required, which included a hospital, a primary school, a market, a park, and a church with a nursery. The Catholic Church built in one corner of the park raised more than a few eyebrows. The nursery and kindergarten attached to it were for the exclusive benefit of the residential housewives. So, with Hisashi at kindergarten each weekday morning, and the housework and Eiko taken care of by Matsu, Ryoko enjoyed a pleasant lifestyle, with plenty of time to chat with neighbours.

Shortly after the family moved into their new home, 19-year-old Tomoko, Ryoko's half-sister, was sent to live with them. Before he died, Jitsuzen had asked Jinjiro to take care of Tomoko once she reached high school age. He wanted Tomoko to attend Japan's first female college, which was located in Tokyo. Jitsuzen knew his son-in-law would ensure Tomoko received a suitable Western education. Although Tomoko, like Ryoko, had never lived with her father, even after his death Jitsuzen still made all the decisions. Tomoko's mother Sato was unhappy, but honoured his wishes.

Ryoko and Jinjiro welcomed Tomoko, treating her as they did Hisashi and Eiko. The money for her keep was meticulously administered by Jinjiro and, with Jitsuzen's prior approval, some of it was used for his grandchildren. As a result, the family maintained a most comfortable existence with modest luxuries they would not otherwise have afforded.

Gently sloping and offering cooling breezes and agreeable views, Sangenjaya on the western fringe of Tokyo was quiet and peaceful. It was bordered by small farms, rice mills and tea plantations. Their sunny, sheltered site enclosed within its bamboo and twig fence, was halfway down the street, with its frontage west-facing. The back alley was between it and the house next door, and provided a tradesman's entrance, with fast growing *sugi* hiding the alley from the neighbours.

L-shaped on its square section, the wooden, tile-roofed house was identical to all its neighbours. Contemporary yet traditional, it was one room deep with the *engawa* running along the front and opening to the garden. Its floors were covered with *tatami*, and its rooms partitioned by *fusuma* and *shoji*-screened windows, with ceilings and trim in pale unvarnished *hinoki* (Japanese white cedar or cypress).

As well as the kitchen, bathroom and toilet, there were four rooms. Jinjiro and Ryoko's bedroom became the reception room during the day, Hisashi and Eiko's the living/dining room, while the other two rooms were used exclusively as bedrooms for Matsu and Tomoko. During the daytime bedding was folded away in the wall cupboards in each room. Just inside the front door was the *genkan* (entrance hall) where outdoor shoes were removed.*

While the east-facing back door was sheltered by three-needled black pines, a trellis flushed with sweetpeas separated the household well and storage bins for bulk charcoal and rice. Along the northern edge, flowering daphne supplied year-round interest, with camellias, dahlias and cosmos adding seasonal colour. Providing a backdrop in summer, morning glory grew with abandon along the bamboo and twig fence. Nestled in the corner Hisashi had a coop for his two hens, with a row of spinach growing beside it for their feed.

Dominating the front yard was a magnificent Magnolia Apollo. The tree had been originally growing in the temple garden and the house had been built around it. In spring its star-like blooms opened deep violet on the outside, paler within. To the side of the magnolia, a large mound was covered with a plum tree, low growing bamboo, a maple and rhododendron and, just in front, was the pond where Hisashi kept *kingyo* (goldfish). Lessening the look of newness, ivy scrambled up the front of the house, while under the eaves, wisteria drew attention to the extravagant glass panels in the front door. Laden with *bonsai*,† a shelf clung to the wall, with miniature pine and azalea carefully trimmed by Ryoko, and potted geraniums below.

---

* Indoor slippers did not become popular until several years later.

† With so little space available, landscaping in urban spaces attempted to create nature in miniature: *bonsai*, the growing of miniature trees, was introduced 1 000 years ago.

Chapter 21

Balmy Spring Days

Shochu no tama
A jewel in one's hand
(The apple of his parents' eyes)

To THE YOUNG HISASHI, everything seemed happy. *Okasan* indulged him, giving him far more attention than she would have been able to if the twins had survived. Striving to be 'a good wife and a wise mother', Ryoko attended numerous seminars for women, this being the fashionable approach to becoming a better housewife.

The years passed happy and uneventful.

As she does every day, 363 days of the year, 15-year-old Matsu scrambles up from her *futon* at 5 a.m. Hours earlier, a farmer has wheeled his handcart from house to house collecting night soil destined for ladling onto his crops. First fetching the milk from the back doorstep, Matsu returns to gather up the *daikon* and cucumber left by the farmer in exchange for his fertiliser. No sooner has she taken them inside, when the fishmonger arrives on cue with his early morning catch; shortly after, the iceman delivers two large, melting blocks of ice.

Street vendors called on the household regularly, their stentorian voices shouting their wares. Hand-carts ladened with *natto* (fermented boiled soybeans mixed with soy sauce and *negi*), noodles, *tofu*, steamed corn, steamed bean-jam buns, and baked sweet potatoes encouraged the housewives and maids outside to buy. There was even an old man, the distinctive whistle of his small boiler instantly recognisable, who mended Jinjiro's tobacco pipe. And itinerant peddlers, their bamboo poles sagging under the weight of heavy tubs, still wandered the lanes of suburbia dispensing knick-knacks and hobby goods.

To shut out the searing summer sun, Matsu lowers the rattan blinds that hang beneath the eaves, then squats in front of the wood fire burning in the small earthenware stove. As water in the iron kettle begins to bubble, steam wafts from under the wooden lid of the rice pot sitting on the second stove. For breakfast it will be boiled rice topped with *natto*.

In the living room the sun shines through the finely latticed *shoji*, the glare diffused through the rice paper. Legs together and her arms by her sides, Eiko sleeps soundly on her back. Five-year-old Hisashi quietly gets out of bed, rolls and puts away his *futon*, then dresses.

He loves to rise early to feed his animals and spend time with Matsu before the rest of the family demand her attention. He pops his head around the kitchen door. The wood fires give off a pleasing aroma and he feels happy to be up when everything is quiet and peaceful. Stirred by the softest breeze, the sound (chirin-chirin) of the bronze *furin* (wind chime) tinkling under the eaves brings a sense of coolness; the sound forever associated with his early morning idyll.

Carefully, Hisashi carries the bamboo cage with his pet finch outside to hang on a low branch of the magnolia tree. Then, after collecting the newspapers from the letterbox, it is time to help Matsu sprinkle water on the garden and the road in front of their gate. Ryoko considers her garden at its best when wet with dew, so the front garden and gateway are sprinkled daily. The bucket is almost too big and heavy for Hisashi to carry, but no matter, he loves to do it, though dressed ready for kindergarten, he has to be careful not to slop water on his navy blue sailor suit, as he will surely be scolded if he gets wet.

After breakfast, *otosan* goes off to work, and *obasan* (legal aunty, referring to Tomoko) to college. Matsu cleans up, then walks with

Hisashi to the kindergarten.

After a quick, boyish bow, he eagerly runs off. Entering through the church, he can never resist trailing his hand through the water in the baptismal font. He enjoys kindergarten, especially sitting on the *tatami* listening to bible stories (in Japanese) and the hymns the organist plays.

Back at home, keeping an eye on Eiko toddling about, Matsu sweeps the *tatami*, wipes the woodwork, and does the laundry, while Ryoko arranges flowers: cosmos in a bamboo basket for the reception room *tokonoma*, positioned just so in front of a scroll. In the *genkan* a bowl of dahlias placed on the shoe cupboard. Accomplished as she is in the samurai art of *ikebana*,* the creation of a beautiful arrangement brings her peace amid the bustle of daily life. Next, she begins unpicking one of her cotton *kimono* for Matsu, inverting the fabric for strength, re-stitching with new thread and using the old thread for less important stitching. The smell of sandalwood lingers on the fabric. As a girl she had spent considerable time learning how to stitch, launder, repair and store her expensive *kimono*. Her skilful fingers move easily over the fabric, but it is painstaking work and she will need the help of the family seamstress before the season's end to complete the job of unpicking, washing, starching, drying and ironing their currently worn *kimono* ready for storing and re-stitching the following year.†

Carefully folding away the work-in-progress, she opens her father's writing desk to write a mid-summer greeting card to Jinjiro's adoptive parents.

In the high heat it was customary to determine the well-being of

---

* *Ikebana*, the art of flower arranging, is a contemplative pursuit and, until the last century, strictly a masculine activity. Introduced by priests as offerings to Buddha, the *samurai* then took it up as a mental discipline to quiet their apprehension before battle, and to calm their minds afterwards. Each branch or leaf used is symbolic.

† As well as different seasonal accessories, there are four different seasonal weights: light silk in summer, thicker weaves for spring and autumn, and heavy quilted cotton in winter.

elderly friends and relatives. Ryoko still felt obliged to show fidelity to her elders. Aware that at all times she was watched closely by friends and relatives, she knew it was important to do the correct thing. Her desire to conform overrode her desire to live a modern Western way of life.

Matsu's mornings were always busy. After the cleaning, being a rare occasion when there was no water left in the household well, she had to walk to the nearby river. Ryoko insisted the water be boiled before use, as contaminated water and food was a constant concern. Ryoko was especially anxious about milk and would never buy ice-cream, so she learned to make it herself. She loved Western cooking and for years attended classes. She was proud of her talent that she felt distinguished her from other, more ordinary housewives.

Fresh produce could be kept for a only day in the wooden icebox, but the neighbourhood market provided everything they could possibly need, having a butcher, fishmonger, greengrocer, dry salter, charcoal dealer, dairy, and even a tailor and a tiny library. Every day after lunch Matsu went shopping, chatting with the shopkeepers being the highlight of her day.

> The greengrocer fusses over the freshest fruit and vegetables, expounding the qualities of the *nasu* and yams that Matsu weighs in each hand. In the dairy, the ageless matriarch whispers the hottest gossip as her daughter measures and strains vegetable oil into Matsu's kettle.
>
> Returning home, Matsu puts Eiko down for her rest, and then starts to make pickles with the *daikon* and cucumber delivered earlier that morning. Each day while they are in season she will preserve some for winter. *Kimono* sleeves tied out of the way, Matsu stands at the sink, the afternoon sun streaming through the window above. Now covered with a wooden chopping board, the sink has been turned into a bench.

Matsu would work on the concrete-floored, lower level of the kitchen, where there was a wooden tin-lined sink, a bucket to take to the well, and the two earthenware ovens. Two steps above on a timber floor, Ryoko would sit at a low table to dish out the meals. A large *tansu* stood against one wall; another wall was lined with open shelves. A trapdoor in one corner of the room gave access to daily supplies of charcoal and rice stored under the house. An atypical feature of the room was the metre-square pit in the middle of the floor, which was covered by a table-like frame. In winter they sat on the edge of the pit with the *kotatsu* (a heating ceramic device that burns charcoal) and a quilt keeping them warm.

After lunch, in the shade of the huge paulownia, Hisashi potters in the children's community garden; then when it gets too hot, he climbs up into the tree's canopy. From his splendid perch, safe in the knowledge the older boys are at school, he flaunts his superiority when younger boys, too small to climb, arrive.

With Hisashi busy in the garden, Eiko asleep and Matsu pickling, Ryoko changes into a light silk 'visiting' *kimono*. She has an easy friendship with the neighbours, all members of their *gonin-gumi*, and looks forward to their daily gossip over a cup of *sencha* (green tea made in a pot and given to guests or the elderly). Prying into neighbourhood affairs, their chief topic of conversation is still the scandalous permanent-wave hairstyle worn by the daughter of a family down the street. A crop of glossy, illustrated monthlies are helping shape their tastes and desires and, flicking through the pages, Ryoko and her friends tut their disapproval at the latest fashions of white bridal gowns and permanent waves.

In the dim interior of his office at naval headquarters, Jinjiro listens to the hum of the electric fan, feeling uncomfortably hot and sticky. He is bored with his work, compiling the navy's account of World War I. Knowing he will soon need to find a new job, he wonders, not for the first time, if he should have stayed in America, or even cooperated with his adoptive family.

The household is at its busiest during late afternoon. Tomoko has to do her practice on the treadle organ Jinjiro bought with Jitsuzen's money. The washing has to be brought in and put away. The evening meal has to be prepared and the trays set.

Eiko wakes up. Fractious and hungry, and with *okasan* and Matsu busy, she demands attention from *niisan*, who is playing with his blocks. She snatches some off him. Just in time Hisashi remembers the new rule *okasan* has taught him, and rather than grabbing the blocks back, he gives them all to Eiko. 'To lose to win' is greatly respected, and sure enough Eiko's attention is soon diverted elsewhere and he gets his blocks back.

Meanwhile, Matsu sets up the table in the living room, arranging four cushions around it. In the kitchen she sets individual trays, each with six containers: two covered bowls, one for rice and one for soup; three others for fish, vegetables and *tsukemono*; and a small *chawan* for green tea. Each tray also has a pair of *hashi* resting on a small pottery fan.

Along with rice, which could be baked, boiled, fried, steamed, wrapped or ground, in keeping with traditional wisdom, Ryoko served eight colours per meal, and altogether 30 different foods a day. Based around *nori*, *tofu*, seasonal fish and vegetables, she accentuated natural subtleties in flavour, colour and aroma.* Portions were bite-size, simpler to pick up with *hashi*. And even for a casual family meal, everything had to be artistically arranged in the proper container.

Dishes and cooking implements, some with lids, some without, were readily available on the open shelves: wide-mouthed dishes for stewed food; medium-sized dishes for grilled food; rectangular plates to serve a whole fish; square plates for sliced *sashimi*; small rice bowls, large noodle bowls, serving bowls, bowls for pickles, bowls for hot-

---

* There are many subtle variations in seasonings and methods according to region: cooking in Kyoto generally has a lighter taste, with salt used to retain ingredients' natural colour, whereas in Tokyo cooking is spicier, using more soy sauce for seasoning and colouring.

pot, and pouring bowls for soy sauce and vinegar; ceramic teapots, handless cups for green tea, some delicate, some sturdy; *sake* bottles, servers and cups; and trays and tiered boxes. There were dishes of blue and white porcelain, black or vermillion lacquer, rough pottery, plain wood, and bamboo.

> A delicious smell arrives as Matsu comes in with their dinner, Tomoko and the children seated with Ryoko. Placing the fourth four-legged tray on the floor outside the open *fusuma*, Matsu steps into the room, kneels and brings the first tray in through the door. Standing, she picks it up, places it before Ryoko, kneels, bows, and then repeats the pattern for each of the children. Tuna is in season, cut in chunks and covered with grated yam and dried *nori*, served with a dish of grilled *nasu* marinated in *miso* spiced with sugar, *sake* and ginger. This is followed as usual by: a serving of *tsukemono* to add texture and sharpness of flavour, tonight, sliced cucumber and *daikon* preserved in soy sauce; a bowl of glutinous rice; a bowl of *miso* soup;* and a *chawan* of *bancha* (lower grade coarse tea for home use).

Okasan and the children murmured their usual grace – Itadaki masu – its literal meaning 'I sincerely thank my fellow creatures who have sacrificed their lives that I may eat'. As they begin to eat she reminds them to chew each mouthful 30 times, and to use their hands and *hashi* to bring the food to their mouths, not to bend over the table.

> Straight-backed, Hisashi finishes his rice and places the lid back on his bowl. He places his *hashi* neatly on the chopstick rest, tidies his tray, and bows his head appropriately to say: Gochisosama deshita (Thank you for your hospitality, I enjoyed my meal).
> As a reward he is permitted to ride around the park on his new red tricycle and, watched enviously by other children, he swells with pride. Also the envy of many, Tomoko goes off to her organ lesson at

---

* Made from fermented soybeans, *miso* soup is usually topped with chopped *negi*, *tofu* and dried *nori*, which soften in the hot broth.

the Catholic Church; and finally Eiko finishes her meal.

Just as the electric street lamps come on, Jinjiro steps off the tram for the five-minute walk home. Seeing his father, Hisashi knows it is time to come home.

In the twilight, the *shoji* are still open, and the family enjoy the cooling breeze and the summer orchestra: accompanied by the hum of ground beetles, a male nightingale carolls his refrain. Inside the house, the distinctive aroma of *tansy* (mosquito repellent) pleasantly pervades the rooms.

Sitting with Jinjiro as he eats his dinner, the family share their day. Hisashi proudly recites a new Mother Goose rhyme he has learned in English. Then as Jinjiro turns the handle of their gramophone, Hisashi sings along with the tinny music and crackling voices of more English nursery rhymes.* Finally, his tedious day behind him, Jinjiro lights his evening pipe and, puffing gently, he is soon deep in the first newspaper.

Jinjiro spent considerable time with Hisashi, who always waited expectantly for *otosan* to come home. An avid reader, Jinjiro would have been a good teacher, and he discussed many things with his son: why a cicada sang so beautifully, how to identify when chestnuts were ripe, and why clouds stayed up in the sky and how they changed their shape. Eiko and later Yayoi were left to their mother.

As *okasan* lays out the *futon*, covering each with a mosquito net, Hisashi closes the *shoji* screens. Matsu makes up the bath [just as in Tatsuko's day], carrying water to the wooden tub, then, lighting the fire in the copper oven at one end. By the time everyone else has bathed and she has cleaned up the kitchen, it is time for her bath.

---

* The first gramophone record was recorded in 1900 by the Italian tenor Enrico Caruso.

Chapter 22

Eggplants Don't Grow on Melon Vines

Kokku-suru, me-ue-ni-shitagawu, shin-shin-wo-kitaeru, na-wo-agaru
To discharge one's filial duties, follow the instructions
of one's elders and superiors, build one's physical and
mental constitution, and make one's mark in society

BY STIMULATING HIS CURIOSITY and a love for learning, Jinjiro had an enormous influence on Hisashi, but so did his mother.

Ryoko, striving and determined, was Jinjiro's complete opposite. She was ambitious for her husband, wanting him to make money, or at least to become someone of importance in the community. Always wanting to show that she was above others, Ryoko expected too much of Jinjiro, and even the young Hisashi felt her frustration and irritation when Jinjiro could not fulfil her aspirations. Jinjiro retaliated by detaching himself from her nagging, spending hours with his son or reading old literature.

Ryoko's isolated background and lack of awareness of normal family life meant she was unable to see how her attitude and efforts to control her family affected her son. Her restrictions fed his innate self-sufficiency to the exclusion of social interaction, creating a boy somewhat 'out of specification' with his peers. He was a boy excessively protected and confined by an anxious mother, who had not only lost two children, but who was dedicated to providing her son with a so-called modern education.

Occasionally feelings of resentment stirred, but Hisashi never thought to rebel. He believed it was his duty to eat what *okasan* made for him, even if he would have preferred the bought snacks the other children ate. It was his duty to give up games other children played, such as card games, and which *okasan* considered inappropriate for educated children. It was his duty to play only with children approved by *okasan,* even though it created a wall between him and the neighbourhood children.

Though isolated, he never thought of himself as lonely and, like most Japanese children, he could play for hours without an angry word. He was a resourceful child, able to create his own play, and was always busy looking at books, making crafts, growing vegetables and flowers, and caring for his pets.

In many ways he was spoiled, allowed to do as he pleased, but from an early age he had learned how to behave correctly at all times, any naughtiness stifled. He knew he had to endure everything without a groan, to suppress his fear, sorrow or pain; expressing emotion was considered impolite, as it would mar the composure of others. He knew he had to suppress his impulses; impulses could hinder a successful life, and only through restraint would he learn self-respect. He knew he had to observe his own behaviour, judging it according to what others would think and say, and through restraint he would make himself more valuable.

Though he was only five years old, he knew his 'proper place'. He knew what was expected of him, and the respect he must show to his elders and authority. He knew the debt he owed not only to his parents for their care, but also to his extended family and friends, and even his forebears.

Chapter 23

Appeasing the Gods

Kurushii toki no kami-danomi
To invoke the gods only in times of distress

JINJIRO'S YEARS ABROAD had purged his need to follow some customary ways, and when he returned to Japan religion played little part in his life. In any case, the burgeoning middle-class subculture was moving away from traditional behaviour.

For Ryoko, being 'modern' was a way of maintaining status but, with a typically Japanese attitude, she included new ways of doing things alongside traditional customs and beliefs. Hisashi's attendance at the Catholic kindergarten was a convenience rather than a religious choice. As the daughter of a priest, she could not, or would not, attend the Catholic Church, though she was happy to avail herself of the opportunity they provided for childminding.

It was common to intermingle the beliefs and ceremonies of Buddhism and Shinto in their daily lives: having a Shinto wedding service, visiting a Shinto shrine when Hisashi and Eiko had been born, but preferring a Buddhist funeral. The Furuya home, like all others, housed the compulsory Shinto shelf shrine; however, unlike other homes that smelt of incense burning on the altar, the Furuya home smelt of Jinjiro's tobacco smoke, which completely masked the occasional whiff of incense lit for the sake of appearances.

New Year was a festival that no one could ignore, and everything shut down. All business and household affairs had to be completed and debts cleared.

Hisashi remembers his mother and Matsu working from early morning until late at night, spending the prior week in a flurry of shopping, cleaning, cooking and decorating the house. The *tatami* had to be recovered and new paper stretched over the *shoji*. But preparations actually began a month before, both women devoting long hours in the kitchen turning out New Year delicacies. And late at night Ryoko would still be up, writing New Year greeting cards, customary since the introduction of the postal service, not to mention wrapping Year-end gifts expressing gratitude for kindnesses throughout the year.

Jinjiro finished work on 28 December, and next day he and Hisashi were out in the backyard in the freezing cold cutting branches of pine and stems of bamboo for Ryoko to fashion into decorations for the front gate.

It was the first time Hisashi had really appreciated the meaning of New Year and, when everything was finished, he wandered around in amazement. Sprays of white-backed ferns with white streamers, one placed above the front door, another at the back door, showed that the house had been purified for the god's visit on New Year's Day. The living room was transformed with paper lanterns and branches of pine. A prized scroll inherited from Jitsuzen had been unrolled and hung in the *tokonoma*. It showed 'long-living' cranes flying towards a sun rising above a forest of pines and bamboo. Beneath the scroll were offerings to the Year God: one large and one small rice cake in the centre; to their left, an arrangement of bamboo, pine, plum and winter cabbage; to their right, a jug of spiced *sake*.

Preparations for the New Year had to be completed by 31 December. Just before midnight, simultaneously in every temple throughout the land, the New Year's Eve bells would toll 108 times. Finishing on the stroke of midnight, the final toll released one and all from their 108 evil worldly desires, and made them pure once more and ready for a fresh start.

On 1 January, dressed in festive *kimono*, Hisashi, Eiko and Tomoko accompanied Jinjiro to the Meiji-*jingu* (*jingu*, a high status shrine), which deified the late Emperor Meiji. Cocooned in the centre of a dense forest, it attracted a huge crowd, all who prayed for health and happiness in the coming year. Then everyone stayed at home until 3 January.

New Year was a time for family reunions. Distant cousins on Ryoko's side always visited. However, apart from Tomoko's mother Sato, their only close family were Mariko (Jinjiro's sister), whom they never saw, and their uncles Michitaro (Jinjiro's brother) and Shozo (Ryoko's brother). Sato and Shozo travelled to Tokyo each New Year but, even though he lived closer, Michitaro visited rarely. The relationship between Michitaro and his brother had soured after Jinjiro married. Ryoko disapproved of her sister-in-law the *geisha*.

The adults sat about drinking *sake* and sampling the delicacies, diligently prepared and charged with wishes for happiness and prosperity. Hisashi played cards with the Onishi boys, his older cousins once removed, both in their early twenties and studying at *Todai*. It was the only time *okasan* allowed him to play cards. He hero-worshipped the boys and fondly remembers how patient they were with him.

A couple of years later, when Jinjiro bought a radio, their New Year celebrations changed. Like everyone else they tuned in to minute-by-minute 'on the spot' concerts at temples and shrines, as well as broadcasts covering the first events of the year. First events were highly regarded. Although radio broadcasts by NHK* had begun in Tokyo in 1925, Jinjiro had waited before getting a receiver, purchasing instead the costly Columbia gramophone.

And there were other festivals the family enjoyed. Women and girls always looked forward to *Hinamatsuri* (Girl's Day) on 3 March.†

---

* NHK is the government-run broadcaster, 'Nippon Hoso Kyokai'.

† The ancient Chinese believed the sins of the body could be transferred to a doll and throwing the doll into the river would wash away their misfortune. Reaching Japan, the custom had been linked to girls playing with dolls, hence *Hinamatsuri*.

A week before the festival, *okasan*, *obasan* and Eiko carefully unpack the fragile miniatures given to Ryoko by Jitsuzen when she was little: dolls costumed after the Imperial Court, with dishes, furniture, musical instruments, vehicles and trees. On the top shelf of the stepped dais, in front of two gilded screens, the Emperor and Empress sit in regal splendour. Below them are three ladies-in-waiting, then five musicians, then two *daimyo* and, on the bottom, three drunken servants.

Kodomo-no-hi (Children's Day) on 5 May is a national holiday. Originally for boys, it had developed into an occasion to celebrate the growth and happiness of children in general. In the Furuya family this was Hisashi's day, father and son decorating the *tokonoma* with minute heirloom warriors and heroes the evening before. Hisashi can still picture himself enthralled as Jinjiro recounted the Ancient Chinese tale of the *koi* (carp), which fought their way upstream against rapids, even up waterfalls, overcoming all obstacles to become dragons.

Next morning Hisashi dresses in his best black *kimono*. On the back of it, an embroidered silver *koi* leaps up a waterfall. With *otosan* standing by, he hoists a long, coloured cloth *koi* up a post erected in the garden. Swelling in the wind, the *koi* swims vigorously against an invisible current.

Odd numbers are lucky in Japan, and on 15 November the whole family celebrated the Seven-Five-Three festival, these three years considered important stages in a child's growth.

Holding *obasan*'s hand, five-year-old Hisashi dressed in his first *hakama*, visited Meiji-*jingu*.

Against the boisterous sound of a brass band and the babble of voices, vendors compete to be heard. Indulgent grandparents, aunts and uncles mill around as exasperated parents fuss over their offspring, conscious of 'others' eyes'. Alerted by the disapproving looks of their parents, Hisashi and Eiko watch quietly as other gloriously attired, exuberant children chase each other about, younger ones playing hide and seek around their parents' legs. After wishing longevity for three-year-old Eiko, at one of the numerous *yatai*, *otosan* buys them each a small cloth bag decorated with a lucky crane, inside which is a red and white stick of 'thousand-year candy'.*

Hisashi remembers how, when they got home, his mother had proudly shown them her first *obi*. Her father had given it to her when she was seven; so beautiful, the *obi* had been the envy of her classmates. Made of the finest quality, it showed rows of silver and vermillion peacocks fanning their tails on black cloth. It had been woven especially for her at the famous Nishijin factory in Kyoto.

---

* A child who eats the candy is blessed with a thousand years of happiness.

Chapter 24

The Master Said So

Toryu-mon
The gateway to honour and success

Hisashi started primary school in April 1926 at the age of six.* Everyone in Japan was guaranteed a minimum six years of education, which included basic literacy in language and numbers, callisthenics, and *shushin*. However, only a few went all the way to university. Conscious they belonged to the new professional intelligentsia class, Jinjiro and Ryoko were keen to provide their children with a superior education.

According to Confucianism, boys and girls had to be kept separate, so all schools were single-sex with girls' schools less academically focussed. From their daughter, Eiko, they expected no more than that she become a 'good wife and wise mother'. From an early age she had learnt her '*on* to the world', taught to recognise that the boys of the family were superior and took priority. If the new baby due in August was a boy, Sato had requested that he be trained as a priest to inherit her position at the temple. It was expected that, after primary school, he would move to Kyoto to Hieizan-*ji* for his training. With all financial support to be provided by Sato, Jinjiro and Ryoko had agreed, and when their second son was born, he was named Yoh by Sato, 'a lucky, sophisticated name appropriate for a priest'.

---

* The academic year followed the fiscal year, which traditionally began in April, prior to the start of the new rice cycle. Hirohito was crowned Emperor in 1926.

For their eldest son, Hisashi, they were highly ambitious, primary school being the first step in a long path leading to a career that would offer him a good salary, promotion and high social status. Like many others, the Furuya parents were grooming their son for a future in a large corporation or in central government. Planned from his birth, both parents determined Hisashi would attend *Todai*, the most prestigious university in the country and from where the civil service recruited its elite employees. Thus his whole 15 years of schooling was geared towards passing the ultimate examination to be accepted for *Todai*. But competition was fierce. Entry to a prominent university was easier for graduates of a superior high school. And to get into such a school, it helped to attend a highly ranked middle school, which in its turn chose its entrants from the top primary schools. Jinjiro and Ryoko decided to send Hisashi to the primary school attached to the Teachers' Training College, and from then on he faced a demanding schedule of study and exams.

Although education was free, sending a son to an elite school incurred additional expenses in providing tailor-made uniforms, extra textbooks, class excursions and tram fares. Jinjiro worried constantly about money: he had no inheritance, no land to sell, inflation was rising, and the allowance for Tomoko's upkeep would stop when she married. However, he considered the struggle worthwhile to ensure Hisashi had the best chance.

Most children could walk to their local school, but Hisashi had to take a 40-minute tram ride, changing lines twice. Jinjiro accompanied him until he was sure his son knew where to get on and off. There were no taxis or buses, and everyone rode the trams. At home, each person had their 'proper place' at the table or in the living room, but on the trams it was first-come first-served, a sweeping change and the beginning of modern society. Twice a day for six years, Hisashi rode the trams. He found the familiarity of his daily routine reassuring in the largely adult male environment.

Smelling of oil and cheap varnished wood, trams were uncomfortable, with seating for 20 passengers on benches along the windows, and another 20 standing, clutching leather rings suspended from the ceiling. Holding on to the door pole, Hisashi would take in everything around him. He would study and memorise the letters from the few framed advertisements above the windows: a famous department store, a confectionary shop, a trade college. Hisashi would read anything written, anywhere

He soon recognised landmarks from which he could calculate the time to school. On the local line to Shibuya the roads were unpaved, the tram bumping alongside carts. From the farmhouse with the unusual blue roof, he had 30 minutes to go; from the magnolia, like the one at home, he was nearly at Shibuya and set to change lines. From Shibuya the paved tree-lined streets were flanked by banks, small retailers and hospitals. At the second hill, where on a fine day he could see Mount Fuji, he had 10 minutes. By the time they reached the grounds adjoining Meiji-*jingu* he was nearly there. But just before then, the tram would lurch as it slowed to pass the shrine. On the conductor's words, seated passengers stood, males removed their hats, and everyone bowed. When he could see the giant gingkoes leading to the *torii* (a shrine gateway) he had only two minutes to go.

Passengers on trams passing Yasukuni-*jinja** (*jinja*, a shrine for people at large), or running along the outer moat of the Imperial Palace, were also expected to bow and pay their respects, a government tactic to encourage nationalism. In the palace, Crown Prince Hirohito had recently ascended to the 'chrysanthemum throne'.

Subject to strict rules, with heavy fines for carelessness, slow, safe driving was the order of the day. But Hisashi would still hold his breath, as, going in opposite directions, two trams would carefully slip past each other, only an arm's length apart.

Soon he recognised each tram driver though, much in awe, he never spoke to them. Middle-aged men dressed in navy blue, military

---

* Yasukuni-*jinja* was the shrine dedicated to fallen soldiers.

styled uniforms, white gloves and peaked caps, they were highly respected for their status and skill. Like many of his schoolmates, Hisashi had aspired to become one, inspired as he watched a driver use his whole upper body to move the large control arm of the hand brake; their showy handling contrasted with his own skill when riding his tricycle.

Jinjiro gave Hisashi a dictionary when he entered primary school.* With 50 000 *kanji* to learn, as well as *katakana* and *hiragana*, rote learning was inevitable, and it was not until he entered his teens that he could read Japanese with ease. Jinjiro's childhood dictionary had had three times that number of characters to learn, while Jitsuzen's had 250,000. Adopting the Chinese system of ideographs, the ancient Japanese had devised a means of reading Chinese characters in a Japanese way called *kanji*, though only privileged males learned to read and write. Later a simpler script called *kana* (made up of *katakana* and *hiragana*) was developed for wider use. However, even in 1926, the Japanese language was complicated and required lengthy study.

The State regulated every aspect of school life. Reverence for Amaterasu and her descendant, the Emperor, filial piety, and respect for tradition were supreme; Confucianism and State Shinto were deeply embedded. Pupils owed every teacher a debt for helping them along the way, their *on* increasing with the years. Discipline was strict and uniformity the key. No one asked questions and no one dared be different.

Hisashi has always remembered 20 August 1929. On that day, at the same time all over Japan, boys of the same age were studying the same calligraphy lesson from the same syllabus using the same text.

> Hisashi dips his brush into the ink then, holding it awkwardly upright, he tries to produce the stylised ideograph. Moving between the rows

---

* Japanese language uses a combination of three alphabets, even in one sentence: *kanji*, which is based on Chinese ideograms; *katakana*, an angular form of syllables; and *hiragana*, the cursive form of syllabic writing.

of desks without comment, the teacher takes Hisashi's hand, letting him feel the correct rhythm. He does not scold or praise, yet expects him to try even harder.

Reading follows calligraphy. Textbooks are opened, phrases and verses chanted over and over, with the words drummed into their heads. Over half the day is spent in class recitation, with texts and tables learned verbatim. But no one checks to see whether the 40 boys have grasped the lesson.

Using a slide rule to calculate his multiplication table, Hisashi is startled by a shout from one of the other boys. Looking out of the window he can see a giant thing floating in the sky. The teacher lets the class outside for a better look and, against the sky, the zeppelin airship passes in front of their eyes.

Hisashi's school was more liberal and progressive than most, using such events as a learning experience. Compulsory texts were supplemented with other creative materials and methodology, including class excursions to the *Diet*, shrines, museums, the zoo and the movies. Pupils were also expected to write a diary with illustrations over the holidays. By the time he was ten, diary writing had become a daily habit.

From primary school the regimentation and restraints increased. Every evening, weekends and holidays, Hisashi had homework. By seven he recognised his '*on* to the world'. He knew if he was disobedient or disrespectful, the world would laugh at him, bringing shame and rejection upon himself and his family. He knew that, as long as he was approved of by others, his parents would support him. By eight, physical control and manners were embedded. By ten, he knew it was a virtue to resent an insult. He learned '*giri* to his name', recognising when and how to clear his honour.

Three years after Hisashi started primary school, Sato arranged for Tomoko to marry into a wealthy temple family that was sponsored by affluent merchants. For Tomoko, who had received a modern Western education, living with her husband's widowed mother was difficult, especially as she wanted to train as a priest in order to run her mother's temple until Yoh was old enough to take over.

Her marriage also had far-reaching effects on the Furuya family. Hisashi, having always been sternly directed against association with girls, even with Tomoko, missed her being around. But of greater significance, Tomoko's allowance came to an end, unfortunately at the same time as Jinjiro was made redundant from the navy. Although he went straight into another job, his salary was nowhere near the family's previous combined income. The company, Kawanishi, specialised in manufacturing flying boats for the navy, which were used for long-distance patrols over the Pacific Ocean. With his accounting skills, knowledge of the navy and his proficiency in English, Jinjiro was appointed manager of the Tokyo branch.

After Tomoko left, Eiko inherited her bedroom. She was becoming too old to share with the boys in the living room. However, with another baby on the way, and Hisashi needing study space, a new room equivalent to six *tatami* was built for him.

Hisashi loved his new room, not just for its privacy but the room itself. Waking each morning, he would watch the flickering shadows of the *sugi* moving in the breeze. By daylight, bright and cheerful, the room was flooded with pools of sunshine. Come evening, by the mellow glow of his lamp, the setting was subdued and relaxing. The room was organised and neat. There was a cupboard and *tansu* along one wall, while another wall was taken up with bookshelves on which favourite books and treasured objects were arranged tidily: a piece of gnarled driftwood, water-worn pebbles, a polished shard of agate. Apart from the *tansu*, the only other furniture was his desk, which he kept relatively uncluttered.

Sadly, just after Hisashi had moved into his new bedroom, four-year-old Yoh died of pneumonia, a month before a new daughter, Yayoi, was born. Hisashi missed his little brother, but kept his grief to himself.

Sato asked that Hisashi take Yoh's place to be her successor, even paying several times for him to go to Wakayama in the holidays to be introduced to temple supporters. However, Hisashi had his own dreams, and one day he actually dared voice his scepticism about priests. If Buddha helps both the good and bad, why were priests needed? And if Buddha helped everyone, why attend temple meetings and donate money? Why be good if it made no difference? Sato saw him as an 'undisciplined, unrescued 11-year-old, a disgrace to his mother'. By the time he entered middle school his parents had decided he should continue his original path. Tomoko, by now an ordained priest, would fill her mother's shoes.

In Hisashi's sixth and final year of primary school, the whole year was devoted to passing the entrance exam for middle school. Out of 100 male primary school graduates only 15 entered middle school, of which only two proceeded to professional schools and three to high school. That one exam set a boy's entire future, so all year they studied past exam papers. There were only a few public middle schools in Tokyo, public schools ranking higher than private. The oldest and most prestigious, 'The First Middle School', was known as the best, and it was there that his parents intended Hisashi would go. To ensure he was well prepared, as with most boys, he had a home tutor.

In 1931 the Great Depression prevailed, and jobs were hard to find, so the right career path was essential. Eleven-year-old Hisashi sensed his parents' tension, their 'big project' to get him into the best school. In fact, the entire extended family pressured him to do well, the hounding resulting in stomach problems. He pushed himself to fulfil his *on*, as did his classmates, all hopes pinned on the eldest or only son. Typically, younger sons went to middle schools where there was less pressure.

Each middle school had its own exam. In February 1932, Hisashi was one of 2 000 boys examined for 250 places. He passed with flying colours, and started his new school just after his twelfth birthday. He knew his parents were proud of him, but they never said so.

Hisashi's enforced social isolation ended when he started middle school. Ryoko now considered his peers to be his social equal, and Yoshio-*kun*, Yoshiji-*kun*, Tetsuji-*kun* and Shinji-*kun** visited often after school. The *genkan* was always full of footwear, with outside shoes exchanged for house slippers.

Having his own room was a bonus, being somewhere to entertain his friends away from prying parental eyes and annoying sisters. And he enjoyed finally being allowed to make friends. Though not the type to be a leader, nor was he a follower, even then his friends recognised him as a 'high-point boy', self-sufficient and independent.

Hisashi questioned everything: an unanswered question usually resulted in Jinjiro buying him a new reference book. He would read for hours on end, undisturbed in his room, his dream of achieving distinction in science boosted by a series of biographies on great men. One of these, Doctor H. Noguchi, the bacteriologist who isolated the yellow fever bacteria and syphilis, turned his aspiration to pathology.

Within the social constraints of the day, Hisashi was a boy going his own way. Superficially, his upbringing adhered to the norm: the eldest son of an elite, intelligentsia family following the appropriate pattern. But no matter the camouflage, in this culture of conformity the family stood out. Even in the new middle class, Ryoko's open home was unusual. Hisashi knew of no other family where classmates were welcomed after school, and it often made him wonder why.

---

* Christian name then *kun* denotes a close friend of one's own age.

Chapter 25

Spoiling for a Fight

Chiri mo tsumoreba yama to naru
Dust amassed will make a mountain

WHILE JAPAN'S RAPID INDUSTRIALISATION had brought prosperity for some, it also resulted in the population more than doubling to 65 million. The country seemed too small to hold everyone. The huge majority of people were still engaged in tenant farming, fishing, cottage industries and small-scale retailing: half of them as desperately poor as they had been since the Tokugawa era, their plight even more precarious as Japan, like the rest of the world, plunged into economic depression. There were too many farmers, and being a mountainous country, there was too little habitable land.

Beneath the surface new forces stirred. Fuelled by exposure to Western thought, increasingly aware of their rights, the general populace seethed. Within the army particularly, the government was perceived to have betrayed those who lived in rural Japan. This was where the majority of soldiers came from, the military a means to escape poverty. Despair turned to anger, and communism* found fertile ground. Unrest was widespread, whipped up not only by militant communists, but also by nationalists who superficially supported the

---
* Encouraged by the prevailing recession, communism was flourishing in the lower socio-economic groups and intelligentsia. In 1921, various small labour movements merged into a stronger single organisation. The Japanese Communist Party, an offshoot organised in 1922, condemned the government for its lack of policy in coping with the escalating level of poverty. Internationally, a Communist Party had been established in China in 1921, Italy came under the dictatorship of Mussolini in 1922, and the Nazi Party was formed in Germany in 1923.

rights of the lower classes. The government responded with the 1925 Peace Preservation Law. Assisted by an extensive police network with a police box wherever you turned, anything threatening peace and order was suppressed. Police raids destroyed many left-wing groups, or drove them underground.

The 1929 New York stockmarket crash ushered in the Great Depression that spread to Japan early in 1930. Still recovering from the 1923 earthquake, the collapse of world trade worsened the situation, causing mass unemployment, with the rural sector hit especially hard by plunging prices for rice and silk. This, coupled with the population explosion, resulted in endemic agrarian poverty.

Imports exceeded exports, and the country's growing reliance on imported foods and raw materials made Japan vulnerable. Bankruptcies were common. But the power of the capitalists was increasing, *zaibatsu* expanding as they established their dominance over the economy.

Ultra-nationalistic societies simmered secretly, increasing in numbers, with support at all levels, including senior military officers and members of cabinet. State Shinto ruled, as *on* transferred to the Emperor, now restored in his rightful place as ruler of the universe.

Continuing Western efforts to oppose the Japanese joining their ranks had created a deep brooding resentment within Japan. International slights were recalled, the 'Unequal treaties', and 'Yellow Peril' adding to the insult engendered by the 1924 Oriental Exclusion Act passed by the US congress, a law seen as targeting Japanese migrants. The world had tipped and dust amassed was becoming a mountain. Xenophobia increased, shifting influence towards the extremists who quietly planned revenge. Compelled by their '*giri* to the world' they had a duty to clear Japan's reputation, and bring the world back into balance with Japan in its rightful place.

Back in the Meiji era, the government had used emigration to alleviate overpopulation, unemployment and poverty. With the door now closed to America, Canada and Australia, the extremists favoured expanding Japan's empire through war, with the closer expanse of China offering the easiest solution. In particular, resource-rich Manchuria was ideal: it was able to provide markets for manufacturers, access to raw materials, and land on which to settle the excess population.

But Manchuria had been under Russian dominance since 1900. The confusion following the overthrow of the Manchu dynasty of Emperors in 1911 meant China was ripe for takeover. It sounded straightforward, Japan had a modern army and navy and a strong industrial base. China's large, but old-fashioned army was poorly trained, poorly equipped, clothed and fed, and her heavy industry would never supply a war effort.

During World War I Japan had sided with The Great Powers, who showed their appreciation in the Treaty of Versailles* by acknowledging Japan's permanent occupation of Korea, giving tacit approval to her supremacy in Manchuria,† and transferring the Chinese port of T'sing-tao from German to Japanese control. Japan thus indebted had assisted in quelling anti-British, American and French riots in China. According to many, this apparently noble gesture suited Japan's expansionist plans. Britain, France and America regarded Manchuria as a buffer between the newly created Nationalist China and Communist Russia. The Great Powers tolerated Japanese involvement, hoping it would prevent the Russian communists advancing south.

The dreams of the Japanese extremists extended far beyond Manchuria. Headed by the Emperor, Japan would lead Asia into a new era, their duty and destiny to free all Asian peoples from European colonialism. At the same time, it would secure strategic defences, access to raw materials, and prevent encirclement and colonisation

---

* The Versailles Treaty had been introduced essentially to punish the defeated countries with the loss of territories, disarmament and reparation; it targeted Germany in particular. Rejection of the treaty became one of Hitler's most effective propaganda themes, the first open violation occurring in March 1935 when Germany re-introduced compulsory military service.

† Except for the Russian-occupied Liaotung Peninsula.

by the West. This grand plan became known as 'The Great East Asia Co-Prosperity Sphere'. As 'the first race in the universe', Japan would take up arms on behalf of its younger Asian brothers, its role as 'elder brother' justifying its actions in deciding what was best for the younger, subordinating it for its own good, with each nation taking its 'proper place' in the hierarchy. Only through fighting could Japan reclaim its 'proper place' in Greater Asia and eliminate the Western powers from the area.

From the late 1920s, weakened by factional infighting, respective Japanese governments generally survived a few months only.* Military control over civil affairs spiralled. Civilian politicians wanting cooperation with the West were increasingly out of step with military leaders, who wanted a military dictatorship that would immediately take over China.

Disregarding the government's non-expansionist policy, extremist officers stationed in Manchuria unilaterally engineered a coup in September 1931, attacking Chinese troops. By the following February, Japan had annexed the whole of Manchuria, which was transformed into the Japanese puppet state of Manchuko. The Chinese, unable to resist, were counting on rescue by the League of Nations, which had been established in 1920 partly to solve international disputes.

The Japanese extremists were a new breed of warrior and, while *Bushido*† was part of their creed, they followed the old ways when it suited and ignored them when it did not. After the coup, they thought they could do as they pleased in China. The government's failure to punish those responsible for the coup and other rebellious actions, made it seem as if the government condoned their conduct.

Militarism and nationalism were now entrenched in domestic life. After centuries of military dictatorship under a *shogun*, the people deferred without question to a military power sanctioned by the Emperor. The military would rescue Japan. The answer was war. And,

---

* Eleven men formed 13 cabinets between 1932 and 1945.

in any case, it was said conflict in Manchuria had been inevitable; if it had not been Japan asserting herself, it would have been Russia. In May 1932, when Prime Minister Inukai tried to moderate the army's actions, he was assassinated. His assassins, young military officers, were lightly punished. In 1933, the League of Nations unanimously declared that Japan should evacuate Manchuria. Japan simply left the League. Also that year Adolf Hitler became Chancellor of Germany.

By now members of the military and their sympathisers dominated senior government positions. Increased arms production stimulated the economy, which now depended on heavy industry, such as steel, shipping and vehicle and machine manufacture. Mitsui, Mitsubishi, Sumitomo and Yasuda were still the most important *zaibatsu*, but new *zaibatsu*, Nissan, Hitachi, Matsushita, Toyota and Toshiba had emerged, most of them subcontracting their component manufacture to smaller firms. Small subcontractors, along with *zaibatsu*, reaped the benefits, the *narikin* class growing proportionally.

The economy peaked in 1934 as demand from the military grew. Industrial production boomed, creating full employment and attracting newcomers to the cities. At this stage, war was an exhilarating prospect and most people saw only its advantages. Apart from the likes of Jinjiro, posted to Europe at the conclusion of World War I, people were completely unaware of the downside.

Chapter 26

Seasons of Change

Ichi-yoh ochite, tenka no aki o shiru
A falling leaf forewarns of the coming of autumn on earth
(The smallest sign gives the clue to the decay of a country)

HISASHI'S MIDDLE SCHOOL, located several stops past his primary school, was close to the *Diet* building in Nagatacho and took over an hour to get there. The labyrinth of roads enduring from Edo days was not conducive to modern traffic, but transport into the central city had improved. Buses and taxis were now readily available, and the first subway competed with the trams.* Usually, Hisashi took the local tram to Shibuya, met up with friends and caught a taxi, the cost of the 25-minute ride split between five boys being cheaper than the tram.

Tokyo's population now topped five million. Older neighbourhoods in the city centre, overbuilt with factories, warehouses and cheap lodgings were filling up with rural migrants. With steady employment and rising incomes, previous residents were relocating to the more affluent suburbs mushrooming in uncontrolled development on the periphery of the city. The Furuya's suburb of Sangenjaya was still fashionable, but semi-detached housing estates, apartment buildings and small factories now sat alongside the single-family detached homes. Everyone in the area had power, gas, running water and

---

* Asia's first subway began operation in 1927 from Asakusa to Ueno, then in 1931 from Shibuya to Tokyo-*eki*.

telephones. The farmer who previously collected night soils with his cart had been replaced by a truck.

Not far from their house, a new tailoring business had opened. The seamstress had been previously employed to tailor Western-style garments at a department store, but she had been laid off. In the increasingly ultra-nationalist environment, the store was no longer allowed to make or sell Western goods. Ryoko was one of her first customers at her new shop.

> She wants something that will set her apart: a warm, woollen coat, but not a typical Japanese coat, nor a Western copy. The seamstress knows exactly what Ryoko wants.
>
> Her woollen fabrics are of the finest English quality. Seated comfortably, Ryoko examines each bolt of cloth brought for her inspection. The black is too conformist, the houndstooth too different, the tweed too Western, the green too bright. The soft grey cashmere is perfect.
>
> A month later Ryoko stands proudly in her ankle-length, hand-stitched, grey, cashmere coat, admiring her reflection in the shop's mirror.

From 1931, while educational policy had become increasingly ultra-nationalistic and, despite the fact that many of their fathers played strategic roles, Hisashi and his friends at middle school were oblivious to the war in China. These privileged boys enjoyed their young lives. The government clearly stipulated that higher education should educate elite youngsters with a broad schooling, sport and physical training taught alongside classics and calligraphy. Hisashi even started to learn written English, memorising passages from *Aesop's Fables*, and Hans Christian Andersen.

Hisashi proved to be an outstanding student. The 250 boys had been divided into five classes of 50. At the end of every academic year, they were tested, ranked numerically, then divided into five new classes. Each year the top ten were prefects. Each year, coming either first or second, Hisashi was a prefect.

He still dreamed he would follow the intelligentsia ideal, proceeding to a permanent high-salaried, high-status position in a large company like Mitsubishi, staying there until retirement at 50, with a generous gratuity and the possibility of becoming a Director. He also dreamt of getting married after university, and assumed he would have children. As the eldest son, he had an obligation to maintain the family name. However, in 1936, the education system swung from educating the elite to educating all young people, training them for war. The world turned upside down, and nothing was ever the same again.

Classes became much stricter. The curriculum literally changed overnight, with sport, English, literature, anything cultural removed. Science was left, but only because of its possible benefit to the war effort. All pupils now learned about military strategy and preparation for battle, including how to use a rifle. They were drilled with propaganda to instil fervour and pride. Patriotism had always been stressed, but now *shushin* and indoctrination in Japan's supremacy became even more obsessive.

The underlying attraction of militarism was inherent, reflected even in the identical military style uniforms worn at schools and universities since the institutions had been established after the Meiji Revolution; cropped hair and high-collared suits, modelled on the uniforms of the European naval academy. They wore navy blue at middle school, black at high school and university. The traditional family and caste systems fostered uniformity, discipline and obedience. In war time, this austere uniform, anonymous and intimidating, effectively enhanced the martial atmosphere, and a united determination to resist failure. Dressed so, schoolboys strongly reflected the authority and obedience of Confucianism, patriotism and militarism.

The boys' pattern of life was shattered, as preparation for combat encroached increasingly on their lives. Western songs disappeared off the radio waves, and luxury goods like Ryoko's coat disappeared. Privately everyone grumbled, but never in public.

Buoyed by Shintoism, people at large were easily manipulated by the government's propaganda. The ingrained structure of the family system saw to that, and it suited both Shinto and military leaders to encourage this mutually advantageous union. Shintoism could drum up support from a population spurred by the vision that Japan was a divine nation, specially favoured by the gods, with a destiny to liberate and lead all Asian peoples. *Giri* and *on* ensured their compliance and overruled any doubts.

Nationwide call-up began, ending chronic unemployment, with all men from 18 to 45 years old conscripted. Women, too, were expected to help. With so many men fighting in China, women had to take over jobs usually done by men. They went into business, worked as farm labourers, tram conductors and van drivers; some became nurses and went to the front line. But most went into the munitions factories to help make weapons.

In 1931, the Patriotic Women's Association, the first-ever women's political organisation, had been launched by right-wing nationalists. The following year it was legalised and renamed the National Defense Women's Association. Initially, merely a show of cooperation with the military and an expression of loyalty to the nation, ultimately the association proved to be an excellent means of manipulating women for military purposes. Women became the mainstay of fundraising campaigns, recycling metals for armaments and renouncing luxury goods. They were also used to frustrate communism, by dissuading their menfolk from joining the movement.

Fighter planes were top of the fundraising list, but with the average salary at 38 *yen* per month, raising the 70 000 *yen* per plane was a big ask. Rather, women were expected to donate their jewellery for the banks to sell: the cash was then used to buy aircraft. Like many women, Ryoko made token donations. The women also prepared and sent comfort kits to soldiers overseas, and organised farewells for those leaving on active duty. They provided lodgings for out of town soldiers who were waiting to be shipped out. Hisashi came home from school one day to find the household in an uproar. Ryoko had been given two days' notice to billet ten soldiers leaving for Manchuria.

The billets were farmers in their forties, and had been requisitioned as low-ranked servicemen. It was said, a conscripted man's life was worth 'only the cost of sending his call-up card', but they were excited to be going to war and unconcerned they would not be paid. Now they would wear a uniform, have sufficient to eat and free accommodation. They were honoured to be doing their duty in the name of the Emperor and, if they should fall, they would be enshrined at Yasukuni-*jinja*.

Hisashi had gone to the station with his mother to see them off. The platform had been packed. As the train pulled away, with hats off, everyone bowed. The silence had been palpable. Though still an adolescent, he knew his own life would soon be affected, but assumed that in the end he would achieve his personal dreams.

Chapter 27

Poverty Dulls the Conscience

Yoshi no zui kara ten nozoku
To peep at heaven through the tube of a reed

A RETICENT MAN, OFTEN DISTRACTED, Jinjiro showed his affection only to Hisashi. The two of them spent many evenings discussing politics and the unsettling changes in Japan. Dark rumours had been circulating. Jinjiro had heard that ultranationalistic extremists were deliberately setting out to bring down the government and provoke a world war.

In January 1936, father and son sit quietly waiting for the evening news broadcast, the familiar sound of the naval march signalling the beginning of the bulletin. The announcer drones on about this battle and that, then in a short, low-key message declares Imperial Headquarters has renounced the naval treaties previously signed with the Western powers. The navy expresses regret.

It is not news to Jinjiro. Staff at Kawanishi, with its close naval connection, have had advance notice. Usually Jinjiro carefully considers his words before speaking, but tonight he makes no attempt to hide the scorn in his voice or on his face. He had been alarmed at what they had been told that morning and upset hearing the responses of staff. Listening to their vehement attacks on how badly America and Britain had treated Japan, he had kept quiet, as every voice had been jubilant that finally the tables had been turned on the West, and that Japan had recovered its pride.

As he explains to Hisashi, by abrogating the treaty, Japan can build up its naval fleet. But America and Britain will simply follow suit, and their access to oil reserves and their superior capability to replenish hardware lost in battle will widen the gap even further. Renouncing the treaty is pointless and short-sighted, a world war now inevitable. Japan is 'deliberately and meanly becoming a bugbear in international society'.

Behind the scornful words, Hisashi senses his father is genuinely saddened relations between Japan, America and Britain have so deteriorated. Jinjiro's fondness for Britain is real and, after living in America for 10 years, he still has a sincere attachment to that country. His experiences in both cultures had dramatically altered his thinking and expectations.

Until now, Jinjiro has been proud of his country's maritime heritage. Japan had been trading with China, Korea and other Southeast Asian countries long before the arrival of Europeans. When the country opened up, British maritime procedures had been quickly adopted, and steamships bought from Scottish shipyards had been copied to develop the shipbuilding industry. In a short time Japan had created one of the strongest navies in the world, powerful enough to conquer the Russians in 1905. But now, Japanese arrogance has clouded her judgement. Japan does not know her enemy. How do the militarists think they can get away with challenging the might of a combined America and Britain?

In 1921, America had initiated the Washington Conference for nations with interests in the Pacific and Asia to discuss collective security arrangements, at which time Japan was forced to return the Shandong area to China. At the First London Naval Conference in 1930, it was determined that Japan be permitted to build only three warships for every five for Britain and America. Yet again the Japanese felt they had been humiliated. Their naval negotiator was severely reprimanded for giving in to American pressure.* Now, for the second time failing to gain approval for naval parity with the British and Americans, Japan had renounced the treaties.

The Japanese military prepared for war. Military expenditure had increased from 28 per cent of national budget in 1930 to 47.2 per cent in 1936. In a deliberate breach of the Washington and London agreements, Japan had designed 18.1-inch diameter projectiles, the largest shells in the world. These were to be fired from guns mounted in two colossal new battleships, the *Yamato* and *Musashi*, also to be the biggest in the world.

The morning of 26 February 1936 started out like any other school day. Hisashi was nearly 16.

> A chill wind blows briskly from Siberia. At Shibuya the taxis have stopped running, so he takes the tram to school. The weather is at its worst; a day of heavy snow, heavier than anything in ten years. But muffled in his coat, it does not dampen his spirits as he gets off the tram to walk the short distance to school. He enjoys the world around him: the ground blanketed with snowdrifts, the frozen river, and the trees covered with snow.
>
> As he enters the warm school building he looks forward to the day's programme. Lessons begin, then mid-morning, a knock on the classroom door. Fifty pairs of eyes turn. On instruction from the principal, the school will be shut for two days. All boys are to go home directly, no loitering.
>
> Doors open, a thousand pupils discharged from their rooms. Suddenly the corridors are packed with boys hurrying to collect their belongings from their lockers. Jostling together, they chatter in a babble of anticipation at the unexpected holiday. Hisashi is excited, but apprehensive as to why they are being evacuated. Above the

---

* In 2003, Hisashi found out that the negotiator in 1930 had been the father of one of his middle school classmates. During the war, the Vice-Admiral was decommissioned for openly opposing war with America, and spent many years living in fear of his life.

hubbub, class teachers direct their boys into lines. The boys wait expectantly, thrown into relief under the harsh corridor lights: austere dark uniforms, straps of their caps under their chins; metal badges and buttons glinting; satchels and canteens hanging across their chests.

Outside, grim-faced, armed police and soldiers surround the school. The exodus of boys is efficient, but tense. Not a word is spoken. The gravity of the situation pervades the mass and the school grounds are soon deserted.

The day is darkening and, in the monochromatic landscape, black shapes stand out starkly. An abandoned bicycle lies half buried in a snowdrift. Clipped pines rise like sentinels. Clusters of soldiers are setting up machine guns, harsh commands echoing sporadically in the silence. Hisashi sensing their mood is disturbed by the sinister scene silhouetted in black and white.

At a safe distance everyone scatters. Inhaling the icy air he slowly makes his way home on foot. Snow lies deep on the roads and roofs of houses. On main routes labourers shovel fruitlessly as snow continues to fall. Disconcerted by something he cannot understand, Hisashi's thoughts are in turmoil.

His face is pinched with cold, his hands and feet so chilled it is difficult to pull off his boots. Sliding open the *shoji* from the *genkan* into the house, warm air and the smell of cooking welcome him. In the dim light he sees Yayoi lying on the *tatami* reading. *Okasan* is writing letters and Matsu is busy at the stove. They look up, startled by his early return. Matsu quickly brings hot water to soak his feet, fussing around him, wanting him to drink hot tea. All he wants is to talk about what has happened, but they are not really interested.

Not until much later in the day did Hisashi hear on the radio that a coup attempt had been staged by mutinous young officers. Most were from poor backgrounds and poverty was fundamental to their cause, and they dreamt of a divine rebirth of a non-Western Japan. Fifteen-hundred armed soldiers had seized key buildings, assassinated several politicians and demanded the reorganisation of the government: the first step of their dream to rid the country of capitalism and bring down the *zaibatsu* and *narikin*. The proximity of Hisashi's school to the *Diet* had rendered it unsafe.

> That evening, with Jinjiro home early from work, the family dine together. The kitchen is warm from the *hibachi* (charcoal brazier) and the *kotatsu*, and a hearty hotpot bubbles on the gas ring. Chicken and fish, shimeji mushrooms, sweet potatoes, carrots, gingko nuts and bamboo shoots simmer in *miso*, at the last minute Ryoko adding *tofu*, *negi*, pea pods, and slivers of *yuzu* peel. After they have eaten, a quilt is placed over the table and their laps, trapping in the heat. Finally, Hisashi has a listener who pays him attention.

The rebellion was suppressed within days. Several known ring leaders committed *seppuku*. The others were executed, and their supporters sent to the Manchurian Front; better they be killed in the name of war than for their rebellion. The army duly made use of the uprising to increase its control over the government, arguing this was the only way the malcontents would be contained. One extremist faction had been crushed, but another would rise in its place.

> Weeks later, father and son sit in the garden. Spring has arrived and a recent shower has refreshed the air. Jinjiro relates what he has heard that day.
> General Heisuke Yanagawa, the father of one of Hisashi's classmates from primary school, is one of the 'secret wire-pullers' of the coup.* Hisashi's head whirls, remembering how in class he had always had a view of Seiwu Yanagawa's back.† Seiwu had carried on to Hisashi's middle school, but has just left to enter the military academy.

---

* This is one of Hisashi's phrases meaning the leader pulling the strings behind the scenes.
† Seating was allocated according to height.

Chapter 28

One is Free From Shame on a Trip

Daiji no mae no shoji
To concentrate on priorities and ignore trifles

THE NAVY AND ARMY WERE RIVALS. Each had its own arsenal, disciplines and strategy: the navy was modelled along British lines; the army on German and French lines. Initially, the navy had objected to the army's expansionist plans. Navy recruits were generally better educated and more experienced. Most fought in World War I and, like Jinjiro had travelled overseas, so were more realistic about Japan's place in the world.

Jinjiro did not believe in Japan's destiny to rule Asia. He considered the war in China a massive blunder, without consideration of the realities and consequences, likening it to an almighty game of chess. Closing its eyes to military activities, he felt the government was worsening an already tense international situation. As yet neither side was ready to shatter the peace, both perceiving communist Russia as a bigger threat. However, he believed that the Japanese attitude only served to warn their opponents, allowing them to prepare for a war against Japan. And the media cooperated, fuelling anti-Western feeling.

He was also curious as to how the army was funding its schemes. The cost of maintaining troops in China would be astronomical. The economy had suffered terribly in the Depression, yet there were still sufficient funds for the campaign. Even though the military received a huge portion of the national budget, with much of that going to the army, he asked, was it enough to advocate war on such a scale?

Like the British, French and Americans before them, Japan over the years had experienced difficulties quelling communist uprisings in Manchuria, and had undertaken joint action with the Chinese Nationalist government. The strongest force for stability in the new Republic of China had initially been Sun Yat-sen. On his death in 1925, leadership fell to Chiang Kai-shek, whose task it had been to organise an army to resist communism. However, in 1936, Chiang Kai-shek was kidnapped by the communists, and released only in return for promising he would join with them against the Japanese. Benefiting from Russian arms, and British and American subsidies, the Nationalist government and the communists commenced joint hostilities. Japan was now obliged to focus its energies in China. Expansion plans to Thailand, Malaya and beyond were postponed. The navy, though continuing its own activities, changed stance to support the army's ambition.

By 1937, war fever was mounting and in Tokyo rumours abounded that something was afoot in China. Mid-year, the then Japanese Prime Minister was forced to resign. Likening the military to 'an untamed horse left to run wild', he claimed that, 'If you try head on to stop it, you'll get kicked to death'.

In July, following a clash with Chinese troops near Peking (now Beijing), Japanese forces began a full-scale invasion of the rest of China. This was not war as they saw it, but known as 'The China Incident'. Sweeping southwards, they committed terrible atrocities against civilians. By December, they had overrun Peking, Shanghai, and Nanking (known today as Nanjing). To the Japanese, the war had to be won. Failure was unthinkable.

As hostilities increased, militarism flourished back home, instilling a strong sense of national identity. Educational policy turned militaristic. Citizens were persuaded to donate funds to the war office, and the National Spiritual Mobilisation Campaign commenced.

Like Jinjiro not everyone agreed with what was happening; however, coercion and intimidation brought doubters into line. New laws empowered the government to do pretty much anything. The National Security Law and the Special Penal Law of War-Time denied even the freedom of thought and speech. Backed by the *Kempeitai* (Military Police) and its civilian equivalent the *Tokko* (Special Higher Police or Thought Police), the military strengthened its grasp. A network of informers infiltrated every building, street and community in Japan. Suspects were deemed guilty upon arrest, with torture a common occurrence.

Criticism was banned. Press censorship was imposed. Telephones were tapped. Letters to and from troops in China were intercepted. Dwindling numbers of opponents were eliminated. And people retreated into silence.

Early 1937, Hisashi had overheard his parents talking. They were shocked by the defection of the actress Yoshiko Okada to the Soviet Union. Until then, communism had been a quiet, underground invasion. Accompanied by producer Ryotaro Sugimoto, Yoshiko had travelled to Sakhalin to visit the Japanese garrison on the Russo–Japanese border. On 1 January, during a driving snowstorm, the pair crossed the border that was thought to be impassable; their daring portrayed a glamorous image of communism.* In reprisal, and to quash other possible attempts, the *Tokko* persecuted the communists.

Also that January, Jinjiro's brother Michitaro died. Over the years the two men had had little contact, but Hisashi noticed that after Michitaro's death, his father became more reserved.

A few months later, Eiko received a chain letter that was circulating worldwide, promising happiness if she participated. Suspicious of the novelty, the *Tokko* had declared the letters were the action of foreign spies sourcing military secrets, so Eiko threw away the letter.

---

* Much later Jinjiro heard they were arrested as spies; Ryotaro executed and Yoshiko imprisoned. Released after the war, Yoshiko stayed in Russia working as an announcer for Moscow radio until 1972, when the Japanese government allowed her to return home.

Paper and ink were now scarce. Only two daily newspapers were published, reduced to propaganda news-sheets informing the public of the government's version of progress, with a little local news thrown in.

> Jinjiro looks up from his newspaper. Another satisfactory military achievement has been reported, this time in Nanking, the city's seizure hailed as a splendid triumph over the combined nationalist and communist armies. No details of the slaughter are reported. Recognising the report will have been censored, Jinjiro wonders what really happened.

What did happen became known to the West as the 'Rape of Nanking'. People worldwide were sickened and incensed by the ruthless massacre of so many people. The wanton, gratuitous violence created the savage reputation of the Japanese soldier, fixated beyond reason.

In each area they captured, the Japanese army had managed to drive out the communists. Nanking was full of soldiers: Japanese, as well as Chinese communists and nationalists, the population doubling almost overnight. The communist army was so poor, their soldiers did not wear uniforms. This made it impossible to differentiate them from civilians.

Japanese military leaders wanted a swift victory to hasten their march south. Word had come from Imperial Headquarters, 'to concentrate on priorities and ignore the trifles'. The quickest method for the best result was to kill everyone. A well-disciplined army, responding under orders, meant they were free to annihilate the enemy as quickly as possible. It was commonly believed one was 'free from shame outside one's home and immediate environment', especially outside the country. Varying from 30 000 to over 250 000, the death toll is fiercely disputed.

Antagonism against Japan hardened even more. The American government wanted to forcibly halt Japanese aggression, but public opinion favoured staying out of foreign wars and concentrating on getting people back to work after the Depression.

'The China Incident' spiralled into a 'Holy War'. More men, more tanks and more aircraft were marshalled. Nearly two million Japanese soldiers were stationed in China. With the National Mobilisation Law passed in April 1938, the nation was formally on war alert, and the army's budget increased even more.

Throughout 1938, Japan continued to take Chinese cities along the coast, and had reached as far south as Canton by October. They had expected a quick capitulation, but the Chinese were fighting back. The army had wanted to conquer China, then to confront Soviet forces on the Manchuko border. Though risking war with America, Britain, France and Holland who had interests there, the navy favoured continuing southwards to resource rich Southeast Asia. To strike the north and south simultaneously was not viable. The army prevailed. In late July 1938, Japanese troops had clashed with the Soviets on the Manchuko border, both eventually agreeing to a ceasefire.

From within their middle-class milieu, Jinjiro and Ryoko observed the escalating fanaticism with growing horror. But at this stage it did not impact significantly on their lives.

Meantime, across the world in Germany, the Jewish community were being persecuted. Many, including numerous scientists, sought refuge in America. In 1938, German scientists had discovered that if the uranium atom was split over and over again, it could cause a chain reaction over a very short time that would result in a massive explosion. Three of these scientists persuaded Albert Einstein to write to American President Roosevelt describing the potential bomb and urging America to develop its own bomb before Hitler did. Even though America was at peace, Roosevelt instructed his officials to look into Einstein's suggestions. Behind the scenes, as the situation worsened in both Asia and Europe, American defence efforts were being hurriedly expanded.

Chapter 29

Innocent Paradise

Nikko o minai uchi wa kekko to iu na
Don't say wonderful unless you have seen Nikko

ONE OF HISASHI'S CLOSE FRIENDS at middle school was Yoshiji-*kun*. Yoshiji-*kun* owned a German camera. Today, everyone in Japan has a camera, but then it was rare. The Furuya family could not afford a camera, but with Yoshiji-*kun*'s 'camera mania' at its peak during middle school, sepia records of that time exist today, with Hisashi, Eiko and Yayoi his chief subjects. He took dozens of photographs, including some showing the toys given to the children by the younger Onishi brother. Now an economist, the young man had gone to Europe to investigate techniques for watermarking bank notes. He brought home an electric toy train from Germany and an English doll for the Furuya children, and these status symbols were proudly immortalised by Yoshiji-*kun*.

In the summer holidays of July and August 1938, hopefully his last year at middle school, Hisashi was delighted when Yoshiji-*kun* invited him to spend two months in Nikko to avoid the heat of Tokyo. About 300 kilometres away, Nikko was famous as the burial site of the first Tokugawa *shogun*. With its elaborate Chinese inspired mausoleum, Nikko Tosho-Gu was different from other shrines. Set in the mountain foothills on the edge of the vast evergreen forest, the ancient shrine was camouflaged by trees.

Both sets of parents thought the two 18-year-olds would study better for their exams in the cooler climate. Their exams were fast approaching the following spring. Yoshiji-*kun* was preparing for the entrance examination to the military academy, where one in six was accepted; Hisashi for entry to the top public high school, with only one in ten successful. Hisashi was blissfully unaware he had been given a once in a lifetime opportunity, as Yoshiji-*kun*'s mother paid for everything. Yoshiji-*kun* had few close friends, so all his mother expected in return for financing the holiday, was a good companion for her only child. As a wealthy widow, she was a nervous mother and carefully selected his friends and, much to Ryoko's gratification, Hisashi was considered suitable.

The two boys stayed at the Buddhist temple Rin-no-*ji*, occupying a priest's empty hermitageu that backed onto the shrine, an opportunity made available only to those closely connected to the Tokugawa family. Here they discarded the restraints of everyday life, enjoying their first-ever taste of freedom. Their mothers expected them to study hard, but they spent much of their time outdoors. Neither knew how to cook, but walking down to the railway station café for their midday meal, they then only needed worry about a simple breakfast and evening snack.

The days slipped by. Up early to get their study out of the way, the boys spent the rest of the day doing as they pleased.

> The afternoon is bright and sunny, woolly clouds racing across the sky. They wander up the steep hill behind the shrine to see the white lilies growing a metre high, then down into the lush valley, where a stream meanders through the forest. In the distance they can see the mountains.
>
> Beneath the pyramid-shaped *sugi*, the boys stretch out on the grass, hands behind their heads, enveloped in the resinous scent of the trees. Birds sing with clarity, while cicadas chirrup in chorus. Perched at the top of a persimmon tree, a crow preens its satiny black plumage. A hawk fixes its gaze on the undergrowth, then, abruptly, with a soft swish of air, soars upwards, wheeling on motionless wings.
>
> Suddenly a red flame slides down a tree, leaping onto the grass.

> They sit up slowly, careful not to frighten it. Its tail puffed out like a brush, the squirrel is almost near enough to touch, as it watches them with bright beady eyes.
>
> A fox trots out of the trees. It has not caught their scent and stands calmly, ears pricked. Minutes pass, then in the forest a twig snaps, the fox vanishing in a flash. They are so thrilled to have seen the real thing, neither the villain of folktales, nor the stone messenger of the gods.

Exhilarated from their afternoon adventure, they took a canoe and paddled upstream in the early evening.

> In a quiet stretch of water beneath overhanging trees, they stop to watch an otter on the bank. Frisking in and out of holes, over fallen trees, it toboggans down a slope into the river. It sculls along on its back, then with a smooth dive, twists and turns fish-like through the clear water. Dragonflies, silver wings outspread, skim the surface. A kingfisher with iridescent blue wings alights on a branch. A rock swallow flits among the pebbles on the riverbank, while a cormorant dries its wings on a nearby rock.

At dawn and dusk, otters visited the shrine to eat the food offerings left by visitors for the gods; the priests tolerated the clandestine callers.

> As Hisashi and Yoshiji-*kun* settle down to wait in the tall paulownia overlooking the altar, two otters stop, furtive. Standing tall on hind legs, their ears are alert. Then, sure they are safe, they rummage greedily through the offerings. In all their lives the boys have never seen such wildlife as they have at Nikko; have never thought to see, in the flesh, the animals and birds they read about in books.

The boys discussed many things: their dreams, the impending exams, *bushido* and marriage. His mind released from the pressures of home and school, Hisashi could see his life was falling into place. By working as a research scientist in a big company, he would not only follow in his grandfather Hajime's footsteps, but meet his parents' ambitions and society's expectations. Such a position would also allow him to fulfil his own dream of achieving distinction by working on projects benefiting mankind.

That period was one of the happiest of Hisashi's life. Yoshiji-*kun* took numerous photographs of Hisashi at that time, catching expressions of curiosity, mischief and delight. His was an optimistic face, showing a boy with no qualms about his future; a boy highly educated and disciplined; a boy never doubting what he knew.

It was the last summer the two boys ever spent together.

Chapter 30

Luxury is Our Enemy

Ichioku isshin
One hundred million people, one mind

THE NATIONAL MOBILISATION LAW passed the previous year had mobilised the entire nation. Temples, shrines, and schools were now in complete submission to the State. Factories had been requisitioned to produce military goods, all raw materials diverted for military production. Metal objects, even household cutlery, had to be donated and recycled for armaments. Men not called up for service had been absorbed into the munitions industry; not just the unemployed, but street vendors, peddlers and labourers, prohibited from working for anything other than military purposes.

Apart from the mail, which continued spasmodically, home deliveries had stopped. Expensive clothes, cosmetics, jewellery and food were more and more difficult to procure. Sports equipment and art materials were banned, as were leather goods: the leather was required for soldiers' boots and horse harnesses. Increasingly, retailers had to find jobs within the war industry, Ryoko's seamstress one of the casualties. Her customers dwindled as they were required to adopt a less luxurious style; *mompe* (women's work pants) now more appropriate for the wartime atmosphere.

As a symbol of patriotism, women had also been asked to cut off the sleeves of their *kimono*. This reduced the value of the *kimono* and demonstrated the women's readiness to abandon status symbols. Rather than spoiling expensive *kimono*, Ryoko had new ones made with short sleeves.

Membership of the National Defence Women's Association was still voluntary, so well-off housewives usually sent their daughters or maids. In this time of increasing equality, still being able to employ a servant was a test of status. Ryoko sent Matsu.

> The streets are splattered with slogans systematically selling the extremists' beliefs: on billboards along the roadside, on banners across open spaces, and posters plastered on walls. Standing on a busy corner downtown Matsu hands out leaflets to passersby urging them to refrain from luxurious living. Over the top of her new short-sleeved *kimono*, her white apron and shoulder sash identify her membership of the association. The woman beside her, similarly dressed, invites them to sew a stitch on a '1 000-stitch good luck' band to be given to a departing soldier. Matsu, willingly swept up in the militaristic frenzy, relishes the opportunity to serve her country. A common foe binds people together, turning them towards the vision of a better society after the war. Filled with a sense of divine mission, she believes implicitly in Japan's destiny to rule Asia. Coming from a rural, lower-class background, she welcomes military action that has brought employment for her parents and brothers.
>
> The stirring strains of the naval march blares from loudspeakers, and so many people go rushing by. After spending years confined to the house and immediate neighbourhood, for Matsu being in the midst of so much activity is thrilling. Gradually a crowd gathers, attracted to the impassioned tones of a campaigner urging abstinence and frugality, and the need to unite.

In July 1939, an outright order mobilised all workers. Those in private companies, as well as Koreans and other ethnic minorities, were forced to work in military factories. Women and university students were mobilised. Matsu left her job of 17 years to work in a factory making parts for military machines. School children were mobilised to pack medical supplies, make bandages and uniforms, and later weapons.

People were focussed on Japan's divine destiny overseas, not thinking about poverty at home, thus providing a smokescreen for the government and removing them from blame. Citizens responded with patriotic fervour, rushing to help and going without although, in fact, nobody could refuse.

Chapter 31

Force of Habit

Jinji wo tsukushite tenmei wo matsu
Do your best and leave the rest to heaven

EARLY IN 1939, Hisashi was ready to take his application to 'The First High School'. He would soon be 19 years old. Out of the blue, dressed in her grey cashmere coat, Ryoko told him she was coming with him. Surprised and resentful, he tried to dissuade her, but her mind was made up. Formalities at the school did not take long then; even more surprisingly, his mother suggested they go to Meiji-jingu to pray for his success in the exam. His parents were not the type to turn to the gods in times of worry, but worship at a shrine at this time was the sign of being a true citizen.

Walking under the massive *torii*, mother and son are purified and set to enter the sacred world. The gravel crunches underfoot, almost too loud for the tranquil surrounds, the screech of crows the only other noise disturbing the peace. The air is fresh, the scent of *sugi* uplifting, and the wide sweeping avenue meanders through the forest, creating a sense of seclusion from the outer world. Curving, the avenue at last brings them to the shrine. It is a busy day, many others already congregated on the forecourt of the Hall of Worship.

Framed by majestic trees, the blue copper roof ascends to the heavens. The symmetrical main sanctuary, its heavy top supported by sturdy pillars, is a shining example of Shinto architecture. After recent rain, water lies in puddles on the pavers, mirroring the pitch of the roof as if connecting the deities above with their believers below. The shrine resounds to the sounds of ritual. Humouring *okasan*, Hisashi follows her lead, cleansing his hands and rinsing his mouth at the sacred ablution trough.

Facing the altar, both toss a coin into the offertory chest. From a small bag carried in the sleeve of her coat, *okasan* withdraws a tasselled rosary, threading it through her fingers. They tug the bell rope under the eaves and clap their hands twice announcing their presence to the deities enshrined. Palms together they bow slightly, then twice more praying for success in Hisashi's exam.* Fragrant fumes of *sugi* curl skyward, bringing to mind the presence of ancient protection.

Hisashi inscribes his name and a prayer on a tablet purchased at the shrine office, which, like thousands before him, he hangs on the noticeboard. Making doubly sure, *okasan* also buys him an amulet. Nearby, a mass of paper charms tied to trees by hopeful worshippers flutter in the breeze. With exams looming many are seeking help.

'A kind of tragic resolution' stirs in Hisashi's heart as he realises the upcoming exam is his last chance to achieve his dream. The one thing over which he has some control is that exam and, if praying to the *kami* will ensure his success, he is glad he has done so, a notion which up until then he had always despised. He knows instinctively his future is slipping out of his own, or his parents' control, so, as a safeguard, he finds himself falling back on tradition. He clutches the amulet. Despite the gloss of his modern upbringing, he is surprised at the comfort he finds in a religious object and, by the time they reach home, he is resolute, his ambivalence reconciled.

Ryoko, too, is glad they have gone. Things are changing too quickly and everyone feels vulnerable. But having taken her son to the shrine, she has done everything she can to spur him to success.

That night, she puts away her grey cashmere coat, unsure whether

---

* They bowed deeply twice again, clapped twice, finishing with a single deep bow, followed by a slight bow.

she will ever wear it again. Running her hand over the soft grey fabric, she folds it meticulously and places it in its carton box.

The precious coat would receive scrupulous care, camphor balls replaced six-monthly to keep away the insects. Stored on the middle shelf of Ryoko's *tansu*, it would avoid the high moisture of the lower shelves.

After months of strenuous effort the exam arrived. Hisashi passed, and entered high school in April, which in the old Japan would have opened the gate to distinction. However, in the turbulence of wartime society, a 'high-point' boy had less value than in peaceful times. But, at least he was protected from being conscripted, like most other boys of his age.

Boys attending public high schools were required to board, and Hisashi appreciated the opportunity, though went home for weekends. The school was lenient about attendance and, like most of his friends, he rebelled. Having achieved his goal and been accepted into the top school, the pressure suddenly came off. For years he had been unfaltering in his commitment, never missing a day of school. At high school he barely made half his classes, spending many a happy day 'just idling'. Alone or with friends, he would go into central Tokyo to watch the odd movie, but mostly he mooched around in the bookshops in Kanda. The only films available were Japanese productions stressing patriotism and sacrifice, and they were of no interest to him.

He loved Kanda. Bursting with bookshops, distributors and publishers, student lodgings and cheap cafés, it was crowded with dark uniformed students. Some shops specialised in second-hand titles; others in art, classics, comics, contemporary works, or foreign languages. Most were tiny stuffy shops crammed to their rafters and overflowing onto tables outside. It was in Jimbo-*cho*, a street famous for its second-hand bookshops, that he loved to rummage through dusty, musty tomes. His bookshelves at home were lined with a miscellany of topics and authors, all having been translated into Japanese: the history of aluminium; Marxism; the great scientists of the nineteenth century; books by Tolstoy, Dostoevsky, Maupassant and Flaubert; and even the romantic *The Moon and Sixpence* by Somerset Maugham.

> In his favourite shop, ceiling-high shelves butt the door, bulging with obscure titles, Buddhist encyclopaedias side by side with Russian architecture, American medical manuals and Indian philosophers. Providing they do not sit down, customers can stay as long as they like. Though entering a browser, Hisashi usually leaves a buyer.
>
> Departing with his precious purchase, he ducks under the indigo *noren* (a shop door curtain) of a small *soba-ya* (noodle restaurant). The *soba-ya* is cheap and cheerful, the food filling, and he can eat standing at the counter. Mounds of circular swirls of uncooked noodles are stacked behind the counter. Sometimes he has the thick *udon* noodles,* other times the *somen*.† But today he chooses *soba*,** the thin, nutty flavoured noodles served with deep-fried *tofu* in a hot savoury broth. Placing his payment on the tray provided, he heads off to spend the afternoon happily sipping cheap coffee in a café, and reading his latest acquisition, Ibsen's *A Doll's House*.

Hisashi was growing up. When he went home each weekend with his washing, he saw familiar things through new eyes. On the evening of 3 September 1939, the family were seated around the radio listening to a concert of new folk songs.

> Suddenly the naval march interrupts the programme. Through the neutral tones of the announcer, Imperial Headquarters informs the citizens of Japan that, following the German invasion of Poland, Britain and France have declared war on Germany.
>
> For ages they have been hearing about Hitler's awe-inspiring power, so it is hardly a surprise; but even so, Jinjiro is dismayed. He

---

* *Udon* noodles are made with wheat flour.
† Also made from wheat flour, *somen* noodles look like delicate vermicelli.
** *Soba* noodles are made from buckwheat and wheat flour.

loved England. He hardly hears the rest of the concert, his mind filling with images of the time he spent in his London homestay. After the concert finishes, the females wander away, uninterested in a European war, or what Jinjiro has to say about it. Hisashi stays behind, and Jinjiro surprises his son, reminiscing about the stray cat that adopted his host family. Jinjiro had found it strange, but soon fell for the tabby who sat on his knee. His hostess had suggested that he name him. And *Dola* duly came when he was called.

Dola (a homeless person) was a word with which Jinjiro empathised, his own fate similar to that of the cat, an orphan as he thought of himself. Hisashi is intrigued. Few people in Japan have pet cats; cats are workers. *Otosan's* unusual openness prompts him to see his father in a new light, and makes sense of some of his favourite Western habits.

Nothing had ever been allowed to interfere with Jinjiro's Sunday rituals of his English breakfast with toast and salty bacon, and his cup of afternoon tea. For a short time each week he could close his eyes on the frustrating and depressing times in Japan. If other family members were home, they joined him; if not, he was content on his own. Growing up, Hisashi had always enjoyed Sunday afternoon tea but, as he got older, he noticed *okasan* was there only if the children were, too. He had come to sense the tension between his parents, observing they avoided being alone together.

He detected the differences in their attitudes to life, and it came as no surprise to realise they actually did not get along. Tonight he could see *otosan* was unhappy. And this was no new thing. He noticed for the first time how a framed photograph taken by Yoshiji-*kun* a year ago had caught the family dynamics, the relaxed manner of the three children, the staunch expression of *okasan*, and *otosan* slightly ill at ease, almost detached from the group.

* * *

Rowing was a status sport in Japan, the eagerly contested interschool/university struggle on the Sumida-*gawa* having been popular since the first regatta in 1884. Races were run twice yearly over the 1.3 kilometres between the second and third bridges spanning the river. Soon after starting high school, Hisashi had been scouted to join the nine-man team as cox. He had not been keen, but Jinjiro had rowed as a student, and thought it would be good for his studious son.

Traffic between the bridges was suspended during the race, spectators watching from the bridges, the river banks or an official boat.

> Three crews wait, poised to begin. Hisashi, facing the rowers and the finish line, tries to relax, to control his breathing and keep his weight evenly distributed. The white flag drops.
>
> Favoured with calm conditions and accompanied by vociferous encouragement from school mates, the boats race smoothly towards the finish line. Suddenly, just over halfway, out of the corner of his eye Hisashi sees a small, crowded craft moving at right angles to the race. Attempting to slow the vessel, the single rower of the unofficial craft has laid down his oar and now the boat is drifting out of control, right in Hisashi's path. He has two choices. He can divert and lose the race, or continue knowing a crash is inevitable.
>
> They are closing in. The fishing boat is only 100 metres away, then 75. He can hear the hazy murmur of the spectators. At 50 metres, it is his last chance to take action. He makes his choice. They are in the wrong. He is not. He will hold fast; 40 metres, 30 metres, 20.
>
> He can see the scared faces of the boat's passengers. Ten metres from the finish line, the team from 'The First High School' stop rowing to slide in on the current. Next moment, *zushin* (a Japanese sound effect), they pass over the low-lying bow of the fishing boat, which overturns. No one is injured, and neither of the boats is damaged, but the race is disqualified and run again later with a replacement cox. Hisashi is damned by his crew, but his teachers and the police recognise it as an 'excusable outburst of youthful vitality'.

Chapter 32

Self-sacrifice is Our Honour

Hoshigari-masen katsu made wa
Waste not, want not until we win

AFTER CRUSHING POLAND, Germany turned its sights on Norway, Denmark, Holland, Belgium, Luxembourg and France. Then, on 10 June 1940, Italy entered the fray, allowing the Germans to continue their westward thrust with bombing raids on Britain. Japan now controlled most of the Chinese coastline, but they wanted sole access to China's economic benefits. If Japan cut off foreign help, China would have to accept Japanese domination; however, supplies were still reaching China via French Indo-China and Burma. Rather than face military action with Japan, Britain closed the Burma Road in June, while France's surrender to Germany offered a golden opportunity. With the Japanese occupation of parts of French Indo-China, China's supply line was closed, and Japan's presence was consolidated.

America retaliated by placing an embargo on sales of scrap iron and steel. Seventy per cent of Japan's supply came from America, and up until now most imports had been obtainable. Over time they had been quietly stockpiling essential resources, but to fuel the Japanese war machine, they had to be self-sufficient. Oil, rubber, iron and steel, most of which came from Britain, America and the Dutch East Indies, were urgently required to increase production. British Malaya, French Indo-China and the Dutch East Indies (now Indonesia) had the resources Japan needed.

In July, a new government was formed, its 'new structure' meaning the military held sway and, with no single body strong enough to challenge the militarists, the civilian government existed in name only. Political parties were banned.

Preparation for war against the United States began. Recognising it would be fought mainly at sea, the navy assumed leadership.

Japan had been politically and militarily linked with Nazi Germany and Fascist Italy for years. General Hideki Tojo, the new Minister for War, was an ardent admirer of Hitler and, in September, Japan became the third member of the Axis Alliance. For America, it was a clear warning that their own entry into the war on behalf of the Allies would entail a war in the Pacific against Japan.

In World War I, Japan had sided against Germany. For this war, a German win was predicted. Confident in Hitler's support, the Japanese considered the pact would mean freedom to act as they pleased in China. European powers, concentrating closer to home, would be less likely to take on Far Eastern activities.

Rationing in Japan commenced in June; first was sugar and matches. Sugar could no longer be imported, while the sulphur used for making matches was required by the military. In October, charcoal was rationed, owing to a shortage of manpower for production; followed in November by dairy products, which were needed for the military. The beginnings of a *yami-ichi* (black market) emerged. However, with sufficient supplies still available, prices were reasonable and most people could afford to top up with *yami-ichi* goods. Unable to avoid scrutiny, restaurants and institutional kitchens were most affected. Volumes per serving were reduced, quality became poorer, and diners needed ration tickets to buy meals. All Tokyo boys at Hisashi's school boarding house were sent home.

It was now unpatriotic to read Western books, listen to Western music, or play Western sports. Cinemas that had previously drawn huge audiences to American and British films could no longer show them. Classical concerts were prohibited, jazz bands dissolved, and dance halls shut down. Restaurants closed. With the exception of hotels, the use of English or other European languages was banned. Traditional Japanese instruments, dance and theatre were banned, and were replaced with new melodies and folk songs that pushed patriotism, filial piety and reverence for the Emperor.

Jinjiro and Ryoko worried about the interruption to their children's education, but there was nothing they could do about it. Stories abounded of obsessive older male teachers brought in to replace conscripts. In many schools, the 1890 Imperial Rescript on Education was read daily, stirring pupils to a state of fanatical zeal. At Hisashi's school, there was little change in staffing, as most men were already over the age of conscription and, like his father, most were liberals and influenced by Western ideas. They were courageous and radical in the face of military demands, and Hisashi respected them enormously.

Deep down, he worried about his future and tried talking to his father. But Jinjiro had his own worries and no time to sympathise, saying fatalistically that Hisashi was an unlucky boy, living in an unlucky period of Japan's history.

Proof of a man's success was wholly tied up with his status in society: top of the list a directorship in a big company, followed by ownership of a small profitable business, a prestigious post at a famed university, or the highest rank in the military. In his short stint in the navy, Jinjiro had reached only middle rank. Now, although he was a manager, he worked for someone else. Of an age to retire, he had had to stay on to help the war effort, a war he did not believe in. He felt he had failed at life. He loved his son, but he had no words to help him.

A photograph taken by Yoshiji-*kun* showed Jinjiro seated in the garden. Glasses perched on the end of his nose, shoulders hunched, he was engrossed in the newspaper. It showed a tired, disillusioned man; a man who had known some success, but mainly disappointment. An impression of stoic indifference pointed to a man whose expectations had not been met.

People's lives grew more austere. Adults and high school boys underwent military training, and were expected to contribute several days a month to help maintain city parks, streets, and public toilets, and to transport foodstuffs or garbage. Hisashi and his friends resented this compulsion. As in all schools, as a means of teaching cooperation, they were used to tidying their classroom at the end of each day, as well as giving the whole school a monthly clean, but the new chores were unwelcome.

Girls were not left out. 'The good wife and wise mother' slogan was abandoned, and girls were withdrawn from school to work in the factories for half of each school day. Even Yayoi, at primary school, had to work at a plant manufacturing parachutes. The pupils at Eiko's school worked in a factory developing alternative foods to cover the shortage of rice and wheat.

As 1941 dawned, the extremists were close to achieving their ambition to control the country.

Rationing began in earnest: in January, primary school uniforms; in February, milk; in March, socks; in April, flour and rice. The bulk of the rice crop was allocated for the military, with citizens' allocation reduced from an average three cups a day to two-and-a-half. In May, *sake* and beer were rationed; in July, potatoes; in October, eggs; in November, fish; and in December, sweet potatoes, cookies and sweets.

Once rationing began, Hisashi was always hungry, so he was continually thinking of food. He and his peers stopped speaking of sport, art, movies and love, the war now dominating their discussions. Curriculum changes and the effect of rationing meant a completely different school life to what they had anticipated. The competition for badges and grades receded. Summer school holidays were even abolished, and renamed the 'summer training period' devoted to voluntary labour to help the war effort.

For 21-year-old Hisashi, a dark cloud lurked in the shadows.

Jitsuzen Ashitzu, priest of
the Tendai School, 1895

Ryoko, her stepmother Sato, and baby Tomoko, 1906

Jitsuzen Ashitzu, Chief Abbot of *Rinzai* Zen at Eigen-*ji*, 1915

Ryoko with her half-sister Tomoko, 1907

Ryoko and her baby son Hisashi, 1920

Sato, Jitsuzen, Tomoko (child) and Ryoko, 1909

Eiko in her middle school uniform, 1935

Yayoi's first day at primary school, 1936

Eiko and Yayoi, 1937

Hisashi at Nikko, 1938

Hisashi studying at Nikko

Ryoko and Yayoi at the ablution trough at the shrine in Nikko

Ryoko and Yayoi visit Hisashi at Nikko

Happy times at Nikko

The Furuya family in 1938

Hisashi with chocolates sent from China, 1939

Yayoi's class evacuated to Sendai, 1944

Hisashi, Eiko and Yayoi, 1940
(Hisashi in his summer high school uniform)

Part Three

Giri to the Emperor

IN THE FINAL DAYS OF HIS YOUTH, Hisashi tries to grasp and understand the culture of the new world foisted upon him. Insidiously, inexorably, life is changing. Just as Japan spins out of control in turbulent international waters, her people drift like leaves in the tempestuous stream of Japanese society.

Hisashi has been brought up with many advantages, but gone are the soft years of decadence. And now …

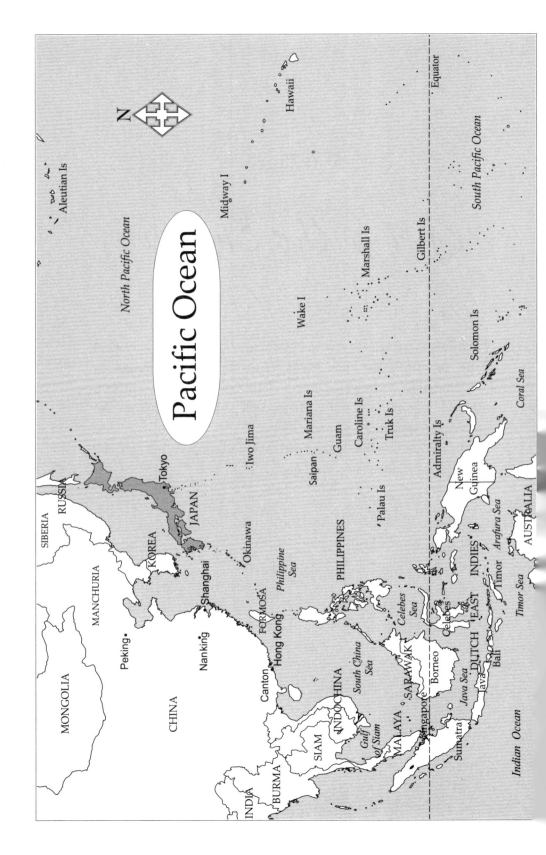

Chapter 33

Surging Waves

Sente hissho
Hit first, hit hard

THE WHOLE WORLD was in a state of flux, carried along on a turbulent stream within which several worldwide movements became entangled, making war inevitable: rapid social and technological change, colonialism and imperialism, competition for resources, population increases and unemployment, communism, and the global financial crisis.

As victors of World War I, Britain, France and America were the most powerful nations in the world. To gain resources they ruthlessly consolidated and expanded their interests within and outside their colonies. Desperate to catch up and build an empire of her own, Japan had entered the colonial race in Manchuria.

Influenced by his father, Hisashi felt that political and military leaders did not care about the number of fatalities their decisions and actions caused. Like grains of sand, people held value in their quantity rather than as individuals. The war in Manchuria provided much needed employment, but would also reduce the pressure of population increase with soldiers being killed in battle. Hisashi agreed with *otosan* that Japan did not have the resources to challenge America, but no matter his opinion, his main intention was to be a loyal citizen with little thought of the future: holding only desperate hope there would be a future.

Both the Americans and Japanese had recognised another world war would arise, but this time it would be over who controlled the Pacific Ocean. Competition to build the biggest naval fleet escalated during the 1920s, and crisis after crisis was triggered as America, Britain, Europe and Japan sought to secure resources. Advances in the development of the aeroplane and wireless,* both promptly adopted by the military, exacerbated rivalry. Aircraft required aluminium, steel and oil, while wireless communication required copper. In Japan, vast quantities of copper wire were available for telephone lines and to send electricity to munitions mills,† but almost everything else had to be sourced from outside the nation.**

Three words sum up this period of Japanese history: mobilisation, acceptance and authority. Everybody was mobilised for the war effort, conditioned as they were to accept that Japan was innately superior and destined to lead Asia. Backed by the traditional family system, acceptance among the Japanese was unquestioning, and with fanatical zeal, they expressed their belief in the supreme authority of the military and in the glorification of war.

By 1941, half of Japan's national income was allocated to the military, but with the economy seriously stretched by its expansionist activities, the problem of acquiring sufficient resources was becoming critical as troops pushed down through Southeast Asia. After signing a non-aggression pact with the Soviets, Japan wholly occupied Indochina in July.

America retaliated instantly, freezing Japanese assets in the US, and imposing a total trade embargo, including oil, on Japan. With the British, Chinese and Dutch reacting similarly, the ABCD [American, British, Chinese, Dutch] Encirclement tightened its grip. Japan was

---

* The Wright Brothers flew the first power-driven aeroplane in 1903. Marconi's first wireless message was broadcast across the Atlantic in 1901.

† The Tokugawa regime had protected the development of the copper mining industry for domestic military purposes.

** Japan did not have large local supplies of fossil fuels, such as coal and oil, nor the other raw materials it needed, apart from copper, so most had to be imported.

cut off from all major suppliers of essential resources. Japanese Military High Command, adamant they would not withdraw from China and its southern neighbours, continued their advance. As they saw it, America was deliberately provoking them to attack.

In October of the same year, following the resignation of the then Prime Minister, military power was finally sanctioned when the Emperor appointed the right-wing, anti-communist General Tojo to the position. Dubbed 'The Razor', General Tojo was revered by some and feared by others: Jinjiro, like many of the intelligentsia, deplored the appointment.

Token attempts had been made to improve relations with the US, but there appeared to be no middle ground, and Japanese tacticians argued for going to war before the American defence forces grew even stronger. The tacticians argued that it would be a short war, terminated as soon as the new Japanese Empire was secure. They calculated that, if Japan destroyed the American Pacific fleet, American interference would be neutralised for at least 18 months. Japan's best chance of victory lay in a surprise attack on Pearl Harbour in Hawaii, the largest military base in the Pacific. However, not wanting to alert the Americans to their plans, negotiations with Washington would continue until Japan was ready to strike.

The US had recognised that a Japanese air strike was possible, but expected it would be directed at the Philippines, a chain of American controlled islands in the Malay Archipelago. The US's main fear at Pearl Harbour was land-based sabotage, so aircraft were lined up close together, making them easier to guard. Warnings of an imminent attack were reputed to have reached the Americans via various sources but, regardless, they were unprepared for an aerial assault.

Late in November 1941, confident of victory, the Japanese Imperial Navy departed for its undisclosed destination, undaunted by having to sail undetected across 5500 kilometres of the Pacific Ocean. On 2 December, radioing the secret code, 'Climb Mount Niitaka', the attack was on: timed for breakfast to have the utmost impact. Keeping radio silence, and shielded by bad weather, the convoy, complete with aircraft carriers, steamed towards Hawaii.

> On Sunday morning 7 December, the Stars and Stripes flutter in the Hawaiian breeze, the naval base concerned only with its usual weekend routine. The vessels of the Pacific fleet pack the harbour, with most crew ashore. Aircraft are lined neatly in the middle of landing fields and most anti-aircraft guns are unmanned, their ammunition in storage.
>
> At 0812 hours, a menacing roar shatters the calm, as the signal 'Tora! Tora! Tora!',* directs 51 Japanese dive-bombers, 89 torpedo-bombers and 43 fighters, to drop their lethal loads. Bombs pour from the sky, pounding Battleship Row, the airfields and shore installations. An hour later, a second wave of aircraft strikes.

In two hours and 20 minutes, 70 per cent of the American Pacific fleet was destroyed or badly damaged. Huge clouds of smoke billowed from smashed and burning battleships and aircraft.

At the beginning of the European war, most Americans, while siding with Britain and France, thought it was none of their business. They assumed the Allies would triumph over Germany, and that an agreement could be negotiated with Japan over China. But this attack was the ultimate in betrayal.† The Japanese saw it differently. Their pilots were patriotic officers attacking military targets.

The morning of Sunday 7 December 1941 was one that everyone in Japan would remember.

> As Ryoko starts the housework, Yayoi, Eiko and Hisashi disappear to their respective rooms, only Jinjiro remaining at the table to finish his toast as he listens to the news. At the end of the broadcast, an

---

* Tiger! Tiger! Tiger!

† Despite little evidence to the contrary, many American citizens of Japanese descent (*Nisei*) living on America's west coast were suspected of disloyalty and interned. However, there were still thousands of others who served in the American forces.

extra bulletin is announced, and as the last notes of the naval march fade away, Jinjiro has called the family back to the table.

Matter-of-factly, the newsreader announces that early that morning, local time, the Japanese navy attacked Pearl Harbour. Recognising that Japan stands on the brink of full-scale war, Jinjiro is stunned, likening the attack to the case of the poor man living hand to mouth too long. With only a few remaining coins, the poor man risks everything in one game, rather than 'gradual pauperisation'. It is widely whispered that the government prefers the risk of 'colossal poverty', to 'a life of continuing hardship'. Hisashi, knowing little of Hawaii and nothing at all of Pearl Harbour, feels indifferent, and having been conditioned to believe in Japan's supremacy, thinks a successful attack is hardly surprising.

The following morning, Monday 8 December, the family breakfast together as they wait for the seven o'clock news. With the naval march playing softly in the background, the announcer, his animated voice at odds with his normal restrained tone, pronounces:

> 'We now bring you very urgent news. The army and navy departments of Imperial General Headquarters jointly announced at six o'clock this morning, December 8, that the Imperial Army and Navy forces have begun hostilities against the American and British forces in the Pacific.'

Later, using the arcane language of the Imperial Court, the Emperor officially declared war, placing the blame on the Americans and British.* The Far Eastern War and the European war had coalesced into World War II. Excitement spread throughout Japan as the news was transmitted over public loudspeakers. Admiral Yamamoto, architect of the raid on Pearl Harbour, was hailed a national hero. What the public had not been told was that the Japanese navy

---

* And he reminded them of the blame, every ninth day of every month of every year until the war ended, his words repeated on the radio and on the front page of every newspaper.

bombers had failed to hit the American aircraft carriers that were on manoeuvres elsewhere.

Jinjiro, reflecting current navy opinion, commented to Hisashi that now they had shown they had the upper hand, Japan should call for peace, even if it meant losing the recently acquired territories. With limited access to fuel, they could hold the advantage for a short time only. 'Bogged down in the mud' of the Chinese continent, Japan had thrust herself into a war she could not win. He recalled Admiral Yamamoto declaring earlier that in the first few months of a war with America and Britain he would 'win victory upon victory', but after that, he would 'have no expectation of success'. Even Prime Minister Tojo's message broadcast that day anticipated 'a long war', his speech concluding with the famous battle song, '*Umi Yukaba*' that ended with the lines:

> *Across the sea, corpses lie in the water;*
> *Across the mountain, corpses lie in the fields.*
> *I shall die only for the Emperor,*
> *I shall never look back.*

Two hours prior to the attack on Pearl Harbour, Japanese bombs had fallen on Malaya, and by the end of the day, crack divisions stormed towards Singapore. Simultaneously, attacks had also been made on Siam (now Thailand), Hong Kong, Guam, the Philippines and Wake Islands.

The *doto** swept relentlessly onwards, 'waves of men thrown into action to form a human sea'. As modern day *samurai*, the Japanese military were highly motivated and cruel in the extreme. Prisoners of war on either side, whether captured or having surrendered, were deemed to have lost their honour, reduced to the mediaeval status of *hinin* in the minds of the Japanese military.

Hoping to establish an impregnable position before America

---

* 'Surging waves', a media expression frequently used at the time.

recovered from the attack, and with Allied forces concentrated in Europe, Japan intended to stop the Western Powers interfering in her Asian conquests. In an island-hopping campaign they surged south, their sights set on India, Australia and New Zealand. Troops were also pushing northwards and eastwards into Siam, Burma, Java, Sumatra and the Philippines, with millions of men locked in deadly combat. Only a week after the Pearl Harbour attack, Guam fell, then on 21 December Siam became a Japanese ally. The Allied Wake Island garrison held out until 23 December, while Hong Kong surrendered on Christmas Day. By 23 January 1942, the Japanese also occupied Borneo, Timor, the Celebes, and part of New Guinea; Singapore surrendered on 15 February.

Japan had now assumed 'Lordship of Asia', and by 9 March was in control of the Pacific, almost to the coast of Australia. Rangoon, the capital of Burma, fell on 10 March, and Corregidor, the last remaining Allied foothold in the Philippines, surrendered on 6 May. American bases in the eastern Pacific were now in Japanese hands, as were southern Asia's main sources of raw materials. On 31 May, three two-man midget submarines were launched outside the Sydney Harbour heads, sinking the HMAS *Kuttabul*.

For a while the Japanese forces were unstoppable. At this point, power of the seas was supreme, and the Japanese navy achieved impressive results. But behind many of their successes was the Allies' arrogance in dismissing Japanese strength and capability. Nonetheless, the Japanese hope of a brokered peace deal did not transpire. The Japanese government had misjudged American and British determination, both allies unwavering in their resolve to fight to the bitter end.

In China, as Japanese forces ventured deeper into the interior, they were losing the upper hand. In January, the Chinese triumphed in the clash for Changsha, the capital of Hunan province. Overconfident, and without heavy artillery, Japanese troops were beaten by peasants defending their homes.

One of Hisashi's friends stationed in China wrote that the vast landmass and enormous population gave him 'a feeling of oppression, as though looking into the frightening, inky depths of a deep lake. In relation to its history and size, the current hostilities [were] nothing but ripples on the surface of the lake.'

Chapter 34
Bright Hopes Grow Dim

Katte kabuto-no-o o shimeyo
Fasten your war helmet tightly
even after a victory

HISASHI HAD DREAMED of a career in pathology for years, and Jinjiro and Ryoko had supported his choice. Having lost three children, they liked the idea he might discover a new vaccine for a virus or disease. But just before he filed his application for medical school, they changed their minds. The demand for young doctors at the frontline was increasing.

Both parents considered engineering a better career option, and the military urgently required middle-level engineers and scientists to work in munitions factories at home. Furthermore, in their way of thinking, not only would he be safer during the war, but also wealthier afterwards. As a new discipline, engineering was considered a prestigious profession and engineers were scarce. Engineers were in the highest income bracket for the salaried middle class, a first job promising a salary of 85 *yen* per month, higher than what the average middle-aged policeman or primary school teacher earned.

Hisashi, not wanting to abandon his dream, applied for both courses, gaining entry to study medicine at Keio University, famed for its medical faculty, and entry to *Todai*, the highest ranked university overall, to study engineering. Always conscious of his parents' expectations, he was in conflict: wanting a career in medical research, yet not wanting to be sent to the frontline. After talking to a friend of his father's, who gave the same advice as his parents, he opted for engineering, choosing metallurgy as his major.

As Hisashi's hopes and dreams ebbed away in the light of reality, the Japanese warlords proceeded as if they believed their own propaganda. But the blow struck at Pearl Harbour did not detain the Americans for as long as Japan had hoped; rather, it mobilised the nation's massive manufacturing power.

In May 1942, only five months after the Pearl Harbour attack, Japanese and Allied forces clashed in the Battle of the Coral Sea. Fighting erupted with furious vehemence, this the first encounter in history where opposing forces never set eyes on each other. It was a battle fought exclusively between carrier-borne aircraft and land-based aircraft, without the fleet firing a single shot. Unaware that Allied cryptanalysts had cracked their communcation codes, the Japanese had planned to seize Port Moresby in New Guinea as a base from which to invade Australia. Tactically the battle was a draw, Japan losing more aircraft, the US more ships. But strategically, with Japanese plans thwarted, it was an Allied success, though Japanese High Command claimed a victory.

The ultimate crisis came the following month in the Battle of Midway in the central Pacific. In what the Japanese deemed as their final attempt to assert their superiority, then broker for peace, Imperial Headquarters aimed to capture the island of Midway, from where they would then take Hawaii. Success would bring the Allies racing to negotiate a settlement.

Determinedly, Japan committed the Combined Fleet, the strongest battle fleet ever assembled: eight aircraft carriers with 685 planes, ten battleships, 24 cruisers, 70 destroyers, 15 submarines, 18 tankers and 40 other vessels. Split into three, one force headed to the Aleutian Islands in an attempt to divert the American fleet away from Hawaii. But, once again, Allied code-breakers enabled American bombers to intervene in advance.

Shadowed by American submarines, Admiral Yamamoto's main strike force, including the carriers *Akagi*, *Kaga*, *Hiryu* and *Soryu*, sailed unsuspectingly towards Midway Island on the morning of 3 June. Mobilised and heading towards them were the American carriers *Enterprise*, *Hornet*, and *Yorktown*, 350 land- and carrier-based aircraft, 14 destroyers, 25 submarines, and eight cruisers. That afternoon, American heavy bombers from Hawaii inflicted initial damage on the Japanese fleet.

The following morning, a torpedo squadron from the *Hornet* attacked the Japanese convoy, but all were shot down. Then, against the odds, dive-bombers from *Enterprise* and *Yorktown* swooped, losing heavily, but finding their mark. Japanese Zeros (fighters), Kan Baku (torpedo-bombers), and Kan Ko (dive-bombers) meshed crazily with American Dauntless (dive-bombers), Devastators (torpedo-bombers), Buffaloes and Wildcats (fighters). *Akagi* was hit and abandoned. *Kaga* was hit and she, too, was abandoned. Bombers dived on *Soryu*, and within 20 minutes she was abandoned as well. Ahead of the others, *Hiryu* escaped, launching two strikes of Zekes (US code-name for Zeros), Vals (code-name for Kan Baku), and Kates (code-name for Kan Ko), crippling the *Yorktown*.

Within quick succession, three of the Japanese carriers had been reduced to burning hulks, then *Hiryu* was hit, hours later joining her sisters. Admiral Yamamoto, sailing aboard the *Yamato*, and unaware of the extent of the damage before him, was expecting an intensive encounter. Instead, in the pre-dawn gloom of 5 June, he ordered his fleet to disperse. Still floating, *Akagi* was scuttled by Japanese torpedoes. *Yorktown* stayed afloat, but the following day was sunk by Japanese submarine I.168.

Despite superior firepower, the Japanese had been outmanoeuvred. They lost four carriers, along with five cruisers, two battleships and hundreds of pilots; three destroyers were damaged. The Americans also lost heavily, many men killed: 150 aircraft lost, a carrier and a destroyer sunk, and others damaged. Back in Japan, official despatches announced another victory. Casualties were withheld, with Midway described as a small encounter with 35 aircraft lost.*

But the tide turned after Midway; the Japanese were forced into a defensive position, never to regain the initiative. Only one large carrier was left in service; the others under repair. More had to be built urgently. The Americans had three carriers still operational, with a further 28 being built. US warship manufacture in 1942 was ten times that of Japan.

Most people in Japan, unaware of the true situation, were happy to believe their troops were all-conquering. But Hisashi heard a different story. One of his middle school friends, Tetsuji-*kun*, a gunnery officer, was wounded in the Battle of Midway. An only child, Tetsuji-*kun* was an accomplished young man who could expect a rewarding future running his parents' cycle shop.

> Regulations at the Tokyo naval hospital allow only one visitor at a time, 15 minutes each. In the small, single room, propped up in bed, Tetsuji-*kun* almost disappears into the white walls and bed linen. His head, covered in bandages, looks like a rugby ball with three holes, two for his eyes, and one for his mouth. Hisashi utters the usual platitudes, though what he really wants to do is ask what happened. Then, surprisingly, Tetsuji-*kun* brings it up.
>
> Conversation is not easy, but haltingly he tells Hisashi that the Battle of Midway was a tactical blunder, resulting in a catastrophic defeat. Japanese planes are faster and more manoeuvrable than American planes, so even though taken by surprise, they should not have been wiped out. Unfortunately, the slower Kan Baku, rather than the faster Zeros, had been sent first. Realising American fighters were already approaching, the bombers had returned to the carriers without fighting, thus blocking the runways for the Zeros to take off.

---

* An official survey post-war alleged 322.

Tetsuji-*kun* had been badly burned, his face grotesque under the bandages. He had no ears and his nose had melted away. His prospects of promotion and marriage were gone. Six months later, he went back to the battlefield to die with honour, soon getting his wish. Japan had lost a capable, young man, and Hisashi a good friend.

In their efforts to conquer Asia and the Pacific, the Japanese had underrated the logistics of their task, and their expansionist plans were working against them. Lengthy supply routes to battle lines had become ideal targets for bombing, and in 1942, less than half the production from their captured oil fields reached Japan. The Japanese merchant marine was no match against Allied submarines and aircraft, and the Japanese's inferior technology, especially in electronics, was weakening their fighting power. New construction did not match losses; even in 1941, Japan's aircraft manufacture was still only a quarter of American production.

In June, Japan occupied Kiska in the Aleutian Islands, but in August, with its best units wiped out, the Japanese navy could not stop the Allies from landing at Guadalcanal, the largest and least developed island in the Solomons. Imperial High Command knew the struggle for the Solomon Islands would decide the fate of the war. Again and again, they attempted to wrest back the island: on the ground, on the sea, and in the air, fanatical 'dare to die' tactics escalated to parallel their desperation.

Two days after the American landing, one of a succession of prolonged naval battles began. Under cover of darkness, in heavy rain, star-shells and searchlights lit up the devastation of blazing vessels, with visibility further reduced by flames and drifting smoke. However, the Americans had the advantage of radar. As a fledgling engineer, Hisashi felt frustrated that Japan had relied on German mechanical weaponry, which was no match for the newly developed American electronics.

With men deployed from other islands, both Japanese and Allied strength increased, but with the land campaign fought in the mud and rain of the tropics, beriberi, dysentery and malaria took their toll. The Japanese army had no frontline medical care. Risking one's life was considered heroic and honourable, and precautions were needless. A wounded or sick soldier was deemed worthless, and often committed suicide or was shot.

By Christmas Day, only a third of the 6 000 Japanese troops left on Guadalcanal could fight, and each man's rice ration was down to half a cup per day. And still the bitter fighting continued, though Japanese hopes of winning the war quickly were growing dim.

Chapter 35

An Uneasy Wait

Ichioku hi no tama
One hundred million people
now a big ball of fire

As AMERICA WAS INITIALLY UNINVOLVED in the wars in Europe and Asia, there was no urgency for it to develop the atomic bomb; however, Pearl Harbour changed everything. Top-secret research, code-named the 'Manhattan Project' began in earnest, with America and Britain aiming to build an atomic bomb before Germany. Even when they found out the Germans had abandoned their programme, the two nations continued.

On 18 April 1942, the first enemy bombs fell on Japan. Named the Doolittle Raid after the colonel who led the attack, 16 B-25 bombers flew nearly 1300 kilometres from the American carrier *Hornet* to bomb Tokyo and other cities. Minimum damage was inflicted, but enough to boost Allied morale and frighten the Japanese, who realised they were no longer safe at home.

Life in Japan changed drastically, and preparations to repulse an invasion intensified, with call-up and shortages impacting on every family. Citizens were showered with slogans and propaganda promoting abstinence and austerity. Rationing was strictly enforced, and volume controlled to exact amounts; and naturally quality was downgraded. Supplies of food, clothing, petrol and other necessities dwindled.

Almost everything was rationed by the end of the year, purchases of fixed quantities per person limited by coupons. In February, a city dweller had 100 points a year for clothing, while someone in the country had 80. A blouse cost eight points, a pair of socks two, while a man's overcoat cost 50. By December, shortages of cloth meant clothing, too, was rationed, and the allowance was cut.

To begin with, food had been rationed according to nutritional value, so for a while many people were actually better fed than before. Years of poor nutrition among the rural lower class had resulted in nearly 40 per cent of recruits being sent home from Manchuria with tuberculosis. However, rationing was not enough to lift most people out of dire circumstances. Delays and even cancelled deliveries were common, and even animals were affected. Without food, all the animals at Ueno Zoo had to be poisoned.

For the Furuya family, with Jinjiro still working even though officially retired, their income was guaranteed. His job was linked to the navy, so they also benefited from extra supplies of food from the Ministry of Munitions. Families without connections to the war industry, especially city dwellers, resorted to the *yami-ichi*; but with prices now up to ten times higher than rationed goods, many moved to rural areas where food was cheaper and more accessible. Despite the inconveniences though, life was orderly and manageable. In fact, there was a tremendous spirit of cooperation and community, focussed on achieving the nation's destiny.

After Pearl Harbour, participation in the National Defence Women's Association was compulsory. For Ryoko, the elegant days were over as, like all women, she undertook air-raid training and stood for hours in rationing queues. Gone was the era of the *kimono*; now she wore the practical civilian uniform. And Ryoko hated it, feeling frumpy in the shapeless, drab, cotton *mompe* gathered at the ankle, a half coat over top, thick *zukku* (canvas duck shoes) on her feet, and a padded rucksack on her back. With her hair drawn back in a bun, her previous fashionable style forbidden, she looked like every other woman. Her most important possessions had become the family ration book, a quilted anti-air raid hood, and a cotton tag stitched on her jacket, giving her name, age, address, blood type and next of kin.

Her middle-class existence had gone awry: one moment she had been looking forward to her round of neighbourly visits; the next, she was faced with a dislocating new world order. But Ryoko was philosophical, reconciling herself to this different life, like her son feeling somewhat detached about the future. Never for an instant did she consider not cooperating, so deeply ingrained were her social and moral conditioning. She coped through the long ordeal, maintaining her home and looking after the family; patching and repairing old clothes; sharing creative recipes using wild foods and substitutes, and making scarce ingredients go further.

Previously, she had had little to do with the wives of craftsmen or retailers in the neighbourhood; however war had equalised everyone, the caste system all but gone. Pride in ancestry or education was irrelevant, and Ryoko's middle-class complacency faded. But anxiety and stress grew as these dutiful, conditioned women were forced to change their role and behaviour in situations far removed from their habitual patterns of conduct. Their lives were filled with the same fears of the unexpected, the unknown, and of death – the same heartache as those of mothers, wives, sisters and daughters on the opposing side.

The Furuya family, like all families in Japan, was now a member of a *tonari-gumi*.* Overseen by the Home Ministry, ten households in close proximity, led by an older man from the group, had their activities managed for the common benefit: distributing rations, patrolling blackouts, digging and building shelters. But most importantly, these groups ensured everyone complied with the rules: that all eligible men enlisted, and that everyone contributed generously in time and cash.

In every neighbourhood, countrywide, the women tried to keep

---

* *Tonari-gumi* were compulsory, self-governing, self-regulating, wartime neighbourhood associations.

life as normal as possible. They cleaned the streets, collected the rubbish, and weeded the public gardens. In cities, they built air-raid shelters, and every 100 metres dug reservoirs for emergency water supplies. Large tubs placed in front of houses and tenements were refilled regularly, and it was not uncommon to see groups of women handing heavy buckets of water along a human chain.

Local fire brigades and *tonari-gumi* organised compulsory air-raid training in order to teach first aid and fire fighting. Each woman was given her own fire extinguisher,* and a bamboo spear to stab parachuting enemy pilots. When the first practice siren warned alert, Ryoko rushed outside with her equipment in one hand, a bucket in the other, feeling extremely nervous; but with regular drills her confidence increased. Immediately after Pearl Harbour, when the sirens went, they really did think the bombers were coming. Air Defence alerts advised citizens to rush to the nearest shelter; but invariably they were false alarms, and gradually a sense of anticlimax, almost a state of complacency developed, and most people stayed home.

Most air raids took place during the day, and were aimed at munitions factories and military depots. But there were often casualties among civilians who lived and worked close by. The Furuya family lived away from such facilities and was less vulnerable. They had plenty of warning via local radio to get into their shelter, spending numerous restless hours underground. Over Christmas, they had dug an underground shelter with a trapdoor in the front garden, their wooden *shoji* shutters used to line the walls. Shelves were fitted to store supplies, and three empty buckets were kept at the entrance to be filled with water and lowered inside when the siren rang. As time went on though, especially at night, they tended to stay in the house, not feeling in any danger.

Every building had to have blackout curtains, with windows

---

* A mop of straw ropes attached to a bamboo pole, the dampened mop used to smother small fires.

covered so no light escaped to help enemy aircraft sight their targets. On nights with no raid forecast, curtains were closed, but lights were allowed. If a raid was forecast, only one light was permitted per house, and street lights were switched off, leaving only traffic lights and car headlights. If bombers were confirmed, it was lights out everywhere.

Ryoko hung curtains in the dining room where everyone gathered if the alert was sounded. With the alerts usually lasting only a couple of hours, and the worst never happening, the family never took the raids seriously. However, they dutifully dressed ready to evacuate if the house caught fire. Each had ready their regulation padded hood and rucksack containing two meals, and hot green tea in a vacuum flask. Jinjiro also packed his cigarettes and matches, and carried an empty bucket for a toilet. As well as her fire extinguisher and spear, Ryoko had the first aid and sewing kits.

While Ryoko spent her days involved with the Association, Jinjiro went off to work. Yayoi, in middle school, had morning lessons, then each afternoon her classroom turned into a production line. The 12-year-old girls made balloons to carry incendiaries that were to fly at the *kami's* behest across the Pacific to bomb America. Made of 64 gores of paper and silk, the large, water-proofed balloons were stuck together with potato starch, chemical glues being used for more important military purposes. Out of an estimated 9300 balloons launched from submarines, 285 explosions were recorded by military authorities on the American west coast. They caused forest fires and killed six people. Japanese propaganda bragged of 'thousands killed'.

One highlight in 1942 was Eiko's marriage. Soldiers were supposed to leave an heir, so marriage was particularly popular, and brokers were kept busy arranging 'quicker than usual' betrothals. Ryoko wanted her 20-year-old daughter wed, and Eiko duly married Hiroshi. 'Her *on* was deeper than the deepest sea, and higher than the highest mountain', and for the first and only time in her life, she kneeled before her parents, her head bowed to the floor, thanking them for arranging such a favourable marriage. Not only was Hiroshi from a wealthy family, but the couple would be moving to Shanghai, where he worked as an accountant at the Mitsubishi plant. An heir was of the utmost importance, Hiroshi's only brother having died in battle. Safe from the battlefields they enjoyed colonial life, and Eiko gave birth to the requisite heir shortly thereafter.

In April of that year, Hisashi began university, Jinjiro and Ryoko's long struggle achieving its end. Located in the heart of the city in the residential district of Hongo, *Todai* was a green and pleasant campus. Entrance was through *daimyo* Maeda's splendid, double-doored estate gate, the very same gate through which Sakuzaemon Furuya, the *samurai* doctor, entered on his return to Edo in 1620. Outside the brick and wrought-iron wall, shapely gingkoes protected pedestrians against the beating sun. Strolling under their shade, and through the red gate, it brought a sense of deja-vu for Hisashi that 80 years earlier his grandfather, Hajime, had also passed that very same way.

Graduates of *Todai*, whatever their field, were assured of reaching the highest positions in government. A photograph of Hisashi's classmates shows a group of proud young men in university black. Little did these privileged young scholars realise the tumult that would surround them on graduation. Several would soon die and the survivors would live in a different world. But that day, what made them stand apart was the metal 'T' badge on their uniform collars, 'T' for technical. Liberal Arts students wore 'L' badges: graduates who were potential bureaucrats, politicians and bankers dropped in status in time of war.

The 'T' curriculum had been designed to meet the demands of modern society. While recognised as academic, it also included the practical techniques needed by industry to achieve Western standards. More expensive to run than other disciplines, not just in set-up costs, but also the ongoing outlay for experiments, such as apparatus, materials and fuelling the furnace, it consumed much of the government's education budget. Limited to 50 places a year, only *Todai* and Kyoto offered the course, but once war started the quota quadrupled to meet the demands of battle. With the increased intake, a new engineering faculty was built in Chiba, Tokyo's immediate neighbour.

Many Tokyoites perceived Chiba as a backwater of smokestacks and potato fields. However, the proximity of so many industries, built since the revolution, meant it was highly suitable for the new campus. There were a few gentle hills, but the area was generally flat with not many trees. In small, independent market gardens, farmers toiled long hours, following the ancient pattern of planting and harvesting produce, the area famous for its sweet potatoes.

For most students it was over an hour's travel each way from home, so the university preferred they board nearby. The first year, Hisashi boarded at Nakamura-*san*'s house,* a farmer who lived near the university. Nakamura-*san*'s family had farmed their land for generations, first as tenants under their *daimyo*, then purchasing three acres after the Meiji Revolution. Since then successive generations had expanded their holding to ten acres.

The house, with its heavy wooden eaves and grey tiled roof, was nestled amidst orderly furrowed fields, one planted with vegetables, enough for their own use and some to sell, with the rest in sweet potatoes. Apple, peach, persimmon and plum trees bordering the house provided a surfeit of seasonal fruit. Inheriting the farm a few years earlier, when materials were still available, Nakamura-*san* had rebuilt the old thatched-roofed farmhouse, and replaced the outside privy with an inside toilet. It was a substantial house, with electricity and running water, an indication of his wealth.

Nakamura-*san* worked hard, endeavouring to repay his *giri* to his ancestors, the farm supporting three generations: his mother, his wife, himself, and two teenagers. A sturdy, broad-shouldered man with greying temples, he was typical of most farmers. He was a good man, congenial and obedient to authority.

---

* Family name then *san* refers to a same or older generation male or female relation or friend; used like Mr, Mrs and Miss.

Hisashi was well looked after and, like most of his classmates, he found living upcountry easier than living in the city. The food was better, as were study conditions. Having to participate in citizen drills and air-raid training, city students' study was often interrupted. In Chiba, apart from a couple of days' voluntary service when Hisashi worked as Nakamura-*san*'s labourer, the war did not affect his course.

The weeks went by in a routine of reading and writing, lectures and experiments. University life was competitive, the reverse of his carefree existence at high school: lectures in Chiba on Monday to Thursday, laboratory classes at the Tokyo campus on Friday and Saturday, study on Sunday. Hisashi was extra busy preparing for graduation, hurrying to complete a three-year course now condensed to two-and-a-half years. He left Nakamura-*san*'s at seven in the morning, returning by six for dinner, then continued his study until well after midnight. He had little contact with home and, in July, when the Staple Food Control Act inflicted hardship on civilians, Hisashi's situation was much better than his parents.

University students at this stage were still exempt from conscription, though graduates were not. At the end of his first year, he had to choose which division of the military he would serve in after graduation. With *otosan* and *ojisan* having been in the navy, Hisashi wanted to follow the family tradition, and his grades were more than satisfactory to do so. Every university holiday was devoted to military training, and several times he worked as a trainee engineer at a naval munitions plant, the only student chosen to participate. The navy needed methods of efficient iron-casting, as well as utilising substitutes for scarce metals, and it was Hisashi's task to assist with the research.

On his first posting he had felt quite intimidated. Located on the Miura Peninsula, the plant was one of hundreds of huge naval factories, depots and test sites that stretched along the 30-kilometre promontory. Travelling by train, past Yokohama, nearly to the end of the peninsula, his view of the Japanese fleet was obscured behind huge bamboo screens. The wall, and the secrets it hid, piqued his curiosity, and added to his feelings of awe and excitement about the seriousness of his assignment. He heard that here was where the super-battleships, *Yamato* (1941) and *Musashi* (1942), had been built.

Each evening after work he was taken to the officer's club at the naval base. His first glimpse of the huge harbour astounded him: brilliantly lit, it was alive with activity. Japan still considered she held the upper hand at this stage, so there was no need to dim the lights. Hundreds of vessels were moored: battleships, barges, cargo ships, destroyers, heavy cruisers, light cruisers, landing craft, oil carriers, transporters, torpedo boats, as well as a few trawlers and fishing boats. There was even a hospital ship with a large red cross on each side. Submarines were at another base close by.

Chapter 36

Backs to the Wall

Keima no taka-a-agari
The knight jumps too far

JAPAN'S WAR HAD MOVED so quickly from triumph to collapse that High Command could never regroup. Continuous fighting on three fronts – in the Pacific against the Americans, Australians and New Zealanders; in Burma against British and Empire forces; and in China against the nationalists – meant the military was overextended. More than six million men were in uniform, with another two million locals compulsorily recruited in occupied territories. But, with communication and supply lines overstretched, inferior technology, and troops too scattered, the offensives were rapidly collapsing.

Heavy casualties at Midway had resulted in more than 70 per cent of their planes and pilots being lost, insufficient fuel causing many to crash into the sea once their targets had been sunk. Since then, the calibre of pilots and planes had deteriorated as training and production had come under pressure. Nevertheless, air superiority was all important for success.

After six months of almost constant combat over Guadalcanal, fighting without support, its drive blunted, Japan relinquished the struggle. Early January 1943, after withering losses, and the increasing strength of the Allies, Imperial Headquarters was forced to issue the order to evacuate, with remaining troops redeployed to Southern Bougainville in New Guinea. The Allies advanced in leaps and bounds, embarking on a two-pronged, mainly amphibious push through the Pacific. One command, led by General MacArthur, was to take the rest of the Solomon Islands and New Guinea, before heading to the Philippines; the other, under Admiral Nimitz, would move from the Gilbert Islands towards Formosa or the Philippines. The Allied 'pincer' operation closed in, island to island, bypassing those islands too strongly defended by the Japanese. Time after time starving Japanese troops were trapped on islands and left to die.

Then in March, the Japanese suffered a demoralising loss when Admiral Yamamoto was killed, his plane shot down near New Guinea.

By mid-year, the Allies were surging up through the Solomons, and in August they recaptured Kiska in the Aleutians, each time up against suicidal resistance. When Allied raiders converged on Tarawa Atoll in the Gilbert Islands in November, only 17 out of the 5 000-strong garrison and a few dozen Korean stevedores had survived.

By now Japan had been fighting much longer than her national resources could sustain. Munitions manufacture had fallen even further, and despite her crude oil requirement having more than halved, only 15 per cent of production from captured oil fields was reaching Japan.

Some years earlier, one of the Japanese dailies had criticised the army for 'looking like a scarecrow'. Officers then had been against using tank forces, saying the tank was a weapon for cowards. To Jinjiro this had meant the army and the *Diet* lagged behind, not only in military capability but thinking power. Japan did not know herself. Correctly acknowledging that their obsolete equipment was adequate against the Chinese communists, they could not admit that against the Americans it was ineffectual. Being descended directly from the gods, they were inherently superior, thus they could not possibly fail.

The army's expectations had always been unrealistic, and Jinjiro could not understand how they had such faith that the Japanese spirit could overcome American military might, and that victory could be achieved on fervour alone. They also believed that American planes could never reach Japan, and that their own navy was superior; but Jinjiro knew that American warship production outstripped Japan fourteen-fold.

The grim reality of war was hitting home in Japan. In March, the government adopted the Urban Demolition Plan, with residents living near at-risk facilities evicted from their homes. The houses were later demolished to create firebreaks for air raids. Fortunately, the Furuya home was not affected. Commodities were growing scarcer, and shortages felt more and more keenly. Parks, grass verges, tennis courts and school grounds – any open spaces – were being used to grow potatoes and pumpkins.

With two roommates at Nakamura-*san*'s, Hisashi had found it difficult to study, so after the first year he decided to move back home. He was young and energetic and, despite the three hours' travel each day, he still managed to find the time to study long hours at the library. What he did miss was the fresh fruit and vegetables Nakamura-*san*'s wife had provided. At home there was no fruit and no meat, only dried fish, dried vegetables, sometimes extra rice supplied by *otosan*, and green vegetables grown in the back garden.

In August, a new law ordered the collection of all things metal for recycling into armaments. Everything was put towards the war effort: elevators, fans, cooking utensils, tin baths, tin cans and saucepans; cast-iron radiators, gates and fences; copper candlesticks, statues and coins; bronze bells, censers and plates; brass vases, statues and carpet-holders. Scrap rubber, rags and waste paper were also required. As well as donating her own iron, copper, bronze and brass goods, including an antique sword and Hisashi's precious cast-iron toys, Ryoko helped collect from temples and schools.

In September, it was decreed that girls would be mobilised to work in munitions factories, and university students, apart from those studying science and engineering, would no longer be exempt from conscription. Aware they could gain exemption by pretending to be ill, or by using parental contacts, Hisashi and his friends never really believed they would be sent to the frontline. But things were changing quickly.

On 21 October, Hisashi walked from university along with his year-group to the National Stadium adjacent to Meiji-*jingu* to attend the send-off of the first intake of drafted students. He was not particularly keen to attend, but going meant points towards his military drill course.

> It is a miserable day and, despite the continuous downpour, raincoats and umbrellas are not allowed. As a result, they are soaked even before they get there. Roped into sections allocated to institutions, 20 000 mainly male students stand to attention in the muddy stadium. In the sea of faces atop black institutional uniforms, the university and college boys rest cumbersome 40-year-old *san-hachis* on their shoulders.*
>
> For over an hour they wait in silence. The rain continues to fall, then, to the accompaniment of the military march, uniformed officials march on to the stage. If the motive has been to inspire impressionable youth, it is not working with Hisashi, who sees the spectacle as nothing but propaganda to pressurise the intelligentsia. Drab and colourless, it feels like a hastily organised school assembly, and all he wants is to be able to get out of the rain. For another hour, bombarded with speeches he cannot hear, the rifle deadening his shoulder, Hisashi recognises his insignificance and his powerlessness to control his future.
>
> Finally the 2 000-odd drafted second- and third-year Liberal Arts students march by, anonymous in their bedraggled university tunics. Seeming to Hisashi like a quiet rebellion, no one appears to have tried to look their best. Most uniforms are shabby and slapdash, and those students wearing military gaiters wear them carelessly. He sees no expressions of nationalistic fervour, merely sullen resignation.

---

* The 38 was a military issue rifle, left over from the 1904 Russo–Japanese war. It was used for practice drills, but ridiculed for its poor firing action.

Still it rains. Then suddenly from the west, through the deluge, a glimmer of sunshine, which follows the parade until it finishes. Afterwards, as everyone heads for the exit, Hisashi notices a woman teacher, conspicuous in her *kimono*. No ordinary day, she has dressed for the occasion. The hem of her *kimono* is mud-spattered, and he knows it will not be easy to clean. So concerned that she will lose her *zori* in the sludge, the teacher has forgotten about the girls for whom she is responsible.

The next day, the rally was in the newspaper and on the radio, reported in glowing terms with attendance inflated as high as 35 000 students. This was quite different to the impression of Hisashi and his friends who were there. Neither had they noticed the 60 000 bystanders also mentioned in the reports.

In December, the drafted students were swallowed up by the army, which from all accounts was doing badly on every front.

At the beginning of 1944, the Japanese thrust into India was driven back, while in the Pacific, step by step they were being forced to give up their conquests. Only five per cent of captured oil production was now reaching Japan. Defeat was certain, but still they persisted in their fight to the death.

A desperate situation demanded a desperate response. A new weapon was needed. 'Flesh bullets' were suggested. Suicide squads of naval servicemen would die in the Emperor's name. Plans for human torpedoes and suicide pilots were revived and the *Tokkotai* (Special Attack Force) was born.

At the end of January, the Americans landed in the Admiralties and the Marshall Islands; in February, the Caroline Islands; in April, New Guinea; and in June, Saipan.

The former German-governed Mariana Islands had been part of the Japanese Empire since an official mandate in 1920. Given its proximity to Japan, Saipan, the largest island, would be an ideal base for the new American long-range bombers to make return raids to

Japan. And with 535 ships and 128 000 men, the Americans were determined to take the island. Considering the Marianas safe from capture, little had been done to strengthen Japanese strongholds. But Saipan was too vital to lose, and Japanese troops refused to budge. However, most of the 30 000-strong garrison, as well as 22 000 civilians, had been killed within days. Hundreds of civilians, driven to the cliffs by the approaching Americans, had hurled themselves off; one mother first throwing her baby, then following.

The Imperial Japanese Navy had now lost over 90 per cent of its carrier-based aircraft. Added to that, the new 'thicker skinned' American Hellcat, modelled on a captured Zero, could outmanoeuvre and outrace the Zero. The glorious Japanese dream of winning the war was fading into grim reality, and the failure to secure Saipan was to impact hugely. Slowly the bad news was filtering through back home. Hisashi read in the newspaper the Americans had nicknamed the battle 'The Great Mariana's Turkey Shoot', likening their actions to turkey hunting. With the islanders having no weapons to fight back, it had been easy pickings.

People in Japan were starting to feel confused and insecure, until now the extent of military failures kept from them. The dissemination of selected information, exaggeration and half-truths meant it had been difficult to know what to believe, the official line always having been that Japan was winning on all fronts. But, the fall of Saipan could not be hidden. Prime Minister Tojo resigned and was replaced by the equally hard-line Koiso Kuniaki.

As much as possible, and in the face of tight censorship, Hisashi followed the conflict between Japan and America, as well as Germany and the Allies. With the true situation becoming clearer, it created a confusion of feelings; ill-feeling against the Allies for dramatically changing his life, but at the same time sympathy for those he knew were suffering under Hitler and the Japanese troops. To him it seemed as if the less educated were better able to blindly obey directives, never considering the consequences. Although the intelligentsia were less caught up in the hype, persistent propaganda had taken hold, and like his peers, Hisashi still thought war had been the only choice.

Prior to Pearl Harbour, a Japanese task force had estimated America could produce ten times the weaponry of Japan. But they had not reckoned with the speed and size of output achieved by American mass production, and its vast natural resources, including two-thirds of the world's oil supplies. The US navy had actually expanded twenty-fold, and the air division of the army, many times more.

In July, the Americans landed in Guam and Tinian, and in September, the Allied pincer movement converged in the Philippines. However, waiting to welcome them was the 'greatest naval force ever assembled'. With 738 ships, it was 400 per cent bigger than their task force at Midway, and 15 per cent bigger than the Americans at Saipan. And it was here in the Leyte Gulf on 24 October 1944, that the *kamikaze* made their debut, their first strike recorded the following day.

Kamikaze means 'divine wind'. In 1905 the name had been given to a destroyer, and in 1921 to a class of destroyers. Early in the Pacific War it had also been used for an army fighter plane in Burma and Malaya, and it was now adopted as the name for the naval aircraft to be used in the subsequent suicide raids. On 15 October, the Commander-in-Chief of the Imperial Combined Fleet had finally consented to the formation of the *kamikaze* corps. Two days later, Admiral Takijiro Onishi, 'father of the *kamikaze*', moved to Manila to set up the unit.

Young men, flying like the wind, would repel the invaders who threatened Japan, just as the *kamikaze* nearly 700 years earlier had vanquished the invading Mongols. On two occasions, Emperor Kublai Khan had attempted to capture Japan, both times in September, *taifu* season. Both times the raiders had been driven away by heaven-sent *taifu*; the prayers of those in Japan, answered by Amaterasu herself, and Susanowo, the Storm God.

After the *kamikaze* destroyed the second Mongol fleet, no invader had ever set foot on Japanese soil. The Divine Winds had also been called upon to help eliminate Chinese and Russian threats in 1894–95, and 1904–05, respectively. And now the government avowed the *kamikaze* would again be Japan's salvation.

Meanwhile, the Allies were liberating a vast part of Europe.

Chapter 37

Samurai Against Samurai

Jinsei choro no gotoshi
Human life is like the morning dew

Images bleep on the radar screen. Disappearing, reappearing, advancing, retreating, the pilot of the single-engined Zero plays cat-and-mouse in the clouds. Suddenly coming into sight, he dives from astern, banking vertically. Down he screams, heading for the battleship loaded with missiles, mortars and machine-gun fire. Rapidly losing altitude, he descends in a deluge of steel. He is hit. A wing shears off. Flames and smoke streaming behind, he crashes onto the deck, 600 kilograms of explosives erupting on impact. The battleship sighs. The teenager is incinerated instantly, his ashes strewn over the deck, and the fire is quickly quenched. Nearby, other fireballs plummet into the sea. Later, an American crewman finds a button stamped with a three-petalled cherry blossom.

THE BATTLE OF LEYTE was a resounding defeat for Japan. Four carriers and three battleships, including the 'unsinkable' leviathan *Musashi*, were lost. However, on 28 October, NHK had hailed the campaign a *kamikaze* triumph.

The young officers in their late teens and early twenties had been carefully selected; risk-takers chosen for their ability to make good decisions and manoeuvre small planes. Young men without responsibilities, they were usually unmarried, second and third sons. However, approaching the end of the war, the age of recruits dropped, and with the shortage of components for aircraft, veneer and cloth were substituted for aluminium, and plywood for glass.

The first marine *kamikaze* or *kaiten* (*Tokkotai* midget submarine) sortie occurred on 8 November. In his final student posting at the naval institute, Hisashi heard talk of the new weapon, production having begun that June, with I-class submarines being modified to carry four or six *kaiten* at a time. The name *kaiten*, literally 'return to heaven', spoke for itself, and he could not help thinking of what it would be like to be one of those young men.

> In the steaming bowels of the mother sub, he dons his *hachimaki* (the replica *samurai* headband), and the sash stitched with strands of hair from 1000 women. He touches the three copper coins in his pocket, ready to pay for his fare to ferry his soul across the *Sanzu-no-kawa* (River Sanzu). The national anthem blares over the intercom. Immaculately dressed, he stands to attention, then ritually sips his *sake* infused with 'Imperial on'. In the Emperor's name, he climbs into the torpedo, his comrades crying 'See you at *Yasukuni*', their spirits to meet again at the shrine.
>
> He is small, but it is cramped inside, and stretched out on his stomach, he can touch his companion's head with his boots. He feels the forward thrust of the torpedo as the submarine releases them near the lagoon. Sealed in, he will sacrifice his life, just as the cherry blossom drops at the faintest breath of wind. He knows they have fuel for only one way. They are not expected to return. He knows he is going to his death. He has left his will behind. He has left a letter to his parents and, like a *samurai* of old, he enclosed a lock of his hair.
>
> Cruising slowly at the bottom of the sea, the torpedo is propelled by compressed air in the tail. He turns the crude periscope to navigate and manoeuvres the 'dead-man's handle' (rudder control lever). Checking with the primitive control panel, 500 metres from their target he switches the steering to automatic, and swallows his last whisky. According to his training, his mother will soon hover before

his eyes. He will hear a sound like the shattering of a crystal, then, he will be no more.

Such honour for his family, his name read over the national news, posthumously promoted a rank.

Hisashi wondered what thoughts would be running through his mind. Would he feel claustrophobic and in a cold sweat? Or be going stark raving mad? How could anyone sit calmly, just waiting ...

Tokyo boasted that on their first offensive, *kaiten* sank five vessels. The Allies recorded one.

Technically, *kaiten* and *kamikaze* recruits were volunteers. During their training, participants were requested for secret, sacred missions. Amid group pressure, and trained specially, it was espoused that to die in this way would honour the Emperor, death bringing full and final repayment for every *on* ever incurred. If any soldier refused, his whole family would lose face.*

The act of dying for the Emperor worked on people's entrenched belief in his divine status. Inferring he was responsible for military manoeuvres ensured people would support government decisions, and using his name helped people rationalise the concept of the *Tokkotai*. While people at large accepted the propaganda, there was unease among the intelligentsia as to the morality and sense of such attacks, but fear of the *Tokko* and *Kempeitai* kept them quiet.

Hisashi thought the notion of dying for the Emperor was a pointless gesture, though knew that if he was 'tapped', he would surrender to the inevitable. But he was confident he would not have to, as he could serve his nation without being sent to the front. His parents had been right, and while he was ashamed to think it, he was relieved.

Whether a general, a 'flesh bullet', or the lowliest foot soldier, those who died were simply discharging their 'Imperial *on*'. However, in reward, each and every one became a *kami*, enshrined at Yasukuni-

---

* Since conscription was introduced after the Meiji Revolution, anyone evading call-up was jailed; the entire extended family was shunned and often starved to death.

jinja. People were indoctrinated to honour their dead soldiers as heroic *kami*, thus allaying a mass aversion to aggression. As a display of loyalty to the Emperor and nation, citizens were expected to regularly visit the shrine, as well as attend mass rallies like those held in Germany.

> Blossoming today, tomorrow scattered;
> Life is like a delicate flower.
> Can one expect the fragrance to last forever?
> (*haiku* by Admiral Takijiro Onishi)

Chapter 38

His Heart is Left Behind

Shuyo
Self-discipline builds up the belly

THE FALL OF SAIPAN and the escalating fear of bombardment provoked mass evacuations. From cities and towns that were designated danger zones, children, pregnant women and the elderly were evacuated to safer areas upcountry: to temples and shrines, or the homes of friends or relatives. For those who evacuated, those who were left behind, and those who housed the evacuees, it created huge upheaval. At the end of June, Yayoi was sent away with her school to the city of Sendai. And, as the possibility of raids increased, Jinjiro arranged access to an empty house in case of emergency. It was owned by a tram driver who now lived in his company's boarding house in Tokyo central, his family having been evacuated. As it was near their house, it might well be damaged at the same time, but at least it was a backup.

In the summer of 1944, as food supplies declined, day-to-day hardship intensified. When delivery of maize and soy beans from Manchuria had stopped altogether, and only locally grown potatoes were available to supplement the ever-decreasing amount of rice, the total food supply dropped more than 40 per cent. Radio Tokyo informed citizens that callisthenics made hungry people strong and vigorous again; and, in fact, coping without food, warmth and sleep actually 'strengthened one's spirit'.

In the cities, the rich could get food on the *yami-ichi*. In the country, as most men were overseas fighting or working in munitions factories in the cities, there were fewer mouths to feed and there was sufficient food for personal needs, with some left to sell. The real sufferers were the middle- and lower-class town and city dwellers, reliant on meagre government rations and what little they could grow themselves. Jinjiro still managed to get a few extras from Kawanishi, though even that source was drying up; but they were among the lucky ones and could still afford goods on the *yami-ichi*.

Night-time blackouts had been made compulsory. Street lights were turned off, cars were driven without headlights, and blinds were drawn before turning on the lights in homes and offices. The only lights remaining were those that swept the skies searching for bombers.

The year 1944 was Hisashi's third and final year of university. Working night and day to finish his thesis on metal forging, he attended the government-funded aeronautical laboratory on the Tokyo campus. A new technique was needed to refine magnesium alloy so it could be used in the manufacture of aircraft. With traditional methods of refining, the metal became too brittle and prone to cracking. Under his professor's supervision, he was using X-ray to examine his experiments to determine what temperature, pressure and speed the magnesium alloy could withstand before it fractured. Using X-ray for medical purposes was popular in Japan,* but for metallurgy research it was very new. In the whole country, only *Todai* had the requisite X-ray machine.

Challenged by the work, proud and excited to be involved in something so important, he felt very possessive of 'the seed he was nurturing'. Not only would success bring huge improvements to the Japanese aircraft industry, but worldwide fame. However, at the end of August he was notified that he had to report for naval training on 30 September, when he would exchange his university uniform for a

---

* The X-ray machine was invented in 1910.

naval kit. Given the urgency for manpower, especially for graduates, his training would be reduced from six to four months, beginning without delay; and without a graduation ceremony. So, even though he had not completed his thesis, Hisashi qualified as an engineer, and handed his research over to a second-year student.

Prior to leaving home, Hisashi helped *otosan* turn the blackout shelter into storage. If the house was destroyed and they had to start again, they would need the basics. Valuable and precious items like Ryoko's grey cashmere coat and *kimono*, Hisashi's books, glass windows, and Jitsuzen's antiques were added for safekeeping. Then, once everything was placed inside, the planks were replaced and covered with soil. With big furniture already having been shifted to the Kawanishi warehouse in Nihom-*bashi*, Jinjiro and Ryoko would camp in the house.

It is early afternoon and a beautiful autumn day. Hisashi stands in his bedroom, sunlight shimmering through the *shoji*. But without his furniture and personal effects, the room has lost its personality. Empty just like him, it is as if nobody has ever lived there; no sign of the boy who opened and closed the *shoji* every day for almost 15 years. Loneliness echoes around the empty shell.

Surrounded and warmed by the gentle sunlight, he shuts his eyes, desperately wanting to hear familiar, reassuring sounds, so long taken for granted. But all he hears is the rustling of the *sugi* brushing against the house, and this adds to his agitation. Even when the house had been alive, his room had been a haven of constancy and calm. He knows every fleeting variation of light and shadow, changing through the day, and by season. But now he must leave his haven behind, its lifetime of memories exposed to the danger of air raids.

For the first time in his life he feels cut off and completely alone. His relationships with family, friends and neighbours have been disrupted, and the sense of loss for his past life is profound. Everything he has been brought up to believe in and aspire to is gone. Everything around him is unpredictable and demanding. Everything is so sudden – hunger, bombs, fire and death – and he is helpless against it all. Fear crowds his mind, half of him wondering what will happen next, the other half feeling dead and vacant.

Study is his life. He loves books, the pursuit of knowledge the core of his life. He does not like that his research has to be placed under restraint. He is not inspired by patriotism and he does not want to think of his country before himself. In fact, he abhors the rowdy behaviour of the military, with its songs and speeches bristling with patriotism. And now, at the request of his country, he must leave his world behind. His duty is to protect his fatherland, and maybe sacrifice his life. His seniors have gone before him to die and his juniors will follow. Now it is his turn. But what is death? What is fate? What is creation? He has no answers.

The only way he will survive is with sincerity and mental concentration, and he must digest the aloneness that has befallen him. The process of building his character will be severe and solitary, just like the young Buddha who gave up his prosperity. After all, to live alone with one's self is nothing but the root of life. But right now he feels numb, then angry. He deeply resents having to hand his research over to someone else. He has completed over 70 per cent of the work, but the credit will never be his. In his hand, he holds his university graduation certificate, a symbol of his past life. He has tried his utmost to achieve that piece of paper, but who he has been, what he has desired, and where he has been heading are all in vain.

How hungry he is.

A temporary training camp for naval officer candidates had been set up near Washizu, in Shizuoka province, from where Mount Fuji can be seen in the far distance. The 450 trainees were divided into squads of 30. They included a cross-section of disciplines, all tertiary educated, with most having attended technical colleges.

Roused at five a.m. by drum call, they have to be up and dressed within two minutes, pulling on khaki pants and white open-necked shirts, black leather boots and baseball caps. They stand still and stiff-backed in front of the barracks in three lines of ten – but not for long.

First there was ten minutes of exercise to wake and warm them up, then, in groups that rotated daily, they began their chores. Some set the breakfast table in the dormitory, others cleaned the latrines and showers, and three collected the day's schedule and the containers of boiled rice and *miso* soup. Eating ravenously, they enjoyed the sensation of fullness, something no longer possible at home or in school and university canteens.

But with the navy's rigid hierarchy, there was a tense atmosphere. The 1882 Imperial Rescript to Soldiers and Sailors dictated their code, the sacred words learned by heart, and meditated for ten minutes each morning, their '*giri* to the Emperor' supreme. Hisashi was left in no doubt as to where his duty lay. Obedience was absolute. As the words extolled:

We [the Emperor] are the head and you are the body. We depend on you as our arms and legs. Whether we shall be able to protect our country, and repay the *on* of our ancestors, depends upon you fulfilling your obligations.

As an individual, Hisashi did not count. The squad was all-important. If he failed his training, he would be deemed a second-rate citizen.

The early weeks brought the biggest shocks. With 18-hour days, training was physically demanding, particularly for graduates used to sitting at desks. Tough, unsympathetic instructors tried to whip the new recruits into shape: transforming them into efficient officers who knew how to march in military formation, how to handle guns and rifles, even how to use Western-style table manners. But their main training was on the cutter boats (the lifeboats on warships), and they learned how to row, to tie knots, and climb rope ladders.

Classes were punctuated by regular bursts of exercise, including the daily ten-kilometre run after lunch. Underpinning all the training was the *samurai* ethic that the more they were tested physically, the stronger would be their fortitude and will to win.

Assuming his 'proper place', according to the intentions of his superiors, and mindful of the honour of his name, Hisashi was keen to learn everything, and plunged wholeheartedly into his training. He gained much needed confidence in his physical ability. Growing up with weak digestion, pale skin and a small physique, he had been led to believe his physical condition was below average. At school, he never got top in running or swimming, but now he saw he was somewhat better than average, which was quite a boost. He even survived the daily ten-kilometre run: though some stumbled and fell every day, he kept going.

Having been a member of the rowing club in high school, he was confident at water sports, and even though the oars were built British-size for bigger men, he quickly mastered the cutter boat. Although most warships had been built in Japan, British naval traditions were still followed; ironically the very skills taught by the British were now being used against them.

In November, Hisashi received one of the weekly letters from home, and for a moment had been thrown back into his old world. *Otosan* wrote that they had received a visit from the wife of the university president, who handed over the gold medal that Hisashi had won as top engineering graduate. It was a day well remembered when he had heard that he had achieved this pinnacle of success; but it came as an anticlimax, as only he and his family ever knew who got the medal of 1944.

If he had graduated before the war, they would have been very proud, but now in the larger scheme of things, it no longer seemed of value. Nonetheless, it pronounced he was suitably moulded, a *Todai* graduate, a clever man, and he should have felt elated. In better times his future would have been assured, but the war had devalued the meaning of the medal, and destroyed his sense of himself, his future and his past.

Those first weeks of training passed slowly, but near the end, each day slipped by more quickly than the one before, and for Hisashi it was a good experience overall. Thanks to their rigorous drilling, the officer recruits were physically fit and ready for action. Having been together for four months, they had made friends, many of whom they never saw again. For the first time in his life Hisashi had contact with men from varied backgrounds. More than half were farmer's sons, both rich and poor. The differences of wealth, class, region and tertiary training made him more aware of who he was and where he stood within society: 'not so rich, not so poor, not so strong, not so weak, not so wise and not so stupid'.

No one was worried about what would happen to them next. They thought about their families and friends, looking forward to seeing them again some day; but on the whole they felt as if they were taking part in a great adventure.

By the end of 1944 the population of Tokyo had decreased from nine to four million, people having been either evacuated or sent overseas to fight. Only those linked to the military were left. Working for a company closely connected to the navy, Jinjiro had to stay. Ryoko could have left, but insisted it was her duty to stay with her husband, though, in their all-but-deserted community, she was lonely. Yayoi, still in Sendai with her school, was unhappy and continuously asking to come home, and just before Christmas, Ryoko went to fetch her.

Chapter 39

Alone Against the World

Shika o ou ryoshi yama o mizu
A hunter on the track of a deer
fails to see a mountain

THE YEAR 1945 DAWNED on a scene of utter hopelessness. Fighting continued to grind on, but gradually the Japanese were being driven back on all fronts. As the Allies' submarines attacked an ill-prepared fleet, they gained naval ascendancy in the Pacific. Japanese losses were ten times those of America, with all but ten per cent of their ships lost. No captured oil was reaching Japan.

In January, the Americans landed on the Philippine island of Luzon. In February, they captured the island of Iwo Jima. In March, the British reopened the Burma Road to China, while the Americans retook Manila.

In Europe, the Germans were close to defeat. Hitler killed himself on 30 April, and Germany surrendered on 8 May. The war in Europe might have been lost, but the Pacific war raged on, Japan alone against the world. Even before Germany's collapse, Japanese leaders would have known defeat was certain, but the mood of 'do or die' resistance prevailed, carrying the 'Holy War' to its bitter end.

The US's next target was the island of Okinawa in the Ryukyu Archipelago,* the capital Naha 1200 kilometres southwest of Tokyo: the final hurdle before an invasion of the Japanese mainland.

---

* The island, with its Chinese-Malay-Ainu origins, was annexed by Japan in 1879, gained political equality as a prefecture in 1920, and by 1941 was under the authority of the Imperial Japanese Navy.

Preceded by a ferocious naval and air assault, the 1 April invasion amassed the biggest American task force yet, and the most concentrated barrage of bullets and bombs of the war. The American military strength was overwhelmingly superior. Initially few Japanese soldiers could be found. Underground in a labyrinth of tunnels and concrete-lined bunkers, they bided their time; and it was not until they surfaced, that the Americans made progress. The invasion quickly became a bloodbath.

Out at sea, the largest ever *kamikaze* incursion was scheduled for 12 April. In a final grand gesture, the *Yamato*, the pride of the Imperial Navy and Japan's last surviving super-battleship, was sent on a one-way mission to avert Allied aircraft from *kamikaze* routes. However, she was sunk before she could get even halfway to Okinawa, and most *kamikaze* were shot down before hitting their targets. Despite their zeal, the 'divine winds' of the *kamikaze* raids proved no match for the 'barbarian hordes'. The Imperial Japanese Navy was wiped out.

Japanese propaganda over-inflated both *kaiten* and *kamikaze* 'kills'. The Allies declared that most of the stories were fabricated. Whether on land or sea, or in the air, suicide attacks failed to turn the tide. It is generally accepted that 2940 men died in suicide sorties between October 1944 and August 1945, nearly two-thirds of them during the defence of Okinawa.

Like Saipan and Iwo Jima, Okinawa suffered some of the most chilling tragedies of the war. To avoid capture, civilians killed each other while waiting in their hiding places; mothers, clutching their children, leapt to their deaths off cliff-tops. Numerous soldiers committed *seppuku*. If Hisashi had been there, he would have done the same. It was the 'Japanese way'; surrender was not an option.

About that same time, rather than kill themselves, hundreds of army stevedores surrendered on islands in the southern sea; that, too, was acceptable as they were vagrants and outcasts, and so had no idea of appropriate behaviour.

Fighting on Okinawa continued for 82 days, but by the end of

June the Japanese troops were severely beaten. The American forces had also taken a hammering, but from the island of Okinawa their bombers could carry out air raids on the Japanese mainland, as well as targeting inbound supply ships. In April, US troops took Bataan in the Philippines, then, in May, the British recaptured Rangoon, the Australians landed in Borneo, and the Chinese regained Fuchow and Nanking.

Right from the start, aerial bombardment had played a crucial part in battles, as well as in non-combat situations. Prior to 1945, periodic bombing on the Japanese mainland had been aimed at destroying military depots, dockyards, ground cannons, water reservoirs, power stations, munitions and aircraft factories. Small bombers carrying a 500-kilogram bomb and machine guns in case of anti-aircraft fire could come and go easily from aircraft carriers stationed near Japan. However, early in 1945 the Americans switched tactics, and bombing with a different purpose was introduced. Psychological air raids were aimed at breaking Japanese morale and destroying the fundamentals of society.

Napalm bombs, manufactured from a compound of jellied gasoline,* broke up and sprayed an area on impact before igniting. They then burned slowly and with high intensity, destroying everything around them, leaving the area flattened like a carpet. Carpet bombs, as they came to be called, were available in two weights: 220 kilograms and 1100 kilograms.

The carpet bombing of Tokyo was possibly far more devastating than the bombing of London or Dresden, the flammable nature of Japanese wood and paper buildings igniting into huge fireballs that burned vast areas to ashes.†

Squadrons of lumbering B-29 Superfortresses executed the civilian

---

* Commonly known as Molotov baskets.

† The overall death toll from carpet bombing was also larger than from either of the two atomic bombs, yet little has been written about the fires.

attacks. The B-29 was the largest aircraft of the war: 33 metres long, with a 48-metre wingspan and four massive 2 200-horsepower engines, each turning a 5-metre propeller. Taking off from Saipan, Tinian or Guam, over 2 500 kilometres from Tokyo, and flying at a maximum of 570 kph, there was little room for error given its operating range of 6 000 kilometres. Twenty per cent, on average, failed to return after each raid. They were either shot down, or ran out of fuel and crashed into the sea. Several reconnaissance B-29s, boat planes and submarines kept radio contact along the route to pick up survivors.

The American tacticians were confident that by terrorising and demoralising civilians through sustained fire bombing, they could force Japanese leaders into submission and end the war. However, the more the Americans bombed, the more determined Imperial High Command was to continue.

The Emperor did nothing to direct the military to stop. Even before the war began he rarely ventured outside the palace. To Hisashi, as everyone else, it was normal behaviour for the Emperor 'to sit behind a curtain', out of touch with daily matters. However, after the Manchurian Incident he had been intentionally shut away, not only to keep him from hearing things he may disapprove of, but to protect him from assassination by leftists or communists. An awe-inspiring Emperor was needed by the militarists to keep the populace subservient and motivated for war.

The morality of bombing civilians had been discussed at length after World War I. In 1923 Britain, France, Japan, Italy and America had agreed to prohibit aerial bombardment of civilian-only areas. At the 1932 Geneva Disarmament Conference most nations agreed that air attacks on civilians violated the laws of war; however, nothing was ratified. Between the beginning of February and the end of May 1945, 16 major operations targeted Japanese civilians, six against Tokyo.

Citizens were courageous and resilient, and everyone joined in fighting fires, digging for survivors, tending the injured, clearing the streets and demolishing ruins. But, three years of living under gruelling conditions was taking its toll. Everything was in short supply, accelerating the demoralisation of the population and, with air raids increasing, people were becoming discouraged and beginning to doubt the military, which continued to play down losses in radio and newspaper reports.

There are heroes on both sides of any war, with innumerable brave men dying. Many of Hisashi's classmates were killed in battle, and every time he heard of yet another, he realised the senselessness of it all; the waste of young lives in their prime. There was Seiwu Yanagawa, for example, his classmate from middle school, who died on the Burmese battlefield that March.

After graduating from the Military Academy, Seiwu, an exceptional athlete, had gone to China for several years, returning to Tokyo in 1944 to assume a new posting as a battalion commander at the academy. Six months later, he voluntarily enlisted to go to Burma, knowing full well that Japanese defeat was inevitable. But, in true warrior style, he wanted to help postpone that day.

A pleasant and affable man, the twentieth-century *samurai* Seiwu would be remembered by his peers at the academy and the men under his command as a warrior, representing the end of a disappearing world. His friends and comrades erected a monument dedicated to his memory at a nearby shrine.

Hisashi felt great sympathy for Seiwu. As the son of a famous general, he had the deepest duty to become a warrior. Did Seiwu wrestle with his conscience at this critical time in Japan's history? Did he wonder if he should remain safely in Tokyo seeking promotion? Or transfer to the front to most likely die? With an influential father, he could have stayed in safety, but he deliberately chose the same path as his comrades, whose fate was at the discretion of Imperial High Command.

Chapter 40

Deny Oneself and Serve the Nation

Ichioku taigi ni shisu
One hundred million people
are ready to die with honour

Second-lieutenant Hisashi Furuya arrived at his post at the Naval Engineering Arsenal (Branch I) in February 1945. Even though he was ranked second from the bottom in the hierarchical order of authority, his commission was highly valued by his family.

> Fifty of the newly assigned, young engineering officers travel the 400 kilometres from the training camp to Miura Peninsula, past Tokyo and Yokohama, embarking just before Yokosuka naval base.* Moving at night in case of attack, they leave in the dark, sit in the dark and arrive in the dark. The snow is unusually deep, and the train moves slowly. The carriage had been overheated, and the cold wintry blast hits them as they step outside, daylight a vague hint in the sky. The snow is a metre deep and everything is white.
>
> Hunching their shoulders against the sleet, their woollen greatcoats give little protection. In miserable silence, lugging their heavy bamboo suitcases, they walk the kilometre to the plant. With strict blackouts, there are no street or factory lights. Vast, dark buildings loom either side of the slushy road, which is barely distinguishable between the banks of white snow.

---

* The American base today.

Giri to the Emperor • 227

Having been here before on his university postings, Hisashi is less daunted than the others. Excited at reaching his post after months of training, he is nonetheless tired, hungry and grumpy. Arriving at the institute, they are fed, briefed, ordered to show up for work at noon and released.

Inside the barracks, it feels nearly as cold as outside. Unpacking his meagre belongings, Hisashi changes into his boots and work uniform, transferring his ferry fare for the *Sanzu-no-kawa* into his trouser pocket. He hangs his officer's sword from his belt. The sword cost him 14 yen, the belt 12. Annoyingly, his boots still pinch and give him blisters; how he wishes he had chosen the medium instead of the small.

His whole kit had cost 377 *yen*.* Even with the 100 *yen* government clothing allowance, as a lowly second-lieutenant earning only 28 *yen* per month, it would take a long time to pay off. But, unlike non-commissioned soldiers, at least he got paid.

Assigned to the experimental institute where he had worked as a student, Hisashi was disappointed to find most experiments had been shelved. The plant had been diverted to mass production to meet the day-to-day needs of the battlefield. Ten thousand personnel were stationed there – 200 officers, 300 regular navy personnel and the rest, recruited labourers – spread over five plants each employing 2 000 men. One plant made steel for torpedo and bullet shells, another filled the shells with explosives, while the others screwed the fittings, painted the outside, and tested the finished product.

He was pleased to be assigned to the one and only research project, and began his service in Air Bombardment, helping to test a new one-tonne bomb. The navy was desperate for the new bomb, and testing it was top priority.

The test site was a vast, desolate area where engineers from ten

---

* For example, his navy-blue dress uniform cost 38 *yen*, suitcase 7.2 *yen*, gaiters 4 *yen*, greatcoat 73 *yen*, tie 1.2, and cap 1.7 *yen*.

different fields of engineering examined the detonation and impact of each bomb. The effectiveness of the metal, powder, construction and design of the bomb was tested to ensure the most precise hit, and the greatest coverage. As engineers were scarce, there was only one expert available per field; as the metallurgist, Hisashi checked the fragments of bombshell, quite enjoying the work.

However, after a month, much to his disappointment, he was transferred to the steel-making plant, where he had responsibility for running the furnace. There were three factories in the department: smelting (where Hisashi worked), forging and casting, each with two qualified naval engineers to supervise day shifts. The paucity of naval engineers meant civilian engineers managed the night shift.

The smelting factory was operating at 100 per cent capacity when Hisashi arrived, producing 200 tonnes of steel per day. Production, however, gradually declined. Tonnage fluctuated according to the supply of ingredients, with operational hours changing accordingly. On a worldwide scale, it was not a financially viable operation, but from its inception this had been an experimental rather than commercial concern.

Operating round the clock, the mill turned out the high-tensile steel required for the torpedoes used as *kaiten* and aircraft machine-gun bullets: 65 per cent of production went into the torpedoes. Naval High Command had still not recognised that the aircraft had taken over from the battleship as the main surface combat machine.

Smelting, the smallest section of the mill had 40 regular navy trade engineers and 40 labourers to fetch and carry. The labourers, mainly local farmers and retailers aged over 45, were considered a nuisance. Without the training required to work in a steel mill, most pretended to work, which was highly frustrating for Hisashi and his fellow officers, who were responsible for their schedules. Privately, Hisashi thought the money used for their salaries would have been better spent on buying much needed trucks to transport the manufactured bombs.

He had to be up and ready for workers' roll call at 5.45 a.m. every morning. Week in, week out, his daily schedule rarely varied: 8 a.m. to 4 p.m., seven days a week, the work tedious and monotonous. All 9 500 labourers and the 20 young officers responsible for them lived on site, with only the regulars and senior officers going home to their families housed nearby.*

Hisashi's responsibilities extended to supervising three dormitories. Under the guise of patriotism, thousands of males had been conscripted, literally kidnapped from Japanese colonies: Formosa, Southern Sakhalin (now part of Russia), and the whole of Korea. While the 20- to 40-year-olds went into combat, those under 20 and over 40 undertook menial duties in military plants in Japan. Hisashi's dormitories each housed 80 Formosan teenagers. The dorm song, written by one of Hisashi's fellow officers, and sung each morning at roll call, was intended to ensure dedication, and a sense of unity.

Oh! Fresh cherry blossoms†
we get together,
morale soaring
our supreme target dying for our fatherland.
We put forth every ounce of energy
in the drive for production increases,
praying to god to hit the target
with the first shot of every bullet we manufacture,
on the battlefield thousands of miles away,
praying to win another victory.
In the moonlight of the dormitory windows
we never forget the deep emotion we felt
when we left our parents' houses,
where they still pray to god for our honourable job.

---

* A 'regular' was someone employed permanently in the military, not just during wartime.
† Symbolising Japanese youth.

Hisashi had breakfast with the boys in the canteen, and then attended his same spot in the mill for the following eight hours.

> Its grey bulk, grim and intimidating, is surrounded by a field of mud, prefabricated sheds and dormitories showing signs of wear and tear. Vehicles constantly move back and forth, avoiding the huge mounds of corroded scrap metal waiting to be melted down. Tall stacks spew vast quantities of smoke into the air, the ash settling in a thick layer over the dirty buildings with their unsightly patches of rust, peeling paint, and broken windows.
>
> The three-storey furnace is fearsome. It is badly lit, its rooftop windows permanently covered. Dominating the interior space is the enormous brick tank, measuring 50 metres long, 15 metres wide and 2 metres deep, which is fired from below by coke gas. The fierce heat generated glows in the workers' faces and makes them cough. Two overhead cranes howl incessantly as their wheels screech along the rails, filling the room with sparks, dust and din: one deposits the ingredients, the other extracts the liquid steel.
>
> Each type of steel has its own recipe, and it is Hisashi's responsibility to supply the materials and formula to the furnace, ensuring the correct mix. Under his watchful eye, ingredients are weighed manually into one-tonne buckets: scrap metals, manganese, magnesium powder, lime, calcium and sand. Each ingredient has to be deposited evenly, so he identifies the precise spot for the crane to empty its load, leaving the molten steel to mix itself as it melts. When the mixture liquefies at 1 800°C, gravity forces the contents into two-tonne buckets, which the second crane winches up, and transfers to casting or forging.
>
> As the supply of raw materials declines, a missing ingredient will affect the whole mixture, and it becomes increasingly nerve-racking waiting to see which supplies will arrive. Each shift Hisashi has to recalculate the recipes according to what turns up. Production cannot stop as the molten steel will turn to a solid unmanageable mass.

The monotonous, deafening racket bombards his eardrums: the clanging, clattering and roaring, louder than a fast train passing nearby. Steam, escaping through the valves of the gas inlet pipes, hisses and makes the air even hotter. The lack of ventilation is stifling. With no break in operations, the dust drifts continuously, a choking, coughing grey nuisance.

The minute Hisashi steps inside, his crisp, khaki uniform wilts. Wearing dark blue goggles to protect his eyes, cotton gloves to protect his hands, and covered in grime from cap to boot, he is an eerie sight in this dank world. There are no ear muffs but, even if there had been, he could not have used them. His ear has to listen amidst the din for a deviation in the air blast, or the creak of the crane, perhaps indicating something is wrong.

Standing for hours in the swirl of dust and fumes, Hisashi is mesmerised by the endless repetition. All his senses are disturbed: his skin flushes and his stomach muscles cramp, sometimes so severely that he loses his appetite. The dust dries up his nose, irritates his throat and tastes unpleasant. Sweat soaks his clothes, and often he feels light-headed, a sign that reminds him to eat rock salt from the bucket nearby.

Hisashi suffered from sore feet, backache, dehydration and headaches. He was easily irritated and ill-tempered. Outside, the smoke hung motionless in the sky, but even so, he was always thankful for a lungful of fresh air. While the labourers had set lunch breaks and ate in the main canteen, Hisashi had no official break. When he had time, he dropped into the small canteen attached to the mill, where officers and regulars had lunch, always hurrying to get back to work.

After his shift, he would go back to the dormitory for his supervisory duties: first supper at 5.30 p.m., then the communal bath. He always bathed quickly: the boys thought he was spying on them, and often they picked his pockets while he was in the water. He had already lost several ferry fares, his fountain pen and two wristwatches.

The two-storey dormitories housed 40 boys per floor and were divided by *fusuma* into sections of ten. They were dim and stuffy, their windows boarded over for the winter. By day, their *futon* were rolled up on the *tatami*, with personal possessions wrapped in *furoshiki* (large scarves) and left on top. As a supervisor, Hisashi had his own room, albeit a cell-like space with unlined walls, a wooden floor and no windows; but at least he had it to himself.

Returning from his nightly visit to the officers' club, 20 minutes away by train, he was usually in bed by 9.30, needing to check the boys only if there had been an air raid. With a phone at his fingertips, he could contact his immediate superior, who lived locally. Despite the long days of strenuous physical activity, and the stress of never-ending problems, he rarely felt tired. He was young and dedicated, but he appreciated the privacy when he got to relax on his military issue bed at night, his telephone and candle lamp on the floor beside him.

As an officer, Hisashi was entitled to have his quarters serviced, and a neighbouring farmer's wife replaced his bed linen daily and laundered his uniform. But, despite bathing every night and sleeping in clean linen, minutes after getting into bed, lice and ticks attacked his neck, especially the soft skin behind his ears. He had become adept at telling the biters apart. Lice attacked slowly and continuously all night long, whereas a tick was quicker, with a bite that was more severe, leaving an itchy, longer-lasting pain.

In peacetime, insects were kept under control, so he knew this was a consequence of the times, but it disgusted him. Of course he did not suffer alone but, with insecticides in short supply, he and his fellow officers could find no solution. After a month his skin had become immune and, even when bitten, he no longer itched. But much to his shame, red spots appeared nightly, making him feel unclean.

Granted two days' leave per year, Hisashi went home. *Okasan*, who had been waiting at the gate, took one look at him and sent him round to the back door, ordering him to take off his clothes and go in naked. She had seen the telltale red spots, so furiously boiled his underwear and hung his uniform outside to blow in the wind.

*　*　*

Because of its remoteness on the narrow peninsula, deliveries of supplies to the plant were erratic during the last year of the war. Coastal shipping was non-existent as barges and boats had been commandeered, so everyone depended on the single railway line; but its service was frequently disrupted by air raids.

With priority given to military resources, foodstuffs were in poor supply. It was a worry for Hisashi, always wondering how to satisfy the hunger of the labourers. A bowl of rice, and vegetable and bullfrog soup, were the standard daily fare. It was both better in quality and quantity than civilians had, but they were still hungry. As an officer, Hisashi enjoyed better quality rice, and a bottle of beer at the officers' club each night, but he too was hungry most of the time, and often dreamed of his mother's meals.

Some of the boys stole rations from the warehouse at night, but Hisashi ignored it. However, the stealing quickly got out of hand with forays into nearby fields, where the youths stole tomatoes, watermelons and turnips. Farmers began complaining, but reprimands did nothing to stop the boys, and Hisashi seemed to be forever apologising for them. In the end he compromised. He compensated the farmers with cigarettes and sugar, and they quickly turned a blind eye.

However, food was not the only shortage. After many years of fighting, there was a serious shortage of raw materials and increasingly the mill was operating below capacity, with frequent stoppages. In June, Hisashi wrote his first diary entry:

> *Everything's going wrong, melting capability down to 45 ton [sic] per day, a quarter of standard output. Problems with the overhead cranes, the furnace bed, and shortages of electrodes and scrap metals, have*

brought the mill almost to a standstill, and making matters worse, labourers don't show up for work.

As production declined, he was sometimes despatched to commercial mills, such as Mitsubishi and Sumitomo, to collect scrap metals. But even if he managed to find materials, invariably there was no transport available.

Chapter 41

Nothing in Life is Permanent

Fly to Tokyo All Expenses Paid
Join US Army Air Corps

By now Tokyo and other Japanese cities were being repeatedly pounded by bombs. Six civilian raids between 25 February and 25 May razed the capital.*

The American strategists had decided to split the city into six grids, and aimed to burn 177 square kilometres over three months. Capable of carrying 44 000 kilograms of explosives, one B-29 could burn an area 600 by 150 metres, even more if it was windy. Specialising in high-level precision bombing, the B-29 pilots required clear visibility from an altitude of 9000 metres.

The bitter weather Hisashi had experienced when he first arrived at his posting also affected Tokyo. It snowed heavily during February, particularly on the twenty-second and again three days later before it thawed. Hindered by continual bad weather and poor visibility, the Americans decided they could wait no longer, so shelved the idea of precise bombing.

Operation 38, scheduled for 25 February, was based on the same tactics the US had applied over Germany. However, executed during a heavy snowstorm, it was an enormous challenge. Flying at altitudes ranging from 7 200 to 9 500 metres, 229 aircraft bombed Tokyo between 2.15 p.m. and 4.03 p.m. Visibility was so poor only 75 per cent of bombs landed on their designated target.

---

* Six raids were made on Tokyo: 25 February, 10 March, 13 and 15 April, 24 and 25 May.

All three squadrons had departed their respective island bases, with each B-29 flying independently to the meeting point, its flight path up to the pilot. They were to rendezvous at a specific time at specific coordinates just outside Tokyo, and from there work to a precise schedule, as to which aircraft went in first and from what direction. In addition to smoke and turbulence upsetting the timetable, variable arrival times meant many bombers had to wait while the others arrived, thus consuming precious fuel. Instructed to return to base in a group, some with insufficient fuel had to land in China, which was still under Japanese occupation.

* * *

For Hisashi, every day at the mill was usually a repeat of the one before, but several days remain indelibly etched in his memory.

While he slept on the night of 10 March, a series of explosions ravaged downtown Tokyo. Both the army and navy airforces had completely collapsed and ground cannons were now the main means of defence. With the Japanese counterattack deemed so little threat, the B-29s had been modified, with both armament and weaponry removed to increase their payload. When the 'all clear' sounded, Operation 40, the largest of the raids, had destroyed much of the city centre, including *Shitamachi*.

Early the following morning, Hisashi was ordered to go into Tokyo to collect usable parts from vehicles damaged in the raid.

> Soon after dawn they pull out of the plant. The sun rises higher, turning the snow into slush as the dun-coloured lorry lumbers along the rutted roads, jolting the 15 mechanics in the body of the vehicle. Hisashi sits in the cab beside the driver.
>
> A pall of smoke hangs over the city: the hostile landscape before them beyond recognition. Fires are still ablaze in a wasteland where only hours earlier thousands of homes and businesses had stood. Hisashi is incredulous, unable to acknowledge the reality and the

scale of damage before his eyes: a scene of death, destruction and desolation as far as he can see. House after house, street after street are obliterated. There is nothing but ash and charred remains, blackened tree stumps and a handful of survivors scavenging among the ruins. But worse is to follow.

He knows the neighbourhood where the massive iron Kototoi-*bashi* spans the Sumida-*gawa*. One side had been a high-class entertainment district, but businesses had long since closed and the *geisha* evacuated. The other side, not a particularly beautiful area, but peaceful, housed a hive of small factories that had still been operating, employing thousands of citizens. But not any more ...

The area has been cordoned off: no public, no press; military personnel only.

The bridge and the concrete banks are intact. But there are no trees visible, no vegetation of any sort. Apart from several crumbling concrete walls, everything else is flattened; everything burnt, black against the snow. There is no bird song; no movement. The only sound that breaks the silence is running water from a broken factory tap. And Hisashi and his men are the only people alive.

Black watermelons, unrecognisable as human heads, and limbs like logs of wood, lie scattered around them. Hisashi wants to fulfil his duty as an officer, to show no emotion, but he trembles with shock, his pulse racing as, bewildered and battered, he holds back his tears.

It appears that residents had fled in the dark, trying to outrun an insatiable blaze. They had rushed to the bridge from both sides, colliding in the middle, unable to pass. Some burned, but many did not. To escape they plunged into the freezing water. The tide was out, but the water, less than a metre deep, was only 2°C. Hypothermia quickly set in, and falling unconscious, the people drowned.

It is now mid-tide and the mud flats can be seen at the edge of the concrete banks. Under the bridge the river is littered with corpses, mostly face down, floating side by side like timber in a millpond, while on the mud flats lie hundreds more. Swollen with gas and dressed in civilian uniform, they look like life-size balloon dolls, with deep grooves where their rucksack straps fasten; on some their burned and bloodied clothes hanging in tatters.

The water is gentle, the bodies quietly adrift under the dull, smoke-filled sky. A young woman, face down, floats aimlessly, a baby tied to her back. Its pale face is peaceful and serene, as if it is asleep.

In his mind's eye, Hisashi could see the terror: civilians, laden with baggage, many pulling *tansu* crammed with belongings, some on bicycles towing carts, blocking the congested bridge. Hotter and hotter, roaring, greedy flames would have pursued them from both sides of the bridge, closing in. They could not go forward. They could not go back. Everything on the bridge would have caught fire in an instant, leaving no choice but for the terrified citizens to trample over bodies, baggage and furniture. Many would have jumped off the bridge, enveloped in flames. Some would have survived the fall, but heavily clothed, were unable to swim. The baby, its hips brushed by the freezing water would have cried on its mother's back, then, the mother would have succumbed …

It had been lunchtime when Hisashi and the men arrived, so he ordered them to sit on the concrete bank to eat. Legs dangling over the side, one of them spotted the precious gumboots of a corpse below, saying that if he stood in the shallow mud at the bottom of the bank he could easily reach them. An uncomfortable silence followed Hisashi's refusal, but the man obeyed, and finished his lunch.

Returning to base by a different route, the men had been quiet. More charred, smouldering bodies were to be seen lying in heaps beside what was Asakusa-*eki*. At another intersection, a fire truck had been incinerated, those in her cremated. The water cannon lay aimed in vain at invisible buildings, its hose still connected to the hydrant but burnt like a coil of wire. As they passed Senso-*ji*, the sun was sinking. The day before, dozens of small souvenir shops had lined the lane leading to the temple, but now the only thing etched on the dusky horizon was the concrete wall that previously backed the shops. Hisashi wanted to weep, recalling the time when he had visited as a small boy with *otosan*, just before they watched the fireworks over the Sumida-*gawa*.

Incendiaries measuring 1 665 metric tonnes* had been jettisoned over the target area of 29 square kilometres, east of the palace along the Sumida-*gawa*. The Americans had correctly estimated it to be the most densely populated neighbourhood.

February's bad weather had continued into early March, and then, at last, good weather was forecast. The people of Tokyo had enjoyed a fine day on 9 March.

At 12.03 a.m. the following morning, in ideal conditions of a 20-knot westerly wind, reconnaissance Pathfinders had crisscrossed the city, marking the four target areas. They dropped a napalm bomb every 33 metres to form an enormous burning X. Following behind were 325 B-29 bombers.

Learning from their mistakes of 25 February, the US forces had changed their plan of attack. They chose a night-time raid when weak searchlights would give poor visibility for Japanese fighters and ground cannons. A hundred additional bombers had been deployed, and the altitude had been reduced drastically. The 9 000-metre flying height used over Dresden was too high for Tokyo as the jet stream in tropical climates disturbed cruising speeds, increased fuel consumption and affected accuracy. Neither were the bombers required to meet before the attack and bombing could begin as soon as they arrived. Each pilot could decide his return route.

Above the inferno, aircrews had observed and plotted the progress of the four fires. After 40 minutes, fanned by the westerly, each fire was 400 metres long. But soon they raged out of control. At 90 minutes, new flames were recorded, then more and more. The result was over

---

* 3 683 M47A2s (220-kilogram bombs), 3 548 E46s (1 100-kilogram bombs) and 4 971 E28s (1 100 kilogram bombs), a total of 1 665 tonnes.

target, and nearly 26 square kilometres of the city had been reduced to ashes. Pilots reported the smell of burning flesh was so overwhelming crews had to wear oxygen masks to keep from vomiting.

However, not all had gone to plan for the attackers. They had bombed east to west against the wind, so that smoke from the first bombs would not disturb the planes following. But in the gale, smoke from the first wave had covered the area, drifting as high as 7 000 metres, far higher than their flying heights of 1 500 to 2 800 metres. With drop points difficult to find, pilots had jettisoned their cargo before the target. Added to that, the fire draughts were so fierce, turbulence lifted the bombers like leaves, 600 or even 900 metres higher, further reducing visibility, and prolonging the operation. Even so, 86 per cent of bombs were dropped on target.

Japanese Imperial Headquarters announced on the radio that a few fires had been caused, but they were successfully extinguished.

The Sumida-*gawa* flows into Tokyo Bay, so for weeks, decomposed bodies washed ashore. Counting the dead was always difficult on such an occasion, but the death toll of over a 100 000 ranks with that of the Dresden raid of 13–14 February (and later with Hiroshima). Hisashi wanted to know what had happened to the bodies under the bridge. He heard that within three days they were gone, presumably taken to the nearest surviving temple and burnt. At the same time, over 1.5 million people were injured, and 250 000 buildings were lost.

The weather gradually improved, and on 13 April, while what was left of Tokyo enjoyed spring warmth and cherry blossom, President Roosevelt died. That same day, 352 bombers attacked the city again, with 93 per cent success; two days later, Operation 69 was 91 per cent accurate. In this raid, there were only 120 bombers, the others diverted to Okinawa. But between the two raids, another 27 square kilometres of Tokyo went up in flames.

A new Japanese cabinet, led by Admiral Kantaro Suzuki, was formed that April.

The admiral father of one of Hisashi's friends wrote in his diary:

'US raids have intensified, and those staying in Tokyo must be prepared to die, their fate as perilous as candle light exposed to the wind. Japan is now confronted with the weakening struggles caused by the arrogant extremists.'

In parallel with civilian raids, military facilities continued to be targeted.

> One night, just after midnight, a sudden flash lights the sky to noonday brightness. Loud blasts wake Hisashi abruptly, his room shaking as in an earthquake. Sitting bolt upright, his mouth is dry and his heart pounding. Judging by the sound of the departing bombers, he thinks there are probably six aircraft, and given this is a military site, he knows each will have dropped a 500-kilogram bomb. He dresses quickly, grabs his lamp and rushes outside into an atmosphere knotted with terror and despair; his nostrils immediately fill with the stench of burnt flesh.
>
> Out of the darkness, more candle lamps appear, and by their joint light, he can tell one of the dormitories he supervises has been gutted by the blast. Surviving boys are weeping. He feels breathless. Short sentences jerk out of him. There is no blaze to spread to other buildings, but small fires have been ignited by the explosives; clothes, *futon* and blackout curtains set alight. In the moonless night, they cannot see how bad it is, so nothing much can be done other than give first aid to any injured they can find, and organise for survivors to be shifted into undamaged buildings. Then, for a couple of hours it is eerily quiet.

Stationed in Japan, Hisashi had not expected the war to come so close, and it brought a sharp reminder that this was what his comrades experienced daily on the battlefield.

> In the pink light of dawn, he sees the remains of what was once the dormitory silhouetted obscenely against the rising sun. At the first shock he is too confused to think. Having seen the results of raids in

Tokyo, he thought he was prepared and had steeled himself for what lay ahead. However, as he knows the boys who have been killed, this is personal. Being a Sunday morning, some are away on their time off, but 50 boys have perished, and others have been critically injured.

Everyone is milling around, waiting for him to take charge. Wispy plumes of smoke rise from the ground littered with body parts, fragments of glass, and charred timber.

This is by far the most difficult day of his service, and while outwardly he is in control, inside he feels nauseous and his mind screams in horror. Ordered to have the coffins filled and closed by 9 a.m., he sets to mechanically. He organises to have the wooden caskets brought over from the warehouse, which always has a supply on hand.

Then, with volunteers who search through the rubble, body parts are collected and reassembled. He has to ensure that each coffin contains a body with two arms, two legs and one head. But, it cannot matter whether they match, as the parts will be bound together in white bandages, no one will be any the wiser. Supervising his men, he waits for instruction as to what to do with the coffins. Will they be returned to Formosa, or burned locally? He wonders how the Formosan parents will be notified, and is glad it is not his responsibility.

With parts still buried or burnt beyond recognition, several bodies cannot be completed, so he orders his men to bandage thick sticks in place of the missing arms and legs, and to use kettles for two missing heads.

He wants to turn away from the sight, but at the same time he is held in a dreadful fascination by the row upon row of coffins with their anonymous mummy-like corpses. For those not injured, work continues as if nothing has happened.

The factory next door had been the intended target. It was the only one of its kind and manufactured precision instruments. It suffered massive damage and was out of action for the remainder of the war.

American planes, larger than fighters, but smaller than bombers, began flying over the peninsula more frequently. Once, the plant was attacked in daylight, but then they had sufficient warning to organise everyone into the caves dug in the hills nearby: each young officer responsible for 30 men.

> The droning reaches them first, then the squadron of small bombers comes into sight. Approaching singly from different directions and swooping low, they pitch and swerve, vapour trails streaking the sky. Quickly dropping their cargo, they flee back to their mother ship. Bombs erupt in a shower over the mill, their sinister whistles followed by explosions.
>
> One shell scores a direct hit on the labourers' canteen, a little too close to the entrance of the cave where Hisashi's group is hiding. Watching it hurtling towards them, he thinks he might die. One minute the building is there, then in a matter of seconds it is flattened; an enormous crater in its place. The detonation is deafening. The heat in the cave is stifling, and amid the clouds of acrid smoke, the teenagers panic.

Amazingly, there were no casualties, the canteen having emptied after lunch. Hisashi was badly shaken, but in the ensuing confusion there was no time to be upset. Instinctively he got on with the job, and for days was occupied with getting the area cleared and reopening the canteen.

On 24 May, the B-29 bombers returned and Tokyo was hammered once again. With 564 aircraft it was the biggest onslaught yet, with many of the planes having recently been released from the European front. Ninety-two per cent were on target.

The next night of 25 May, Hisashi was on duty, his roster having been changed to nightshift after the dorm was destroyed. As usual, the noise in the mill was deafening, the humidity high, and the ever-present dust swirled. At 11 p.m. he went outside.

It was a fine night with a perfect full moon, no wind, and the air heavy with moisture. Forty kilometres away, the sky over Tokyo glowed red. He strained his ears, but heard only the routine hum of the mill, and the drone of aircraft carrying out test runs nearby. Military radio briefly reported Tokyo was under fire, and next morning Imperial Headquarters announced there had been another air raid. But with much on his mind, Hisashi thought little more about it.

Operation 183 was the last of the Tokyo raids, the final charge that targeted the central business districts. Determined to make a clean sweep, bomb numbers had doubled, and between 10.38 p.m. and 1.00 a.m., in a stable air stream, 502 aircraft dropped 3 646 tonnes of bombs. With 92 per cent accuracy over an 8.5-kilometre area, they claimed nearly 80 000 victims.*

A few days later, Jinjiro appeared at the mill. Travelling anywhere in Japan required copious permits stamped with red seals to justify one's presence in a specific place. But it was easier for Jinjiro to visit Hisashi, as his job entitled him to carry identification that granted access to all naval facilities, as well as priority to board public transport. The shortage of fuel for trains, and electricity for trams meant access to transport was at a premium. Passengers, even if they could get a ticket, usually waited endlessly for a train or tram.

Jinjiro's pass was closely scrutinised at the gate, and as directed, he followed the boundary fence to the furnace. A messenger was sent to fetch Hisashi.

Otosan's visit was so unexpected Hisashi knew something was wrong. Fearing the worst, his heart sank and he stared at his father, unable even to say hello. Shorter than Hisashi remembered, Jinjiro appeared to be barely holding his emotions in check. He explained that their house had been destroyed, but fortunately he, *okasan* and Yayoi were unhurt. Shocked and worried about his family's future, Jinjiro was angry, saying it was time the military acknowledged themselves beaten: shaken that still they talked a web of lies.

---

* It was the second highest death toll.

Hisashi had many questions but, being on duty, he was allowed only 15 minutes. How had they escaped? Had they somewhere to live? Was there anything he could do?

They had fled to the tram-driver's house, which had not been touched, just 500 metres short of the burning carpet. Everything else was being arranged by Jinjiro's office. The very thing Hisashi had anticipated months earlier when he stood in his empty bedroom had happened. But fortunately they were lucky, and had all survived.

Just after 10.30 p.m., Jinjiro, Ryoko and Yayoi hear the familiar, ominous buzz, and the air soon filled with the powerful throbbing of the bombers. Japanese defence is so weak the B-29s are flying lower and lower. The air raid siren has been ringing for some time, and an hour earlier, national radio had announced a squadron approaching. As usual they have had time to prepare, but they have never been affected before so, thinking it will be the same again, they stay in the house.

Hyu~hyu~hyu. Shu~shu~shu. Bombs rain down, Jinjiro yells out. Lying face down on the *tatami*, they close their eyes, and cover their ears. *Go~Go~Go* (booming), *Zushin~Zushin~Zushin* (thumping), *Gura~Gura~Gura* (shaking). As if the heavens are splitting, a bomb explodes directly across the street. They can feel the fearful heat. Their eardrums feel like bursting. Suddenly, air raid drilling is uppermost in their minds and, fitted out in *zukku* and anti-air raid hoods, they run from the house with their rucksacks.

Unable to resist, they turn briefly. Oil from the bombs drips onto their upturned faces and stings their eyes. Smoke rises from under the eaves of the house opposite, then, instantly ablaze, it is lifted effortlessly into the air. Separated by only the width of the street the blaze, fanned by the strong breeze, moves menacingly towards them. Red tongues of fire burst in all directions, leaping the road, ever changing, never resting. The house next door is immediately wrapped in a shroud of flames, its roof caving in to send furious pillars of fire into the reddening sky. Within seconds their own house is alight. Jinjiro bows deeply to the house, as in a matter of moments their home of 20 years is devoured.

They run for their lives, the air so thick with embers, heat, smoke and bomb oil, it is difficult to breathe. Through chinks in the clouds, now in, now out of sight, the bombers glow orange. The air-raid siren continues to wail. Spreading like wildfire, block after block of buildings succumb, and walls of flames block their way. Suddenly they are pushed through the air, caught by a whirlwind,* and debris flies towards them. Holding fast to a telephone pole, Jinjiro decides when it is best to run with the wind. From pole to pole, they race the flames, finally reaching the bare ground of a firebreak where he thinks they will be safe.

A pale flashing light appears, and then another, as wardens with other residents tied together, also reach safety. Where minutes earlier there has been a community, now, their homes, the roads, rice paddies, ploughed fields, even the reservoir Ryoko helped to dig, are gone.

On through the night the 'burning carpet' blazes, lighting the darkness and consuming everything in its path. The black silhouetted pagoda of Zojo-ji† floats on a sea of flames. Slowly subsiding, it is reborn a radiant golden ball.

That first night, after ensuring the fire has changed direction, Jinjiro takes his family to the tram-driver's house, relieved they will not have to sleep in the open

The fire brigade did the best it could, but the area was virtually levelled. In Shinjuku, the Isetan Department store stood alone.

The worst had happened. But the local *tonari-gumi* was prepared, and people knew what they were supposed to do. In the aftermath everything was orderly. The nearby temple, that had already been designated the temporary morgue, had been protected by its garden,

---

* A whirlwind peculiar to the conflagration caused by bombs.
† Zojo-ji is the Tokugawa family temple.

the burning carpet having stopped just short of its boundary. The priest and his family had been evacuated months earlier, but the resident caretaker had been left in charge.

> As dawn breaks, survivors arrive with their dead: in their arms, slung between two people, loaded on carts, dragged on tin signboards; using anything they can find to bring forth bodies and dismembered parts. The caretaker has stripped every *tatami* from the temple, placing them outside in the rear garden where male victims are to be laid. The wooden floor inside is allotted to females and children. Jinjiro and Ryoko help in the reception area, which has been set up to handle enquiries, while others do their best to identify and label the corpses.

Next day the bodies were removed by the police.

A quiet settled over the city, which was now half its original size: 90 square kilometres had been snuffed out.* Then, on 29 May, most of Yokohama was destroyed.

---

* Half of the American target.

Chapter 42

Bear the Unbearable

Gun-mo zo o nazu
A group of blind men feeling an elephant

Y<small>AYOI WAS EVACUATED</small> back to Sendai. All large industrial cities and many smaller towns had virtually been destroyed. Tokyo, Yokohama, Kawasaki, Kobe, Nagoya and Osaka were battered and beaten: roads and buildings blotted from the landscape. So many had been killed, and so many homes and livelihoods lost. There was no hope of victory, but still the government stood firm, and Imperial Headquarters prepared for an invasion.

Bombed almost to impotence, Japan's only option would be to fight a suicidal battle, with every available person and weapon rallied for one final clash. Alongside the two million or so military combatants who served on the mainland, and the four million military civilian employees, nearly 60 million citizens would form suicide waves. There would be a *kaiten* in every waterway, and all remaining aircraft would dive bomb the 'barbarian hordes'. It was rumoured that cyanide tablets would be distributed to the populace.

In their final thrust to subjugate Japan, the Allies were planning for a massive amphibious assault. That coming autumn, Operation Olympic was to land on the southern coast of Kyushu, the southernmost island of Japan, while simultaneously deploying a feint attack off the island of Shikoku. Six months later, in the early spring of 1946, Operation Coronet would invade east of Tokyo, the entire armed might of America supported by units of the British Commonwealth, including the United Kingdom, India, Australia and New Zealand.

By June, American planes were flying over Tokyo twice weekly and scattering leaflets written in the Japanese language. The leaflets claimed Japan had lost fighting power, that American forces were preparing to invade, and that people should campaign to convince their government to surrender. The Japanese authorities denied everything. Nevertheless people worried the claims were true, though recognised that persuading the government was beyond their control.

By July, there were few remaining targets to bomb. Several historic cities had been spared, as were the cities of Niigata, Kokura, Nagasaki and Hiroshima.

As detailed plans for the invasion of Japan were being prepared, the results of the Manhattan Project were revealed to President Truman. The project, finished by the end of 1944, was secretly and successfully tested in July 1945. The day after testing, a conference was being held at Potsdam, Germany, between the new President Harry S. Truman, British Prime Minister Winston Churchill, and Soviet leader Joseph Stalin to discuss the rebuilding of Europe and the defeat of Japan. It was to be the last time the 'Big Three' met as Allies. Stalin agreed to declare war on Japan on 7 August, and to join forces with the invasion. However, there was another plan that Truman shared with Churchill only.

Churchill left the conference on 25 July, returning to London for the British national elections. Swept from power, he was replaced by Labour leader Attlee, who duly travelled to Potsdam on 28 July. The Potsdam Declaration, giving the Japanese a choice between 'unconditional surrender' or 'prompt and utter destruction' had been issued on 26 July. With surrender unacceptable, the Japanese delayed to gain time, 'ignoring [the declaration] with silence'. With a Neutrality Pact having been signed with Russia in 1941, they believed the Soviets would help them sue for peace.

The B-29, Enola Gay, takes off on its secret mission from Tinian Island in the South Pacific at 2.45 a.m. on 6 August. Its destination

> is Hiroshima. On board is the 20 000-kilogram atomic bomb nicknamed 'Little Boy'. Flying farther behind are two observation planes carrying cameras and scientific instruments.
>
> Reaching Hiroshima around 7.30 a.m., Enola Gay circles in the cloudless sky. Then at 8.15 plus 17 seconds, the bomb-bay doors open and 'Little Boy' plummets from the plane. The bombers leave quickly to watch from safety, while the parachutes open and 'Little Boy' floats gently down.

Like the Japanese at Pearl Harbour, the Americans had given no warning, in case American prisoners were moved to the target area.

On the ground, sirens had sounded at 7.15 a.m., sparked by an American weather plane. But people had become accustomed to the plane flying over at this time, so it caused no concern. They ignored the warnings and the three B-29s that followed.

On 5 August 1945, the city of Hiroshima had a population of around 230 000, a third of its people having already been evacuated. The following day, at least half of the population was dead or dying.

> With a blinding flash, 'Little Boy' detonates 200 metres above the city centre. At the instant of detonation, the temperature at the hypocentre exceeds 1 000 000°C. The sky burns at white heat, generating a demoniacal fireball, which no power on earth can bind. The heat is so intense it melts granite.
>
> Temperatures on the surface reach 5 000°C, the searing flashes and whirlwinds wreaking inconceivable damage. Flames rush through the city, burning and crushing everything within three kilometres of the hypocentre. In less than four seconds, 60 per cent of Hiroshima is annihilated.
>
> A massive mushroom-shaped cloud rises above the wasteland. Then, 30 minutes later, black radioactive rain begins to fall. Thousands upon thousands of people are killed, with most never identified.

A new word – fallout – had entered the English language. Those within a kilometre of the hypocentre received life-threatening doses of radiation. An estimated 70 000 died instantly in the blast, but the circle of death spread outwards, with thousands more dying daily from deadly burns. A report published in 1946 put the death toll at 118 661. But later estimates, taking into account those dying of radiation, claim the toll was as high as 200 000.

According to Truman's ultimatum, a second bomb would be detonated unless Japan surrendered. But again the deadline passed. American planes dropped more leaflets over major centres informing people other cities would be destroyed if the government did not end the war.

On 8 August, Japanese diplomats appealed to the Soviets to help bring about a peaceful settlement. The Soviets responded with a declaration of war. Russian troops invaded Manchuria the next day, meeting little resistance from the Japanese army. But so great was their fear of losing face, the Japanese extremists would still not admit defeat.

On 9 August, carrying 'Fat Man' in its bomb-bay, another B-29 set off from Tinian, this time bound for the city of Kokura. But Kokura was covered in haze so the plane was diverted to Nagasaki. 'Fat Man', nearly twice as powerful as 'Little Boy', descended on the unsuspecting city, exploding at 11.02 a.m. An estimated 75 000 inhabitants died: a number that increased to 150 000 in the years that followed.

Reasons abound as to why the bombs were dropped. Two stand out. America wanted to force Japan's surrender as quickly as possible, and before the Soviets declared war against Japan. Dropping the bombs would quicken the end of the war and minimise Allied fatalities. What is more, it gave the Americans an opportunity to measure the bomb's effectiveness in an actual attack. Exploding in daylight against cities less damaged by conventional bombing, the full force of the explosion would be seen. It was thought the Japanese would be so shocked they would surrender. But as usual the Japanese government had not fully informed the people.

The day after the Hiroshima bombing, Imperial Headquarters announced that a new type of bomb had been dropped. Mentioned with their regular news bulletin, nobody was particularly concerned. Following Nagasaki however, the government formally protested against the bomb, claiming it to be an inhumane weapon that violated international law.

The next day the media reported the protest, and for the first time the public were informed that they had been attacked by atomic bombs. However, described as *pika don*,* the report gave people no idea of the scale of the disasters.

Faced with such devastation, along with a declaration of war by the Soviet Union, Japan had little room for hope. Furthermore, the war had continued far longer than anyone had envisaged, and the nation's war debt was astronomical. Many politicians wanted to surrender, but the government was divided.

The country was still governed by the 'Big Six', a supreme war council, the most powerful person among them the War Minister. Three of the six – Prime Minister Suzuki, Foreign Minister Togo and Navy Minister Admiral Yonai – were prepared to surrender: the War Minister, General Anami; the Army Chief of Staff, General Umezu; and the Navy Chief of Staff, Admiral Toyoda, were not. Japan still held Indochina, the Dutch East Indies and the Chinese coasts, and General Anami was sure 'our 100 million people are ready to die with honour'. Convinced the Allies would rid Japan of the Emperor, they preferred to fight to the death.

As they were unable to agree, Prime Minister Suzuki called a full cabinet meeting; however, it also was divided. The impasse could be resolved only by the Emperor.

At midnight of 9 August, the Emperor met with the Supreme Councillors in his underground shelter. Yet again, all arguments were heard, but still the ministers were at odds.

---

* A twinkle of light in the sky accompanied by the sound of an explosion.

Finally, at 2 a.m., Emperor Hirohito directed his ministers to agree to Allied demands.

Cables were sent to the Allies. Japan would accept the Potsdam Declaration, but wanted to retain the Emperor as Head of State. Truman prepared a vaguely worded reply.

The news got out and a group of intransigent, young army officers conspired to stop negotiations. Rumours of a coup spread. But once again Emperor Hirohito called for peace.

The Imperial Rescript of Surrender was recorded by the Emperor on to a waxed disc for broadcasting on NHK the next day.

As coup leaders searched desperately for the disc, others attempted to assassinate the supporters of surrender, including the Prime Minister. They failed. The coup collapsed, and its leaders killed themselves in front of the palace.

That night, in the corridor outside his quarters and attended by his brother-in-law, the War Minister also committed *seppuku*.

> After drinking his final *sake*, General Anami kneels, facing the Palace. Shoving his sword into his stomach, he slashes to the right, then straight up. With his dagger, he severs his carotid artery. His white shirt, a gift from the Emperor, is soon sodden with blood.
>
> For two hours he remains in position, declining his brother-in-law's offer to decapitate him. Eventually, when the General crumples, his brother-in-law stabs him to death in the neck, and covers him with his tunic, which is weighted with medals.
>
> In front of the *tokonoma* beside a photograph of his dead soldier son, is Anami's resignation letter, a poem he had written, and his will that begins with the words: 'Believing firmly that our sacred land will never perish, I – with my death – humbly apologise to the Emperor for the great crime [Japan's defeat].'

The sun shone high in a cloudless blue sky on 15 August in Tokyo. Around 9 a.m., military radio reported that a special announcement would be made by the Emperor at noon. Never before had the people heard the Emperor speak, so they knew this was important news. Everyone expected the announcement to be about ending the war, but by now, knowing Japan could not win, they expected a cease-fire.

> Like many people all over Japan, Hisashi and others from the steel mill assemble outside. In the dusty quad, tension mounts. It is very hot. Sunshine streams over their shoulders, and sweat trickles down their faces and backs.
>
> Preceded by a screech, then the naval march, and a brief introduction by Prime Minister Suzuki, the sacred voice of the Emperor comes and goes through the crackling loudspeakers. Though the court language is unfamiliar and difficult to understand, the message is clear, as the Emperor encourages his people to 'bear the unbearable, and endure the unendurable'. His voice wavers with emotion, and Hisashi has the impression he has tears in his eyes. Contrary to their expectations, his words mean Japan will surrender without condition and, as a final caution, the Emperor urges that there be no *kamikaze* action.

The Japanese public had expected a cease-fire, but by surrendering, Japan was admitting defeat.

> Strained by weeks of rumour, the people have been aware the end is coming, but still it is a shock.
>
> Hisashi, lost in thought, fixes his eyes on top of the surrounding hills. Under the sun, they are vivid green and, much to his amazement, several dazzling white flags flutter in the breeze, startling and dramatic against the blue sky. It is an impressive display and he wonders vaguely who has staged it. He had never expected white flags arranged in advance.
>
> His cap lies damp on his forehead, and his clothes are wet with sweat. His feelings are mixed. On the one hand he feels a huge release, and he is relieved to hear the harsh days are over. His family has got

Reading in the pre-war style, right to left, top down:
1) August 15 1945
2) Asahi Shimbun Press Company
3) Emperor sympathises with victims of the new bomb
4) Japanese Empire accepts the Four Allied nations notice
5) Emperor Showa says Japan will have to 'bear the unbearable' accepting this as the beginning of eternal peace
6) Emperor issues notice regarding termination of the war
(As in all articles at the time the words ultimatum and defeat were deliberately avoided)

off lightly. Why should he not have a happy life, rather than having to devote himself to the Empire's cause? But at the same time, he reels with anxiety, distressed that Japan has lost. Then, pragmatically he wonders what on earth to do the very next moment.

Round about him, Japanese workers wait for instruction. Then, spontaneously, en masse, the Formosan boys burst into song, a Soviet Labour Day song, forbidden for being anti-Emperor. Losing the war, Japan will no longer rule Formosa. Unrest erupts and, transforming into a mob, the boys go berserk, rampaging through the nearby fields.

For several hours, Hisashi felt completely disconnected. Voices drifted around him, but he did not hear the words. He returned to the mill, his head 'white-coloured', his mind adrift, and with only the vaguest idea of what to do next. What would happen to them all? All of a sudden he felt exhausted and, despite the heat, a shiver ran from his neck, deep into his heart.

Part Four

Giri to His Name

A PATTERN OF LIFE VASTLY DIFFERENT from the one Hisashi had led before the war emerged; that previous life all but a dream. Like Japan, Hisashi was irrevocably changed.

Chapter 43

Zero Year

Oi mo wakaki mo nasutokoro wo shirazu
Neither elder brother, nor younger brother
(Utter confusion)

THE PEOPLE OF JAPAN now faced military occupation, the government subject to the authority of SCAP [the Supreme Commander for the Allied Powers]. Occupation, although officially an Allied responsibility, in reality would be led by the United States.* As Supreme Commander, American General Douglas MacArthur would preside over GHQ [General Headquarters]. But it would not be until 24 September that SCAP would issue its first official orders; in the interim, Japan struggled with the concepts of surrender and defeat.

War had lasted so long it had become the norm. Since the Manchurian Incident on 18 September 1931, until 15 August 1945, the people of Japan had devoted their lives to the Japanese dream. For many like Yayoi, ten years younger than Hisashi, war was the only world they knew.

And for so long having believed the military was invincible, defeat was a traumatic blow. However, with a dazed passivity, the majority accepted their new circumstances. Hisashi had assumed surrender would be months away, but judging by the speed with which things started to happen, he realised the occupation schedule had been

---

* The Allied Powers included Australia, Canada, China, France, India, Great Britain, New Zealand, the Netherlands, the Philippines, the Soviet Union and the United States.

prepared well in advance. It seemed everyone except the Japanese had been aware of Japan's imminent defeat.

The day after the Emperor's announcement, Prime Minister Suzuki and his Cabinet resigned. The Emperor appointed his uncle, Prince Naruhiko Higashikuni, to take office in the interim. Hisashi surmised it was merely a show of 'good face'. If the wartime government stayed in power, the Allies would probably take a tougher stance.

No Japanese army had ever been defeated by foreigners. Losing the war humiliated the Emperor's sacred reign, and in the days to follow, scores of civilians all over Japan committed suicide in apology.

In Tokyo, on the plaza near the double bridge that spanned the moat and led into the inner grounds of the Imperial Palace, bodies of civilians lay face down in a tidy row, etiquette scrupulously observed in their final moments. Hundreds of others sat and wept. Over waters filled with golden carp, oblivious to the picture above, swans glided beneath the granite bridge.

Rather than submit to the humiliation of foreign rule, thousands of military personnel performed *seppuku*.

The headlines on 15 August had said little:

>Emperor declares termination of the war
>
>With tears of blood Japan accepts
>the Four Powers Declaration
>
>Hearing the Emperor's affectionate words,
>we 100 million Japanese mingle our tears

Cabinet had reluctantly accepted the outcome of the war, but was not going to lose face by admitting surrender or defeat. Articles referred to *shusen* (the termination of war) rather than *kofuku* (surrender) or *haisen* (defeat); and to *shinchu-gun* (stationary troops) rather than *senryo-gun* (occupation forces). Every article in every newspaper was written in a similar vein, full of old-style platitudes, flowery euphemisms and bureaucratic speak, avoiding the forbidden words. The wartime cabinet was still in power and hiding behind the traditional curtain of authority. People could see the foreign troops arriving, but no one was telling them what was going on. There were no government orders, and nothing from SCAP.

The 40 days between surrender and SCAP's first orders seemed endless, and Hisashi felt as if he existed in a vacuum. Who was the leader? Who was responsible? There were no more bombs. The relief was wonderful. But there was no purpose and people were incapable of managing their affairs. It was *kyo-datsu-jotai* (a state of postwar lethargy).

Somehow life continued. In Tokyo, trams and trains ran on the loop line, newspapers were printed, radio was broadcast, and power was disrupted intermittently only. Everyone was busy surviving, collecting food and seeking shelter. But still reliant on the old ways, they expected the government to guide them; though in reality there was no government to look after them.

In the emptiness of those 40 days, there was little trouble. The Emperor had called on his people to be calm and courteous, and they would obey implicitly. People felt suspicious, but generally they were cooperative. The American troops were baffled. They did not understand that the Emperor had changed the principle of *giri* to fit the new conditions. Up until the time of surrender, *giri* demanded that soldiers and citizens fight to the death. With his broadcast, he had changed the rules, so the people of Japan welcomed their occupiers. The sudden change of face, swinging from foe to friend was nothing new. It was 'the Japanese Way'.

At the naval factory, nerves were stretched as Hisashi and the other naval and civilian workers awaited their fate. No one had any idea about what was going to happen, and the plant was rife with rumours. Then, out of the blue, memos from the occupation forces started to arrive. Production was to cease.

Physically the plant looked the same. It had the same layout and was the same size and the same colour as before. But the atmosphere was gloomy and empty of purpose. Overhead, the pitiless sun revealed every detail of an almost abandoned site. There was no smoke, no movement of vehicles. Buildings and machines stood silent.

For Hisashi, however, there was no easing off. He got up at the same time and meals continued as before. Usual plant activities might have stopped, but his days were just as busy. Young officers were burdened with umpteen duties. As well as supervising the exodus of labourers, they did clerical work and replaced the regular guards, who had simply disappeared.

SCAP, afraid of mob riots, wanted all groups dispersed as quickly as possible. With the exception of the military, crowds bigger than 20 were prohibited. On the Miura Peninsula, out of the some 100 000 naval workers, nearly half were labourers, and thousands were moved out each night by rail. During the day, the one and only train ran exclusively for the occupation forces, transporting their equipment and soldiers. Knowing little of use was left in Japan, the Americans were bringing everything with them.

There was plenty of talk: talk of reparation, talk of trials for war crimes, talk that SCAP would freeze the bank accounts of military personnel. Senior officers withdrew their savings. Hisashi overhead them discussing how clever they had been, claiming they had been civilians. He would have liked to do the same, but could not find the time, and soon his bank account containing nine months' wages was cleaned out.

Hisashi had even heard talk that all Japanese citizens would be reduced to *hinin* status. But, underpinning all the speculation was the question: would Japan remain responsible for its own affairs, or would the Americans overthrow the government? Rumour had it that, as in Germany, Japan would be divided: Honshu under American occupation, Hokkaido under Russian, Shikoku under British, and Kyushu under the Chinese. People were talking of moving to the zone occupied by their preferred country.

At the end of August, Hisashi began to write regularly in his diary.

Aware it could be read by others, his entries were brief, and he avoided anything too personal, expressing more sensitive thoughts on scraps of paper, which he hid among his correspondence. His second diary entry, 31 August 1945, read:

> From August 15th until today, I've been busy distributing rationed goods to labourers. Their exodus takes priority, starting with the Formosans. Clerical staff and senior officers are stealing furnishings and office equipment.

The gates of the plant had stood open around the clock during wartime. Now they were shut overnight. However, the first week, taking advantage of the lack of control, friends and family of senior personnel waited with carts and bicycles for the gates to open. With tacit consent, furniture, stationery, 'Tiger' hand calculators, filing cabinets, desks, anything portable, disappeared. With the military disbanded, naval property belonged to no one. Better that things be retained among the Japanese than left for the Americans, so to them it was not stealing. Hisashi, though, was shocked at the behaviour.

After 15 August, junior officers had been shifted off-site to live in temporary dormitories in Yokosuka city, 20 minutes away by train. Travelling daily, Hisashi observed the increasing American presence as jeeps, trucks, bulldozers and construction vehicles kept rolling in. Small parties of soldiers were everywhere, guiding newcomers, or parking at crossroads watching the traffic. Many of the first arrivals were Japanese faces, *Nisei* (American-born Japanese) from the west coast of America or Hawaii.

Tens of thousands more soldiers were to follow and were stationed in the cities. Providing facilities to feed and house so many was not easy. Hotels were requisitioned for senior staff, commercial buildings for administration, and sports grounds for camps, depots and hospitals. To assist, the Japanese had collected thousands of hospital beds and cutlery. But the beds were too small and, in any case, the Americans had brought their own cots and cutlery.

It is late afternoon and sweltering. Tired and sticky, Hisashi wants a bath. He has night duty so is going back to the dorm for the hours in between. Before leaving the plant he has changed into civilian dress. A memo from GHQ has stipulated uniforms are not to be worn outside military installations; nor are officers permitted to wear their swords.

As he walks from the station, he notices that the streets are alive, with everyone out enjoying their freedom. Snatches of childish laughter reach his ears. Around the corner a jeep moves slowly, its two passengers standing to scatter chewing gum and chocolate to the shabbily dressed children following behind. He stops to watch. The GIs, tall and strong, in caps and well-pressed khaki, wear open-necked shirts, and there are no weapons in sight. Smiling widely, the soldiers seem to enjoy the children's glee. A laughing mother waves her baby's hand at the soldiers. Hisashi's head is in a whirl. Watching the Americans' antics, and the unconcerned innocence of the children, he feels even more insecure than usual. What are the Americans thinking behind their amused expressions?

Constantly in a state of suspense, he worried about the future: how he would get through all his work; when and how he would get back home; whether he would even get back home.

Rumours were multiplying. It was said that all servicemen in Japan would be sent to clean up the battlefields in Asia. He was worried that, if he was thrown into forced labour, he might starve or become sick and die. His most immediate concern was how to send his personal belongings home, and the letter he must write to his parents. He had already begun forming the words in his head.

> Go-ryoshin-sama (*my respected parents*)
> I may be unable to return home. I am expecting to be interned as a prisoner of war. Forced to work outside Japan for the Allied Forces, I may die from sickness or starvation. Thank you for your long years of care. I apologise for my premature death and for leaving you without

my support. I apologise for not meeting your expectations.

Hisashi

The new Prime Minister held a press conference on 28 August to announce he would uphold 'national polity', meaning he would retain the Imperial political structure. '*Ichioku so zange,*' the newspaper declared; '100 million confessions'. The prince's words reflected the feelings of the nation, people wanting to apologise to the Emperor for their failure to protect Japan.

Two days later, 30 August, General MacArthur arrived. He aimed to purge Japan of its so-called evils: Shintoism, militarism, the vestiges of the caste system, and the political authority of the Emperor. In their place would be a democracy that vested sovereignty in the people and that would also prevent communism taking hold in war-torn Japan.

Hisashi's diary entry of 31 August ended with the words:

We stood agape listening to the Arsenal Chief. All military personnel are to be demobilised, only the mill manager and ten workers to remain on site.

On 1 September, GHQ was established in the Dai-Ichi Insurance Building near the Imperial Hotel in central Tokyo. Windows and doors were shaded, and no one knew what happened inside.

Ninety years after the first visit by Commodore Perry and his *kuro-fune*, American ships had reappeared in Tokyo Bay. Warships and supply vessels lay at anchor, the stars and stripes flying in the breeze.

On 2 September, aboard the US battleship *Missouri*, with brush and ink, Japanese officials added their signatures to the Instrument of Surrender. Capitulation was complete.

2 September
I'm going home!

With these words Hisashi's long struggle began.

Chapter 44

The Burned Plain

Kuni yaburete, sanga ari
The country is in ruins,
and there are still mountains and rivers

3 September 1945
Second-Lieutenant Matsumura came home with me and stayed the night. We transported our belongings, and that of ten others, in a truck from the mill, our house the store until they can collect their things.

4 September
Second-Lieutenant Kawafune and Midshipman Fukazawa collected their belongings.

THE SURROUNDING DESTRUCTION was overwhelming; everywhere was the presence of rubble, misery and hunger. Major cities were reduced to nothing. Transport systems were wrecked or dilapidated. Few ports were operative: harbours jammed with wrecks and docks reduced to ruins, merchant ships sunk or damaged, and fishing fleets decimated.

The economy was crushed, and inflation spiralled as the *yami-ichi* raged. Factories, offices and homes had been destroyed. Livelihoods and jobs had been lost, and there was little to eat. Poverty and filth blanketed everything. Sickness and disease were rife. Most people had no home, no food, no fuel, no money and no job.

In Tokyo, families crowded into one-room apartments, or several families lived in one house. Some lived in derelict trams or buses. Some constructed shacks where their former homes had stood; or a shed from an upcountry relative was transported and rebuilt on the site. Some made homes in caves, others in parks, under raised railway tracks, or in the entrances of buildings that had survived.

The Furuya family was not as destitute as some. Philosophical about losing the house, they were thankful they had clothes to wear, bedding to sleep on, and most fortunate of all, that they were safe. And they did have somewhere to stay. The day after the bombing, Yayoi was evacuated back to Sendai, and Jinjiro and Ryoko had stayed at the tram-driver's house until something more permanent was arranged.

On the outskirts of their old suburb, some homes were unburned and Jinjiro organised lodgings in their doctor's house, the doctor having evacuated his family to the village where he was born. Kimura-san had been the family doctor for over 20 years and, being of a similar age and with similar interests to Jinjiro, the pair had developed a good relationship.

Their neighbourhood had been a thriving community, full of activity and gossip, the Kimura house particularly busy with the comings and goings of patients to the surgery. It was a comfortable house, similar to the old Furuya house. The doctor had been concerned that, if it was left empty it would be vulnerable to squatters, so the tenancy was mutually beneficial. All the big furniture was there. Jinjiro and Ryoko needed to bring only kitchenware and bedding from their underground shelter, leaving half their inventory still buried.

With Hisashi home, it became his responsibility to take care of the family. As a good son he never questioned the repayment of his *on*. His diary referred again and again to his frantic search for food, fuel, housing and work. For the time being, with having somewhere to stay, his most immediate concerns were food and fuel. But he knew Kimura-*san* and his family would return soon, so he had to find somewhere else and preferably before the winter.

7 September
Fetched my bicycle from storage at the Kawanishi warehouse.

A bicycle was jokingly credited as being one of the Emperor's three 'divine instruments', the originals being the sword, mirror and necklace gifted by *Amaterasu* to the first Emperor. Now, a bicycle, radio and breadmaker were more desirous than any jewels. With the usual modes of transport restricted or unavailable, a bicycle gave mobility and a vehicle to transport supplies. People were hungry for information, but radio kits were not on sale. Breadmakers provided an alternative use for the flour ration and a change from steamed dumplings.

The Kawanishi warehouse was 12 kilometres away in Nihombashi. No buses or subways were running. Only the trains and trams on the loop line were operating; other lines were idle, either damaged, or without engines or carriages.

> As Hisashi walks to the tram station, silence pervades the air. With most residents evacuated, there is not a soul about. Under ordinary circumstances he would have appreciated the chiming of the neighbourhood *furin*, but in the eerie stillness, their sound is mournful.
>
> Passengers on the tram seem dazed and he wonders whether he appears the same. Shabbily dressed with untidy hair and lifeless expressions, they look vulnerable in their unpredictable new world. As the tram leaves Shibuya, the first couple of kilometres are much the same as before the war: middle-class dwellings, small shops, small farms, bamboo groves and potato fields. He cannot tell whether they have electricity and water, but guesses they suffer from irregular power supply and lack of water the same as his family. Water and power supplies along main streets had recovered quickly, but those further away often went without.
>
> Then, suddenly the landscape changes. No one knows the full extent of the damage to the city, but closer to the centre, whole districts have been levelled by fire. Not just homes and businesses destroyed, but hospitals, schools, temples, parks, water mains, telephone and power lines. Pockmarked with bomb craters, grey powdery ash is all that remains.

Arriving at Tokyo-*eki*, it is a short walk to the warehouse. The railway station has lost its two top storeys, but is otherwise intact. The Imperial Palace nearby has not been so lucky. Heading towards the Sumida-*gawa*, he is surprised to see that a number of large concrete and brick buildings have come through the bombing unscathed, making him wonder whether they had been deliberately spared so SCAP would have offices from which to govern.

Another survivor, drawing attention to itself, is the brick Kawanishi warehouse. Its cavernous interior is draughty and barely lit. *Kyu~kyu* his rubber-soled, canvas *zukku* squeak on the wooden floor. Chilled, he is pleased to collect his bicycle and leave.

The city is crowded: some people wandering aimlessly, others foraging through the wreckage or simply enjoying the luxury of not worrying about air raids. Given the petrol shortage there are few cars, only people pulling carts or riding bicycles with trailers.

Cycling back home, continually on the look out for semi-wild dogs,* Hisashi rides through the blackened landscape of the narrow side streets. Up and down gentle hills, through flat, empty spaces, once prosperous commercial districts and suburban neighbourhoods lie scorched and scarred.

Telephone and power poles lean precariously, at times blocking his way, their hanging cables entangled with broken porcelain, a chair leg, a signboard. Some things stand out: a stone lantern, gushing water pipes, the burnt skeleton of a tram car. An empty safe marks the site of a former shop, stone funerary pillars where a temple stood. It is over three months since the bombing ceased, but there has been no time to clean up.

Hisashi stops. As far as he can see everything is flattened. No familiar landmarks remain. He can see far into the distance, nothing in the way to obscure his view. The only discernable shape on the horizon is a tram, visible as if in open country. Accustomed only

---

* Pets now without owners.

to seeing his immediate environment as he is, this endless expanse distorts his perspective. And apart from the tram, nothing moves. There is no traffic, there are no cats or dogs or birds, no people, no shops, no factory noise. Even the scavenging black crows have vanished. He wonders where all the people have gone.

He feels hot, and notices a shallow pool that has collected where a household tap is trickling. The repetitious dripping is a restful sound. Crunching over the carpet of ash, he crouches at the pool to moisten his face. In the stillness a frog jumps into the water. He starts. Other frogs are there, safe under the crow-less sky.

8 September
GHQ has pushed the Higashikuni cabinet to resign. Otosan says they're too right wing for the Americans. Shidehara is Prime Minister,* but unlike Germany and Italy's fresh blood, the new cabinet still consists of pre-war elite. MacArthur has raised the American flag over the American embassy. Occupation has begun. How will we be treated? How will our family cope? How will I find work? Will Tokyo be rebuilt?

10 September
Took my Curriculum Vitae to Professor Mishima – it's quite uncertain what will happen to the metal industry and to Todai.

Work was scarce. Through his network of friends, relations, alumnae and fellow naval officers, Hisashi scoured far and wide. Hour after hour, day after day, he pored over his desk, copying his curriculum vitae, writing letters, and answering hundreds of advertisements. On foot, by bicycle, tram or train he traipsed the countryside, following up leads, cold calling, registering with every agency, bureau, association, relief scheme, or club suggested to him.

Continually thinking of ways to earn an honest *yen*, he performed all manner of mundane tasks, translating applications for people wanting work with SCAP, acting as middleman for Shinji-*kun* (his

---
* Appointed by the Emperor.

middle school friend) who repaired radios. He even sold some of his precious remaining books.

14 September
This morning visited my Alma Mater in Chiba, then Nakamura-san.* His mother died early this year, so I gave a condolence gift of ten yen. He gave me six kg of potatoes and onions. Chiba city was badly bombed, but the outskirts, including the campus and Nakamura-san's farm, are undamaged.

The lack of daily necessities was worsening. Finding sufficient food for the family was Hisashi's biggest challenge. Economic controls established during the war remained. Ration tickets were still to be used to buy official goods at government nominated prices. Except for musical instruments and books, which no one needed and few could afford, everything was rationed.

Supplementary coupons were issued to those who had lost their homes. However, with insufficient funds to go round the huge number of claimants, the coupons were next to useless. Barter and the *yami-ichi* kept people going. Few goods were available legitimately, and even before the war ended, people had resorted to barter: town dwellers exchanging antiques, books, clothing, nails and glass plates for farmers' vegetables.

Although the unauthorised sale of controlled goods was forbidden, the *yami-ichi* ran free, and now the GIs provided a new source of illegal goods. *Yami-ichi* goods were in plentiful supply and usually better quality than official rationed items, but costing up to ten times more. City dwellers unable to afford such prices were forced to shift upcountry to live with relatives.

In the Furuya family, almost everything was left to Hisashi. Jinjiro had aged. He still went to work, but his salary had been halved, and his savings had nearly gone. Sometimes he came home with *yami-ichi* goods bought through Kawanishi, but generally he had little energy

---

* The farmer with whom he lodged in his first year of university.

to do anything more. Ryoko swapped vegetable information and the rationing schedule with other women.

One day Hisashi collected vegetables; the next day, fuel; the third day he looked for a house; and the next day for work. It was a schedule he repeated over and over for months and months. Each transaction took time, having to go in person to the source, and never knowing whether supplies would be available. Nothing was straightforward, and nothing acquired without an additional gift. Rather than redeeming their coupons for official foodstuffs, he often exchanged them for dried goods from *okasan*'s regular pre-war vendors. When cash was available, he would purchase produce from Nakamura-*san*, but for most of their food he bartered with other farmers.

The trains were always congested with foragers like himself. Rucksack on his back, filled with items from their underground shelter, he would board local lines, getting off to walk randomly in search of a farmer who was willing to barter. Leather shoes, *kimono*, his and *otosan*'s suits, were all exchanged for vegetables. A medium quality *kimono* usually went for 700 *yen*; however for *okasan*'s precious red wedding *kimono* he got 2 000.

Chapter 45

As Perilous as a Stack of Eggs

Naki-tsura ni hachi
On a weeping face the bee attacks

17 September 1945
Presented my CV to the Relief Association for Demobilised Naval Officers; at the Navy Officers' Club filed application for a house; then at the National Labour Mobilisation registered as a scientific technician. A taifu is on its way.

EVERY YEAR IN JAPAN, during late summer and early autumn, the whirling winds of the *taifu* cause chaos. *Amaterasu*'s brother-husband, *Susanowo* the storm god, plays his tricks, causing violent winds and heavy rains. *Raijin*, the spirit of thunder, beats his ring of drums. Frightened, *Amaterasu* hides in the 'Cave of the High Plains of Heaven' and the world goes dark.*

That afternoon, fuelled by warm moist air from the tropics, the *taifu* landed at Makurazaki, on the southern island of Kyushu. Reaching a low of 916.6 millibars and a radius of 1000 kilometres, it was one of the worst recorded *taifu* to hit Japan. Screaming across Honshu (the mainland) at 300 kph, *taifu* Makurazaki crisscrossed

---

* As Hisashi had been growing up, there had been little change to the pattern of weather. Every year *taifu* hit in September and October; monsoon rains arrived in June; snow fell in January and February. Each seasonal occurrence, accompanied by its pattern of damage, disrupted daily life, power and water supplies inevitably cut off for at least half a day.

• 273

the country: north to Hiroshima, west to the Japan Sea, northeast to Sakata, then, as the swirling mass swept back towards the Pacific Ocean, it threatened Tokyo.

The weather has been deteriorating throughout the day. When Hisashi leaves home in the morning, the air is hot and heavy, the smoke from cooking fires rising vertically. Gradually a breeze springs up, causing the smoke to drift. In the afternoon, the light grows darker and the sky fills with thunderclouds. A cold wind whistles, trees begin to sway and it becomes difficult to remain upright in the gale. When Hisashi gets home, radio alerts herald the approaching *taifu*. It is still far away, but said to be a big one, and those in Tokyo can expect a direct hit. Every half hour the radio reports its progress: its diameter and strength of the wind.

The city is hammered by massive gales. Strong winds lash the coastline. The sea swells. Torrential rain buckets down. Nevertheless, routine preparations are well orchestrated. Hisashi and *otosan* nail down the shutters, collect buckets and other containers to catch the rain water if roof tiles are blown off, fill jugs and jars with drinking water, and put candles and matches around the house. *Okasan* prepares cold meals: rice balls with *tsukemono*; and *soba* noodles with *negi* and *wasabi*. Accustomed to dealing with the inconveniences of such weather, they know how to minimise its effect.

Night falls. The news alerts grow more disturbing. City power is shut down. Without lights, it is as if an air raid is expected. Then finally, at midnight, the storm pummels the city. Ferocious winds smash and hurl things about. Colossal waves plunge back and forth, funnelling water up the valleys, submerging the coastline and countryside.

In full spate, the tempest rages, every bit as wild as predicted. Seated on the *tatami*, Hisashi, Jinjiro and Ryoko wait in the darkness. *Hyu~hyu~hyu* the wind roars; *gata~gata~gata* the shutters rattle; *dosha-buri* the sky dumps bucketfuls. They have to yell to be heard.

The house groans as support poles strain alarmingly and furious gusts seem about to take off the roof. Trees pirouette in a maniacal frenzy, and fallen debris clatters along the road. Fences take flight. Power poles dip as power lines dance. Windows shatter.

All they can do is listen to radio reports and wait it out. Hisashi is not particularly worried. So close on the heels of the bombing, what does a *taifu* matter? They have nothing to lose, only their lives. He prepares to meet his fate, accepting his 'extraordinary misfortune. *Come on, do your worst. You cannot hurt me any more.*'

Suddenly, as dawn is breaking, the storm abates. A weird silence falls. Wondering what has happened they go outside. The scene is mesmerising, and for the first time, Hisashi experiences the eye of a *taifu*. Up to 50 kilometres wide, the eye is a peculiar place. Winds and walls of cloud rotate at high speed around a vacuum where no storm dares. In the stillness, framed by leaden clouds, a turquoise sky stretches overhead. Hisashi thinks it is magical, but then, as suddenly as it arrived, it disappears. Raging winds, this time blowing from the opposite direction, push the beautiful sky away.

When it was over, the borrowed house and its occupants were safe. But, the *taifu* had hit a vulnerable population, 'a double punch', ravaging cities and towns, ploughing through communities, carrying away animals and people, and destroying crops. In its wake it left massive damage, multiplying problems and putting even greater strain on scarce resources. Dams and power stations were damaged, causing long breakdowns in power supply. Already wracked by poverty, tens of thousands of inhabitants were again homeless.

Buildings in the *taifu*'s path had been dashed aside like toy bricks: nationwide 90 000 dwellings had been destroyed, 250 000 flooded, and others badly damaged. Nearly 4 000 people were missing, believed dead. Flimsy shanty towns and already weakened buildings, swamped by muddy water, were decimated. Bombarded by floods, mudslides, landslides and rockslides, roads were impassable. Bridges had collapsed, traffic was cut off, and vehicles tossed aside. Communication and power lines were down. Trees were toppled across the roads. There was no water, no power and no telephone.

And those ten terrible hours finished off what was left of Tokyo; the outskirts and low-lying areas the worst hit. What remained of the coastal infrastructure was destroyed. Propelled by battering winds and towering seas, vessels were ripped from their moorings to be piled on top of one another or smashed.

18 September
Taifu Makurazaki raged over Tokyo until 10 a.m.

Under clearing skies, some areas were still ankle-deep in murky water, others buried under layers of stinking mud. Excess water had to be drained quickly; and everywhere was sprayed with insecticides to stop the spread of disease. Power cables and telephone lines had to be repaired, roads cleared and water supplies restored. Once again people had to find food, shelter and fresh drinking water. Many needed medical care. Dangerous buildings and houses had to be made safe; many needed to be demolished.

19 September
Went to Kawanishi and organised to transport the rest of our belongings, then went to the National Aeronautical Research Institute to present my CV.

20 September
Met with Professor Kkikawa, who introduced me to Shimoyama-shi [family name then shi refers to senior males], Head of the Railway Bureau. Had hoped for work with the Railways, but he told me the Bureau is duty bound to accept 1.7 million repatriates returning from Manchuria ahead of those who remained in Japan, so no new employment. Professor Kkikawa says not to worry: he'll introduce me to other companies.

Before the war, Professor Kkikawa had been department chief for engine casting at Nissan, so was well connected in the metal industry. He had taken Hisashi under his wing, and had offered to see if he could get him a job at his old company. Nissan, founded in 1928 and underwritten by the Yasuda *zaibatsu*, was engaged in heavy industry and vehicle manufacturing and had profited hugely during the war. When they rejected his application, Hisashi was extremely disappointed.

GHQ was prohibiting ex-officers, particularly the intelligentsia, from working in large enterprises, and consequently hundreds of thousands of men were without work; but protesting was not their way, and they quietly managed as best they could. The professor was also certain SCAP would not allow motorisation to be revived in Japan for the rest of the century. Hearing this, Hisashi gave up his desire for a job in the automobile industry. At that time, the only jobs permitted were for mechanics to repair American vehicles, and factory workers to manufacture auto parts, again only for American vehicles.

> *21 September*
> Otosan *brought home a pack of frozen oranges* [exclusively military supply]. *I exchanged half with Ogiwara* [the grocer] *for a week's supply of dried fish and beans. In the afternoon went to Ensen-ji to speak to the priest about our land. He's still upcountry, only the caretaker in residence. The* taifu *caused much damage. Purchased a hatchet for 20 yen, an unbelievably high price!*

When their housing estate had been built 20 years earlier, the land had been leased from the nearby temple. The lease still existed, so in theory the family could rebuild. Although that was out of the question right now, they decided to keep paying the rent.

With winter approaching, finding fuel was a headache. Coal and wood chips were available through the ration system, but not enough. Hisashi knew he would have to get out and chop wood himself, so a hatchet was a priority, no matter the cost. Twenty *yen* was nearly what a month's salary had been when he was in the navy, but on the *yami-ichi* retailers could ask what they liked.

22 September
Collected a bike load of kitchenware from Kawanishi, and then went to the Ward office to find out about the assistance scheme for air-raid victims to rebuild their houses. Okasan has gone to Sendai to bring Yayoi home; another mouth to feed. The Asahi Press reports the taifu seriously damaged rice, potato and sweet potato crops.

With hundreds of thousands of houses destroyed in Tokyo alone, providing accommodation to resettle the victims was a huge problem. Funding for redevelopment, albeit very limited, had been distributed to each local authority. Hisashi heard the Tokyo Metropolitan Government had pledged to build 3 000 units a month. Bulldozers lumbered across the burnt wasteland, and new housing estates literally sprang up overnight. Their design was simple: one room 4 x 4 metres, a wooden roof and walls, two windows, a lean-to kitchen and toilet, and access to a communal well. It was tolerable shelter until there was time to build something better, but best of all it was cheap.

Invariably there were ten times the applicants for the units available. Priority was given to families with elderly, sick or infant dependants, as well as those repatriated from Manchuria. The Furuya family was low priority.

Although each house took only about three hours to assemble, overall progress was slow in relation to the number of dwellings required. But it was not just houses; other buildings also had to be replaced. Since 1937, a considerable proportion of the nation's funds had gone into the military, neglecting the much needed building and maintenance of roads, housing, schools and civic facilities. The widespread destruction of homes in the air raids, and now the *taifu*, exacerbated the already enormous backlog.

Chapter 46
The Difference of Clouds and Mud

Konzetsu
Laying the axe to the root of evils

24 September 1945
Yoshio-kun dropped in for a chat. Navy Officers' Club replied saying that all their houses for rent in Tokyo are taken.

* * *

HISASHI SLEEPS LATER than usual. Seven o'clock, eight o'clock, the memory of a dream plays on the periphery of his mind, transporting him back to his boyhood: the joy of New Year preparations, he and *otosan* cleaning the *shoji*; his favourite smells wafting through the house as *okasan* and Matsu prepared special dishes, chestnuts simmering in sweet syrup, and dried herring eggs marinating in soya-bean sauce and *sake*. It was a time when his parents communicated amicably.

But now, he awakes to the familiar sound of Ryoko goading Jinjiro. Her voice rises higher, complaining about their lack of money and his lack of ability to provide for the family. Exposed to the *narikin* suppliers and dealers on the *yami-ichi*, she is growing increasingly resentful. Although contemptuous of the *narikin*, considering their conspicuous spending vulgar, she envies their rising status and comparative wealth, while hers is in reverse. She expects Jinjiro to restore the family to their old way of life.

Hisashi can identify with his mother. He, too, desires the return of their prosperity. It is unfair. Those who did not lose their houses are not suffering the same hardship. And, knowing he has the ability to make money on the *yami-ichi*, but refuses to do so, makes him feel guilty. In the military everything had been supplied, and he had not realised how lucky he had been in comparison to his parents. His initial feeling of liberation has faded. Civilian life is far more severe, and family life upsetting.

The sound of his mother's strident tones has finally stopped. He knows *otosan* will have left the room feeling useless. Though Hisashi can see both sides, his sympathy goes to his father. However, he feels helpless to do anything and wishes *otosan* would stand up for himself. Emerging from his room, he flicks through the newspaper headlines. It has been 40 days since hostilities ceased. SCAP is taking control.

Japan to be demilitarised permanently

Ex-Prime Minister Tojo and major war criminals imprisoned

Japanese militarists to be stamped out

US government gives MacArthur guidelines to dissolve Japanese industry, including the zaibatsu, finance and heavy industry

Reports from all manufacturing and mining companies required within 30 days

Orphans to be housed in dormitories

No plan to give food and clothing aid to the Japanese people

Terms were harsh. He accepted change must come, and that their fate was bound up with the Americans, but he had hoped things would happen more gradually, and that the Americans would have been more sympathetic. But MacArthur was beginning a complete and immediate shake up of society that included a thorough reform of the political structure and Imperial system, as well as the landholding, labour and educational systems; demilitarisation; the trial of war criminals; the purge of militarists and nationalists from government and civil service; and dissolving the *zaibatsu*.

Hisashi recognised that 'laying the axe to the root of the evils of Japan' was the only way to ensure Japan would fulfil the terms of surrender, but he had not expected that the very foundation of society would hang in the balance. Occupation policies were rapidly being developed. By December, MacArthur would be subject to restrictions imposed by the Joint Allied Far Eastern Commission, so he was taking advantage of the time he had.

26 September
Today went looking for work around GHQ, afterwards taking my first stroll down Ginza Street. The street was packed with people, mostly GIs buying Japanese dolls and ukiyoe [woodblock prints of life in Edo]. *Went to* Ameyoko *for something to eat, but left before night fell – crime increases after dark.*

* * *

Melting into the crowd, Hisashi soaks up the changes. Much of the street has been destroyed, only concrete buildings standing amidst the wreckage. The grand department stores have survived but, having been occupied by government or military organisations since the war, their windows are still covered in brown paper; though several now sport the stars and stripes or the words 'WELCOME, WELCOME'. The granite fastness of the Hattori Building houses the American PX [the Post Exchange, the GI supply store].

He walks a couple of blocks to a famous restaurant but, with insufficient food available, it is shut: the few eateries that are open are for GIs only. Most shops are also boarded up, empty of merchandise. With rationing still in effect, there are few goods to sell. Those that are open are selling exotic knick-knacks to the Americans, the US dollar going a long way. The Japanese are shopping at *yami-ichi* stalls along the gutter in front of the shops. Hisashi buys a *manju* (a steamed Japanese muffin).

Strolling unhurriedly, he observes the lively scenes. Dressed in drab *mompe*, a woman of *okasan*'s age is peering from a doorway. But most of the Japanese about are men, and dressed like him, in shabby khaki uniforms worn with a coloured tie. The street teems with American soldiers: GIs, marines, and air crew; uniforms of khaki, navy blue, mid-blue, white and grey; and all manner of skin tones. The mainly male, well-pressed soldiers tower above the Japanese. The well-built Americans, many two metres tall, radiate confidence and authority, making Hisashi feel small and ineffectual. He can understand why *okasan* and his sisters feel intimidated. For years the Americans were made out to be monsters, and now that they are here, people are waiting for something to happen, keeping their distance, and their thoughts to themselves.

The language is predominantly English, spoken loudly, and incomprehensible to Hisashi. Different words, different tones, even the laughter sounds different. And laughing cheerfully, a group of younger men in khaki fatigues walk towards him, one eating an apple. Hisashi is shocked: eating on the street is rude. Not only should apples be peeled, but eating while walking is 'the poor man's way'. Others are smoking and tossing away their used butts. Not far behind is a street cleaner, with his spiked bamboo stick poised at the ready. Street cleaners had not been necessary before the occupation.

Another new trend is the use of the sandwich man for advertising. Two unshaven, red-eyed, down-and-outs trundle down the street, their American-style sandwich boards hanging before and behind: one side in Japanese, the other in English – one advertising a bar, the other cigarettes.

Then a third sandwich man comes into view. Hisashi has heard of him; the son of an admiral branded a war criminal. Well-dressed in his dark suit, he looks more like a teacher, his noble face smooth and shaven. Why does he do such a degrading job? Is he atoning for his father's sins? Or is it that he cannot find a job because of his father? Pedestrians part as he makes his way, heads turning and following his progress. Looking straight ahead, his jaw set, the sandwich-man's eyes make contact with no one. He seems like an actor playing a part.

Curious to see more he continues his sightseeing, roaming the narrow side alleys. As before, they are chock-a-block with wooden houses, shops, bathhouses, and a temple or two, but the district goes only two or three blocks deep, the rest burned. Being early afternoon, everything is shut, but he knows that tucked away in these alleys, gambling dens and bars open in the evenings, eager for American business. Approved brothels are displaying their licences in their windows. Medically certified and registered, their girls are protected by the Japanese police against Japanese gangsters; though most shops and girls are unlicensed.

At sunset the sandwich men, street cleaners, vendors and shoe-shine boys will disappear from the Ginza. The street girls will appear and the Americans will go on the prowl.

Hisashi knows from his sisters that most women covet Western luxuries. A pair of stilettos, a dozen nylon stockings, or a silk petticoat from the PX can be earned in return for sex. *Otosan* has a doctor acquaintance who practises in the Ginza. Some of his patients are street girls, and he has noticed that their underwear has improved since the Americans' arrival.

Late afternoon, mindful he wants to be home before dark, Hisashi takes the tram to Ueno to get to *Ameyoko* (Confectioner's Alley). As the tram arrives, the waiting throng surges towards the door. Some passengers are unable to get off and have to travel to the next station. As always people are so jammed in they are immobilised, and as the coach sways, so too the passengers sway en masse. Even when Hisashi loses his grip on his satchel, it stays wedged in the crush. He shuts his eyes. He hears voices around him, though nothing registers. Suddenly the tram jerks, and he opens his eyes, looking at the man in front. Is that a grain of rice on his collar? Slowly, the speck moves.

Relieved it is only five stops, he gets out at Ueno-*eki*. *Ameyoko* under Ueno-*eki* was a pre-war market, which had done a roaring trade in confectionary made from sweet potatoes and beans. Now it does a roaring trade on the *yami-ichi*. Around most railway stations and vacant lots, legions of illegal street stalls have mushroomed, but *Ameyoko*, famous for its variety, is the best.

Hundreds of smoky, lamp-lit stalls are tucked beneath the raised railway track, where black marketers join candy sellers peddling pickles, fruit, kelp, dried fish, cakes stuffed with bean paste and sweet potatoes coated in sugar syrup. The GIs are also there, not just buying, but selling cigarettes, bulk tea and coffee, cheap shoes, jewellery, and silk stockings acquired from army stores. Pushing his way through the crowd, Hisashi is overwhelmed at the array of merchandise available.

It has been whispered that a family from their neighbourhood makes a living at *Ameyoko*. Buying sweet potatoes, they on-sell them, steamed, at ten times the price. He hopes he does not see them as their *haji* would be great, and he would not know what to say.

Feeling slightly ashamed, he eagerly tastes his favourite Hokkaido dried herring, and oranges from southern Japan.

Leaving the market, Hisashi passes a group of barefooted children begging. He knows there are thousands of homeless orphans and has heard they roam the streets stealing to survive. Periodically the police round some up, and cage them in an asylum on the island of Odaibo, an Edo era fort just off the Shinagawa shoreline.

Huge numbers of homeless live in squalor under the station, or in Ueno Park. He sees a woman and three children, one a tiny baby, huddling nearby, their only possessions the rags they are wearing and a battered old pot. Other crumpled bodies lie under a tattered blanket. Hisashi knows other people are worse off, but it is hard to think of others while suffering yourself. He feels embarrassed but can do nothing to help. Looking the other way, he leaves quickly.

Chapter 47

Patience Through the Unbearable is True Patience

Hyakunen kasei o matsu
It's like waiting a hundred years for the waters
(of the Yellow River) to clear

27 September 1945
Applied for a job with Occupation Personnel; then, at the Metropolitan Police Office asked for work as an interpreter; also enrolled at the Ex-servicemen's Relief Association, who referred me to the Kato Steel works.

30 September, Sunday
Visited Yasuwo-kun [university friend] and went with his mother to buy cucumbers and green pepper, ten yen. Train was terrifically congested. Kimura-san [san applies to Mr and Mrs] and her son have returned to their home from the country. From now on, they and our family will live together.

3 October
Dai-Ichi Hotel was advertising for staff – amazed at the queue of applicants, I gave up. At the bicycle shop exchanged our welding rods for a bicycle carrier.

4 October
Heavy rain and strong wind all day, so stayed inside and wrote letters asking friends and relatives to share their vegetables with us.

7 October, Sunday
Looked for a house, but nothing – every house has two or three family name plates.

10 October
It rained all day so wrote more letters. In the evening listened to the radio. A postcard arrived from our ex-neighbour Kajikawa-san. His mother has died from injuries she received when the atomic bomb fell on Hiroshima.

As during the war, censorship was tight. Criticism of SCAP or its policies was forbidden. Restrictions were also placed on information related to the atomic bomb: full reporting of the damage did not come to light for years.

12 October
After a long spell of rain, it was a fine day, so visited our old house to dig up the sweet potatoes okasan *had planted before the bombing.*

* * *

Rounding the bend beside the last of the surviving houses, Hisashi rides towards where he knows their house should be. He knows the house is gone, but still it gives him a jolt. There is nothing there, nothing to tie him to the place where he lived for so long. The entire neighbourhood has vanished.

The view is endlessly vast, and no matter how many times he sees it, the emptiness and flatness amazes him. Only in the far distance can he see buildings and the purple outline of the eastern hills. He listens for birdsong and other noises, but there is nothing. He misses the song of the nightingale and the cooing of the doves in the temple next door. Memories threaten to overwhelm him: tending his pets and plants, riding his tricycle in the park, climbing the paulownia tree in the community garden. He recalls that last time in his bedroom. He had known this would happen.

His eyes wander over the waste ground as he picks his way carefully towards the potato plants. Several have survived to send up shoots; leaves sprouting through the ash, maybe an omen for a new beginning. But at the same time, their fresh, green leaves look obscene against the scorched earth.

Looking closely he sees signs of the past. The stone posts mark their front gate. Nearby lies the concrete trough that *okasan* kept filled with water in case of fire. Broken roof tiles glint in the sun. Fragments of garden pots poke from the ash, and a charred stump is all that remains of the Magnolia Apollo. Walking round an incendiary half buried in the ground, his eye is caught by a familiar metal cup. He picks it up. As a child he had loved watching the rain spilling from the roof, cascading down the rain-chain strung with small cups. Lastly, he checks that the underground shelter is still secure.

13 October
Delivered a bottle of cooking oil to Shinji-kun – he was absent, but his mother took me mushroom gathering. Also helped a farmer dig potatoes and for my efforts got 12 kg for the cheap price of 25 yen. Nukui [a relative] wrote saying he'll endeavour to find foodstuffs for us.

14 October
Up early to visit Nakamura-san. My letter of 4 October reached him only yesterday. He sold me 20 kg of potatoes.

* * *

Hisashi rises with the dawn, hurriedly eating a small bowl of rice. He walks quickly to Shibuya-*eki*. In the misty damp there is just enough light to see, but he listens all the while for footsteps following. Even before the rush hour, the train is packed. And after changing lines for Chiba at Tokyo-*eki*, he dozes where he stands, as for over an hour the train jolts from side to side, its windows rattling.

The farm is six kilometres from the station. Slowly warming up, Hisashi strides swiftly, praying that Nakamura-*san* will sell him plenty of produce. Autumn mist shrouds the area. The air smells of dead leaves and, in the silver-frosted fields, occasionally the shadows of workers move. As the mist begins to clear, he turns off the lane onto a dirt dyke that stretches across the fields to Nakamura-*san*'s house.

It is as if time has stood still. Grass and wild flowers grow along the gravel drive, with hens pecking in the soil. The persimmon trees are laden with ripe fruit: some already picked and hanging from the eaves of the house to dry. Bales of charcoal are stacked by the shed, and pumpkins are laid in rows beside the bamboo fence. Stoneware storage pots line the front of the house: big beaked jars for water, wide-mouthed tubs for *tsukemono*, and narrow-necked bottles for *sake*.

As he walks towards the house the door opens, reassuring him he is expected. Nakamura-*san*'s mother-in-law smiles in recognition, bowing deeply: she had moved in after Nakamura-*san*'s mother died. Removing his boots, Hisashi follows her into the kitchen. Brown eyes beam from her lined face, her sparse hair neatly knotted under a white cotton towel. Despite being bent over from decades of weeding in the fields, she seems well. Her daughter comes hurrying in from outside. A vigorous woman, she is hospitable, but garrulous and somewhat ambitious for her husband. In her early forties, she is dressed in grey *mompe* like her mother, and her ruddy, oily skin glows with robust health. Self-supporting, they have no need to depend on rationing.

A fire crackles in the hearth. Hisashi inhales the scent of wood smoke and the smell of potatoes boiling on the stove. The cosy glow of an oil lamp falls on the small household shrine, beside it sepia-toned photographs of earlier generations. Nakamura-*san* (referring to the wife) bustles about, fetching him a cushion, and offering him tea. In the warm, low-ceilinged room, with its comforting smells, he feels revived.

Nakamura-*san* (referring to the husband) arrives, exuding an air of contentment. He had been over the age of conscription, and now at nearly 50, he is in a fortunate position. In fact, life has never been better. His produce sells easily on the *yami-ichi*, and at far greater profit than in normal times. Transaction completed, Nakamura-*san* offers him a meal. Breakfast was hours ago and Hisashi is ravenous. Seated at the low table, they commiserate with him over his difficulty finding food and work. But as much as he wants to, he cannot stay: they have work to do, and he has to get home, his duty to get back as early as possible. He knows that with 20 kg of potatoes, it will take longer to reach the station.

Lugging the heavy rucksack in full sun, the scenery is nowhere near as appealing as when camouflaged in haze. It is an earthy monotone of browns merging to greys, only green potato leaves adding contrast. With the elderly and children still evacuated, and the soldiers not yet returned, over half the small holdings stand vacant: their houses dilapidated, and their gardens and fields overgrown. What a waste, he thinks, when so many people are starving in the cities. He trudges on, his rucksack growing heavier and heavier.

It is close to noon when he reaches the station. Returning, it is never easy to get on the train as it is overloaded with foragers, their bulky rucksacks getting in each other's way.

15 October
Went to the War End Administration Bureau to apply for a job as a translator, but was told they needed staff with experience as foreign traders. Put in a mail order for a grain grinder.

The food shortage was now particularly severe, so much so that GHQ had arranged for supplementary supplies to be sent from America. The Furuya family, like other city dwellers, was obliged to go through the degrading experience, not only of eating unfamiliar, but also poorer quality foods. In fact, Ryoko refused to cook tinned American beef and soya beans.

Local rice was sold only on the *yami-ichi*, and was now too expensive to eat every day. The American corn substitute was alien to their diet, and of such low quality it was rumoured that it was used for cattle feed in America. At best the corn was pitted, but often it was mixed with chopped straw and powdered husk, and sometimes it was infested with insects. However, they still ate it, cooked up in steamed dumplings. Ryoko had heard that, by adding local cereals and re-grinding the corn, she could make bread that would taste better. All they needed was a grinder and a breadmaker.

17 October
Saw Professor Kkikawa who's helping me to find a position at Fujiwara Technical University, which is developing a new department of metallurgy.

Fujiwara Technical University was the newly established engineering college connected to the prestigious private Keio University. Fujiwara, whom the college was named after, had developed a successful mining company during the Meiji era, and had bequeathed money to set up an educational fund, from which Keio University had been built. Professor Kkikawa expected to become the new Head of Department, and he wanted Hisashi as his assistant, though they were working secretly as the professor still worked at *Todai*.

18 October
Will we Japanese survive under occupation? The Minister of Finance said in today's Asahi Press, *'Under the present conditions, approximately ten million people will starve to death or die of illness over the next few months.'*

21 October
It rained all day.

24 October
Searched for a house, then, left my name card at the tobacconist shop.

25 October
Am experimenting, trying to dry sweet potatoes in the sun. Miyazaki-san [university friend] wrote he'll purchase flour for me – God be praised! Repaired my gumboots, and started to make a kitchen oven in the backyard using burnt bricks.

27 October
Japan is to be reorganised. MacArthur wants Cabinet to prepare a new draft constitution – a Committee to revise the 1889 Meiji Constitution. Today I completed the outdoor oven. Otosan's assistant from Kawanishi brought vegetables and information on houses for rent. A reply came that the grain grinder won't arrive until mid December (costing 77 yen), so we'll have to put up with dumplings till then. Meanwhile I'll organise the breadmaker.

Gas supplies to the city had not resumed normal operations, and with power prioritised for lighting, people were supposed to cook on charcoal or wood fires, either on an open hearth, or in a *hibachi* if they were lucky enough to have one. However, it paid to have options. Jinjiro had bought a *konro* (a small portable stove) made of cement that burned wood chips and paper rubbish. Another primitive, though common method, was cooking on a large tin. With holes punched in the sides, and a fire burning in the base, the top of a tin could be used as a hot plate. At Kawanishi there were plenty of military, five-litre oil tins lying around, one of which Hisashi had brought home on his bicycle. However, everyone with access to power mostly ignored the restriction, though this increased the number of power cuts.

Breadmakers were illegal because they used power, but people devised their own. Shinji-*kun* had graduated as an electrical engineer, so it was simple for him to make one. Galvanised metal plates were screwed to the ends of a small wooden box, the wires soldered to each plate, then connected to an electric light. American corn and local potato powder were ground together, mixed with water and a little salt, and poured into the box. In 20 minutes, it produced a greyish, gritty, crumbly loaf of bread, bland to taste, but it filled their stomachs.

28 October, Sunday
*Got up at 5 am and visited Nakamura-*san*, purchasing 24 kg of sweet potato and 4 kg of onions for 60 yen.* The* Asahi Press *reports* yami-ichi *prices as follows:*

	Illegal prices	Official prices
rice	70 yen per sho†	0.53 yen
refined sugar	1,000 yen per kan**	3.75
sweet potato	50 yen per kan	1.20

---

* Nakamura-*san*'s good prices went some way to repaying the *on* he owed for the cash Jinjiro had paid him when Hisashi boarded at the farm.

† 1 *sho* = 0.477 of a US gallon (a little less than a litre).

** 1 *kan* = 8.267 pounds.

If I'd purchased today's sweet potatoes on the yami-ichi *they would have cost six times more.*

29 October
Visited the Housing Section of Tokyo City Office and confirmed their housing plan is identical to the Japan Housing Corporation. Went to the Association of Iron and Steel for a second interview, and was told all applicants will be employed. I can have 15 hours a week clerking until the end of the year. The Asahi Press *opines that to live on 'rationed food alone means death'.*

30 October
Everyone knew glass would be hard to get after the war, so we carefully stored our windows. Went to our old house to get them from the underground shelter, but since I was there on the 12th, everything had been stolen.

Precious items – scrolls, lacquer-ware, porcelain and furniture inherited from Jitsuzen were all gone – as well as things they had stored: the windows, *shoji* and *fusuma*, metal kitchen utensils, storage jars, photographs, personal documents, books and clocks. Hisashi now felt completely fatalistic: everything that could go wrong would go wrong. But so what if historical items and photographs were lost. To absorb the new Western way of thinking, the past had to be forgotten.

31 October
It rained all day so loafed at home. The Nippon Keizai Press *reports that, despite the necessity to improve Japan's gold-mining capability, large mining companies are following the government and taking a negative attitude. Smaller mining companies, who are more positive, are suffering from a shortage of materials and labour.*

The war had left so many problems: ruined cities, shattered industries, dislocated trade, and a displaced population. Government funds were limited, and it was difficult to prioritise. Jinjiro had heard that only 40 per cent of factories were operating. Like others in the aircraft industry, Kawanishi was suffering, with production almost nil, and Jinjiro worried about his future.

Textiles, iron and steel, chemicals, and cement production were all badly affected. And it was a vicious circle. The country urgently needed coal, oil, raw materials and equipment to restore war-shattered industries. But with shipping inoperative, and the *yen* of little value internationally, it was difficult to import the necessary materials. Lacking raw materials, they were unable to manufacture, export or earn foreign currency to restore the economy.

The Japanese government and SCAP wanted to revive domestic industry, but American military needs came first: repairing vehicles, vessels and aircraft. Thus heavy industry thrived, as did aluminium refining, shipbuilding, and vehicle manufacture. Companies such as Mitsubishi began producing American-designed trucks to carry military personnel. A huge percentage of the Japanese budget was geared towards such industry, with minimal allocation for rebuilding domestic production. Seventy per cent of power was used for American military purposes. This was the occupation after all.

1 November
Went to Chiba hoping to see Professor Kkikawa, but he wasn't there.

2 November
In the morning Kimura-san [referring to the doctor] returned home from the country. In the afternoon I searched for a house. In the evening otosan and okasan argued about us shifting. Our two families live separately within the house, but it can't continue. We must find somewhere else.

3 November, Saturday
Meijisetsu, a National Holiday. The search for a house continues, but in vain.

4 November
Professor Kkikawa wrote asking me to contact Keio University in a hurry.

5 November
In the morning went to the Mobilised Military Service Staff Relief Association, who referred me to JG Diesel Co. Yoshikawa-shi, a senior of my Alma Mater, interviewed me, asking if I wanted a job repairing bulldozers. Also went to Keio University. They want me to work for them, but having been an officer may prevent my appointment. In the afternoon addressed envelopes at the Iron and Steel Association.

At university, Hisashi had come top in every subject each year. But now it seemed to mean nothing. It had come as an enormous blow to him to find that the Americans did not appreciate graduates from public universities. Rather, they ranked private universities higher. Hisashi had heard that public universities in America were for 'non-whites' only. Such a contrast to the Japanese system where, since the Meiji era, everything associated with the government had greater prestige. However, even if in a practical sense, his gold medal gave him no advantage, he was glad to have been educated under the traditional system.

He had enrolled in the navy rather than the army thinking he could continue his research at the naval laboratory, which had been one of the top labs in Japan, especially in metallurgy. Well funded and well equipped, it had been a good place for academic study. But in the end, his degree and the fact he had been an officer were obstacles in postwar job hunting.

7 November
In the morning cycled to Kawanishi to fetch coke, then went back again in the afternoon for another load.

Usually during October and early November there are many mellow autumn days, but this year the rain never seemed to stop, and by the end of November it would be cold. Already the temperature had dropped, and their fuel supplies were dwindling. What remained had to be carefully conserved. Fortunately Kawanishi, protected during the war by the military, had a good supply of coke, which Jinjiro arranged for Hisashi to collect. Several times he made the 20-kilometre round trip, sometimes twice a day, resting the heavy load on his bicycle, and wearily pushing it home.

> 8 November
> Went to Keio University and met with Professor Kkikawa, who wants me to go to Nikko to prepare an inventory of naval assets at Furukawa Mining. No pay, but am hopeful it will lead to a permanent job.

During the war the navy's engineering department had been evacuated from Tokyo. The metallurgy section went to Furukawa Mining, which operated a copper mine and smelter in Nikko. They had taken their own furniture and equipment with them, and now the new Fujiwara College was to inherit it all. However, a detailed inventory was needed in order to gain approval from GHQ, who controlled military assets.

> 8 November continued
> Titled 'Death March', the Asahi Press *reports the following statistics for numbers dying from starvation over the last 2 months:*
>
> | Nagoya city | 702 | Kobe city | 148 |
> | Kyoto city | 300 | Osaka-eki | 42 |
>
> For Yokohama they say 3 per day, Tokyo 2.5 per month. That's nonsense. Otosan's Ginza GP friend says most doctors' record 'cause of death' as illness, which sounds better than starvation. He says on average, 6 a day die of starvation in Tokyo.

> 9 November
> GHQ has said farmers must be released from kosaku [tenant farming].

> 11 November
> Today, Sunday, the railway around Tokyo was used exclusively by occupation troops, so I had to give up going to buy charcoal. And foraging trips around Tokyo are banned next week.

14 November

Otosan *thinks he's found a house.* Okasan *also heard the Haraguchi house may be available. But the urgent need today is to obtain fuels.*

In the fuel crisis they shivered in front of their almost empty stoves. To begin with there had been a supply of tree stumps in the neighbourhood, which even though burnt and blackened could still be used for firewood. But now with the start of the wintry weather, they were well picked over. Widening his search through the *yami-ichi* and the 'good offices' of friends and relatives, Hisashi unearthed new sources. Twice he went as far as the military drilling ground adjacent to Meiji-*jingu*. He knew he would not be the only one to remember its trees, so he had to get there as soon as possible.*

Meiji-*jingu* has been destroyed in the bombing, but the red brick military prison stands unburned in the corner of the drilling grounds. It was here the young rebel officers of the 1936 coup had been imprisoned before they were shot. Hisashi's mind wanders, remembering those young men who had then been about 25: his own age now. Had their sacrifice been worth it?

A chilly breeze blows. He had better get a move on; no time to brood. The stumps are massive, some standing perhaps seven metres tall. Some are even sprouting new shoots. On one hangs an incendiary a metre long, its scorched parachute still attached. Nearby, a man throws stones at a lone crow sitting on a stump. Most birds died in the bombing, and any left are being killed to eat. Part of a stump is big enough to cut into five good-sized logs, about a month's supply of firewood. So his 20 yen for the hatchet is a good investment, but without his bicycle he could never retrieve the wood. It is a 15-minute cycle to get there, but pushing the bicycle home is a two-hour slog. Hampered by his heavy, unsteady load, it is tricky keeping the bicycle balanced, and he is often tempted to let it go.

---

* The area became Washington Heights, a camp for American military and their families.

Chapter 48

One Inch Ahead is Darkness

Senri no ko mo ippo yori hajimaru
Even a thousand-mile journey begins
with the first step

THE AMERICANS WERE INTERESTED in the big picture only, pushing Japan on its journey to democracy and creating a nation in their own image. They made their first move on 16 November when they announced that all *zaibatsu*, starting with the Big Four (Mitsui, Mitsubishi, Sumitomo and Yasuda), would be dissolved. In the end, when the dissolution rules were applied, ten *zaibatsu*, which included 73 companies and represented over one-third of Japanese corporate capital, were stripped of their shareholdings and company control.

For people at large, their priorities were the minutiae of daily life: where to live, what to eat, and how to pay for it. The nearest they got to a bigger picture was attempting to come to terms with the shame of defeat, which they did by absolving themselves of responsibility. But they were so embroiled in day-to-day survival, they had forgotten they had yet to pay for going to war.

Until Hisashi found work and a new house, he had no time or energy to think of America's grand plan. His sights were set on securing a position at the new college, and on 17 November he took his first step towards his goal.

17 November 1945
This morning I arranged Monday's visit to Nikko. In the afternoon went to Miura-san's [remote relative] with okasan to organise a rice purchase.

Every two months he made a trip to the west coast, north of Kanazawa on the Niigata Plains, to purchase 20 kg of rice. A 20-kg sized rucksack was tacitly permitted by police, who made surprise inspections on trains looking for the illegal transportation of staple foods. The rice purchase had to be organised well in advance. Correspondence to and from Kanazawa confirming the availability of rice and possible pick up dates took several days. Buying a long-distance rail ticket took another few days, and missing out meant lining up again the next day.

18 November, Sunday
Fetched sweet potatoes from Nakamura-san, then, went to Asakusa to buy my rail ticket to Nikko.

Getting back to Tokyo from Chiba around one p.m., he went straight to Asakusa-*eki*, spending hours in the queue hoping to get his ticket before they sold out. Placing his heavy rucksack on the ground beside him, he had to be alert. Thieves were rampant at rail and tram stations, often walking away with someone else's bag and leaving an empty, similar looking one in its place.

19 November
Left home at 7.30 to catch the 10 a.m. train from Asakusa-eki. Taro-san [the Keio University clerk] was late, but fortunately we got seats. It was after two when we arrived at Nikko – only Japanese got off the train. We checked into the hotel, arranged our food rations, and then took the tram to Kinugawa to the smelter to meet the accountant and manager from Furukawa Mining.

Hungry! Ration amount not enough – a bowl of rice each, miso soup and two dried fish.

Expenses paid out of my pocket, to be reimbursed by the university:

Return rail fare Asakusa to Nikko	980 yen
Return tram fare Nikko to Smelter	140 yen
Hotel Charge	2027 yen
Chippu [tip for porter and bedmaker]	1000 yen

* * *

Despite the destruction wrought elsewhere by the war, Nikko is untouched. But the picturesque village is not as Hisashi remembers from his visit six years earlier with Yoshiji-*kun*. The evergreen forest covering the mountains has not changed, but the thriving tourist attraction has vanished. The souvenir shops are shut. There are no tourists, or even locals walking about.

Leaden-coloured clouds hang low, settling in a thick blanket so low the mountains are barely visible. Cold winds have stripped the maples and *nanakamado* (mountain ash or rowan tree) bare. Turning the collars of their greatcoats up over their ears, Hisashi and Taro-*san* walk quickly out of town to the hotel. A couple of American jeeps speed past, the stillness broken by the sound of their loud engines, and the stones bouncing off their tyres as they raise clouds of dust on the unpaved road.

After checking in to the hotel, the two men head to Furukawa Mining. And, like the town, it too has a neglected, desolate look. Since the Meiji era, the huge refinery has made copper cabling. Operations have now ceased, with the mine, smelter and manufacturing plant sealed by the Americans, who want to examine Japanese naval documents and inspect the performance of the *zaibatsu*. During the war there were around 20000 workers at the plant, but now only a skeleton staff remains to liaise with GHQ.

The armed, immaculate, black GI at the gate checks their papers, nodding them in the direction they should go.

The copper-rich mine is positioned at the foot of the mountain.

Enormous dilapidated structures stand against a backdrop stripped of trees and vegetation, mostly caused by deadly fumes and waste. A myriad of mining, smelting and manufacturing processes have wreaked havoc, decades of excavation and contamination ravaging the immediate surrounds. As the refinery had greedily consumed vast quantities of the mountain's ore, its giant conical-shaped chimney had spewed pollutants into the air. It saddens Hisashi to see the destruction of what would have been an abundant *sugi* forest, wiped out in the relentless push for production, with nature completely overwhelmed. Today the atmosphere is clean, but it is easy to imagine the sight when the plant was operational, smoke and heat scouring the area.

Supplies of ore and scrap copper are dumped in piles. A ramshackle configuration of rail tracks wends a trail from the smelter into the mountain, switchpoints now defunct, conveyor belts standing still. Derelict tug engines have rusted on their rails. Uncoupled wagons, open bins for carrying ore and flat beds for copper cables lie abandoned, some overturned. And everywhere everything is coated in orange dust. Dust, flushed through ditches, has left a yellow froth along the sides, and although the water looks clear, it is full of poisons. Seeping into streams and rivers further afield, this concoction of acids, chemicals and sulphides is passively tolerated. From a distance the settling pond looks beautiful, but is even more lethal.

This was all there when he and Yoshiji-*kun* had holidayed at the temple, but as youths, they had seen only the beauty and not the bigger forces at work.

Preliminary meetings go well, but it is getting late when they return to the hotel. Fog descends and the air smells of the syrupy fragrance of *sugi* resin. Arriving at the hotel, the foyer is full of high-ranking, khaki-clad Americans working with Furukawa Mining, along with some on rest and recreation with their families. Lower ranks are billeted in the dormitories at the refinery.

The Americans have claimed the best accommodation, but

Hisashi's small Western-style room is still an agreeable refuge; his window opening on to the forest. Staring out into the mist, he can distinguish the moon rising silently between the mighty stands of trees. Judging by the noise, the courtyard below his room extends from the bar, and in the gloom, the glow of burning cigarettes reveals a group of soldiers, arms casually crossed, as they regard each other with nonchalant arrogance.

He often thinks back to the happy, summer days when he and Yoshiji-*kun* roamed freely through the forest. How idealistic and naïve that boy had been, confident in his future, a successful life on target. Now look where he is. But at least he has made the first step in his postwar life, working towards a position in the new metallurgy department of Fujiwara Technical University.

20 November
Took the bus to Imaichi. At the Furukawa Research Institute we met the engineer stationed there during the war. Went with him by train to Kinugawa to the smelter where he guided us over the laboratories. Nobody was about, and everything, inside and out, was covered in orange dust. Takahashi left and we began labelling and cataloguing equipment and furniture.

Expenses for two:

Hotel Charge	*4800 yen*
Bus fare Nikko to Imaichi	*120 yen*
Train fare Imaichi to Kinugawa	*100 yen*
Meals out	*400 yen*
Cinamon [fruit]	*2000 yen*
Chippu at hotel	*1000 yen*

21 November
Began work at 5.30 a.m. as we needed to catch the 2 o'clock train. Paid 3000 yen for persimmon to take home as a souvenir. Slept all the way to Tokyo.

1 December
Today the newspapers are full of reproaches for the war. They want someone

to blame, but infer people at large had no responsibility; they say 'We were deceived into cooperating with the military'.

4 December
Ten hours from Ueno to Kanazawa, returning the following evening.

* * *

Travelling inland, the train rattles through the countryside. Across flat plains, over gentle hills, the distant tree-covered mountains draw closer, their majestic green silhouette slowly changing to purple in the waning light. In the unheated carriage full of foragers, Hisashi tries to sleep. He tries to ignore the darkness, the cold and the uncomfortable wooden seat. He tries to ignore his loneliness and the rumble in his stomach. But sleep will not come, and he spends the long night dozing fitfully and brooding about his uncertain destiny.

Emerging through the mist, the dawn light reveals they are on the rich Niigata Plains, and nearly at their destination. Little has changed over the centuries. The countryside has not been affected by the bombing, and its sea of irregularly shaped paddies continues to be worked intensively. Tiny towns lie scattered. Narrow lanes twist between paddies, crisscrossing ancient irrigation ditches that snake through the fields.

As Hisashi leaves the station, the wind picks up. His cold breakfast of three rice balls and *tsukemono* has not satisfied his appetite. But hunching against the cold, hat pulled down, he starts out.

Wooded slopes shelter the rice paddies, which are separated by low earthen dykes fringed with vegetables and mulberry trees. Winding paths meander between farmhouses, the smoke of cooking fires curling upwards from their steeply pitched roofs. He trudges on for three kilometres, in no mood to appreciate the changing colours of the paddies, nor the flooded plots mirroring the tentative sunlight, the muddy water ready for the transplant of seedlings. Women in conical hats, some with toddlers on their backs, stoop, knee-deep in mud. Fields of golden grain wave in the wind as they await harvest. In fields newly harvested, bundles of rice are tied to poles and lined in orderly rows. On straw mats along the roadside, unhusked rice is spread out to dry.

The peaceful valley, disconnected from the pressures and problems of Tokyo, could be an illusion.

6 December
The US–Japan Reparation Committee presented President Truman with a report that recommends 'dealing harshly with the Japanese people'. The grain grinder has arrived. So has winter, bringing clear skies and low humidity.

15 December
Wartime Prime Minister Konoe has committed seppuku *before being branded a war criminal for failing to stop the militarists in Manchuria.*

GHQ has separated Shinto from the State: the Emperor from the people, and religion from politics. They're convinced Shintoism is too entwined with militarism and, of course, they're right. They're also saying the Imperial dynasty isn't the originator of the Japanese people, and that the extremists used the Emperor. Sentimentally I'm still drawn to the Emperor, but logically I feel it's better for Japan that the Emperor is separate from politics.

Historically Japan had been relatively tolerant of other religions, although with official sponsorship fluctuating between Buddhism and Shintoism, to the disadvantage of the one out of favour, it was not true freedom.

The Shinto Directive, another step in the Americans' grand plan, aimed at stopping the politicisation of religion. State Shinto as a compulsory national faith was disestablished and all religions were placed on the same footing. The doctrine 'that the Emperor of Japan is superior to the heads of other states because of ancestry' was condemned. Bowing towards the Imperial Palace when passing on the tram was banned, as it was when passing the Meiji and Yasukuni shrines.

Shinto was abolished from public schools. Shushin was banned.

Texts were censored. Ceremonies and expressions of reverence for the Emperor were prohibited, as were school visits to shrines.

> *29 December*
> *GHQ is allowing us to hoist the Japanese flag over our doors to celebrate the New Year.*
>
> *A new Trade Union Law has been released. Union membership, strikes and collective bargaining, previously prohibited, are now allowed. Otosan and I believe this will encourage communism. The Socialist and Communist parties were recently revived, and we think GHQ allowed this in the hope they will crush any lingering signs of militarism and nationalism.*
>
> *Tokyo is gripped by cold and hunger. We live hand to mouth. Yami-ichi prices have gone up 20 to 30 times. Not only food, but all commodities rise almost daily. My most urgent concerns are still how to obtain food, work and shelter. I've heard nothing about the job at Fujiwara College. We Japanese have been too optimistic, assuming we would continue to be looked after in the traditional way.*

Japan as a nation was spiritually diminished. Excerpts from the *Asahi Press* of 31 December 1945 show how traditional societal norms had been eroded:

> At Ueno-*eki* at least 60 robberies are reported per day. Police rounded up 153 loafers there on the 26th, and 65 on the 27th. In December alone, 21 babies were abandoned there, and 2 men found hung.
>
> *Yami-ichi* sales outrival department stores, which are confined to selling official rationed goods. Over Tokyo's 10 districts, there are some 53 000 street stalls. Shim-*bashi* the 'Mecca' has 1000. The entire *yami-ichi* is headed by a *yakuza* (gangster), Matsuda-gumi based at Shim-*bashi*. Only Tokyo citizens can do business, but if Matsuda-gumi allows it others are permitted.
>
> Tokyo orphanages are bursting with 1655 orphans, mainly the abandoned babies of street girls. However, this is a superficial

government statistic, hiding the real problem. Thousands more have been taken in by neighbours or upcountry relatives.

Tokyo Rail has announced commuter services in Tokyo will cease over New Year. If service continued the union would request a bonus. After a month's strike, the management have accepted the union's demands, including a 500 per cent wage rise.

A few weeks ago a baby was pressed to death on its mother's back in a crowded train carriage, and the mother was charged with accidental homicide. In a survey by the newspaper, half the respondents thought the mother was careless, and half that the railway company should have been charged.

With most people unable to wash, lice are thriving. The Metropolitan Police Office is encouraging public *sento* to stay open over New Year to give workers the opportunity to have a bath. With power cuts, *sento* can usually open only in the daytime, so labourers cannot go.

Pre-war fertiliser company, Showa Denko, has sent out its first production of fertiliser since before the war, to 'superior farmers' around Tokyo. These farmers met their quota of rice to be used for rationing, rather than selling to the *yami-ichi*. During the war Showa Denko manufactured powder for explosives.

Yet another new word had been created: '*tokko kuzure*' (kamikaze crew gone wrong). Last night, claiming they were ex-*Tokkotai* with no homes, or money, four men broke into a house downtown. After tying up the family, they cooked and ate a meal, drank half a gallon of *shochu* (low class spirit) and two bottles of beer, then left, taking all the rice they could carry, 560 *yen* and several sets of clothing.

The 4.36 million military personnel stationed nationally have all been demobilised. Repatriation of the 3.5 million military personnel stationed overseas has begun.

Chapter 49

Recompense

Kateba kangun, makereba zokugun
If victorious a national army, if defeated a band of traitors
(Winners are always right, losers are always wrong)

EVENTS MARCHED SWIFTLY. SCAP's sweeping programme of reform would touch every individual, regardless of their gender, generation or standing.

However, the majority of people had other things on their minds, and by and large were unaware of the changes. Functioning in a strange state, engulfed by a sense of insidious helplessness, they carried on as best they could, absorbed by just trying to stay alive. But accustomed to living under strict direction, and spoilt by centuries of being looked after, they were rudderless. Change had always been imposed from above, from Amaterasu, the Emperor, and the *shogun*. Now the people needed a new hero to tell them what to do. And seemingly General MacArthur fitted the bill. He was dubbed the 'blue-eyed *shogun*'. For Hisashi, it was not so much a case of wanting a hero, rather that 'the winner is always right', so let him get on with it.

By January 1946, the Furuya family's hope had vanished. Their living conditions had worsened. Hisashi still rose at six every morning, his days dominated by the search for food, work and shelter; Jinjiro still went to the office and Yayoi to school. And somehow, from somewhere, day by day, meal by meal, they managed. But they were running out of cash and items to barter.

The food shortage in Tokyo was at its worst. Finding food required even greater ingenuity and effort. Quantities of rationed foodstuffs had been cut. Quality had deteriorated. Prices on the *yami-ichi* were beyond the purse of most. And with rampant inflation, the minimum sum required to survive had escalated. Even farmers had limited supplies. Less land had been cultivated because of the bombing. Then the *taifu* on 17 September and 10 October had ruined crops. Rice output was barely 60 per cent of 1944, and wheat was down 30 per cent. But it was not just produce that was affected. Even water was scarce. The fish catch was 20 per cent less. Insufficient transport did not help, nor did the shortage of manpower. Females aged 15 to 49 outnumbered males by 6.5 million.

There were fewer jobs, and no improvement in housing. Social unrest was soaring. The same stories of starvation, rape and robbery Hisashi had read about happening in Germany were now being experienced in Japan. Rumour had it over a million had starved to death in the four months since surrender.

It was one of the harshest winters in years. Icy winds blew across from the Mongolian plains. Tokyo usually received only occasional snowfalls, but this winter the snow settled for weeks and fog shrouded the city for days on end. Heavy snowfalls buried countless makeshift homes. Everyone looked pale, thin and grubby. With insufficient food and fuel, people were at the mercy of the elements, unprotected by their usual man-made comforts. In the hostile environment, Hisashi felt like a wild animal relying on his senses: poised, listening, sniffing and watching for opportunity or danger.

> It is a grey day with a nasty wind and, like the weather, Hisashi feels dull as he makes his way, rucksack on his back, to Kawanishi for supplies. Like every other day, he has put on his shabby, winter uniform and military boots. Fortunately, he has kept his woollen greatcoat, gloves and hat. Going out of doors is treacherous, but the family needs food.
>
> Trees are weighted down with snow. Roads and paths are hidden

in deep drifts. Only the main tram routes are being cleared, with ice chipped from the rails. As he walks to the tram stop, the snow is deeper than he expects, and he struggles through the heavy wetness. The temperature has dropped and the wind sweeps the snow over his footprints. A flurry disturbed from a laden branch whooshes to the ground beside him. The cold is numbing, and he yearns for spring.

Off the tram, crunching over the icy snow, he stops behind the warehouse. Standing on the frozen bank of the Sumida-*gawa*, alone in the landscape, he studies the scene. As his eyes look slowly about, the snow beckons, drawing him into its white depths. There is no sky, only acres and acres of snow converging with the pale horizon; in the foreground the dark forbidding river. The world has been transformed. Everything looks new. All traces of the bombing are hidden beneath the wintry depths: the bomb craters are filled with snow and mounds of debris blotted from view. But with the scene devoid of anything to distract his eye, and in the deathlike silence, the sheer scale is awesome, assaulting his senses, and giving him the feeling he is the only person alive.

The family still ate three meals a day, but small helpings and never enough. Pre-war, being able to afford fresh fruit and vegetables, dairy products, fish and meat, they had eaten a balanced diet of around 2 400 calories a day. Rationing had been calculated to provide 1 100 a day, with people expected to supplement their diet with produce they grew themselves, or from the *yami-ichi*. This worked for those living in the country, but, not for the majority of city dwellers. The Furuya family counted themselves lucky if they each consumed 1 400 calories a day, even less than when the war ended and lower than in other defeated Axis nations. The potatoes and peas they had tried to grow had not survived.

Grains and sweet potatoes were the staples of their diet. Everything else was dried – dried fish, dried *tofu*, dried *nori* and dried vegetables – and all had to be soaked and softened before use. Perhaps once a month they had a few grams of chicken or fresh fish. Ryoko had to resort to ingredients she would never have considered before, and not just American rations. Before she would have thrown out the stalks and leaves of the sweet potato, but now she used everything. With their diet 80 per cent carbohydrate, it was nutritionally inadequate and in such limited quantity and quality that it left them undernourished and prone to sickness.

New words and phrases were appearing regularly in the Japanese vocabulary, among them *eiyo sshicho* (unbalanced nutrition).

Nationwide power cuts were now in force, with regular interruptions every other day. To economise on heating the four of them ate and slept in one room, at night the four *futon* filling the space. One of their neighbours had recently burnt his floorboards for fuel.

New Year's Day was normally a joyful time, but that of 1946 had been the complete opposite.

> As a concession to the day, Hisashi has not gone foraging; but with the family cramped together in the small room, they get on each other's nerves, any one of them liable to burst into temper. So they hardly speak. The breeze creeps beneath the *shoji*. The feeble heat from the *hibachi* and tin stove gives little warmth. Ryoko is continually piling slivers of wood on the tin stove and nudging the flames with waste cooking oil. Dressed in several layers, then wrapped in blankets, they huddle around the two stoves. Each has only four changes of clothing, two for winter and two for summer, and today they wear them all. Of their other outfits, more than half have been used for barter, while the rest have been put aside to exchange in the future.
>
> Used to eating rice at nearly every meal, they are down to once a day, but its quality is deteriorating as more *koryan* (a kind of corn produced in Manchuria) is added for bulk. As a treat for New Year's Day they will have it twice: 100 grams for breakfast, a third of their pre-war serving, with *tsukemono*, and again at midday with hotpot.
>
> Most days after a breakfast of leftover hotpot Hisashi and Jinjiro

eat out for lunch, using coupons to buy noodles, and Yayoi has lunch provided at school. If they are home, like Ryoko they have bread with bean paste, then hotpot again for dinner. Today, with everyone at home they have hotpot in the middle of the day. Ryoko has managed to get her hands on a little fish paste made from ground shark.

First thing this morning, she leaves several sundried sardines in cold water to make stock. An hour before cooking, she soaks dried brown *nori*, dried turnip and dried potato: soaking triples their volume. Yayoi helps her, pouring hot water onto dried *tofu* to remove the excess oil, then cutting it into strips. Once drained, everything would usually be fried, but oil is scarce, so instead the ingredients are placed in the ceramic pot, covered with the sardine stock, a dash of soy sauce, a spoonful of *miso* paste and a sprinkle of bonito flakes, and simmered for two hours, with the shark paste added 30 minutes before serving. But, even with long, slow cooking, postwar hotpot is tasteless.

As they eat, Hisashi dreams of the hearty, wholesome hotpot served in winters past. With the kitchen warm from the under-floor *kotatsu*, coming inside, chilled to the bone, the warmth would seep into his system, his body slowly thawing. Mouth-watering smells would be wafting from the steaming pot sitting in the middle of the table and they would eat as much hotpot, rice and *tsukemono* as they wanted.

With so much on his mind, he is not that interested, when over the radio the Emperor renounces his divine origin. For the second time ever, the one-hundred-and-twenty-fourth Emperor addresses the people. 'I am a man, not a god.' He also announces that the Japanese are not superior to other races, and fated to rule the world.*
Jinjiro thinks it is about time. He believes Japan should have become a democracy back in 1868 after the Meiji Revolution. He wants to

---

* Around that time it was also announced that Hirohito's reign would be known as the Showa era or Brilliant Peace. Prior to the war an Emperor's reign was named posthumously.

thank MacArthur for forcing the Emperor to renounce his status, but he regrets the Japanese people have not initiated it themselves.

By five o'clock it is dark outside. After their tea of steamed dumplings, they read by candle light, then, at 7.30 p.m. unroll their *futon*. Hungry, restless and cold, Hisashi is unable to sleep.

As 1946 rolled on, Hisashi had no inclination to fill in his diary. Enduring the bitter weather, overwhelmed by everything and everyone, it required too much effort to record his thoughts. For a while after surrender, he had anticipated a new start, believing their circumstances were temporary, and that somehow, miraculously things would improve. But, reality is crueller than he expected. He knew survival was a matter of physical and mental fortitude. But now he switched off, sleepwalking through time, hoping he would survive.

They hardly saw the Kimura family. Superficially both families got on. There were no bad words, but tension had increased. Clearly the Furuya family needed to move out as soon as possible. But it took until mid-February to find somewhere else. Moving round the corner, they rented three rooms from the eldest Onishi son, whose brother, Hisashi had hero-worshipped as a boy. Onishi-*san* awaited repatriation in Singapore and with only his wife and baby in residence, there was space to rent out. Ryoko and Jinjiro took the best room; there was one each for Hisashi and Yayoi; and there was scheduled shared use of the bathroom and kitchen.

These were important times politically. There had been three generations of politics in ten years: the old guard of the 1930s, the militarists and now the new ruling hierarchy.

On 4 January, SCAP announced Occupation Purge. To accelerate reform and to ensure that war would never be waged again, they purged pre-war and wartime leaders, banning thousands of military, political and business leaders from public life. Officially, only men in the highest positions of authority were targeted, but Jinjiro speculated that it would also include the intelligentsia.

And yet another acute problem had emerged: what to do with the millions who had fled to the countryside and now wanted to return to the city, not forgetting the six million citizens, civilian and military, who had to be repatriated. Faced with severe shortages of food, work, housing and other infrastructure, many cities were ill-equipped to cope with an influx. Although Tokyo had dropped from nearly seven million people in 1940 to three million at war's end, the city could not cope even with the number it had. And as the soldiers started coming home, the crisis grew.

Repatriation had started immediately after surrender, but was soon restricted. Recognising the seriousness of the problem, the government announced a five-month ban on re-entry to 25 cities on 10 January. Repatriates were sent to rural areas, joining the urban emigrants who also had to stay in the country.

Five days later, 15 January, radio NHK commenced a segment called 'Demobilisation News', broadcasting the names of ships due at Kure, the only port of disembarkation. When an incoming ship was announced, wives and mothers from all over Japan would arrive at the wharf, hoping their husbands and sons were aboard. Ship after ship after ship, they would watch and wait.

And now Japan was dealt another blow. It was time for the losers to pay for going to war, and for the winners to collect their booty. On 20 January, 393 industrial plants were designated for reparation. Machinery, equipment and research materials were confiscated from munitions-related industries and research laboratories. This included precise equipment such as wristwatches and wireless sets, either removed for American use or destroyed on the spot. Nor did the victors forget the gold bars in treasury. Contact with international markets and the rebuilding of heavy industry was also prohibited.

With over a quarter of Japan's national wealth destroyed, production down to an average of 20 per cent of pre-war levels, and the national treasury disbursing enormous amounts in reparation, the country's finances were in ruins. Inflation escalated out of control, causing even greater privation.

On 17 February, SCAP announced emergency anti-inflation measures. People were ordered to declare their financial assets, including cash. All wartime *yen*, bank deposits, savings and trusts were compulsorily frozen, with all pre-1946 currency invalidated. Jinjiro's stocks and bonds became useless scraps of paper. However, those fortunate to have converted their cash into goods before this date increased their fortunes by selling on the *yami-ichi*.

New notes were to be issued, but there had been no time to print them. So until August, temporary notes would be used, old *yen* pasted with a certificate stamp, thus providing a lucrative opportunity for the sale of forged stamps.

The government took tight control of frozen accounts. Society had been flattened, and every individual was entitled to the same monthly amount. The head of a household could withdraw 300 new *yen* a month, but other family members were allowed only 100 each. Taking into account rationing and barter, the government assumed the allowance would cover expenses requiring cash, such as rent, power and gas, with some left over for *yami-ichi* goods. However, for a family of four like the Furuyas, 600 *yen* per month went nowhere. And the price of commodities kept rising. A book Hisashi bought for two *yen* on 5 February cost 25 *yen* two weeks later.

Early in February, hearing a rumour of what was about to happen Jinjiro had gone to the bank. However not wanting to carry all the cash in one go, and assuming he had time to go back for the rest, he withdrew only half his money. Unfortunately he was too late. With access to the remaining 5000 restricted to 300 yen per month, what was left was eaten away by inflation.

Introducing these drastic changes destroyed the ruling class. Supposedly SCAP was afraid their influence could disturb the development of democracy. Losing their assets and influence placed the ruling class on the same level as everyone else. And with the nation's financial resources effectively destroyed, it also ensured the Japanese economy would not recover quickly. By keeping the people down, Japan would be easier to control, and less of a threat.

This should have meant everyone started their new lives on the same footing. But farmers and those dealing on the *yami-ichi* had a head start, having little need to spend their new currency, thus becoming rich. It was quite the opposite for town dwellers, especially those who had lost their homes. But everyone accepted the situation calmly. Everything was in the hands of Buddha. And people had neither the weapons, nor money to fight.

By 25 March, the country was suffering a currency crisis. The *yen* had devalued dramatically, the exchange rate lowering from 5.5 *yen* per US dollar in 1940 to 120 in 1946. Though in reality, the basis for daily commercial transactions was the *yami-ichi* rate of 400 *yen* per dollar. Despite the exorbitant rate, prices continued to soar. Some people had more to spend than the government or SCAP had realised. Based on past experience the government had not expected people to conceal what they had.

All physical assets, but not ordinary household items, were also to be declared and handed over to the Ward office. But again, the directive was so hasty there was no time to print and distribute the declaration forms, so on 28 March they were published in major newspapers. Antiques, art, classical literature, gold bars, and so on, were all to be confiscated. To many, it was stealing: but 'the winner is always right, and the loser is always wrong'. However, with most large cities destroyed there was not much left, and few people owned up to having what they really had.

Consequently, on 29 March, the government announced the head of the household could withdraw only 100 *yen* from the bank, the same as other family members. Now, officially, the Furuya family had only 400 *yen* to live off each month.

Land reform was also a hot topic. SCAP wanted to eradicate the feudal system of tenants. Albeit full of good intentions, but knowing little of rural Japan, the reformers had assumed a small group of landlords dominated a huge tenant class, failing to notice the great number of middle-level farmers, like Nakamura-*san*, who cultivated their own land.

Absentee landowners were to lose their land, which would be seized and sold off cheaply to tenants. Occupier landowners, like Nakamura-*san*, who had more than 2.5 acres were supposed to sell their surplus. To ensure reallocation was fair, committees of local farmers were set up to redistribute the land. But evasion was easy, and like most, Nakamura-*san* disposed of his excess by re-registering it in the names of his extended family.

In early April, temperatures started to rise, which eased the effect of the power cuts introduced in March. Now the cherry blossom bloomed, and on 6 April the first group of civilians repatriated from Korea, China and Manchuria arrived back in Japan. Included among them were Shozo, Ryoko's brother, who had been in Shanghai for the last ten years, and Hiroshi, Eiko's husband.

Yayoi also started college. The three-year programme trained well-to-do young ladies to be a 'good wife and wise mother'. Attending the college was considered a status symbol, and definitely gave a graduate greater opportunity to find a superior bridegroom.

On the road to democracy, the new constitution would be the road map. After rejecting the cabinet committee's efforts to produce a new constitution that had effectively retained the Emperor's position, MacArthur instructed GHQ to prepare an entirely new version.

Since surrender, the Emperor had been in a vulnerable position. Was he answerable for Japan's decision to go to war? How aware had he been of the atrocities committed in his name? Hisashi and Jinjiro assumed that, along with Prime Minister Tojo, the Emperor would be tried as a war criminal. They accepted he had been ultimately responsible for military activities, but believed he had been used by the extremists.

Despite considerable international opinion that the Emperor should be brought to trial, MacArthur decided otherwise, sure SCAP would face a Japanese revolt, and risk a communist insurgence if it did. He intended to retain him as a token symbol to ensure changes were accepted. It was not until much later that it became clear the Emperor had been fully aware of the atrocities, and had played a significant role in decision-making.

On 13 February, GHQ's draft constitution, approved by MacArthur and the Allies, was presented to cabinet, when it was spelt out that, if the government did not present it to the people, then MacArthur would. Everything was in the hands of god: a god with an aureole emblazoned with 48 stars had replaced the aureole with a red circle. Though initially opposed to GHQ's draft, cabinet duly published it as their own work. The first page of every newspaper announced the new draft constitution on 18 April.

Though the Emperor remained 'the symbol of the State',* he lost his sovereignty of the people. His former subjects, 'acting through [their] duly elected representatives in the National Diet',† were assured of their voice in government, with the authority of the State clearly divided into legislative, judicial and administrative functions to prevent the misuse of power.

The Diet had its legislative function divided between two chambers: the House of Representatives and the House of Councillors. 'Executive power shall be vested in the Cabinet', which consisted of a civilian prime minister and other Ministers of the State.** Local and *prefectural* assemblies elected by the people would oversee local governments. An independent judiciary was established, the newly formed Supreme Court authorised to oversee the lower courts and to ensure the government acted within the constitution.†† However, the

---

* Article 1 of the Constitution.
† From the preamble of the Constitution.
** Articles 65 and 66.
†† Articles 76 and 77.

administrative function with its conservative central bureaucracies of graded officials, where power truly lay, was barely touched, perpetuating the government's involvement in private as well as public life.

Numerous social issues were addressed. Articles in Chapter three listed the 'Rights and Duties of the People', guaranteeing the basic minimum of work, housing, opportunity, security and standard of living for every citizen. And women were finally given the vote. But the most publicised Article was number nine, which renounced war as a 'means of settling international disputes', and specified that 'land, sea, and air forces … would never be maintained'.

Next came another unavoidable reckoning: the Allies had a lengthy list of wanted war criminals. Leaders were brought to trial in Tokyo, but the Tokyo Tribunal would hear only a fraction of the total number of prosecutions. Represented by the Allied Powers, the International Military Tribunal for the Far East commenced in Tokyo on 3 May. Twenty-eight 'A-class' defendants were charged with war and humanitarian crimes: four prime ministers, four foreign ministers, five war ministers, two navy ministers, four ambassadors, 14 generals, and three admirals.* Thousands of others charged with brutality, rape or murder were tried all over East Asia.

After the Emperor's New Year address, efforts had been made to popularise the Imperial family, encouraging the idea they were united with the people. Goodwill tours began, and for a fortnight in May the Imperial Library was open to the public for the first time. Eiko, who received a complimentary ticket from her old college, gave it to Hisashi. Curious to see if it was better than other libraries, he was disappointed. He decided SCAP's intention had been to show that the Imperial family were the same as everyone else.

While many people continued to revere the Emperor, others were anti. Believing the Emperor had a hoard of rice, demonstrators sat on

---

* Two died during the hearing; one went mad; the remaining 25 were found guilty: Prime Minister Tojo, Foreign Minister Hirota and five generals were hung, the other 18 imprisoned.

the palace plaza on 19 May appealing for him to distribute it to the people. Reading about this in the newspaper, Hisashi was shocked. He understood their hunger and desperation. But it was not the Japanese way of doing things, and he strongly disapproved. Loyal subjects who had been prepared to die for the Emperor in the war would not have demanded rice. Supporters of the new democratic Japan would have made their claim to government. So what was their real motive? Were they pawns of the communists?

Communist activists were pursuing their agenda with a confidence impossible a decade earlier. Some days later there was another demonstration, this time openly organised by the communists. One newspaper alleged 300 000 had congregated in the palace plaza. To Hisashi, it seemed as if the Communist Party was showing off its power, while the Americans wanted to besmirch the Emperor's name. 'Both parties shared the same bed, but different dreams.'

By May, the weather was becoming warm and pleasant. On the first day of the month, as they had done for centuries, everyone changed from winter to summer dress. Hisashi's spirits lifting, he began writing his diary again.

Chapter 50

It Can't be Helped, We Lost the War

Kunshi hyohen
A wise man changes (suddenly)
like the spots on a leopard
(The wise adapt themselves to
changing circumstances)

21 May 1946

These past few months have been chaotic: eight months since war ended, and everything is still uncertain. Nobody knows where Japan is heading, or what our new lifestyle will be. In limbo, we obey GHQ. So busy trying to survive, we manage the shortage of food and other necessities, but everything is beyond our control. We've no independence. We can't show initiative. We must accept the downfall of the intelligentsia and the slow recovery of social order. But it can't be helped; we lost the war.

In Hiroshima and Nagasaki, patients are being diagnosed with leukaemia. GHQ has announced 190 000 Allied troops, many with families, are stationed in Japan. Using up most of our electricity, coal and gas, they leave little for us.

22 May

I hear nearly 70 per cent of eligible women voted in the first democratic election held back in April. Okasan went with otosan and I. Political parties had been re-formed, but in the chaos, no party won even a quarter of the vote. An alliance of conservatives formed a government, on May 3rd electing

Hatoyama as Prime Minister. But GHQ rejected him, putting out a warrant for his arrest. We don't know why. Shigeru Yoshida has now been sworn in.*

25 May
Repaired Matsushita-san's [Ryoko's cousin] *home heating unit; afterwards raised a beer to observe the first anniversary of the bombing of our house. A letter came from Eiko's otto* [referring to Eiko's husband Hiroshi] *saying their marriage is in trouble. Despite the rain Matsumura-san* [naval friend] *delivered charcoal in a straw bag on his back.*

Eiko was finding it difficult juggling her roles as wife, mother and daughter-in-law. Sent back to Japan from Shanghai in late 1943, she had moved in with her in-laws until Hiroshi returned. But his recent promotion to Mitsubishi's plant in Kurashiki was threatening to wreck their marriage. It was a new trend for young couples to be independent, and Eiko wanted to go with him. But a stroke had confined her father-in-law to bed, and Hiroshi's parents, typical of their generation, wanted Eiko to stay in Atami city with them. Conditioned to the old ways, they expected her to obey unconditionally.

Eiko resented their attitude and thought her wealthy in-laws should employ a nurse. Caring for a new baby, squeezed between the traditional family system and the American lifestyle promoted by Mitsubishi, Eiko's troubles increased. Hisashi had explained her rights under the draft constitution. As well as being able to vote, she could initiate divorce, own property, share in an inheritance, and have the same opportunities in education and employment as men. Article 18 even stated that involuntary servitude was prohibited, which meant she did not have to obey her in-laws.

Unfortunately Hiroshi found it difficult to stand up to his parents, so Eiko sought help from Yoshida-*shi* (Hiroshi's superior at Mitsubishi), who had arranged their marriage. Yoshida-*shi*, who was in his late fifties, had been promoted postwar to senior management. During the

---
* Out of 700 seats in the Diet, 39 were won by women.

war he had been middle management only so had not been purged. Advocating Western values, and having been a practising Christian for years, he was the image of new Japan, and had been approved by GHQ as a suitable director. Siding with Eiko, he advised Hiroshi to be independent and to let her live in Kurashiki.

> *26 May*
>
> *It was wet, so cancelled going to Nakamura-san's, and instead milled flour. Professor Kkikawa wrote asking me to stay with the Fujiwara project. A middle-aged couple called Kobayashi, relatives of Onishi-san's, have moved into our house, but fortunately not affecting our space.*
>
> *27 May*
>
> The Mainichi Shimbun *published an opinion poll in which 85 per cent of respondents, including me, think that the new draft constitution was not imposed on Japan. I am also one of the 70 per cent who believe Article 9 renouncing war is necessary.*
>
> *28 May*
>
> *Today Shinji-kun and I started with the Fisheries Agency, assisted by a Fisheries clerk. Only 1000 yen each for 2 months' work, but we celebrated with coffee – 5 yen a cup. GHQ wants reports written in English to explain the technique used for extracting cod oil, and how the product is used; the same for seaweed processing.*

GHQ had increased the number of industrial plants for reparation to 505, including textile factories manufacturing silk parachutes, those extracting vitamins from fish oil, and others manufacturing synthetic rubber for tyres.

Japan was virtually the only country extracting cod oil for commercial use and, interested in utilising the oil, the Americans wanted information on the cod fishing industry. Consequently, every fishing company had to submit their last ten years' records to the Ministry of Agriculture and Forestry.

The Fisheries Agency, a branch of the Ministry, had been assigned responsibility, but had no one to translate. During the war, with most fishing boats having been commandeered for the navy, and most fishermen conscripted, the office had been downsized. GHQ, reluctant for people to know of their interest, did not want the agency advertising for translators, so it had been spread about in certain circles that openings were available. Hearing through their naval supervisor, Hisashi and Shinji-*kun* applied. Given it was a government department, they were lucky to be employed. The work was tedious, the pay poor, but cash earnings were scarce, and so anything for cash was worthwhile.

Many of their friends, also ex-officers, were unable to find jobs anywhere, let alone with the government. As Jinjiro had predicted, Occupation Purge had spread to include the intelligentsia. In this case, few men, apart from those of the intelligentsia, would have been able to do the job. With the language having been prohibited for so many years, the pool of men able to speak and write English was limited. And, no self-respecting teacher or lecturer of English would apply for such a low-level position.

Though Hisashi had been exposed to English since kindergarten, and learned it formally from primary school onwards, he had used it only for reading technical texts at university. So each day he would take some of his work home, seeking his father's help with difficult translations.

29 May
Milled flour, then, in the afternoon the two desks and chairs we purchased from the Kawanishi office were delivered – costing three instalments of 600 yen. The re-entry ban to cities has been extended until November, so with recent repatriates added to evacuees, villages now face similar problems to cities.

1 June
*Ex-Captain Kuriyama came to the house offering Shinji-*kun* and me work*

at the Agricultural Association after we finish at Fisheries.* The government and GHQ want to boost the rice yield, so the Association aims to have Japan 100 per cent self-sufficient in rice production.

2 June, Sunday
Cousin Furuya-san came to visit, complaining about his sister. Moved with sympathy, took lunch with him. Afterwards went to Yoshida-shi's house to see Eiko and the baby, who had left home without her in-laws knowing. Yoshida-shi did not approve. I agree, but Eiko is desperate. Her in-laws still insist she looks after them. Eiko continues to refuse. Now they've told Eiko's otto to divorce her, so Eiko ran to Yoshida-shi for help. Yoshida-shi rang Eiko's otto in Kurashiki threatening to fire him if he didn't tell his parents he wanted Eiko with him, and that they would have to pay for nursing help. Pleased to be asked to take a bath at his house.

Spring was fading into the muggy rains that dominate June. In the damp, debilitating heat, a bath was the perfect ending for a trying day. Before the war Hisashi had bathed every day, but now he was lucky if he bathed once a month; and he washed his hair only every two months. He felt grimy and greasy, continually wanting to scratch his hair and skin. Without soap, shampoo or washing powder it was hard to keep clean. But it was the same for everyone.

And with the fuel shortage, being offered a bath was a precious gift. When that was not possible, he and *okasan* walked 20 minutes to the public *sento*, where they bathed, even at the risk of catching lice or someone stealing their belongings. Few *sento* were operating. Most had been destroyed, and those that had survived were affected by the fuel shortage.

Swapping fabric slippers for plastic, he enters the *hinoki*-lined bathroom that backs onto Yoshida-*shi*'s kitchen. Even with a sliding door to conserve space, the bathroom is so small there is only room

---
* The Agricultural Association was a farmers' co-operative.

for the tub, which sits in the middle on a slatted wooden platform. A metre long, the tub takes a single bather: at the far end a brick chimney connecting to the wood-chip oven that heats the water. Yoshida-*shi* has just bathed, so the room is wet and steamy, the aroma of the damp *hinoki* pervading the space.

Removing the lid, Hisashi dips his hand into the brimming water to test the temperature – about 40°C – perfect. He swishes it, appreciating the sound as it laps over the edge onto the concrete floor and gurgles down the drain. Satisfied that the heat is evenly circulated, he undresses and places his clothes on the shelf. Sitting on the wooden stool, using a wooden bucket, he scoops water from the tub, pours it over himself, and scrubs his body as best he can with soap substitute. Made with waste cooking oil, the oily smell lingers, and like his clothes and bed linen, his skin feels greasy to touch. The tub overflows, as slowly and gratefully, he sinks into the steaming water. The wood of the aged *hinoki* feels smooth on his skin. Light floods in from a low window, and submerged up to his neck, he shuts his eyes, breathing deeply. For a while his worries and fatigue take flight.

3 June
Bought barley (1.5 gallon), broad beans (100 oz), peas (60 oz) and rice cake substitute from Nakamura-san – in total 110 yen.

4 June
Had a dull day at the office, then after dinner visited ex-Captain Kuriyama to see if he would buy grandfather's scroll. He agreed, and for his trouble gave him a gift of dried fish. Eiko went to her husband in Kurashiki.

With space at a premium, and with most Fisheries buildings having been bombed, Hisashi and Shinji-*kun* worked in a laboratory that had been closed down at the end of the war. Situated at the mouth of the Sumida-*gawa*, not far from the Kawanishi warehouse, the lab had been used to measure the quality of the river water, its temperature, flow and salt content. As the building had still not reopened, Hisashi and

Shinji-*kun* were the only ones there, which gave them considerable freedom to come and go.

And, right from the start, they seized their precious opportunity. Taking advantage of being in a laboratory, they manufactured salt for use at home. Still a *yami-ichi* item, salt was expensive and difficult to come by, so it was much appreciated as a way to make tasteless food more palatable. Arriving at work they would place a pan of river water on the electric heater. By evening the water would have evaporated, and they could both take home about a tablespoon of salt, and sometimes a bonus of a miniscule amount of dehydrated fish or octopus. By the time the job had finished, they each had made about a year's home supply of salt. It was an 'unusual perk grasped from a thousand junk opportunities', and gave them both a feeling of secret enjoyment, as well as much satisfaction for getting one over the government.

Chapter 51

Once a Samurai, Always a Samurai

> Bushi wa kuwanedo taka-yoji
> A *samurai* uses his toothpick
> even when he has not eaten

5 June 1946
After tea visited Kobayashi-san to see how to get the frame house we've won.

FOLLOWING THE WAR, the lottery had increased in popularity. People grabbed at anything that inspired hope, dreaming of winning some small item that would improve their daily life: a toaster, a bicycle, or a portable light. But most worthwhile was the Housing Lottery, with millions of people staking a wager with their local Housing Corporation. Each month a number of new houses were won by a fortunate few, with the option to buy or rent. The *narikin* with cash earned through the *yami-ichi* could buy, but most winners had to rent.

The Furuyas' name was drawn and, if they used all of Hisashi's earnings from his Fisheries job, they could afford to purchase. However, the one-room houses were cheaply constructed of plywood. The 20 square metres included a toilet and kitchen, but there was no running water or waste disposal. (Toilet waste would have to be disposed of on the small garden.) Ryoko did not like it, but then neither did the others. For some, it would have been a dream come true, but no matter that most people now suffered in the same boat, they still exhibited their pre-war differences in status and lifestyle.

6 June
Was surprised at the cost of our monthly gas bill, especially when use is spasmodic – 51 yen for 66 cubic metres. Our expenses are rising, and now there are doctor's bills and drugs for otosan, who isn't well.

7 June
On the way to work walked through the bombed district where Matsu [their maid] lived when she left us – we have no idea whether she's dead or alive. At work, ground rice cake substitute into powder, and was pleased to receive an advance of my June wages. As neighbourhood representative went to a meeting of tonari-gumi to discuss ways of overcoming the food shortage.*

8 June
Coming home from work got a haircut, then tried tilling a corner of the nearby school grounds to grow potatoes, but was stopped by the custodian.

9 June
Sunday, stood in the heat for 3 hours to purchase cigarettes for otosan.

Hisashi did not smoke, but pretended he did to collect double rations for Jinjiro.† Produced domestically, there was plenty of stock: ten packets per person per fortnight. Jinjiro had been a heavy smoker all his life, first a British brand of cigarette, 'Airship', and then the American 'Golden Batt'.

---

* GHQ had abolished *tonari-gumi*, getting rid of anything remotely military, but although illegal, many re-formed to manage food distribution.

† Tobacco consumption was an age-old habit, popular with men and women, the finely cut leaves smoked in a bamboo pipe. Prior to the Meiji Revolution, *daimyo* ruled the industry, but after it the government took control, tobacco exports ranking second only to silk. The British had wanted cigars, the Americans cigarettes. Wanting to please the Americans more, the government manufactured cigarettes. While most rural people still used the bamboo pipe, the urban middle class could afford cigarettes and a new fashion had developed.

11 June
Kobayashi-san wants to know if we're taking the lottery house – we're not. And anyway, it's not so urgent we move. Onishi-san likes our rent money.

12 June
Shinji-kun and I went to Kanda to sell some of his books. He got 900 yen, of which I'm holding 550 to buy dried potato for him.

Hisashi's favourite shop in Kanda had not been bombed. Long and narrow, it was still a gem of a bookstore, rich in history and renowned for its antiquarian books.

> Scuffed and pitted from a century of *geta*, time and traffic have mellowed the wooden floor. Floor to ceiling shelves ranging along three walls are overstuffed with the musty, dusty tomes amassed over the decades. Some books are stacked vertically, others horizontally, with the precious books behind glass. The wooden fan, creaking in the middle of the ceiling, ineffectually circulates the stuffy air and, even with the door open, it is stifling inside. Entering casually, they place the bundles of books on the counter, hoping the owner will buy. Selling the books is a wrench, but Shinji-*kun*, ready to accept anything, is pleased when a good price is offered.
>
> Onishi-*san* (referring to the wife) wants her radio fixed. On the way home, they call in to Akihabara, where shoe-horned under the railway tracks, the *yami-ichi* sells spare parts for radios. Out of his fee, Shinji-*kun* will pay Hisashi a commission.

13 June
Attended the Local Fisheries Conference, then, met Eiko's otto, who's in Tokyo for meetings at Mitsubishi HQ. He wants me to stop interfering in his marriage. After supper, I reported our conversation to Yoshida-shi.

16 June
Sunday went to Nakamura-san's farm.

17 June
Attended work, obliged to stay all day as one of the senior staff came to visit, though he wasn't much interested in what we're doing. No one checks our work. At home found ojisan [his uncle, Shozo], *who has recently returned from Shanghai. How he shocked* okasan *with his story.*

Shozo had been in Shanghai since 1937, managing the family owned hotel, Dai-Ichi-Ro. He had only just been repatriated.

In the early days of imperialism, America, Britain and France had extracted trading rights with China and, following its success in the 1895 Sino–Japanese War, Japan had strengthened its industrial interests there. Increasing numbers of Japanese, including five of Ryoko and Shozo's maternal aunts and uncles, had migrated to Shanghai. By the 1920s, the Japanese were the city's largest foreign community. Shanghai offered a cosmopolitan lifestyle abounding with commercial, intellectual and social pursuits. Separated into three sectors: the Chinese Municipality, the French Concession, and the International Settlement, where the Americans, British, Japanese, Jews, Russians and Poles resided, each country had its own enclave where it had transplanted the habits and amusements of home.

The siege of Shanghai had begun on 13 August 1937, when the first Japanese bullets were fired in the city, and the Chinese Municipality soon fell under Japanese occupation. The international enclaves remained neutral, though clearly the Japanese wanted them, so most residents left. However, it was not until January 1943 that the Western treaty powers relinquished their rights to the city.

Early in 1937, one of Umeko's relations had purchased the International Club, the prestigious expatriate hub on The Bund,* turning it into a hotel that included restaurants and a house of prostitution. Accommodating senior military officers and residential representatives of Japanese companies, it was a most lucrative

---

* The Bund, overlooking the Huangpu River, is a magnificent boulevard known as a 'miniature Museum of International Architecture'.

business, buzzing with men entertaining friends and brokering deals. Shozo, who was appointed General Manager, loved the life, living in grandiose style, operating as middleman between the Chinese suppliers and army HQ. When Hiroshi and Eiko had shifted there in 1942, he had taken them under his wing. However, by the summer of 1943, most wives and children, including Eiko, had been sent back to Japan, making businessmen like Hiroshi 'temporary widowers'. Looking roguishly at Hisashi, but making sure he had his sister's complete attention, Shozo began his story.

> Dai-Ichi-Ro is chock-a-block, when one day a man asks to see him. The stranger, a sickly looking Japanese, is about 40 years old, his shabby clothing drooping from a gaunt frame. He is insistent, and will not leave until he has seen Shozo. Shozo does not usually deal with such people, but for some reason he listens to the man, and never in a million years, would he have anticipated his words. The man is his own half-brother, Jitsuzen's other son. Brought up as a priest, he has spent the last few years in China with the army.
>
> Shozo has heard of this fourth child, but has never known any details other than that he is illegitimate and born in Matsushima, where their father worked for several years. He believes the priest standing before him, for he has a look of their father. From that day on, the priest comes to the hotel daily to eat a good meal and to play mah-jong with Shozo; their regular foursome including Hiroshi and a doctor friend.
>
> A year later, Shozo realises he has not seen his half-brother for several days; however, he has no idea where he lives. Then a runner arrives with a message: the priest is dying and wants to see him. Accompanied by the doctor, Shozo rushes from the hotel. Along the majestic Bund, into the labyrinth of alleys on the seamy side of the city they hurry to the address he has been given. The noisy lanes are lined with tenements, cheaply thrown up to house the poor, and no self-respecting Japanese would live there. Barbers, cobblers, coolies,

coffin-makers, and fortune-tellers congregate in dank corners; the smell of rotten vegetables and blocked drains is appalling. Shozo is even more shocked when he sees how his brother has been living. Sadly, the priest is eaten up with disease and dies days later.

After the war the hotel was captured by the Red Army, and the family lost everything. However, Shozo had already ensured his livelihood back home. Realising the war was coming to an end, he had purchased Chinese rosewood furniture, which he had shipped back to Japan on the last boat out. With so much destroyed in the bombing he knew there would be demand on the *yami-ichi* for high-class goods. And, in fact, he lived comfortably off the proceeds for the next five years. Born and brought up a merchant, in his mother Umeko's home, the *yami-ichi* was Shozo's natural environment, unlike his higher-minded sister who was unable to let go of her *samurai* heritage.

Chapter 52

The Power of 'On'

Nana korobi, ya oki
To fall seven times, to rise eight times

18 June 1946
Attended the Local Fishing Conference to pick up the manuscripts I wanted from fishermen – only half ready. Otosan caught a cold sitting up late helping me translate them into English. Now it's developed into asthma and he suffers day and night from a hacking cough. Shortages of sleep and food have hastened his deterioration, as have Eiko's marital problems and the family budget. He drags himself through each day, his mental and physical fatigue doubled in the oppressive heat. He is a sorry sight as he leaves for the office; I fear for him in the congestion of the tram, one hell of a crush.

AT A TIME WHEN 55 was the average life expectancy for a man, Jinjiro at 63 was considered fortunate to have lived so long. But now, suffering from asthma combined with poor diet, he had little stamina. The drug efedrin could help his asthma. It was available on the *yami-ichi*, but it was too expensive for them. So Hisashi walked and walked in vain, hunting for an official supply.

19 June
Visited Professor Sato at Keio University to see how things are going with the Fujiwara project. It's still not certain whether Professor Kkikawa and I will be purged from the teaching profession. White-collar servicemen are being deliberately excluded from restructured commercial companies, government service and educational institutions. Professor Sato has asked me to continue preparations until things become clear, but with Professor Kkikawa having

been a Rear-Admiral, he says our chance of success is low. After supper, ex-captain Kuriyama came to the house with an advance payment of 1500 yen. He wants Shinji-kun to build him an all-wave radio.

Before long, the purge had expanded to include politicians, career military officers, government and religious officials, and members of the 'tokko' and patriotic organisations. Not all had been supporters of the war: some had simply been following orders or fulfilling their duties. Generally, those in the bureaucracy were not purged as they were needed to implement reforms.

21 June
According to the radio, today was the hottest day in 66 years.

27 June
Fatigued after copying manuscripts for several days, but am finally finished.

29 June
Bound the manuscripts and toasted the completion of our work. I brought fried fish, Shinji-kun some greens, and the Fisheries assistant marinated octopus.

30 June
Sunday stood all morning for our cigarette ration. I've started smoking.

1 July
Delivered the manuscripts to the Fisheries Agency, and GHQ. A Japanese fishing boat, Fukuryu Maru, has suffered in an H-bomb test at Bikini atoll.

5 July
Sat the entrance exam at the Japan Agricultural Association [JAA].

12 July
At lunch time went to Mitsukoshi Department Store to have my photograph taken for JAA. JAA has written asking me to start on 22 July.

13 July
Picked up my photograph at Mitsukoshi – who is this man? In odds-and-ends

> *style dressing: a shabby uniform with a civilian tie, this stranger is a man tossed about in the storm of life, absorbed in daily struggles. His features reflect the social conditions: anxiety stamped on his face, with eyes older than his 26 years.*

It was a face both familiar and unfamiliar. It had the same features, but it was a listless face. The eyes were dull, and the quirky expression of youth had gone. It was 'the face of a man in hibernation, as if defeated by life, he was doing no more than exist. Not weeping, not regretting, just doing nothing, expecting nothing, keeping quiet, akin to death'. What a contrast to the face of the boy at Nikko in 1939. On a bridge, a fit young man, tousled and wry, posed confidently for the camera.

> *14 July*
> *Saw Professor Kkikawa who says the Fujiwara project may be called off. I'm relieved – am tired of working without payment. Without the war, I could have walked into any university position. Universities, colleges and schools are being staffed by men who previously wouldn't have been employed. The Americans want to colonise Japan, and by downgrading the education system they can keep people under-educated and easier to control.*

In the end, neither Hisashi nor the professor were employed at Fujiwara College. Both casualties of the purge, others took over their project.

> *15 July*
> *The awful heat continues.*

> *21 July*
> *Translation work all day, but hard to concentrate as it was terribly hot.*

> *23 July*
> *Through Yoshida-shi have been offered a job at Kawasaki Kiki, part of Mitsubishi Heavy Industry. After supper, went to let him know, shaking hands with true gratitude. At last, a steady job with good prospects. My luck is turning, and my foraging days are over – I can buy food and fuel from the company union.*

The Mitsubishi *zaibatsu* had been established in the 1870s, with mining, shipbuilding and heavy industry their core business. During the war they had expanded into the production of small fighter bombers, such as the Zero, and other machines and equipment required by the military. Now they repaired and modified imported trucks into buses.

25 July
Spent the morning sorting my employment contract, then went for a physical check at Mitsubishi Hospital. Delivered sardines to Yoshida-shi, then visited ex-Captain Kuriyama to obtain his consent to cancel my contract at JAA. He was not happy, and no agreement was reached.

Hisashi's salary would be 2 700 yen per month. It was not particularly high because he was on probation, but on par with his officer's salary of 28 yen a year ago, inflation having raised the cost of living drastically in that period.

26 July
The Kawasaki plant [later Mitsubishi Auto] manufactured tanks during the war, and now makes American diesel-engined trucks called White. Assigned to the steel mill, I'm responsible for supplying the materials used to forge the chassis. The Plant Manager says the forging plant has some problems, but I should observe quietly and 'sheathe my sword'.

29 July
Went to the Fisheries Bureau and said goodbye. Received consent from ex-Captain Kuriyama to be released from my contract at JAA.

30 July
Heard the Ministry of Home Affairs is clamping down on the yami-ichi.

1 August
Obeying senior management, I've signed up with the union. GHQ wants to topple the zaibatsu, especially Mitsubishi for its involvement in the war. Currying favour with the Americans, senior management are doing

everything to democratise the company, so everyone must join the union. GHQ mistakenly sees unions as a means to spread democracy, but unions are pawns for the communists. Like my fellow engineers, I've no intention of going to meetings. I hate the influence of the communists and unions.

From the start of occupation, reformers had pushed for radical changes to labour laws and working conditions. Unions were emerging in the private and government sectors. Japanese preference was for enterprise unions, whose members came from the company where they worked, a mixture of white- and blue-collar workers who deferred to the group. Confucian thought, with its focus on social order, allowed the contemporary Japanese company to portray itself as a family unit with common interests, comradeship and long-term relationships. Cooperation, harmony and hard work would bring success to the company; and in turn its success would contribute to the success of the nation.

Company based unions, lifetime employment and the seniority system were the mainstay of Japanese management, with rank and salary connected to length of service. Regular employees expected to be employed at the one company until retirement. In return, they put the company first before their family and personal life, worked overtime, took the minimum of holidays, and accepted transfers uncomplainingly.

2 August
Sketched the forging process, then everyone went to the finals of the inter-departmental ping-pong competition – we lost. After supper visited Yoshida-shi, who advised me that physical strength is of key importance in life. He also advised me to become a 'true head of plant', rather than a clerk stamping seals.

3 August
Engineer Obama and I joined a calligraphy course.

Ryoko and Jinjiro, 1942

Attack on Pearl Harbour, 7 December 1941. US Department of Defense

Yoshiji in uniform with his officer's sword, 1940

Hisashi in his university uniform, 1943

USS *Pennsylvania*, behind the wreckage of the USS *Downes* and USS *Cassin*, 7 December 1941, Pearl Harbour. US DEPARTMENT OF DEFENSE

Labourers' dormitory at the steel mill, 1945, later flattened by a bomb

Hisashi and friends, 1946

Hisashi in 'odds and ends style dressing' 13 July 1946

Yayoi, 1958

Hisashi, Eiko and Yayoi, 1954

Ryoko, 1958

Hisashi at Standard Vacuum, 1955

Yayoi, Ryoko and Hisashi in 1960

The Furuya family with Tomoko, her husband and sons aboard the *Mikasa* in 1935

Hisashi and Eiko aboard the *Mikasa* in 2004

Hisashi, 2004 REG GRAHAM

Chapter 53

Hang One's Head in Shame

Shoja hitsumetsu, esha jori
The living are destined to perish,
those who meet are bound to part

1 September 1946
Otosan went to the doctor, who prescribed him complete rest. Returning home he took to his bed. The end is near. I have failed in my duty to provide for otosan in his old age and ill-health. I have failed to earn sufficient money to purchase drugs and foods on the yami-ichi that could have eased his suffering. I failed to speak up when okasan and Yayoi nagged him for money.

HISASHI'S SHAME WAS INTENSE. He knew that, even in these days, a person was still watched and judged by his deeds. And he turned his Japanese susceptibility to failure and slurs against himself.

By the end of the war Kawanishi was in a shambles. Otosan was dismissed but still obliged to attend. Neither office nor home offered him comfort. At the office he was no longer useful, and at home okasan spoke snappishly about household expenses. When he was dismissed, if only I could have said, stay home at your leisure. If our house hadn't burnt, he could have sold his assets, which would have relieved him of his burdens, both physical and spiritual. I cannot but curse myself for my lack of ability to rescue my family. I cannot but curse the war that destroyed our house. But even in such circumstances, I, my sisters, and okasan *could have saved him. If everyone had worked, instead of relying on his income, and, if everyone had slashed their expenditure, it could have been different.*

In March, despite otosan's *and my opposition, when Yayoi graduated from middle school, she and* okasan *were adamant she would go to college. Surely they were aware of our situation. If so, insisting on getting their way was deliberately done to worsen* otosan's *mental condition. Coming into summer,* otosan *getting weaker day by day,* okasan *showed no consideration, just kept pushing for money and more money. And what was the money for? If she wanted it for food, then Yayoi going to college was nonsense. And if it was for Yayoi's satisfaction, then it was selfish. Yayoi got to college on money borrowed from* obasan's [his aunt, Tomoko] *maternal inheritance. So why did they keep nagging* otosan?

15 September
Otosan's condition worsens daily. The last fortnight, on top of a fever, he experiences feelings of languor and no appetite. His skin is jaundiced. His face, legs and hands are swollen. His heart weakens by the day. Kimura-san comes every other day, injecting him with glucose and a cardio-tonic drug. But today Kimura-san has given up. Okasan rang at noon telling me to come home urgently. I spent the afternoon sitting beside otosan. *He knew I was there and spoke once. Obasan* [his aunt, Mariko] *and other relatives came.*

Hisashi sat with his father.

Jinjiro lies in the front room opening off the corridor leading from the *genkan*. Even with the *shoji* shut, sunshine bathes Jinjiro as he lies on the *futon* in the middle of the room, his head facing west towards Buddhist heaven.

The hours pass in silence. A lonely vigil, time goes slowly, as Jinjiro drifts in and out of consciousness, the quietness broken only by his laboured breathing and bouts of coughing. At times he lies inert, but then he becomes restless, his active mind trapped in his decaying body.

As afternoon turns into evening, shadows cast patterns on his emaciated, yellowed face. The son, ever watchful, senses his father slipping away, then, unexpectedly, Jinjiro opens his eyes. With a slight movement of his hand, he gestures for Hisashi to come closer. Rheumy eyes blinking, he wheezes noisily. Hisashi listens carefully. Eyes fixed, Jinjiro whispers his last words. 'Your first priority must be to look after *okasan* and Yayoi. You must protect them from the occupying soldiers. You must change your goal. Instead of status in a large company you must seek money. And in that way harmony will be maintained in the family.'

Satisfied that he has fulfilled his final duty, Jinjiro peacefully closes his eyes. Knowing his son will bow to his fate, he slips into a coma. By dying, Jinjiro will escape his *on*, released from managing the family in the postwar chaos. That burden is now transferred to his son.

Shaken to the core, Hisashi finds his father's words smash his dreams to smithereens. It is an impossible degree of *on*; and just at a time when his dreams have begun to materialise. Hurting, as if he has been punched in the stomach, Hisashi has to get outside before he screams. He is desperate for a smoke.

Hisashi recalls *otosan*'s words of a few days earlier, recognising now why he had spoken of his experiences in the aftermath of World War I. How incredulous *otosan* had been, seeing the devastation wreaked, not only on the losers but also the winners. In England, whenever he had left the ship, with sugar so scarce, he had always carried sugar cubes for his cups of tea. But the unforgettable images that had upset him the most were the innocent victims of war. In Germany, he had seen many mixed-blood children, offspring of black Allied soldiers and German women. With Japan now in Germany's position, uppermost in his mind was the thought that the same would happen in Japan: that women would be raped and many unwanted coloured babies would be born.

23 September
Otosan *remains comatose.*

1 October
Worried about otosan, *but have to sit the annual service exam at Mitsubishi. For several days* otosan *has been in a stupefied state, though sometimes he moves restlessly. Eiko attends his bedside. Kimura-san's doctor son visited, and gave him injections and sweets.*

Hisashi's chief concern was how to find an undertaker with sufficient petrol for the hearse and processional cars, and coal for the cremation. Fortunately, at Ryoko's request, Shozo took charge, organising and paying the undertaker's exorbitant fee.

2 October
At 8:10 a.m. otosan *passed away. I was home from work by noon, by which time the priest and the undertaker had been called, and Kimura-san had certified* otosan's *death. The immediate cause of death was a heart weakened by emphysema and malnutrition.*

In the evening otosan *was en-coffined. Okasan, my sisters and I,* obasan [*his aunt, Mariko*], ojisan [*his uncle, Shozo*], *Cousin Masaaki-san, and friends kept a watch over his body. He died smartly and in good timing for him, envied by his son.*

On a clear, mild day, Jinjiro Furuya was freed from his earthly troubles.

Apart from the cushions, all furniture was removed from the room. Still on the *futon*, Jinjiro's body was turned so his head faced north, on the 'north-facing pillow' used only in death. As his closest relative, Ryoko cleansed him with a wet towel, then covered his body with a white silk sheet and a cloth over his face. Beside his head, perfumed vapour wafted from a bowl of incense sticks.

The undertaker had delivered the coffin, altar, white flowers, white burial robes and black mourning bands.

As Hisashi enters the gate, he sees preparations are well under way, the notice of mourning already posted on the front door. Resting on wooden tripods, two on either side of the door, are four large, doughnut-shaped arrangements covered in white lacquered water lilies,* white ribbons displaying the donor's name: two from the family, one from Kawanishi and one from Mitsubishi.

The house is silent. Head bowed, legs tucked beneath her and hands folded in her lap, Eiko kneels on the *tatami* beside her father. A haze of smouldering incense shrouds his head. The ascending smoke veils 'his manifest form': to protect him from evil, purify his soul, cleanse his physical body, and ensure favour with the gods.

A three-tier altar, covered in a white cloth, has been placed against the back wall with offerings set to the *kami*. At either end of each shelf, white candles burn in white holders. On the top tier, between two vases with artificial white flowers, is Jinjiro's photograph, beside it the *kako-cho* (the book containing the family records). On the second tier, rice paste, freshly picked chestnuts, a pear and persimmon have been left so Jinjiro has food for his journey across the *Sanzu-no-kawa*; in their midst is a vase of fresh white chrysanthemum. On the bottom tier, a brass hand bell and a white porcelain censer rest on a small table.

Kneeling before the altar, Hisashi lights the tip of an incense stick, blows out the flame, and places it into the censer on the bottom shelf, aware of a delicate curl of smoke drifting upwards. To catch the attention of the *kami*, he rings the bell and then, his palms together, he bows.

All afternoon they keep watch over Jinjiro's body.

Early evening, the priest arrives. Two of the *fusuma* have been pushed apart, extending the space to accommodate everyone. The smell of *hinoki* is almost overpowering in the crowded room.

---
* Symbolic of Buddhism. Four tributes was a mark of moderate regard.

Wearing a brightly coloured *kesa* over his black robes, with his palms joined in prayer, and his *juzu* (rosary beads) threaded through his fingers, the priest blesses the body. The kneeling mourners face the altar, listening as he intones extracts from the sacred books, punctuating them by ringing a bell.

Hisashi observes *okasan* as she virtuously accepts her role as widow: her fingers move over her purple *juzu*, counting the 108 beads as the priest recites 108 prayers to remove the 108 worldly desires. Hisashi also holds his *juzu*, but prefers to rub the beads between his hands. In keeping with ancient ritual, he knows he should ask Buddha to show favour to *otosan*. However, a change in thinking since Tokugawa times espouses that this is a moment to farewell the deceased. He does both. Sad at the loss of his father, who has been a true friend, full of guilt and remorse, and now burdened by his overwhelming responsibilities, he is leaving nothing to chance.

Following the short service, refreshments were served. The priest entered Jinjiro's details in the *kako-cho*: his worldly name; age and date of passing; his posthumous Buddhist name, and his status in the next world, the latter chosen in relation to his generosity to the temple. Jinjiro received the lowest status.

When the immediate family were alone again, they dressed Jinjiro in his white burial robe, right side over the left as for a corpse, and laid his body in the coffin. Ryoko placed a walking stick in his hand to help his passage to the other side, and then covered him again with the white silk sheet. Afterwards as custom demanded, an all-night vigil was held: taking four-hourly shifts, each family member sat with Jinjiro. It was required that one person at least had to be there to ward off ill-intentioned forces that might disturb his spirit.

As night deepens, an insistent wind arises, rustling the last leaves on the *zelkova*. In his mind's eye, Hisashi sees *otosan*'s spirit lurking in the shadows, his soul carried away on the breeze. 'Hallelujah! I am safe

Giri to His Name • 343

at last, relieved of the turmoil of mortal life.' Suddenly, the six altar candles sputter and are snuffed out.

Hisashi breathes in the comforting scent of *hinoki*. He feels profound grief, but is thankful for *otosan*'s good luck in dying on the *tatami* rather than in an air raid. *Otosan* has fulfilled his roles as husband, father and employee, faithfully and selflessly. *On* enmeshed with *giri* has dominated his life. And battered by all life has offered, Jinjiro has been defeated. Hisashi feels pity that he had had no opportunity to enjoy a peaceful retirement, reading and writing poetry.

In the early hours of the morning, himself now cornered by *giri*, Hisashi grieves not only for his father but for the death of his own dreams. Knowing his duty, he accepts his inheritance. On the surface uncomplaining and compliant, he bears the burden that is his destiny.

Otosan's last words have left Hisashi a 'great estate', all future problems falling on his shoulders: Eiko and her marriage, rebellious Yayoi, and *okasan*. It is his duty. There and then, he determines he will never marry while *okasan* is alive. If he did, there would be more mouths to feed, and there would certainly be antagonism between *okasan* and his wife. He knows *okasan* would ensure his bride made the requisite sacrifice. She would expect her daughter-in-law to take care of her, and learn her way of doing things. His wife would have to submit, surrendering any dreams of a modern marriage. *Okasan* is too traditional to change, and he knows he would end up trapped between two women.

3 October
The farewell ceremony for otosan was held from 9 to 12, and at noon we carried the coffin out of the house to the hearse. Staff from Kawanishi were there, as were Yoshida-shi and his wife; okasan's friend Ichimura-san; Kimura-san and his wife; obasan [his aunt, Mariko]; and ojisan's [his uncle, Shozo] family.

Otosan lived through Japan's prosperity and five wars: the Sino–Japanese

War (1894–95), the Russo–Japanese War (1904–5), World War I (1914–18), the China Conflict (1931–45), and the Pacific War (1941–45). But on the day of surrender of World War II, he lost his means to earn his daily bread, as well as the hope to live. And, today, he became a handful of ash.

The presence of the body in the house gave relatives, friends and neighbours the opportunity to pay their last respects. Throughout the morning, the black dressed mourners arrived to present their *koden* (the monetary offering to the departed spirit), according to Jinjiro's status, 20 yen each. Each *koden* was in an envelope folded from thick rice paper, and tied with strands of black and white silk.* Being a small funeral, one cost they could dispense with was a security guard to screen mourners. Professional mourners were on the increase, going from funeral to funeral, and stealing the *koden*.

Following a short service at the crematorium, the cremation began accompanied by the sutra bell; and thanks to Shozo, using the best grade coal. While waiting, they were served with tea and confectionery, and 90 minutes later Jinjiro's widow was presented with a mound of ash in a *kotsutsubo* (earthenware urn).

Years ago, encouraged by his brother Michitaro, Jinjiro had had several of his perfectly good teeth removed, replacing them with gold teeth. Michitaro's *geisha* wife had been a shrewd woman. *Geisha* wisdom advocated that gold teeth were the best way to hide assets, no risk of being stolen, and no need to tell the tax office. As a small boy, on the odd time he saw him, Hisashi had loved to make *ojisan* smile, fascinated by his glittering mouthful of gold. Before they left the crematorium, using *hashi*, Ryoko sorted through the ashes to find the tiny melted ingots.

---

* Five black strands entwined with five white were glued into flat, ribbon-like butterfly wings.

Chapter 54

The Best Luck Comes Back to Bad Luck

I no naka no kawazu taikai o shirazu
A frog in the well does not know the ocean

4 October 1946
Purchased 'return gifts' of sencha from the 10 yen 'gift shelf' at Takashimaya.

9 October
Seven days since otosan died, so today the undertaker will collect his things. My week off is over too soon. At work faced many condolences.

ACCORDING TO TIME-HONOURED BELIEF, life carries on after death, and the deceased continues to receive 'warm hospitality' from his or her descendents, 50 years later becoming a *kami*. When a close relative dies, under normal circumstances, mourners must keep mind and body clean for 49 days, and every seventh day hold rites around the household altar where the *kotsutsubo* is kept. For the Furuya family, no rites were held. They were not a devout family, and the altar was only on loan from the undertaker.

Within the 49 days, the ashes must be buried at the family tombyard. But the tomb-yard built by Hajime had been bombed, and Jinjiro had not been able to afford a new one. So Ryoko asked her stepmother if Jinjiro's ashes could be buried at her temple in Wakayama, beside their twin babies who were buried there. Sato's temple had been bombed, but the twins' tomb was undamaged, and Sato agreed. One headache was solved, but the bigger problem was obtaining the return rail ticket to Wakayama. Although on sale through the rationing system, most were bought for resale on the *yami-ichi*, and it took Hisashi four months to get a ticket for Ryoko. Under normal circumstances, such a delay in burying the ashes would have caused great shame.

11 October
Yoshida-shi informed Eiko and me of the outcome of his talks with her father-in-law. Whether Eiko and Eiko's otto divorce, it is up to Eiko's otto. Eiko is going to meet him. Over the troublesome months, hoping for guidance, she often discussed her situation with obasan [their aunt, Tomoko]. But unable to find comfort in Buddhism, and encouraged by Yoshida-san [referring to the wife], a Christian like her husband, Eiko has turned to Christianity. What will Eiko's otto say?

    GHQ announced the Emperor 'will escape prosecution as a war criminal'.

13 October
Yoshio-kun [middle-school friend], and his mother, and Yasuwo-kun kindly called offering a koden for the repose of otosan's departed soul.

14 October
Disease is rampant. So far this year 3351 people have died of typhus, 3029 of smallpox, and 560 of cholera. Last week I saw a newsreel showing the homeless looking like white rats after being sprayed with DDT. Yesterday we received notice soldiers would spray our district – we thought around houses and ditches. Today they came, two Americans and three Japanese, walking straight into the house, shouting at us to sit on the floor, and to stretch our necks forward. We were so astonished we obeyed, each of us sprayed inside our clothes, and on top, and just like the homeless, we were covered in white powder, which was difficult to wipe off. Only people were sprayed, supposedly so we dirty Japanese won't infect the Americans.

15 October
All day the autumn rain fell. Engineer Okawa and I attended a lecture, then lunched at a recently reopened soba-ya. The menu clearly said noodles were

available, but what a let down, noodles made of low-grade flour mixed with dried nori, *water and a few pieces of* negi. *Yet it cost two ration tickets. Afterwards went to an American movie.*

Plastered on walls and hoardings, colourful, larger-than-life movie posters coaxed the public back to the cinemas. Exotic, sub-titled foreign films provided a perspective on a world hitherto unknown. And thirsty for knowledge, searching for a future, Hisashi saw as many as he could: good and bad, funny and sad. In his mind, he roamed abroad, seeing new places, meeting new people, viewing new foods and fashion, and learning about economics, history and politics.

American melodramas in particular created in him a desire for something different: the need to cut old ties with religion, the family and caste systems. Everything seemed so much easier in America. Everyone seemed to have ample money, opportunity and spare time. The hero and heroine invariably moved through a splendid hall with crystal chandeliers, and ate at a long polished table, waited on by a hovering servant. And, unlike the chasm in Japan, society seemed to encourage an integration of the sexes. Despite the portrayal of lifestyles tantalisingly out of reach, movies opened up new possibilities. And he dreamed of a Japan that was a mixture of America and Europe; peaceful, free and with wealth for all. Jinjiro, like others of his generation, had thought Americans were overindulged and he had been scathing about Western movies, seeing them as a kind of brainwashing, promoting the three Ss – screen, sport and sex; all part of American colonial policy. Hisashi partly agreed, but at the same time, movies opened his eyes and made him realise what was missing in Japan.

Surprisingly, entry charges were reasonable so theatres were packed. Chilly theatres, stale air and hard benches did not matter. Western films appealed. They were in colour, and their background music created a magical atmosphere, quite unlike Japanese movies. Viewed through the lens of the movie camera, Western relationships and sentiment fascinated and perplexed Hisashi. The range of feelings expressed between Western parent and child, husband and wife, friends and business colleagues, were as far removed from Japan as they could be.

And, as for American music, how it transformed life. After years of nothing but military music, deprived of cheerful melodies, people went wild over the new sounds. Encouraged by the occupying troops, jazz was revived, and was a fabulous success. Like a spring wind it swept through Japan, beautiful, expressive and a symbol of freedom.

Whenever he could, between power cuts, Hisashi tuned in to WVTR [American armed forces radio], which relayed a steady stream of tunes amid news from the US. Lying on the *futon*, alone in his room, he would close his eyes, as the sounds flowed over him: fast and energetic, languorous and smooth, friendly and happy. With squeaks, groans and bangs, the sometimes unearthly sounds, unusual chords and improvisation were nothing like Japanese music. The contrast of rhythms exhilarated him, and embraced in their depths he escaped reality: 'Little Brown Jug', 'Amor', 'I Got Rhythm', 'Chatanooga Choo-choo', 'Moon River', 'Jeepers Creepers', 'Over the Rainbow' and 'Lady Be Good'. He loved Swing with its vitality and easy flowing rhythm, the Bebop with its complex harmony and upbeat rhythms. Glenn Miller and his orchestra, saxophonist Stan Getz, and crooner Bing Crosby were among his favourites, not forgetting the 'King of Swing' clarinettist Benny Goodman.

Hisashi hated the dark, dirty world in which he existed, a world he was powerless to change. And in the days succeeding Jinjiro's death there followed the inevitable reaction: weeks spent lamenting his inability to provide for his father. But even an hour of listening to music 'rescued' him for a while and improved his mood.

26 October
Saturday went with Eiko's otto to the Ginza, and then had an early dinner in Yurakucho.

The city centre was lively, the Ginza buzzing once again. Many consumer goods, especially clothing, remained scarce but shops were starting to fill again, and new Western-style ventures lured the public to a variety of entertainment. People flocked to movies and plays, dance halls, jazz clubs, strip clubs and hostess bars, while performances of traditional *kabuki* theatre, masked *noh* plays, and *bunraku* puppets languished.

> Heading south from Yurakucho-*eki* on their way to the *yakitori-ya* (a restaurant selling *yakitori*, kebabs), they meander through the street market. Everywhere they look they see change. Hand-in-hand or arm-in-arm, lanky uniformed GIs escort Japanese girls, in Western dress and wearing heavy make-up. To Hisashi, most of the girls, tottering along in their high-heeled shoes look chunky and cheap, their build better suited to the *kimono*. And a recent phenomenon since repatriation, dressed in hospital gowns, military caps and shabby *zukku*, are small groups of disabled or wounded ex-servicemen begging on the pavement. Most are probably in their mid-twenties, his and Hiroshi's age, but they look more like 50.
>
> Eventually they reach the late-night cubbyhole restaurants under the elevated rail tracks, which are filling with men content to drink, snack and chat. *Yakitori-ya* are less affected by shortages, and chicken is plentiful. Drawn to the appetising smell, they duck through the rope curtain,* and are immediately greeted by the chef – 'Irrasshai' (Welcome! I'm glad you come into my premises and not the one next door) – who at the same time as he is grilling chicken, manages to keep an eye out for the next customer.
>
> Swallowed up in a haze of cooking fumes and cigarette smoke, service is fast, the rhythm of the shop flowing continuously, creating its own background music: convivial conversation, raucous laughter, sparks hissing, dishes banging, and the one and only waitress's shrill voice. Seated on high stools at the wooden counter, they face the

---

* A rope curtain is symbolic of a cheap eatery.

sweating red-faced chef as he grills chicken on bamboo skewers: tongue, heart, liver, meatballs, the intestine, and skin, flames and smoke wafting in the air. The proverbial white band around his head, the chef fans the charcoal fire, turns the sticks, brushes the meat with marinade, and spices it with pepper.*

Removing their *hashi* from paper wrappings, the two men begin to eat. *Oishii* (how delicious), the chicken is flavoursome and moist. And over the *sake* Eiko's *otto* tells Hisashi that, even at the risk of being disowned, he will follow Yoshida-*shi*'s advice, choosing his job and marriage over his parents. Hisashi is relieved Eiko will not become his responsibility and he envies Hiroshi that he can ignore his filial duty.

27 October
To stop farmers selling on the yami-ichi, *the government is raising the price of rationed rice from 300 yen per* koku *[5.11 US bushels or 186 litres] to 550. Good for an honest farmer but, with the selling price nearly doubling to 450 yen per* koku, *not good for the customer.*

8 November
Had a cold most of October, and then, dropped a steel bar on my left foot damaging my big toe, so have been limping. Don't feel good these days. Had a massage, which relieved the stiffness in my shoulders, but not behind my left ear.

9 November
Lame in left leg, hard of hearing in left ear, bad weather, all continue.

14 November
*At last Eiko's problems are settled, thanks again to Yoshida-*shi *who advised her in-laws to give tacit consent for Eiko and their son to continue married life. Not wanting to lose their only surviving child, they've given in, though Eiko and Eiko's* otto *will have less to do with them. Throughout the stormy*

---
* The pepper offsets the fatty taste.

times, okasan *and* otosan *said little, and even now* okasan *shows no emotion, pleased or otherwise.*

17 November
Power cuts during daylight hours are to be increased again.

19 November
With everything still in short supply, the government has extended restrictions on re-entry to cities. Ex-residents with no house or job are banned until March next year. Those whose houses survived can re-enter, even if they've no job. The situation is unfair, and we were lucky we weren't evacuated. And rationing is a joke – there's nothing to ration, goods hoarded for sale at higher prices. The yami-ichi *rules. The volume of rationed rice has been increased to 2.5 cups per day per person but, because of the* yami-ichi, *there's no guarantee we'll get any.*

21 November
Onishi-san has been repatriated from Singapore. Kobayashi-san and his wife have moved to a new house 200 metres away. Becoming Section Head at the Housing Corporation enabled him to jump the queue. Onishi-san now wants us gone, and is pushing Kobayashi-san to find us a house.

20 December
From today, gas has been restricted to an hour a day.

24 December
1946 has been a year of confusion and chaos. Reparation payments have been tough with strict American control over resources, resulting in the slow reconstruction of the infrastructure and severe shortages of electricity, food, work and housing. The gap between people who lost their homes, and those who didn't, has increased. It's estimated over six million are unemployed. And the Population Committee attached to the new Ministry of Health and Welfare is campaigning 'Bring forth no more. Increase no more.'

GHQ seems oblivious to peoples' hardship, one-sidedly issuing directives for society's reform. But it's their version of what's a good society. We accept

> reform will and should happen, but how can it be carried out smoothly when everyone has their own version of what's needed? Directives come one after another. But most politicians and bureaucrats are narrow-minded and conformist, stupidly thinking they can maintain the status quo. So busy coping with directives, they've left us to manage ourselves, unsupervised after centuries of being looked after. We're like neglected orphans left to chance. And now the tail wags the dog. The yami-ichi *has been allowed to spiral out of control.*

The Emperor's speech at New Year had signalled the death of traditional society. Whether the government agreed or not, opposing reform was difficult, as SCAP were doing as they pleased. Democratisation had stimulated the recovery of the Communist and Socialist parties. Those previously at the centre of power had been downgraded, the former ruling class overpowered and replaced with the pragmatic, less-educated *narikin*. In theory that was fine. But it weakened the fabric of society, which was also fine if there was something to put in its place. GHQ promised democracy was wonderful. People did not disagree. But what was the framework of this new society? How would they attain this utopia? Many people thought it was just rhetoric. While movies helped make democracy seem more real, there appeared to be no clear plan of how to achieve it. The nation was in the throes of rebirth, and the people were experiencing the agony of coming into a new world.

Glancing through the *Asahi Press* of 31 December 1946 shows a society under pressure:

> For most people it was a cheerless end to the year, with many citizens raising money through brokers and commission agents. The wife of a *sararii-man*, disposing of her last asset, the final layer of her 'onion-skin living', cried for 3 hours to persuade the merchant to increase his price.
>
> Before the war, banks and post offices would have been crowded

with people depositing their year-end bonuses and withdrawing funds to visit their birth places. This year, the bonuses were a 'mere particle of pre-war bonuses'. People had nothing to deposit and nothing to withdraw. The only ones making deposits were department stores, theatre operators, builders and restaurateurs. All main shopping districts in Tokyo recorded poor sales.

A letter to the editor of the newspaper from a public official complained that people unfairly criticised the recent strike of public officials. As a single man he earned 700 *yen* per month, of which 60 per cent went on food and board, his diet giving only sufficient calories to stay alive.

Chapter 55

Extreme Labour Pains

*Kokoro no omoni wa ude ga moteru omoni
yorimo omoku naru toki ari*
What you carry in your mind can be heavier
than what you carry in your arms

THROUGH MOST OF 1947, Hisashi made no entries in his diary. Then on 30 November, he suddenly felt the urge to review the last 12 months, reconstructing events as best he could remember.

30 November 1947
This last stormy year has been a period of the hardest ups and downs, but at the same time I gained the greatest degree of enlightenment in my life. I walk a long dark tunnel, but now I see a glimmer of brightness in the gloom.

Thanks to my parents' money I attended university. In devotion to my country I served in the military. But after the war, I encountered three almost insurmountable problems: being bombed out of our house, otosan's death, and the difficulty of finding employment, which combined were a heavy burden. I was like a small sheep straying from the flock, bleating at shadows, 'out of specification' with my peers. However, this period marked my rebirth whereby I could find myself. I gained insight into my personal link with the outside world, a precious harvest for my life, but how high the price I paid.

The bitter days of winter 1947 passed all too slowly, but at least with a regular income, I had no need to go foraging. On New Year's Day, 10 people froze to death under Ueno-eki.

With regard to my three problems, on 20 February I obtained a new house, which we moved into straight away. I, okasan and Yayoi must give

> *deep thanks to Kobayashi-san for his efforts at the Housing Corporation, and to Onishi-san who pushed him to help us.*

Hisashi could have rebuilt on the site of their old house but, with the scarcity of building materials, it would have been difficult and too expensive to source supplies, so he gave up the lease on the land.

Despite frenzied construction, the rebuilding of Tokyo was not meeting demand, especially for urban dwellings. Progress was being delayed by other priorities. However, Kobayashi-*san* pulled strings and got the Furuyas a house on the same estate as his own.

On a flat strip of bombed land, a sprawl of identical dwellings had sprouted: square wooden boxes, roofed with iron-plate and fenced with bamboo stakes. Built in close rows, the houses crisscrossed narrow dirt tracks. Any rain and the neighbourhood turned into a sea of mud. The Furuya house, on the outermost street of the lattice, like all the others, was only ten *tsubo*,* or 33 square metres. But it was bigger than the lottery house, and they had security of tenure, a low rental, and the option to buy when Hisashi could afford it.

There was only one room, so during the day it was used as the living room and by night as a bedroom for Ryoko and Yayoi. Built out to the side of it was a small *genkan*, where Hisashi slept, adjoined by a cupboard-sized kitchen with running water and a gas ring; off the back, was a toilet with a hand basin. Bare and basic, it was like camping indoors, but at least it was theirs. Having no bath or shower they had to use the public *sento*. Electricity was supplied, but with power cuts every other day, the voltage was low and was to be used for lighting only. The naked electric bulb emitted a feeble glow; however, there was some advantage in being an engineer. It was illegal but, using thick fuse wire, Hisashi converted their supply for cooking as well. Even so, given the erratic supply of both gas and power, Ryoko often had to cook on the *hibachi*, *konro*, or primitive tin stove.

A new city, with different appearances, was taking shape. Inner-

---
* One *tsubo* is equivalent to two *tatami* mats.

city tenements looked like military barracks. In the suburbs, new detached or semi-detached houses contrasted markedly with those homes unscathed by the fires. Partially burned homes with new extensions stood alongside newly built prefabricated estates. But vast tracts of land still awaited redevelopment.

A new society was also taking shape, a different structure with a different pecking order, different lifestyles, different ambitions and different values. Some people were the same as they had been before the war, however, and had simply picked up their lives from where they had left off. Many of the intelligentsia whose houses had survived seemed more entrenched than others, and were less willing to adapt, less willing to give up the privileges of their previous existence.

Right after Christmas 1946, Hisashi had a harrowing time. Incomes were declining drastically, eaten up by inflation. Still brooding over his father's death, spiralling money worries brought the crisis to a head.

> *Diary continues*
>
> Otosan's *death and the shortage of household funds were overwhelming. And in February, the month we moved, I surrendered to reality, obliged to resign from Mitsubishi. Getting the job at Mitsubishi was all I had desired. I should have been giving thanks for such a prestigious position, but after only a few months I needed a job with higher pay. My Mitsubishi salary was insufficient to support* okasan *and* Yayoi. *For my family's survival I was obliged to make a new life, with money my aim. I hesitated to make up my mind, but to fulfil* otosan's *wishes I had no choice. I couldn't surrender to dealing on the* yami-ichi, *thus I'd no choice but to find a higher paying position. Pre-war engineering careers, enjoyed by past graduates, no longer exist, and I didn't think my principles as an engineer would be compromised by the study of money. But to give up a good job – the envy of my peers – was a drastic step, and, no going back once the decision was made.*

Against all advice Hisashi resigned from Mitsubishi to take up a higher salaried job in a 'new rich' company. It was a moment of gut-wrenching disappointment, but there was no question about what he would have to do.

> *I lost all I had left; my reputation, connections, senior backing and friendships, my years of training a waste of time and effort. Many of my school mates damned me for not acting as a true member of the intelligentsia, thus I was isolated from all but a few. Even in these unsettled times my action was too serious to overlook, too many people rooted in outmoded ways, making no allowances for the shifting tide.*
>
> *Yoshida-shi tried to dissuade me, advising me to continue with my engineering career, that I shouldn't be beaten by difficult times. I should disregard okasan and Yayoi's grumbles, and like Eiko's otto, not allow my career to be destroyed by the family system. He reminded me that, as well as obligations to my family, I also had obligations to the people who helped me get the job at Mitsubishi. Hirayama-shi, the Plant Manager, also advised me to continue my career as an engineer, and that I should remember my obligation to Yoshida-shi. I was so tired. It was difficult to get up each morning. So few understood my situation, or sympathised with my point of view. Most people looked coldly upon me, thinking I was tainted, downgraded. To be judged so wanting was shocking and hurtful. Giri is the bane of my life. There's rust on my body, and without the respect of others; how can I respect myself?*

Hemmed in on all sides, Hisashi was trapped between social obligation and natural inclination. In meeting one obligation, he failed others. Staying at Mitsubishi should have taken precedence, but he failed to follow the signposts of expected behaviour. He failed to balance his obligations, his *giri* to repay the *on* he owed to his fellows. Voluntarily breaking *giri*, even though it was where his duty to his father lay, he reneged on what people saw as the more important obligation. Overburdened with adversity, grief and responsibility, his father's words loomed large, swinging his decision in the direction of family obligation. And the consequences of his action were far-reaching.

As it did for his grandfather Hajime, and his father Jinjiro, the world tipped. He was condemned: a man who did not know *giri*, shamed before the world. It was his *giri* to keep the Furuya name and reputation unsullied, to live by the code of his inherited class position, to observe the conventions of the hierarchy, maintaining his 'proper place', stoic and self-controlled in adversity, shamed into good behaviour. People cut him dead in the street. He cared deeply for what others thought, and it hurt. And, even though he lived close by, Yoshida-*shi* never acknowledged him again, never invited him for a bath. But it was not only his sponsorship and friendship that Hisashi had lost.

Long before Jinjiro was bedridden, Yoshida-*shi* had earmarked Hisashi to be his son-in-law. The scarcity of eligible men was such that prospective brides outnumbered the men 40 to one, and Hisashi, with his education and prospects, was a good catch. One evening, after Jinjiro had taken a bath at his house, Yoshida-*shi* had told him he wanted Hisashi to marry his only daughter. Leaving Mitsubishi ended that. Though after Jinjiro died, Yoshida-*shi* had cooled off slightly. In Japan, marriage was a union of two families. Lacking the head of the household, the Furuya family was no longer suitable, particularly so when Yoshida-*shi*, as a director of Mitsubishi, could choose anyone he liked. Even in times of shortage, a one-parent family was a handicap on the marriage market. It was just understood that a middleman would never arrange such a transaction. Yoshida-*shi* had persevered with Hisashi only because of his potential.

> Ojisan [referring to Shozo] *recommended me to Hinode, a small private company manufacturing car parts, where I got a better salary as secretary to the president, newly rich from the war. Prior to buying Hinode, President Hasegawa had been in the money-lending business as a runner for an old widow. While Hinode is a legitimate business, at the same time he makes huge profits on the* yami-ichi *selling scrap iron, textiles and paper.*
>
> *Even now, months later, I believe I'd no alternative but to change jobs. Priorities shift when disaster strikes. Maintaining my family's way of life outweighed other obligations, and my own feelings. Many times since, I've marvelled at my daring in making such a decision, and more than once*

I've resented the burden of my inheritance. But good fortune and misfortune are intertwined, like twisted rope, turning good, turning bad. Yoshida-shi, Hirayama-shi and others have branded me as a man who abandoned his principles for money. But time will tell. What would otosan *have advised?*

In Hisashi's mind what he did was entirely justified. He had thought Japanese society had changed. But, too late, he realised that, despite American efforts at democratisation, *giri* still maintained the hierarchy among the intelligentsia. He saw his action as a hidden cost of the war and, disappointingly, his sacrifice was not recognised or appreciated by his mother and sister.

Hisashi's original dream of being a pathologist had been taken from him. His almost completed thesis research had been passed on to others. He had been the top engineering graduate, but his achievement was never celebrated. He had worked under punishing conditions in the mill. He had been overworked. He had huge responsibilities at the age of 24, managing unwilling labourers, men twice his age, and delinquent boys. He had experienced bombing and fire. He had dealt with the dead and the dying. He had been surrounded by the physical destruction of his country, his city, his workplace and his home. He had watched his culture subverted as the structure of society crumbled around him, and people were reduced to survival mode.

He had taken on the responsibility of his family. He had lived day by day, struggling in the search for food, fuel and housing. He had watched as the Americans sought to purge and punish his society. He had watched as men were offered jobs he was better qualified to do. Yet again, he had watched helplessly as his father suffered an appalling death. He had put on hold any thought of marriage or happiness. He was sleep deprived and he had been hungry for ten years.

After all this, it was hardly surprising he made the decision he did. He was depressed and unable to see ahead to the consequences of his decision. He could see nothing other than carrying out his father's behest. He did not want to add to the guilt he felt over his death.

Chapter 56

Betwixt and Between

Oka ni agatta kappa
A water sprite on the river bank
(Out of one's element)

NATIONWIDE, THROUGHOUT 1947, financial conditions had become even worse. Undercurrents of unrest festered, and unions, including Mitsubishi, had become more militant, many linked to the Communist and Socialist parties. But SCAP was in charge. On MacArthur's say so, a general strike scheduled for 1 February by united government workers' unions had been called off. Up until then, SCAP had been anti-militarist and anti-nationalist, supportive of the unions and Communist Party. Now, they 'reversed course' to become anti-communist and anti-unionist.

The *yami-ichi* was unrestrained. On 5 March, endeavouring to divert goods back into the ration system, the government announced police would prosecute those who concealed and hoarded goods. They would increase checks on trains and trams, and round up dealers and couriers. New expressions, *intoku busshi* (concealed goods), *uraguchi eigyo* (backdoor dealings), and *karikomi* (round-up) were introduced.

Numerous new laws had been introduced to implement the constitution. Numerous structures had been established to carry out the new laws. However, with the government so disorganised, changes were often slow, which made it easy for SCAP to discredit the conservatives in power. The right-wing Yoshida government lasted only a year, and a new coalition was formed in April, with Socialist

Katayama taking office as Prime Minister. Then, on 3 May, the new constitution went into effect.

> *30 November 1947 continued*
> *We're shocked at the many sudden changes GHQ has instituted, but there's nothing we can do. Used to being directed, most people have adapted quickly, welcoming the changes, showing how malleable we are. How easily people have changed allegiance. How easily people have forgotten. During the war everything American was rejected, now everything American is admired.*
>
> *Most changes seem positive. Pensions, workers' compensation and unemployment insurance are now offered through a proper social welfare system. Local Authorities have greater control over local taxes, education and the police. And marriages can be arranged only with a couple's consent. Okasan is opposed: in her mind is the old saying 'a mother will inevitably be robbed of her son by his bride'. She maintains it's her responsibility to choose my wife, though she doesn't want me marrying while Yayoi's at home. Yayoi would be disliked by my bride and 'it would be like living with a thousand devils'. I can't but agree.*

Reflecting the shortage of young men, it was said there was 'a truckload of brides for every bridegroom', so Ryoko could have made a good arrangement if she had wanted. But, with Hisashi being a 'half-orphan', it would more likely have been with a *narikin* family who had cut their ties with tradition. However, she preferred to live without a stranger in the house, and rejected a number of proposals without even telling her son. Likewise, he declined those that went directly to him. Given he had already decided he would not marry, recognising his mother's feelings confirmed his decision. He would postpone marrying until she died.

> *What of my progress as secretary to Hasegawa-shi? For a while things improved. I broadened my skills. I learnt how a company was run, how to source materials, manage financial matters, establish and maintain customer service; all of which has been a precious experience. However, sometimes*

I'm tormented by thoughts of what could have been, but I won't admit I was wrong. At Hasegawa-shi's suggestion I'm studying the new labour law. In the past, given low status, labour issues were monitored by the Welfare Ministry. Today, a separate Ministry carries out the new Labour Standards Law, which provides basic protection for all workers.

And, what impact did my increased salary have on our household expenditure? For 3 months life was easier. But, by May, okasan and Yayoi were grumbling again about their lack of spending money. Inflation had increased more than my salary. And soon I was in a slump again.

Urban consumption levels were less than half of what they had been in 1935, and 1947 was the worst year of all. The rice harvest did not meet even half the country's requirement. And never a day went by when Hisashi did not yearn for better quality food and more of it. It was taking 70 per cent of his income to feed the three of them, the remainder used up by electricity, gas, fuel, rent and transport. Everything else, he did without. He even gave up smoking. A new pair of shoes would have cost a month's salary.

On the other hand, borrowing the money for Yayoi's college fees from Tomoko, Ryoko was able to afford small luxuries for herself and her daughter. Whatever money she had, she spent and never thought of contributing to the housekeeping. As the widow of a naval officer, every month she received half of Jinjiro's annuity. She had also sold his gold teeth for a good price. Having been indulged as a girl, she was ill-suited to adversity. She had never learned the discipline nor developed the wisdom that would have enabled her to cope with hardship, and now she was too inflexible to readjust. And when Jitsuzen died she had inherited her childhood home, which had been rented out ever since. In return for managing the property, the rent went to her stepmother Sato, but knowing the income would eventually be hers made Ryoko think she was better off than she was.

There was little pleasure in Hisashi's life. During his time off work he tuned in to WVTR if the power was on. Aside from that, he filled the long hours with study. Somehow, living a day at a time, he carried on, searching for that glimmer of hope. And the weather certainly did not help. The rainy season brought one dreary day after another, to be replaced in July by high summer. Endless days of glaring sun and high humidity exacerbated already fractious tempers. Then, in the middle of August, with temperatures soaring, came a new family crisis.

> *Yayoi is impossible. As youngest she's always been spoilt and a little wilful. Now she's aping American ways without understanding the environment they've come from. Her favourite word is 'Boring!', which she says describes Japanese culture. She dreams of changing places with Hollywood stars, wanting fun and freedom like she sees in the movies. She wants a Western-style marriage, with a husband chosen by her, forgetting that in any marriage, Western or Japanese, she'll lose her freedom. Her frivolous chattering, American slang and mannerisms drive me to distraction, and I have to consciously restrain myself from arguing with her. Before the war she would never have dared act this way. As I'm head of the household, she's my responsibility. Okasan has no idea how to cope with her, and keeps silent. But who am I? A man in rough seas unable to steer his own life, let alone a contrary 17-year-old girl.* When the crisis struck, like okasan, I too, was ill-equipped to cope.
>
> *During the mid-year college break, Yayoi worked as a typist in the newly opened office of an American magazine. She's fresh and attractive. A colleague fell in love with her, and wanted them to marry. One day after work he took her out for coffee, then back to his parents' house, where she stayed for several nights, without telling us where she was. Who knows what went on? But I think the worst. At best it was thoughtlessness. She must have known we would worry, especially when we were told she didn't turn up for work. Okasan was out of her depth. What was I supposed to do?*

In desperation, Hisashi contacted Suzuki-san, who questioned staff at the magazine and eventually found out where Yayoi was. Mid-thirties, unmarried, Suzuki-san worked as an interpreter and translator for GHQ, where she had met Hisashi when he was on contract to the

Fisheries Agency. He held her in high regard. She was the daughter of a rich farmer, and a graduate of the same elite women's college as Tomoko.

Together Suzuki-*san* and Hisashi went to the young man's house to meet with his parents. Like Ryoko, they were old Japan, and bewildered and anxious they admitted they were at a loss over what to do. They did not even know Yayoi's family name. Suzuki-*san* threatened to contact the police if Yayoi did not go home straight away. And with nervous bobbing bows, apologising profusely, Yayoi returned home within a couple of hours.

Such a thing would never have happened before the war. Yayoi would never have been allowed to work at the magazine in the first place, so there would have been no opportunity to meet a young man, let alone have coffee with him. Before the war she would have been disowned, as such a scandal would have been a huge handicap for the family. Naturally there was gossip, but nothing serious. Fortunately they were in the city: living in a more conservative rural area, they would have been shunned. Luckily also, Hisashi worked at Hinode. At Mitsubishi he would have lost all chance of promotion.

> Okasan *should have reprimanded her, but so worried about how the incident would be seen by others, she kept silent. Whether it was the young man's fault or not, to save Yayoi's reputation the matter had to go to the local family court, and Shimazu was charged.*

It was obvious to Hisashi that everything was against Yayoi completing college. Ryoko was spending far beyond her means, and with rampant inflation, her funds were dwindling fast. But, she was staunch in her belief that graduating would improve Yayoi's chances of making a suitable marriage. Although he never said it out loud, Hisashi knew that would not help. Given the competition for bridegrooms, as well as the fact that she was a 'half orphan', Yayoi was at an even bigger disadvantage than him. As he saw it, her only solution was to get a job.

He hoped that, with Suzuki-*san* as a role model, Yayoi would aspire to become one of the new breed of professional working women.

> *In these uncertain times it's difficult to know where you are. Everything is off-centre. What is the real Japan? Sometimes the old ways apply, and sometimes they don't. What are the new rules of behaviour: Japanese or American? Is the American vision the best for Japan? At least following tradition we knew how to behave.*

Chapter 57

Metamorphosis

Yoraba tai-ju no kage
If seeking shelter (use) a big tree's shade
(Seek influential people when patronage is needed)

IN EXCHANGE FOR ALL he had lost in leaving Mitsubishi, Hisashi gained new opportunities at Hinode, and he glimpsed an entirely different world, where money counted more than status. He had been unaware of the existence of such a society. Now, most people with whom he came in contact were *narikin*, less educated than him, but capable, adaptable men well suited to the new Japan. Thus he gained new ideas and attitudes, new skills, new connections, new ways of business, and a new set of acquaintances.

> *30 November 1947 continued*
> *One light in the darkness, working at Hinode, I met Yanagida-shi, ex-president of the Bank of Japan, who had just retired. In reality he had been purged. He needed pocket money. Hasegawa-shi recruited him as an advisor, which before the war, would have been unbelievable. Such an esteemed man: he rescued me from my slump, advising me to make the best of my present position by learning as much as possible, and to read every spare moment.*

Senpai–kohai (senior–junior) exists between those of the same background who went to the same high school and university. In the role previously filled by Yoshida-*shi*, Yanagida-*shi* now offered support to the anxious young man.

Their relationship developed quietly. They shared not only a love of books and learning, but a similar standing in life. Yanagida-

shi empathised with Hisashi. He too was unable to make the best use of his background and training. The former banker encouraged Hisashi to talk. Loathe to be a bother, Hisashi was cautious at first, but Yanagida-*shi* was warm and understanding, his conversation without reserve or ceremonious speech.

And the floodgates opened for Hisashi. He had a job. He had pinned his hopes on everything being all right if he found a higher paying job. Why then did he feel so depressed working at Hinode? Was it his fault, or that of society? Yanagida-*shi* would listen courteously, sympathising, making the odd suggestion, but never giving direction.

Yanagida-*shi* was an acknowledged admirer of Zen, and his words had huge impact on shaping Hisashi's future thinking. Yanagida-*shi* taught the younger man the skills he needed to get on in life, 'spraying water so the buds would grow'. Hisashi must polish himself to be the best he could. His mentor emphasised self-reliance, both spiritual and financial. It was only by his own efforts, through mental training, that he could tap his potential strength. He must make peace with the Creator of the Universe, and aspire to achieve spiritual peace and enlightenment, calmly resigned to his fate.

Yanagida-*shi* emphasised self-control, both mental and emotional, which would enable Hisashi to meet any situation 'with neither too much nor too little effort', controlling 'his mischievous mind' and 'polishing away the rust of his body'. Such was 'The Way of the Warrior': that neither external threat nor internal ardour could bring him down. But self-control could be achieved only by recognising the transience of life.

Yanagida-*shi* also emphasised self-governance, and to raise his thoughts to the highest level, Hisashi would need to widen his view. Yanagida-*shi* suggested he read everything he could, studying the past and interpreting it for himself. Reading widely would give him the knowledge and wisdom needed to get along in this new world.

Ultimately, books became an invaluable source of support for Hisashi, encouraging him to think outside the square, and giving him the wherewithal to endure future adversity. It did not solve all his problems, but reading opened his eyes, and taught him to think and to question. Previously his reading had been mainly confined to technology and science, but now he found books in the university library about people and philosophy, psychology and sociology, archaeology and theology, and classics from all over the world.

His own library was much smaller than before the war, with many of his books having been stolen from the shelter or bartered for food. But his collection was growing again – Maupassant's *A Life of a Woman*, Hilty's *Of a Happy Life*, Fredrich Nietzsche's *Look at This Man* – now nearly a whole shelf full, serving to fill the empty hours alone with his thoughts. He had just re-read *Kokoro*, a study in loneliness by Soseki Natsume. Realising it was all down to him in the end, he was making desperate efforts to discover himself.

> *Good news in September, my salary increased to 4 200 yen a month.*
>
> *An insidious remnant of the war has been the increase in social problems that hinder Japan's reconstruction. In October, I read of a young judge who starved to death after strictly observing the rationing system. I cannot decide whether his action was right or wrong. The government turned a blind eye.*

Yoshitada Yamaguchi had eaten nothing from the *yami-ichi*, although he knew he might die from starvation. Crime related to illegal profiteering was increasing daily. According to his conscience, Yamaguchi felt it would be hypocritical to judge these criminals if he was still prepared to eat food from the *yami-ichi*.

Of concern was also the number of people affected by sexually transmitted diseases brought back to Japan by repatriated soldiers. Onishi-*san* (the cousin in whose house they had previously been living) had passed syphilis to his pregnant wife. The baby had been born diseased and died soon after. His wife slowly went mad, day after day sitting in the backyard, muttering inarticulately, as she stirred the cesspit. She died blind and paralysed.

1 December
Over the last few months, thanks to Yanagida-shi, my desire for knowledge has increased. I read on the tram to work, and whenever I have spare time, and through the study of mankind and money, my malaise is fading away.

2 December
Today is okasan's birthday. Our neighbour, Tanii-san, joined our humble meal of festive red rice, dried sardines and bean soup with rice cakes.

9 December
Last night, Yasuwo-kun came to visit, depressed as Nissan workers are staging a go-slow. I sympathise over a situation similar to what I experienced at Mitsubishi. He mentioned he'd seen an old classmate just back from Burma. Three-quarters of their unit died. With few ships remaining, or seaworthy, repatriation is slow. Some areas, like Burma, are particularly late as troops must trek out through the jungle.

24 December
Met Miss Takenaka and enjoyed a snack near the subway station.

Miss Takenaka was a 'long-service office girl' at Hinode. The use of 'Miss' was a postwar title for young working women, but not one Hisashi felt comfortable using for women of his equal, such as Suzuki-san. Though initially he had not had much to do with Miss Takenaka, he had noticed her.

A few months earlier, on the way home from work, he had seen her standing on the landing at Mitsukoshi-mae station (literally 'in front of Mitsukoshi Department Store'), and suggested having a cup of tea. From then on, every week, as he thought, 'just by chance', she would be waiting for him in the same place. In fact, her apartment was in the opposite direction, on a completely different line. She was small and vital, and he was attracted to her vivacious personality. An upcountry girl, she was worldly-wise, knowing how to manage alone in the city, a girl who would always be a 'wife older than her husband'.

31 December

Power cuts have increased. Inflation has increased. And over the year as more and more soldiers have been repatriated, basic necessities have become even scarcer, the narikin *the only ones to gain.*

Mid-year, the definition of democracy became clear, a new political structure we could see. Through 1946, and well into 1947, there was almost anarchy, a messed-up period between the death of old Japan and its rebirth, a metamorphosis of political and social life. Japan was like a dragonfly. Its eggs hatch under water into fierce nymphs. After two years an ugly nymph climbs up a reed out of the water, clinging to the stalk as it sheds its skin, and emerges as a beautiful dragonfly. At last, we thought, a break from confusion. No more chaos, no more bad things. Life is beginning to improve. Unfortunately the basis of the new society has already been adopted, including its bad elements.

1947 has been the worst year of my life. What has happened to the nation has happened to me in miniature. I, too, moved into a new society, changing style. Obliged to dispose of my past into the rubbish, I live as a man not tied to the old ways, not basing my career on my educational background, or the senior system. I am a man newly born, seeking only money. As an Edo era proverb proclaims, 'A man who has no money is a man without a head, and nothing but a slave.' Living through hardship has tested my character and given me a better understanding of the art of living. I must forge ahead on this new path, preparing myself for other struggles along the way.

A metamorphosis had also taken place in American plans. Late in 1947, the Lieutenant General of the US Eighth Army declared Japan would be used as a democratic stronghold against Chinese and Soviet communism. Initially, reparation had imposed a retaliatory, reformist peace that would weaken the Japanese government and halt economic recovery. However, by 1947, as Cold War tensions between America and the Soviet Union grew, the US changed tack. Japan was now seen as a friend who needed to become an economically stable barrier between the Soviet and Chinese communists encroaching on Korea.

US demands for reparation weakened. One by one appropriated factories were released as policy shifted to reconstruction, while a programme of recovery provided loans and reduced import restrictions. Foreign trade, halted by the 1942 ABCD embargo, had resumed in August, but was restricted to certain goods from certain countries. With limited government funds, imports were prioritised, the first priority being foodstuffs: rice from Egypt and India, and soybeans from Manchuria.

At the same time, Government and Relief in Occupied Areas [GARIOA] had been added to the American budget so that nationwide food relief could be provided in Japan. GHQ directives were slowly turning into policy, but the *yami-ichi* still hindered recovery plans.

Chapter 60

Sport of Fortune

Manande omowazareba sunawachi kurashi,
omoite manabazareba sunawachi ayaushi
Learning without thinking, darkness;
thinking without learning, danger

O N 18 July 1948, Hisashi wrote in his diary:

January to July 1948, the blank period of my diary, what have I been doing? What was I thinking during that half year?

Thanks to Hasegawa-shi's generous year-end bonus of three months salary instead of the average two, I had a better New Year holiday with okasan and Yayoi. I was glad I could please them with such a small thing as material happiness, but at the same time I felt disappointed and lonely.

I worked as secretary to Hasegawa-shi until March, by which stage I was comfortable with the job, but becoming bored. Then, quite unexpectedly, at the end of March, without anyone consulting me, I was released from that position. Hasegawa-shi plans to modernise and expand the business, and apparently he has plans for me. At the beginning of April, he kicked out old-timers and wartime staff, and I, though a mere stripling, was appointed Chief Purchaser. Unfortunately my new job is quite disagreeable. My two immediate seniors, the only old-timers remaining, treat me like an outsider.

I'm now in a huge slump, not helped by hearing the outcome of my university research. The two students who took over the work I'd nearly completed have received worldwide acclaim and doctorates. On the one hand, I was proud the seed I'd sown in the bare ground had grown and borne fruit. On the other hand, I was resentful the opportunity had been taken from me.

The other reason for my slump was Yayoi's school fees. In June, realising she couldn't pay the next instalment, and influenced by ojisan [Shozo], okasan decided to ask Hasegawa-shi for the money. She even asked Suzuki-san to act as go-between. Fortunately, Suzuki-san contacted me first. We both agreed it was a foolish idea, so she wrote to okasan telling her she'd had no luck. I know it was the right thing to do, but I hated taking such action. Aside from believing such expenses should be raised by one's own efforts, I know Hasegawa-shi isn't a man to loan money for nothing. In asking him, okasan was innocently offering Yayoi as his potential mistress. And ojisan had no qualms in using them to get closer to the president. In his barter business in Manchuria, it would have been an ordinary occurrence.

Last month Hasegawa-shi shocked us all, revealing his natural shape and original form, declaring he was Korean. With the police clamping down on the yami-ichi, genuine Japanese are being severely punished if caught; Americans, Koreans and Taiwanese less so. Hasegawa-shi, loathe to abandon a lucrative business, could continue only if he declared himself as a Korean.

On 22 July, Hisashi again started regular entries in his diary:

Reopen my diary here. I'm 28 years old. From today I'll write in English. The worrying issues of our household budget and Yayoi's school expenses aren't resolved, but I've recovered some of my composure. And today I ask myself two questions. First, by what job should I earn my living? I don't know, but I must study English. We Japanese must increase our international knowledge, and learn to communicate in English. Second, what or whom should be my God guiding me to ever-lasting composure? For this I have no answer.

In his talks with Yanagida-*shi*, Hisashi had listened carefully, recognising the wisdom behind his mentor's words. But in his present environment, and at his age, it was too difficult to become self-sufficient. He still wanted to rely on someone else for guidance, some other spirit who would provide him relief.

In the meantime, he would occupy his mind learning English. His father's influence continued to be strong. He remembered *otosan* had pushed him to learn English nursery rhymes and hymns at kindergarten and primary school. At university, then in the navy, and Mitsubishi, he had been accustomed to reading technical reports in English, along with French, German and Russian. He had also learned the terminology needed to carry out his translation work at the Fisheries Agency. But there had never been the opportunity to read, speak or listen to everyday conversation. The classroom he used was inexpensive, practical and effective: *The Japan Times* written in English, and American radio broadcasts. Using frequent repetitive expressions, the weather forecast was the easiest to understand. He could judge the temperature, and of course, he knew whether it was raining or fine. World news overlapped with Japanese newspaper headings, so when he read or listened to the news, he was already familiar with the basic information.

> *23 July*
>
> *It was exceptionally hot today, 90 degrees, maybe the maximum this summer. And the house is mine at last – I paid the final instalment of 8 100 yen to Yasuda Bank. Hard to believe it's three years since the air raid.*

Officially costing 81 000 yen, about $US200 at the *yami-ichi* rate, their house purchase had been subsidised by the metropolitan government, assistance given on a case by case basis to those who had lost their homes: for Hisashi, supporting his widowed mother and sister, 60 per cent was deducted from the cost. Ryoko had paid the initial deposit with the traditional 'condolence money' given by Kawanishi, and a good sum had come from Hisashi's year-end bonus. By being frugal, even with 70 per cent of his salary spent on food, he had paid the house off in 18 months.

> *24 July*
>
> *In the afternoon walked down Ginza Street with Yoshiji-kun and Miss Takenaka. I long for mental serenity but won't find it until I decide to what job I should devote the rest of my life.*

29 July
Hasegawa-shi has put me in charge of a new project.

Hasegawa-*shi* knew how to recognise a good opportunity. It had been a clever move contracting advisors like Yanagida-*shi* and other purged, pre-war financial leaders. Through them he acquired confidential information, such as learning that GHQ was looking to revive the car industry.

Pre-war, the woven asbestos cloth and moulded natural rubber used for brake shoes was expensive and wore out quickly. A cheaper, longer lasting material – resin reinforced with cotton fibre – had recently been developed, but was not available in Japan.

Kyodo Asbestos was a failing, family owned factory that manufactured pipes, plates and trays from resin. Gladly accepting Hasegawa-*shi*'s offer of financial backing, the owner had agreed to diversify into making resin brake shoes. Hisashi was given responsibility for nurturing the project.

1 August
Today was very hot. The house smells of ka-tori-senko,* *bringing back memories of my childhood. Visited Kobayashi-san with okasan and Yayoi, and feasted on watermelon.*

Hisashi could never smell the distinctive fragrance of *ka-tori-senko* without being beset by nostalgia. The scent of the wild grass *yomogi*, deeply rooted in his childhood, signified the magic and charm of summer. Unconsciously springing back to life was the scene of a small boy, who, throughout the hot, humid months, just before bed had the special job of lighting the flat coils of *ka-tori-senko* placed in each room. At the close of a busy, interesting day, secure in the midst of his family, the invisible smoke had wafted through the house, its smell evoking warmth and contentment.

---

* Mosquito-repelling incense.

2 August

This morning stormy rain fell, then slowly the sky cleared, and the rain clouds lifted. My project hasn't yet begun. I've nothing to do at Hinode, but too much in my brain and private life learning English.

3 August

Hungry! Is it because Egyptian rice has been rationed again, or the increase in prices? Prices multiply annually by 5: something costing 10 yen in 1945 increased to 50 in 1946, 250 in 1947, and now 1250 yen. Retail prices have deliberately been raised so the government can pay farmers more for rice, but now we all suffer under wild inflation.

4 August

Was angry when I read a verdict of suicide had been pronounced for Shimoyama-shi. I met him only once, back in 1945 with Professor Kkikawa, but he didn't seem someone who would commit suicide. It's rumoured that GHQ provoked the communists to kidnap and murder him. But although forensic doctors suggested homicide, the case has been closed.

Since Hisashi had met Shimoyama-*shi*, he had risen to become president of JNR [Japan National Railways].

GHQ wanted mass employment cuts, with the first wave to come out of the rail sector. A million had already been laid off across related industries. The employment situation was complicated by the flow of repatriated soldiers, the sizeable workforce now expecting their old jobs back. Wedged between GHQ and the unions, Shimoyama-*shi* had been in a precarious position.

Negotiations between Shimoyama-*shi* and the JNR union, which blamed Shimoyama-*shi* for the huge number of unemployed rail workers, had been scheduled for 5 July. Around 8.45 a.m., before going to the office, Shimoyama-*shi* had dropped into Mitsukoshi Department Store. But he was never heard from again. The next day his remains had been found strewn across the railway track near the Sumida-*gawa*. Soon afterwards 100 000 workers lost their jobs at JNR.

There had never been such a crime. Stunned that the communists resorted to such violence, Hisashi concluded SCAP policy had given them licence to do as they pleased.

5 August
Heard Yokoyama-shi of Yasuda Bank has been arrested for taking a bribe from Showa Denko. Such a scandal will end his banking career. Many others have also been charged.

The RFC [Rehabilitation Finance Corporation] established in 1946 had helped rebuild key industries, namely, synthetic fertilisers, coal, ship building and steel making. Fertilisers would increase agricultural output and self-sufficiency, and coal would fuel industry. Restoring the commercial shipping fleet would generate the demand for steel and earn foreign exchange. Steel making would have spin-offs for other industries. All would create jobs. Import restrictions, albeit with heavy stipulations, had been lifted on items required by these industries.

Showa Denko had been a middle-sized fertiliser manufacturer. However, through Sugawara-*shi*, a politician whose brother-in-law Hinohara-*shi* also happened to be president of Showa Denko, the company borrowed over 50 per cent of the fund allocated by the RFC for the whole of the fertiliser industry. Hinohara-*shi*, in his efforts to secure the greatest share of the fund, had passed out bribes. On 23 June, he was arrested on suspicion of corruption.

6 August
I've been rescued by my new project with Kyodo Asbestos. I'll nurse the egg, and then the chicken. Success or failure falls on me.

7 August
Yoshiji-kun came to my office this afternoon. I don't know why, then soon afterwards Miss Takenaka arrived and we all went to Mitsukoski Department Store. Why? These two are collaborating about something, and intend to speak to me, but what about? Isolated soul!! I'll never find peace of mind.

Chapter 59

At the Whim of the President

Koshi-kinchaku
A loin purse, part of the boss's outfit

8 August 1948

Sunday, a constant chorus of cicadas lasted from dawn till dusk, impossible to escape. Trees in the nearby bush are thick with them. Hasegawa-shi is adopting the daughter of a zaibatsu family, the girl's father tacitly agreeing to give his daughter in exchange for an appointment as an advisor to Hinode. Hasegawa-shi expects me to eventually marry his new daughter. I'm not interested. I want to resign.

* * *

HISASHI WAKES TO THE CARESS of the early morning sun. It is going to be one of those white mornings so common in summer. As he lies there, contemplating his day off, thousands of male cicadas join in full voice, railing against the shortness of life. With their transparent wings shimmering in the sunshine, they quiver on the branches, the air crackling with the sound.

Dormant for years, the mature larvae have emerged from underground to shed their horny armour and find a mate. Under the sun, they sing and sing, making the most of their short time on earth, only to die a week later, their transience likened to the life of man. Hisashi is still underground, not ready to surface. He is in no mood to find a mate, or sing out loud. And now this added complication.

Even if his mother had not been a consideration, this is not the right woman. And, he knows for sure, it is not the right job.

Once again Hisashi has been handed a future promising wealth, status and power. But the offer depends on his taking a wife, which has made him realise that not only is he not ready for marriage, but his inclination lies elsewhere. He cares for Miss Takenaka. He knows they have no future and, even if marriage were possible, his mother will never accept someone from her background. However, it confirms he does not want to marry one of Hasegawa-*shi*'s discards.

It was common practice for a rich man to adopt a daughter of marriageable age; an 'open secret', she would be a temporary mistress, then discarded with payment to a subordinate. For the young man, there was double benefit: plenty of money, and legally becoming a son-in-law and heir. But it also tied a string around his neck, like a dog, so he would not run away.

10/11/12 August
On a business trip to Osaka, I was able to meet ojisan *and* obasan [Tomoko and her husband] *to canvas their thoughts on Hasegawa-*shi's *plan. They agree I should refuse his offer. He has a legal wife, and a second young wife. Why does he need another?*

Hisashi had never met the first wife, who lived in Kyoto, but on a number of occasions he had glimpsed the younger wife. Whenever Hasegawa-*shi* left town, ostensibly on a business trip, he arranged for his 'number two wife' to meet him at a high class *ryokan* (inn). For the sake of appearances Hisashi had to go too, and about twice a month, he and Hasegawa-*shi* were driven in the black American Plymouth to Hakone, an area of hot springs. Hisashi usually saw her arrive. Dressed in an expensive *kimono*, she was very attractive and at least 30 years younger than Hasegawa-*shi*.

Yamagoshi, who drove them, was a good source of gossip. The essence of a dutiful servant, he was deferential, head-bowing, but his eyes missed nothing. He and Hisashi shared a room away from the president's luxurious suite, whiling away their boredom by gossiping, though Hisashi was always careful of what he said.

13 August
There are so many problems at Kyodo factory. Like Japanese society, it's in a sick condition, lacking the cooperation and harmony needed to create social order, and recovery will take time. The sample of the first trialled brake lining was unsatisfactory. Hiruma, the factory supervisor, doesn't like Hasegawa-shi pushing him around, so he niggles over minor things and passes shoddy work, blaming it on Hasegawa-shi's order to reduce costs. How pathetic is the man who continually troubles about trivia!! His petty hurt makes him avaricious, so he produces inferior goods. Like Hiruma, the old-style craftsmen at the factory can't or won't change their technique to suit the new product. They should be replaced, but, Chiba-shi the owner, while wanting Hinode money won't cooperate either.

14 August
Kamiyama-shi of Nissan Heavy Industry met with me at the factory. Returned to Tokyo in Hasegawa-shi's Plymouth, sampling its superlative handling through pools of water, demonstrating the dignity of science and mechanical power. Couldn't help but notice the jealous looks at the car's narikin owner. Or was it me they despised – the boss's loin purse – part of his outfit?

15 August
Today is the third anniversary of the War-End. Yamagoshi the steward has resigned, but no one knows why. I regret his leaving, and recollect the Shakespearean tale of King Lear *and his daughters.*

16 August
I must do something with my life. I'm frittering my youthful years on trifles, allowing time to elapse without improvement. What of the words of Rene Descartes, 'I think, therefore I am'? What do they mean?

19 August
Today we found the wrong ratio of materials had been mixed for the trial resin. Was it deliberate? Also decided local phenolic resin isn't satisfactory. We must import higher grade, more heat-resistant resin from America.

21 August
In the afternoon delivered a letter to Hasegawa-shi's second wife. It's the beautiful bird that invariably gets caged. I took tea with her, listening as she talked of trifles. I sense, like me, she's lonely. Lonely souls!! Where is their place of rest? That place is only found after suffering many tests by God!!

Hasegawa-*shi*'s second wife lived with her parents in a house owned by Hasegawa-*shi*. Paid a generous monthly allowance, it enabled them to live a comfortable lifestyle, albeit in a restricted society. Her patron educated her with care and lavished her with expensive gifts of *kimono*, *obi*, fans and ornaments for her hair. His demands were her first priority, and she was expected to tell him every detail of her life.

Taking tiny steps across the *tatami* she ushers Hisashi courteously into the reception room where, with straight back and barely a rustle of her *kimono*, she kneels at the low table to serve him tea. It is the first time he has met her in person, and up close she is even younger than he had thought; similar to Yayoi, but there the similarity ends. Versed in the ancient arts, her life revolves around tradition – the traditions that Ryoko had learned, but which Yayoi had rejected. Nevertheless, imperceptible details hint she belongs to a different world, the world of fleeting affection.

She is most attractive, her face lightly powdered, lips rouged and, in *geisha* fashion, her eyebrows have been shaven and redrawn. Her *kimono* and hair accessories are expensive. She is the picture of health: her skin is like porcelain, her eyes bright, and her teeth white and even. She is charming and intelligent, with gentle, thoughtful manners. A middle-ranked *geisha* destined for a rich merchant, she is a shadowed person living in obscurity, 'a pendant for her master's eyes'.

To all appearances, Hisashi thinks, she seems happy. But as she speaks, there is a look in her eye, and the odd veiled remark indicating that she would prefer a different existence. Maybe it is the best way for her and her parents to survive, but it is apparent that she longs for more. In fact, she is just like him, with few options, and in his heart he sympathises.

Both were constrained by their parents, and obliged to give up their dreams. Both were frowned on by people, and both were dependent on the president's whim.

23 August
In my garden the corn can be picked. Then I must plant radishes and spinach.

26 August
Went to the theatre with Hinode staff and saw the Meiji era play Shingeki*: the percentage of proletariat in the audience has risen. A postcard arrived notifying me I've passed the Labour Ministry's written examination.*

29 August
At last a fine day. Okasan and Yayoi have agreed Yayoi will leave college. On the one hand, I'm sorry for them; but on the other, I congratulate them that they have finally accepted the reality of our new society: defeated Japan.

With more fees due, the time had come to exert pressure on Yayoi and Hisashi's mother. For months he had canvassed them for Yayoi to give up college. With only his salary coming in, he could no longer make ends meet. Yayoi had to find a job. Despite the words of the new constitution, it was still frowned upon for a young lady of a good family to work for money, but there was no choice. Fortunately, Yayoi seemed to yearn for something different, and *okasan* would have to accept that there was no going back to her pre-war world.

30 August
Chief Accountant Iimuka-san says Hasegawa-shi has been evading taxes

on his yami-ichi dealings, but he's been reported. As customary, he has a scapegoat, Iimuka-san.

3 September
Iimuka-san has lost his job.

23.8.3. Hungry. I don't know whether it is due do the Egpt rice — rationed lately — or the general advance of prices of commodities (rised up to about 200% in the end of July)

23.8.4. I was much impressed by reading "Shinjin-roku", which was presented from my uncle Sonoda.

23.8.5. Radio broadcasts that Mr. Yokoyama, serving in Yasuda Bank, was arrested on suspicion of on the charge of taking a bribe from Shōwadenkō K.K.. I am afraid that this scandal put an end to his banker's life.
Takeo Sonoda, my cousin in Wakayama, came to Tokyo to the aid of the baseball match between Ichikō and Sankō which will be held on 8th of August.

23.8.6. I make up my mind to be a good assistant of Kyōritsu Asbestos Co.. I feel great pleasure to be engaged in this assistance, regarding the fruitful future of gum moulded goods, the main products of Kyō-ritsu.

Diary entry from August 1948

Chapter 60
'Out of Specification'

Shirasagi wa karasu to majiwarezu
Shirasagi wa shirasagi to nomi tomoni iku
The snowy heron cannot live with the crow
The snowy heron should live with snowy herons

4 September 1948
Through the good offices of Suzuki-san, Yayoi has been taken on as a typist at the American City Bank in Marunouchi. She's joined the new breed of young working ladies embarking on a Western lifestyle. I'm glad she found an occupation she earnestly desires. From this year many foreign companies have opened offices in Tokyo, creating positions for young ladies. Pre-war, only young men would have been employed.

AS A SCHOOL GIRL, Yayoi had always worn Western dress. Now as a young, working woman she coveted nylon stockings and high heels, and even bought second-hand clothing from an American colleague. The cardigan and skirt, and coat and trousers, were expensive, but they were fashionable, and 'American'. And, much to her mother's horror, Yayoi had her hair permed, and had shaved off her eyebrows to pencil in a new shape. By changing the location of her eyebrows she hoped to change the line of her face and appear more Western. To counter this trend, Ryoko had insisted that Yayoi attend *kimono* school after work, but she went only twice then stopped, astonished at their expense and how bothersome they were to wear.

5 September
Sunday, fine weather, so shampooed my hair for the first time in five months.

The Morning Glories are at their best in my garden, as they romp with abandon along the fence, as are the flowers of the Sponge Gourd, which creep over the trellis in the vegetable patch. Throughout summer into early fall, my Morning Glories open their faces to the sun, closing up and dying as the sun sets; the next day, new flowers break out afresh. Busy bees fly merrily amongst them, muttering to themselves, their hind legs dusted with pollen, as they gather food for their families. What are they muttering? Why are they so merry? Do they know the will of God, can they carry it through? If so, I envy their wisdom. I, a descendant of Adam and Eve, have not achieved their wisdom. Forever straying between God and beast, unlike the bee, I am barely able to satisfy my stomach and that of my family.

7 September

Animalistic, malevolent human spirit!!! I curse it because I must struggle with it all my life. How should I behave? Judging by what I do each day, I'm just an animal, a low grade animal, Hasegawa-shi's dog, killing time to obtain food for myself and my family, contributing nothing to anyone else.

9 September

Materials expected for Kyodo didn't arrive. Was it malice, laziness, or lack of ability? It's rumoured Hasegawa-shi's adopted daughter has returned to her parents after incurring the displeasure of his number one wife. I've escaped!

11 September

Saw the American movie Sentimental Journey. *Foreign film tickets are difficult to get. Miss Chiba got them.* But why ask me?*

12 September, Sunday

Couldn't concentrate on my study of the labour law. Was it fatigue, or lack of will?

15 September

Against his will, Yoshikawa-shi has been made chairman of Kyodo, pushing aside Chiba-shi, who's been moved into a 'do nothing job'. All along

---

*Miss Chiba was the only daughter of the owner of Kyodo.

Hasegawa-shi's wanted the company and the process, not the staff. But this isn't the way. He should have waited a month, by which time Chiba-shi would probably have left of his own accord. I'm disappointed in Hasegawa-shi.

16 September
A taifu roared ashore releasing its fury. Rain trickled through our roof in several places. The power was off all evening.

17 September
The loop line and local tram line were erratic due to taifu *damage.*

18 September
In the presence of General MacArthur and the Imperial Prince, the National Fire Works Contest was held at Ryogoku-bashi over the Sumida-gawa. We had a clear view from our third floor office window, and everyone stayed to watch. Red, yellow and green flowers hung on the inky sky, blooming briefly, then disappearing!! Oh beauty! Why are you so transitory!! Can't you hold your beautiful forms and stay a little longer? Is it such a vain dream to hope? Reminds me of the words that 'upon the full tide of pleasure, steels sadness'.

19 September
A fine Sunday; built a shelf for okasan. *Yasuwo-kun dropped by and we enjoyed the moon. The power is off.*

A full moon in a clear autumn sky was an occasion for thanksgiving. An event celebrated for centuries by farmers after a rich rice harvest.

> Seated on the doorstep, they can see the giant yellow orb rising over the rooftops. Silvery light floods the step, illuminating their faces. Moonbeams cast shadows in the garden, transforming the Sponge Gourds into lanterns. Conversation is desultory at first, both young men weighted down by worries. But, as the *sake* flows, the moon weaves its magic, and their despondency disappears, their animated exchange sliding from inflation and rising prices, to politics, unions and love.
>
> A glass of *sake* with a friend is a bright moment in their lives.

With a sweep of his arm and burst of laughter, Hisashi encompasses the moon. On its surface, he can distinguish the shadowy figure of the resident rabbit pounding his rice cakes. Or is it Kaguya-hime, the beautiful girl born in bamboo, who returned as an adult to the full moon?

20 September
At lunchtime went with Yasuwo-kun to Tokyo National Theatre to see bunraku [puppet theatre]. It's an art of the past, people today preferring the cinema. In the evening played mahjong.

Chanted to music, the eighteenth-century tragedy began. Full of twists and turns, a love affair between a *samurai* and *geisha*, where caste clashed with sentiment, the play covered the gamut of emotions: love, misunderstanding, rejection and revenge.

In spirited tempo, the nearly human-sized puppets exchange sweet smiles, weep and fight, their gestures and expressions guided by a master puppeteer and two assistants. In a white robe, his vest in green and gold, the *omozukai* (principal puppeteer) is meant to be seen. Using skills handed down from generation to generation, he manipulates the eyebrows, eyes and mouth with his left hand, while his right hand operates the puppet's right arm. In robes and hoods of black, his two assistants are barely visible, as one operates the puppet's left arm, the other its legs. From an elevated platform on stage, the solo *shamisen* player dictates timing and pace, the melodious tone of his three-stringed, banjo-like instrument throbbing with emotion. Seated beside him, the *tayu* (chanter) delivers the comic quips and flowery monologues, changing smoothly from the raspy bass of the *samurai* to the *geisha*'s silky falsetto.

Arriving at the *geisha* house, observed by his uncle's mischief-making servant, the hero greets his sweetheart whom he plans to marry. Learning of his nephew's secret plans, the uncle pressures the *geisha*, who spurns her lover. Quivering with anger, the usually mild-mannered hero drinks himself into a rage. The strumming of the *shamisen* soars to a crescendo, the passion and pain too much to bear, and he stabs his beloved in the heart. Too late he discovers the reason for her rejection.

21 September
Miss Chiba gave me a neck-tie and a box of cakes. What should I give in return? The snowy heron cannot live with the crow; the snowy heron should live with snowy herons. Played mahjong again.

22 September
More mahjong. I dislike going to work without changing my clothes.

23 September
The Autumn Equinox, a national holiday, a day off work. Thank goodness, no mahjong. Read over my diary, impressed by my experiences over these three years.

26 September
Mahjong again last night – have spent too many evenings playing recently. Today, a dreary Sunday – the stormy weather continues, so went to the movie The Best Year of Our Lives. An irony, but at least it wasn't mahjong!

Monday, we entertained officials from the Ministry of Commerce and Trade to increase our allocation of rationed goods; Tuesday, bankers to get bigger loans; Wednesday, the shipping companies to get the best rate to ship resin from America; Friday, the Car-Parts Manufacturers Association to make a joint petition to the Ministry for better allocations; and last night, car manufacturers to get orders. Hasegawa-shi said that last night with the staff from Toyota, Diesel and Nissan was the most important evening of all. Why? What's he up to?

* * *

The middle-aged *kimono*-clad waitress comes hurrying towards them, bowing in welcome and guiding them to their room, which like the others is elevated a step above the ground. As they slip off their shoes, gusts of laughter reverberate from a neighbouring room. It is busy, one of the best restaurants in the area, and many customers wait without reservations.

The 16 dark-suited, youngish section heads sprawl on the *tatami* around the low table, drinking, joking, laughing and smoking. Jackets are off, shirt collars unbuttoned, and ties loosened. They like to party. It deepens understanding and friendship. Four teams, four players per team, compete for points, with bets on the side. Amidst the clatter of the tiles, a stream of talk eddies back and forth, with no end of gossip and opinions expressed.

Considerable discussion arises about the break up of the *zaibatsu*. Unperturbed at how asset stripping has affected *zaibatsu* families, nevertheless the men are unanimous in their concern at how the resultant loss of jobs and removal of capable business leaders has slowed economic recovery. Hisashi nurses his beer thoughtfully.

The food is non-stop: something grilled, something fried, something raw, something steamed, something stewed and a rice dish; fish, *tempura*, *sashimi*, egg custard, vegetables and *sushi*. And with unlimited supplies of *yami-ichi* beer and *sake*, the noise and laughter rises higher and higher. As hosts, the Hinode team drink little, attentive, ensuring their guests' glasses are kept filled. And, as with the previous nights, they intentionally lose the game, allowing the Nissan team to take the winnings. And, as usual, playing well past midnight, they are supplied with blankets and bed down on the *tatami*. This last week Hisashi has spent four nights away from home.

But, what had been the purpose of this particular evening? What secrets had Hasegawa-*shi* received from his advisors? All Hisashi knew was that he was after a big order from GHQ. The manufacturers were receiving bigger and bigger orders to repair American vehicles, which needed brake shoes. Having Kyodo, Hinode was no longer merely a middleman for vehicle parts, but a manufacturer with an improved technique, the first in Japan. But why was demand for repair so large, and a matter of such urgency, that the Americans could not handle it themselves? Little did he realise that, with the probable breakout of war in Korea, GHQ were stockpiling munitions, including working vehicles, in Japan.

30 September
It was a fine autumn day, but my head bends low. The only times I'm composed are when I'm sleeping, and at work when I'm too busy to think. When work finishes my heart wanders, seeking answers to tough questions about life and death, inequality, suffering, happiness; answers I can't find.

2 October
Kimura-san came to see okasan, *presenting fruits and flowers for* otosan. *Is it really two years since he died?*

The anniversary of his father's death stirred childhood memories. Some Sundays they had taken walks along the river bank, just a stone's throw from the house, *otosan* pointing out birds, insects and plants. Jinjiro had always seemed to know what would stimulate and satisfy Hisashi's curiosity. He remembered *otasan* talking about the wild weed growing along the bank, the small green leaves and white flowers taking over everything in their path. The *goisshin-gusa* (the revolution flower) was an illegal settler from America, arriving in the Meiji era attached to bags of wheat and barley. There was also the *kikyo*, which had always been grown by the men of their family; its importance as a narcotic passed down through the generations of doctors.

He remembered, too, how once *otosan* had picked up an unremarkable fragment of crystallised quartz. Thousands of years earlier, their ancestors had hunted and fished in the area, using the stone as a knife to cut up their catch. As the small boy lifted it up to the sun, the surface deflected the light, separating it into a mystical rainbow of colours. He had kept the precious find for years, only to lose it after the bombing.

How he missed his father.

Chapter 61

About Face

Chorei bokai
Decreeing in the morning and
amending in the afternoon

3 October 1948, Sunday
Rained all day, read books on Labour law.

4 October
Rain again.

5 October
They've announced there will be an election of a committee to reform middle and high school education. They're throwing out our traditional system, bringing in the American method, including co-education, a new curriculum, compulsory middle school, lowering the entry age to university from 21 to 18, and creating local boards of education. Recently someone in the teachers' union remarked teachers are now in the same genre as night-soil collectors.

FEW SCHOOLS HAD BEEN REBUILT. Classes were taken in community halls, abandoned military facilities, even in the open air, in playgrounds and parks. Teacher shortages meant big classes and low-calibre staff filled the gaps. With such poor conditions and low pay, many staff joined the union; however, their determination to democratise the education system brought them into confrontation with the ministry. The union supported SCAP'S reforms to decentralise education, but the ministry wanted the pre-war model reinstated.

It's useful learning about the new labour laws when so much is happening. But no sooner do I learn the new regulations, than they're rewritten. Though, in this case, I support MacArthur's change in policy. The teachers' union and government officials are too influenced by communist agitators. However, it's GHQ's fault, given that at the beginning of occupation, they treated the communists so benevolently. I would like to tell Mr USA, who is finding it hard to justify what he did to Japan and the Japanese people, of an old Japanese proverb. 'If victorious, a national army; if defeated, a band of traitors'. Losers are always in the wrong.

Unions across the board were gathering momentum. Mid-year, when public sector workers were about to stop work, MacArthur again stepped in, pressing the Ashida Cabinet to retract their right to strike, organise unions and bargain collectively. Cabinet complied. Not only did MacArthur think it was treasonous to strike against one's government, but he was increasingly concerned with the influence of communism in the unions. To his way of thinking, public order and political stability assumed greater importance than individual rights.

7 October
Taifu Lily has passed us by. Winter winds are blowing, and leaves drifting from the trees. The Ashida Cabinet resigned yesterday over the Showa Denko Affair. Ashida has been in power only 7 months, 2 months less than Katayama before him.

All told, 44 people had been prosecuted, the Prime Minister and four cabinet members included. It was commonly believed Hinohara-*shi*, the president of Showa Denko, had been set up as a scapegoat, the puppet of his brother-in-law, politician Sugawara-*shi*, who actually controlled the company and pocketed the profits; but, as there was no evidence, he was never charged.*

---

* Ten years later, former Prime Minister Ashida and others were exonerated. The court confirmed guilty verdicts only on Hinohara-*shi*, the president, and a few other lesser beings.

> *8 October*
>
> *Finally, after a long spell of bad weather, a good day. Hasegawa-shi has sold his Plymouth. Running costs have become too high, though I think it's more to do with the fact that using* yami-ichi *fuel won't look good to GHQ.*
>
> *12 October*
>
> *In my garden, the air is fragrant with the scent of freshly growing things, a synthesis of earth, air and sun. Autumnal flowers, cosmos and dahlia are at their best, colours never more vivid, with butterflies waltzing in their midst.*

In true *samurai* fashion, Hisashi had revealed his need for the beauty of nature: flowers, trees and birds, the sun and moon, encapsulated the ever-vanishing, ever-perpetuating pattern of life.

> *14 October*
>
> *It was a cloudy day, cloudy like my heart.*
>
> *14–24 October*
>
> *No entries in my diary because I was studying for the spoken examination for the Labour Department, a week for preparation, then 5 days repose. Shigeru Yoshida is Prime Minister again.*
>
> *9 November*
>
> *November fifth, heard I passed the exam!!*

Passing the exam entitled Hisashi to be a supervisor of the new labour law, his role to facilitate negotiations between workers and management in Hinode's restructuring. Traditional labour law had favoured the employer, while the new law provided better protection for employees. Few people understood it, so the qualification was a good career move with social prestige.

> *10 November–29 December*
>
> *This period has passed too fast to leave anything in my memory. Work has been busy and there has been no time for anything else. But at last the reconstruction of Japan is underway. The infrastructure is slowly improving,*

the yami-ichi *is under control, and rationing finally works. The principal food ration has increased to 2.7 cups of rice per day.*

Occupation policy has shifted from democratisation to economic growth, and we are now treated as an American colony, but only so we can be used as a buffer against communism. The 'Reverse Course' has begun, and GHQ is abandoning its reform of the zaibatsu, *many of whom have been left in power.*

Chapter 62

Kill or Cure

Koketsu ni irazunba, koji wo ezu
If we don't enter the tiger's den,
we don't get the tiger cubs

HISASHI'S DISCONTENT CONTINUED for another year, as he fluctuated between apathy and despair. Out of place, and out of sorts, he kept to himself as much as he could. From now on, his diary entries were spasmodic.

> *1 January 1949*
> *As last year, I landed New Year's Eve night duty. By the time I got home it was raining and I was sleepy, so gave up my plan to go visiting, and passed the day reading.*

Big companies used professional security guards for night-time security, but smaller businesses like Hinode employed a night watchman for the ground floor, with a senior staff member in attendance on the management floor. Hisashi would sit in his office listening to the radio and reading. Before going to bed at his usual eleven o'clock, he would check the windows on his floor, and the door of the safe in Hasegawa-*shi*'s suite. Then, unrolling the office *futon*, and dressed in his suit, he would take a nap.

> *1 January continued*
> *1948 was another difficult year. I knew by going to Hinode I sacrificed status for salary: however, my salary hasn't been enough, and the average salary outside has caught up to what I'm paid at Hinode.*

14 July
The Soviets say they have an Atomic Bomb. A nuclear holocaust would destroy both sides, so Cold War tensions have been neutralised.

The United States and the Soviet Union dominated the world. Ideologically opposed, a rift had occurred. The River Elbe separated the Soviet controlled east from the American, British and French controlled west, which created two Germanys and two Europes. By 1948, to use Churchill's expression, an invisible, impenetrable 'Iron Curtain' was in place.

1 October
The People's Republic of China has been proclaimed. China is now a communist state. Once again, American policy changes – now against China, yet during the Manchurian Incident they supported them. Occupation policy changes often, like a cat's eye: one minute spoiling Japanese communists, the next minute getting tough, vacillating according to what's best for them.

14 October
Once again there's concern over the yen. Does devaluation of the British pound mean Japan will follow? Devaluation will raise inflation; US importers will cancel their Japanese orders, which will cause a nationwide depression, which will affect incomes. Dodge has been ordered back to Japan.

Aside from scarce resources, economic recovery had been delayed through production restrictions and isolation from international markets. And what money was available for reform had been financed by printing excessive currency and expanding bank credit.

In autumn 1948, Detroit banker Joseph M. Dodge had been appointed to repair the fiscal situation. Commonly known as the Dodge Line, Dodge's Nine Principles for Economic Stabilisation implemented in 1949 were aimed at balancing the national budget by reducing inflation, controlling credit and stabilising the currency. People realised drastic measures, 'kill or cure', were necessary for recovery. Production subsidies and loans were terminated. Wages were cut. Production was cut. Staff were dismissed. The exchange rate was stabilised at 360 yen per US dollar. As a result times were hard.

> 15 October
> Why is Dodge keeping silent? Economists interpret his visit to mean we're in a delicate situation. If he recommends devaluation he'll be obeyed – after all he's the financial dictator.

> 16 October
> MacArthur has said we won't devalue. And, ignoring Dodge's strict line, the government has announced a new law protecting exporters.

Dodge's March budget had not only produced a surplus sufficient to pay off a hefty portion of the nation's bank debt, but had also stabilised some companies. At the same time, price cuts had slowed inflation, but not enough. Superficially, the *yami-ichi* had disappeared, but shortages of rationed goods meant manufacturers were still buying illegally, so production costs remained too high. More drastic cuts were required. But, just as retail prices fell, the cost of resources rose. Exports slumped and domestic spending declined, which resulted in the 'Dodge Recession'.

> 8 November
> Last month the car industry waited to be released from production restrictions. Manufacturers, freely able to import raw materials, would be able to reduce their reliance on the yami-ichi, and business could finally recover. With old-fashioned machinery and systems wiped out, we would start afresh with everything modern – the only thing lacking the restart money. Ironically, on the day of the announcement, recommended by Dodge, GHQ ordered car manufacturers and related industries to 'voluntarily' cut production, dismiss 25 per cent of staff, and reduce wages by 10 per cent. Eighteen-thousand parts per car means 18 000 companies like Hinode are affected, including Mitsubishi, Nissan, and Toyota at the pyramid's peak, which assemble the parts.

27 December
*Yesterday I was saddened and depressed to hear Shinji-*kun [a school friend] *died in June, of what I don't know. He was only 29 years old.*

Another year has been swept from us in turmoil, misery and unrest. Looking back I see pre-war Japan was as young as me, with a pure and simple heart, unaware of the necessity to self-guard against adversity.

Chapter 63
The Kamikaze Blows

Tori wa futatabi saezuru
The birds sing again

19 February 1950
At last some things are being released from rationing. Fresh vegetables are now freely on sale, though, with everything else, the wearisome business of points and coupons continue. Otosan's apprehension about coloured children has been realised – there are many abandoned half-caste children.

Japan must export. Until now exports and imports have been for reparation purposes only, with the US military appropriating Japanese repair services, and payment to the government. To generate income and nourish small industry, export by private hands began last December, and imports from this January. Now manufacturers can negotiate lower prices directly with the Americans, which will increase the scale of work and the number of jobs. However, the government was too optimistic, thinking once trade was freed, things would improve quickly. Little is happening. Companies want to increase exports, workers are available, but money isn't. With Dodge saying cut loans, how do we improve production without funds? Private American companies want to invest, but Mr Dodge 'the almighty' says no. Japan must become master of its own destiny.

And so must I. My experiences have given me abundant fertiliser for my future approach to life. I must turn misfortune into a blessing, taking courage that thus far I've managed.

WORKING IN A SMALL ENVIRONMENT with limited activity, Hisashi was feeling increasingly restrained and impatient with people who wanted to stick to the old ways. It was time to find a new job.

The Imperial Hotel had been requisitioned for high-ranking Allied officers and representatives of the international commissions. It had lost a wing during the bombing, but essentially the exterior remained the same as that built by Frank Lloyd Wright. The burned sections had been quickly rebuilt, and the entire hotel modified to meet military needs.

Hisashi had always liked the Imperial, having visited before the war with his father and Yayoi when they went to the movies at a nearby theatre. Built from volcanic rock and moulded terracotta in a Mayan-style design, with a Western art deco interior, the sprawling three-storey hotel was completely different to anything else around. One unforgettable Sunday, they had gone to their first ever American movie, *Zanba*. In soundless, black and white, wild animals roamed the African plains, a live narrator explaining the scenery in Japanese. Afterwards, for a treat, they had called into the lobby teashop of the Imperial for an ice-cream.

Entering the hotel, the soft-greenish hue of the rough stone walls, the thick yellow and green floor rugs, and the refined hush gently enveloped the visitor. Even five-year-old Yayoi spoke softly, overawed by the grandeur. Wright had also designed the décor and furnishings, creating a harmonised blend of custom-made artworks, carpets, furniture, textiles, even wastepaper baskets, and the most memorable, the white chinaware scattered with overlapping circles.

Years later, the hotel was about to feature even more significantly in Hisashi's life. As he had proffered his pass at the revolving door, he could not help but wonder at the changes. The ground-floor coffee shop was full of GIs from GHQ. And the hotel interior had suffered the same indignity as many other requisitioned buildings: cream paint slapped over woodwork, its wooden floors corked and waxed. Lighting, furniture and carpets now had a military air.

18 March

For months, once a week on the way to the office, I've visited GHQ hoping to convince them to buy brake shoes directly from us, rather than through the car companies. Satake-san, a nisei from Procurement is most helpful.

Before going to GHQ, I drop into the Imperial Hotel for a coffee. This morning, coffee in my hand, as I perused the Japan Times, amongst the usual advertisements for stevedores, a small advert caught my eye: 'Salesman wanted. Applicants without confidence in English conversation need not apply.' What is a salesman? I've never seen the word before. There was no company name, but it must be foreign. I'll apply.

25 March
The interview was so short I must have failed, and I still don't know what company it is.

28 March
A short memo arrived. I got the job and, on the letterhead, Pegasus, the flying red horse: a logo I've seen since a boy, Standard Vacuum, the American oil company [today's Mobil Oil]. Getting the job with my low-level English, must mean that few applied, though not many would apply for sales.

Hisashi never went back to Hinode, thinking it better to ask *ojisan* (referring to Shozo) to convey the message that he had left. If he had gone himself, Hasegawa-*shi* would have tried to stop him, offering him a higher salary and a superior bride.

30 March
Met Miss Takenaka, telling her I've left Hinode and that, because of my family situation, I can't marry her. She listened quietly, somehow knowing in advance what I would tell her. She gave me a tea cup. As I made my way home, the title of Tolstoy's novel The Living Corpse whirled in my head.

Hisashi and Miss Takenaka had met regularly over the years, as friends, enjoying a cup of coffee or a snack, their feelings for each other never discussed. Although nothing had ever been mentioned about marriage or love, he knew what he felt, and instinctively knew she felt the same. The tea cup was one of a pair, made especially for a husband and wife, the smallest of the pair used by the wife. Hisashi never saw Miss Takenaka again, but heard later that she had married the middle-aged lawyer at Hinode.

> 1 April
> Turning 30 years of age, I've joined a foreign company. I and the four other new salesmen are a trial to increase sales against British-owned Shell Oil.

As Standard Vacuum was located in Yokohama, it meant a two-hour train trip to and from work. The company had been in Japan since the late 1920s, when private cars first went on sale, its oil sourced from Indonesia via Royal Dutch Shell. Shell, its only competition, held 60 per cent of the market. Pre-war, the greatest revenue for both companies had come from the sale of lubrication oil for industrial machines; next was banker oil, the heavy oil for oceangoing vessels and harbour barges. With so few cars and no commercial airlines, petrol sales were minimal, and both companies on-sold to wholesalers. The wholesalers serviced two market segments: large consumers such as shipping companies, the military, city government and big manufacturers; and small consumers, such as petrol stations and smaller businesses like Hinode. During the war, as allocations had shrunk, petrol stations had merged, as had the wholesalers.*

Commercial petrol sales to Japan did not resume until 1949, the pre-war wholesalers and petrol station owners quickly reappearing. Every day, Hisashi and the other salesmen visited their own small operators, and those of Shell whom they hoped to win over to them.

> 5 April
> My salary is 18,000 yen a month. At 360 yen per US dollar I'm cheap local labour in the eyes of the Americans, but I'm happy, though I don't like

---

* It was said the Allies won the war 'thanks to the waves of oil'. The recent discoverery of oil in Saudi Arabia had reduced America's reliance on its own domestic stockpile. Conversely, while oil supplies to Japan had continued until the 1942 ABCD trade embargo, Japanese supplies had run out more quickly than expected despite hoarding huge quantities.

my business card saying I'm a 'salesman'. A recipient will consider I belong to a miserable job, certainly not a gentleman's occupation. It occurred to me today that I've begun to hear the birds sing again. Have they just reappeared, or is it that I've just noticed?

6 May

Advertisements for stevedores have been increasing. Walking from the station to the office, I pass queues of men at the government recruitment office. Weeks ago rumours began circulating that war was about to break out in Korea and the Americans needed stevedores. All is now revealed – the motivation behind Hasegawa-shi's actions is clear. Through his secret sources he had advance notice war was expected.

25 June

Lucky for us the Korean War has begun and GHQ is obliged to shelve Dodge's doctrine. Production restrictions will be lifted, and contrary to Dodge's policy, funds will be injected into industry to modernise and expand. They say unemployment will completely disappear. I'm reminded of an old Chinese proverb, 'One hundred days preaching will be spoiled instantly by a single loud fart'. That fart is the Korean War.

After surrender, the Japanese province of Korea had been occupied by American and Russian forces, the thirty-eighth parallel separating North and South Korea, the Russian and American zones respectively. Provisional governments were set up and the occupying armies withdrew. South Korea became a republic in 1948. But equipped with Russian weapons, and attempting to reunite the country under communist rule, North Korea had now invaded the South. The United Nations had come to the aid of the South and, under the leadership of America, with General MacArthur as commander, an Allied 16-nation force, based in Japan, was sent to fight in the name of the United Nations. The North Koreans were joined by Chinese communist forces.

The needs of the UN forces stimulated Japan's economy. Ships and vehicles had to be repaired, car manufacturers produced trucks and tanks, the textile industry produced uniforms, and footwear manufacturers churned out boots. Articles not used by the Japanese, like condoms, cutlery and frying pans, also had to be produced.

Over 300 000 foreign soldiers and their families contributed to the Japanese economy. Foreign investors, mainly American, rushed to Japan and exports revived. Profits were ploughed back into the industrial sector. Regular work and incomes increased consumption and savings. An annually balanced budget and a stable exchange rate were all that remained of the Dodge Line.*

> *24 July*
>
> *Supported by the conservative Yoshida government, GHQ has initiated the Red Purge – heard yesterday that, just before he was to be fired, the union leader at Hinode disappeared.*

While the war against communism was taking place in Korea, GHQ was waging war against the vestiges of communism in Japan at the same time.

By 1950, the Japanese Communist and Socialist parties were potent political forces. Apprehensive about the Cold War, uneasy about communist victory in China, and influenced by Senator Joseph McCarthy in Washington, GHQ clamped down on communism in Japan. Journalists and those in the labour movement with communist leanings were purged. Within a decade the JCP and union membership went into decline, and submissive unions supplanted their more militant forebears.

---

* The exchange rate stayed the same for the next 20 years.

Chapter 64

A Debt Discharged

Fukusui bon ni kaerazu
Spilt water never returns to the bowl

29 August 1950
Confucian thought, supported by the caste system, stipulates that keeping quiet, not making excuses, and modesty are worthy virtues, and as I grew up okasan *drummed them into my head. I find American behaviour incomprehensible. Today, an American subordinate contradicted his senior, and last week someone apologised for not having a report ready on time. In a Japanese environment, the subordinate would have been transferred or downgraded, but neither of these men were reprimanded. As for me, I still have difficulty speaking out in meetings.*

A LL HIS LIFE, HISASHI had tried to uphold his 'proper place' in the hierarchy. He dressed and behaved appropriately for every occasion, and spoke cautiously to avoid causing offence. In this new environment he often felt confused, uncomfortable and frustrated. As a salesman, he was caught between his American bosses and Japanese customers. Already on the periphery of Japanese society, by taking a job as a salesman in a foreign company, he had isolated himself even more. But Hisashi was no more 'in specification' at Standard Vacuum.

5 October
Saw an advertisement for the sale of a fridge-freezer at Washington Heights.

One of Hisashi's duties included supervising the refill of the portable petrol tank that Standard Vacuum provided at the military village, Washington Heights. Without a pass, a Japanese could not enter the camp.

> *7 October 1950*
>
> *At Washington Heights the rows of prefabricated houses are bigger and better than mine, and most with a car parked outside. Only the wife was home – nice looking in her early thirties, my company ID reassuring her I wasn't a dealer on the* yami-ichi. *She understood my poor English, and offered me coffee, the same bitter taste as at GHQ. Inside the house, I glimpsed not just the refrigerator, but a record player, vacuum cleaner, and a washing machine with an agitator. How I envy their easy existence. What a wonderful fridge it is, a GE [General Electric] make, unavailable here. I didn't bother negotiating, the cost not such a burden that it will affect my monthly expenditure. I hope our light-weight Japanese floor is strong enough.**

Modern conveniences were appearing in Japan, though most were luxuries and beyond the pockets of the average Japanese. For Hisashi, though, it was a time of progress. After nine years of going without, the family ate better foods, fixed the leaking roof, replaced the yellowed *tatami*; and Hisashi bought himself a new suit, replacing his father's, which he had worn for the last four years. High interest rates encouraged him to save and, like most people, he was putting aside 30 per cent of every pay.†

> *9 October*
>
> *Hired a truck and collected my refrigerator. As we dragged it along the floor, it made a small scratch. 'Oh no!' the husband and wife declared. Why did they raise their voices? We were amazed. It wasn't serious. It wasn't their own house, and they were leaving, so why such a reaction? I kept bowing, saying*

---

* Fortunately the floor stood up to the weight. That grand old lady of fridges lasted another 20 years when Hisashi reluctantly replaced it with a light-weight Japanese brand, which never seemed as good.

† Savings funds were utilised by the government to underwrite public developments.

sorry, sorry, paid and escaped. I'm very proud to have such a fridge. Okasan is inviting the neighbours to visit, most of them still using an icebox.

29 December
It's been a much better year. Our living standard has improved, and step by step rationing is coming to an end, petrol already released. Dodge has gone. The Korean War saved us. There will be no more claims for reparation. Already 3 billion dollars of Japanese overseas assets have been seized, the Soviets keeping the largest share in Manchuria. According to GHQ, 20 000 industrial machines totalling $230 million have been sent to China, Great Britain, the Philippines and the Netherlands.

Japan is finally emerging from the ashes of war. My life, too, is emerging from the ashes. It has taken time for me to understand American ways. They, too, are more aware of our Japanese ways. Once my nervousness subsided, the rhythm of a fresh life flowed smoothly. I've found somewhere I can work safely, and maintain a reasonable standard of living. Working for an international corporation in a budding industry offers promising prospects and this coming January my salary will increase to 25 500 yen per month.

However, it's not been a good year for Yayoi. In February, she and a colleague at the American City Bank were married and, according to the new Constitution, without obtaining parental consent. I supported them. Okasan said nothing, but his parents objected strongly. Their combined income allowed them to rent a small apartment, but right from the start, things didn't go smoothly. With both of them working, it was difficult to do household chores, pay their bills and go shopping. Other young couples would have been helped by their parents, but his wouldn't help, and okasan thought if she did, she would be accused of meddling.

Although their marriage was authorised by the local government, the local court continues to follow tradition, insisting that a newly married couple live with the husband's parents. His parents complained to the court and, as head of Yayoi's family, I was called to attend. The judge was annoyed I supported the new Constitution. He condemned the marriage, calling it yago *[an illicit union], and after 9 months, unable to manage without support,* their marriage ended and both returned home. Fortunately the marriage had been kept quiet, otherwise there would have been a huge scandal and Yayoi castigated by our elderly relatives.

At work no one has ever asked whether I'm married. My single status is not so strange, many men on their own: widowed, divorced or single. At Mitsubishi, my seniors would have been pushing me to marry. I recall someone there asking if I was impotent and if that was why I was unmarried.

Okasan stays confined to her shell. Apart from the retailers who call at the house daily, she has contact with no one. Her friends and acquaintances from the old neighbourhood have scattered, they, too, keeping quiet. I know she worries about Yayoi. Even apart from her failed marriage, Yayoi working is shameful. Okasan says that if I earned more, Yayoi wouldn't have to work. In her eyes, I've deliberately wasted my education and dropped my status. And even worse, I work for a foreign company as a 'salesman'. She continually hankers for the old days and ways, and seems to feel she's the only one in such a miserable situation, so she's happier and safer hidden away from prying eyes.

* * *

21 April 1951
Today is my 31ˢᵗ birthday, and for the first time in 10 years I've eaten my favourite broiled eel, boiled peas with honey, and bean jam with sweet jelly. Oishii! They were every bit as good as I remembered.

31 December
Altogether it was a more hopeful Christmas than those of the past decade. But what has happened over this year? The Korean War continues and, though I'm sorry for the Korean people, without the war, Japanese industry wouldn't have recovered as quickly. In September, the San Francisco Peace Treaty was signed by Japan and 48 non-communist nations. America also made a joint security pact with Japan. US troops are to be permanently stationed at Yokosuka Naval Base. Sure it means America will protect us,

and coming under their umbrella will be good for international trade, but most people say 'It's a stain upon our honour'.

At work, despite our best efforts, petrol sales to small operators didn't increase. Rationed quantities of oil and petrol were so limited that operators still had to rely on the yami-ichi: not only that, but many stayed loyal to Shell. Head office decided the only way to expand was to target big customers by tendering a lower price than Shell. Five client groups were identified: shipping, textiles, railways, mining, and an assortment of businesses: chemical fertiliser companies, the newly established National Police Reserve, the newly emerged Japan Airlines, and the petrol stations. As youngest, I was made responsible for the latter – my new business card saying 'Sales Supervisor', which sounds much better.

My high salary also makes me happy, though it means I'm erased forever from the list of ordinary citizens. Working for a foreign company, I'm labelled a different species of Japanese. In my daily activities I've no contact with people at large, thus I'm isolated like a lighthouse keeper, unable to share the usual pleasantries of life. However, I'm obliged not to mind.

I've fulfilled otosan's wishes.

* * *

30 April 1952
Occupation has officially ended and Japan has regained its sovereignty. Inflation continues to rise, but is overlooked in light of the Korean War boom.

Part Five

Giri Metamorphosed

THE SUCCESSFUL-LOOKING 'SARARII-MAN' in the black and white photograph is in lifetime employment with a regular salary and married to the company, bowing and smiling each day. Judging from the cut of his hair, the style of his suit, he cares about his appearance. The sensitive face, with its mixture of confidence and diffidence, hints at industriousness, maybe introspection, but the reserved demeanour is too modest to give much away.

Chapter 65

My Eyes Have Stared in Wonder

Sugita koto wa mizu ni nagase
Let what is past flow away downstream

HISASHI SETTLED INTO A NEW PATTERN of home and work responsibilities. Life was stable and certain but, while the worries and stress of the desperate days might have gone, they had been replaced by new pressures. Working for an international petroleum company, he was whirled around in the postwar push for technology and globalisation, and there were times when it was difficult to stop spinning.

He had stopped writing a diary, instead putting together an album of photographs and mementos, and a commentary of his past 20 years. The preface was written on 14 January 1959:

> *I, Hisashi, am 38 years old. It is 14 years since the war ended. The 1950s have been a decade of fundamental change, not only for Japan, but the whole world. Life moves faster and in more directions, and my eyes have stared in wonder. In 1950 in Formosa, Chiang Kai-shek was proclaimed president of Nationalist China; in 1951, Winston Churchill began his second term as Prime Minister of Britain; in 1952, General Dwight Eisenhower was elected president of the USA; in 1953, Queen Elizabeth II was crowned in England and Soviet dictator Joseph Stalin died; in 1954, Jonas Salk discovered an anti-polio vaccine; in 1955, Sir Alexander Fleming, the discoverer of penicillin, died.*

In 1956, most likely pushed by America, China changed its writing style. During the occupation they changed our writing style. Ration tickets I found amongst my souvenirs were written top down, right to left. Now, as in America and China, we write horizontally, left to right – though cumbersome, it allows for the insertion of English names or expressions.

In 1957, we gaped in wonder as the Russian Sputnik sped across the sky, the first manmade satellite to circle the Earth: America outsmarted by Russia. Not to be outdone, in 1958, America sent its first satellite, Explorer, winging skywards. Similarly medicine has made rapid advances: the first artificial heart has been used, and an ultra-sonic machine can take pictures of a person's insides; finally today, 14 January 1959, the vice-premier of the USSR is visiting the US – maybe a development in The Cold War.

It's been astonishing putting together this album – as for the wider world, changes in Japan have been massive and far more severe than those experienced after the Meiji Revolution. Again my eyes have stared in wonder. In 14 years, we have experienced democracy, which has brought a new society and lifestyles, with different housing, clothing, music, foods, and types of work. For me, for the first five years, my mother and sister and I lived hand to mouth; then gradually between 1950 and 1955, working at Standard Vacuum, and my salary increasing from 18 000 yen per month to 42 000, life became more comfortable, which restored my confidence. Over these last four years, I've lived smoothly alongside the Americans, my salary now 56 000 a month.*

Today the Imperial Prince, Akihito, sent an engagement gift to Michiko Shoda, who will be the first non-imperial princess. Her selection is a revolutionary step, undoubtedly part of GHQ's plan to eradicate the imperial system. While I agree that their push to wipe out the myth of a 'divine family' was good, lowering their rank to that of the people was not.

The new Constitution is deliberately vague on many issues, thus policy can be interpreted according to political conditions, such as with Article 9.

---

* At 56 000 yen per month, it was a high salary; higher than his equivalent at the Bank of Japan, which was recognised as the top payer in the country. The average monthly pay in urban areas was 18 608 yen, though half of all industrial workers received barely 12 000.

As a result of The Cold War, GHQ reinterpreted the policy to allow the National Police Reserve to be formed in 1950 – a police force with military hardware, aircraft and submarines! In 1954, when it was renamed the Self-Defense Forces, the government still proclaimed it was to maintain domestic security. However, it is my belief that, if Japan had refused to do as America wanted, we would have been vulnerable to a Russian take-over.

Doubtless, reformers were well-intentioned in their enthusiasm to democratise Japan, but often reform was hastily introduced and based on subjective and incomplete information. Changes to education, local government and employment were too radical. Teachers and local government officials continued to challenge central government policies; and when unions became too powerful, they were toppled by GHQ. While in theory, land reform was accepted, it has easily slipped back into the old pattern. It was all very well redistributing the land, but many small farmers were unable to manage and sold out to the narikin, who now own big holdings.

Back during the occupation, we all acknowledged we would have to accept this new lifestyle, this American democracy. But it was like a man climbing uphill dragging a huge rock: no amount of legislation could force people to change. The traditional hierarchy was too strong and it's taken until now for change to be properly accepted. And, during that transitional stage, everything was dreary.

Lucky for us, the turn around that began with the Korean War has continued. The war finished in July 1953, but by then, war orders and an expansion in world trade had enabled Japan to earn the foreign exchange needed to buy the raw materials needed for growth. Output returned to maximum capacity around 1955. In comparison with other bombed countries, where the old systems remain, such as the British textile industry, Japan was able to modernise more easily. Access to raw materials, a stable currency, limited trade barriers, and worldwide demand fostered growth. Initial scientific and technical innovation was aimed at restoring basic necessities, so that now we can concentrate on the production of luxury goods: Japanese cars appear on the streets of the world, Japanese watches appear on the wrists of foreigners.

Unfortunately, even with our dramatic growth, and even though occupation is over, Japan remains under America's thumb, and such is the case with Okinawa Island. The island has become a US military base and last year the yen was replaced by the dollar. I know it's common practice for a conqueror: we ourselves did it during the war. But was it necessary on Okinawa? Many locals there work for the Americans, and I can understand it's easier to pay them in US dollars, and I acknowledge the islanders welcomed the change. However, the Japanese government was weak and showed no resistance. Are the Americans planning the same for the Japanese mainland? What do they want from us? I know they wonder how we 'lowly' Japanese rolled back so quickly. Winning the war, they had everything, yet still they feel the need to put us in our place.

In 1957, notes less than one yen were removed from circulation, and this year 100 and 50 yen notes are to be replaced by coins. The yen's value has been downgraded, and I'm sad for the loss of the 100 yen note. It was so precious a note, that before the war even among the middle classes it never appeared in daily transactions.* I was 19 when I saw my first one, okasan giving me one to pay my school fees – and now it's a coin.

Looking through my mementos, I found things I'd forgotten, such as my 'Vocational Capability Declaration Pocketbook'. Every male was supposed to report for duty with his pocketbook, so that technicians and engineers would be easily identified and mobilised for the munitions industry. But the government was so disorganised that by the time the system was running, the war had ended, my pocketbook arriving six weeks after surrender. Such inefficiency shows Japan to be literally a 'fourth-world country' and destined to remain there forever. With our government lacking ability and leadership, it just caves in to American dictate.

I became intensely absorbed reading my diaries written during the occupation and overall I felt fortunate that I avoided the most severe misfortune. I fulfilled my family obligations. I had good advisors and I found a career. But the memories of bitter experiences came rushing back. I saw

---

* 100 yen notes had been used only for expensive purchases such as a house or surgery. 1000 yen notes were introduced in 1949.

a naïve and uncontaminated boy suddenly exposed to drastic change. And despite the fact that he was in his mid twenties, he was still a boy, okute (literally late rice). His career change was inevitable, and I saw how heavily it affected him, but like everybody, he was influenced partly by factors beyond his control and partly by his own will and efforts. That young boy's character was polished by the hardships he endured, and his personality would have been quite different if life had been smooth.

During the war and for some time after, I and my schoolmates were young boys with pure and simple hearts. However, now I'm obliged to recognise the words 'pure and simple' mean 'weak-headed and stupid'. An old Japanese proverb says 'to be innocent about the world is to live in a fool's paradise'. Within the intelligentsia, we were hedged from the outside world. While in our purity, we were honest and genuine, we knew nothing of international matters. We simply believed Japanese society was best and accepted unquestioningly what we were told, which meant we were stupid.

My final memento of the war is my 'Physical Capabilities Appraisal Pocketbook', which I received in 1942. I was healthy, but many weren't. Many soldiers who died during the war actually died from TB [tuberculosis]. Back in 1931 when the army had conscripted farmers for Manchuria, they had been surprised to find many had TB. Immediately an anti-TB drive was introduced to improve the health of youngsters, but typically nothing was followed up. In fact, statistics weren't analysed until ordered by GHQ.

Thanks must go to Winston Churchill, who encouraged the research that led the late Alexander Fleming to discover penicillin, and the resultant decrease in TB. Though for me personally, it's a matter of regret that the Japanese anti-TB drive was so far behind Germany and Britain.

With these words Hisashi completed the preface to his album.

Chapter 66

A Seat by the Window

Rainen no koto o ieba oni ga warau
Talk of next year and the devil laughs

IN JUNE 1958, HISASHI'S LIFE had turned upside down once again. One day he was at work; the next day he was not.

In the company's bi-annual physical check it was discovered that he had a shadow on his left lung. It was a shock. He felt fine. How could he possibly have TB? Fortunately the company was covered by the national health policy, which meant he was approved sick leave on full pay, 56 000 yen per month, so even though he worried about his health and the future of his career, financially there was no burden.

He spent his days quietly: pottering in the garden, reading, listening to music, strolling in the Ginza; and twice a week he was an outpatient at the hospital, where he received calcium to strengthen the cells of his lungs. He also spent many hours at a seat by the window, writing in his album, pondering over his life and recording the changes in Japanese society.

> *Career-wise, 1957 was a very good year. That February, I was appointed Manager of Aviation Sales, the first non-American in senior management.*

Standard Vacuum had grown on the back of the aviation industry, which itself had made great strides after the war, aerial warfare having prompted great advances in aircraft design.

In 1951, JAL [Japan Air Lines] was inaugurated as the first domestic passenger service. Aircraft and pilots came from American-owned Northwest Airways, while fuel and airport facilities were supplied by the US military. Only the flight attendants and ticketing staff were Japanese. Two years later the Japanese government took over, and the airline was designated the national flag carrier. By a 'touch of sleeve', Hisashi's mentor Yanagida-*shi* from Hinode days, was appointed president of the airline. And late in 1955, thanks to Hisashi and his connection to Yanagida-*shi*, Standard Vacuum was awarded the sole contract to supply petrol and lubricants to JAL. Hisashi achieved the status of 'million dollar salesman'. Although this was not without its challenges.

Radically different decision-making processes meant price negotiations between the two cultures were fraught with potential conflict. Japanese communication places an obligation on the listener to understand all that cannot be said directly by the speaker. An 'absolute no', along with direct requests and opinions are considered offensive by the Japanese. It is preferable to talk around a point until it is understood by all, for in that way no one is required to back down and lose face.

Americans attending meetings had the authority to make decisions on the spot, whereas Japanese representatives had to check up the chain of command and renegotiate the following day. The Americans thought this slow and inefficient; however, the custom of approval-seeking *ringi* prevailed.

An individual in a Japanese company existed only as a member of the group, and responsibility was shared by all. A proposal prepared by Hisashi would work its way through the hierarchy, approval gained only with consensus. The proposal would be examined by the proper officials at each level, with each stamping their personal seal of approval. Foreigners interpreted this as red tape, which it was, as each stamp took around half a day. But it reduced the risk for any one person.

The Japanese thought the Americans were arrogant and pushy, unable to see anyone else's point but their own, and always being in a hurry meant they reacted too quickly. The Americans perceived the

Japanese as procrastinators, unable to make a decision, and frequently accused them of stalling, and answering yes, even when they meant no. Hisashi would try to explain the 'Japanese way': talking flowery words today, but tomorrow changing; yes did not mean agreement, rather it meant, yes, we have heard your opinion, ours will follow. They were not bad habits, just different, and often the Americans did not understand.

Over the next few years Hisashi made steady progress within the company. He discovered he had an aptitude for selling, for diplomacy, and for knowing when to use his personal connections, likening himself to a 'sort of human lubricant'. The Japanese dislike disharmony, and no matter how tough the negotiations, relating well face to face was essential. Showing irritation or anger would lead to a breakdown in negotiations, and ultimately lost business.

Hisashi was still uncomfortable when the Americans continued to argue a point, thinking their system was superior and would work all around the world. While some Japanese became more American than the Americans, most followed Japanese protocol, saying virtually nothing in discussions. Hisashi followed his instincts and took the soft approach. To get around the problem of *ringi* and reach an earlier decision, he would bring the key decision-makers together over dinner to arrange verbal approval, so that the next day the system of seals was quickly expedited.

> *And another piece of luck: in 1958 we shifted into a new house in Takanawa. Takahashi, an importer, frequented my office wanting the latest information on the American chemical market. During the war the Americans had developed uses for synthetic rubber, such as vehicle tyres and waterproof skins for submarines, Standard Vacuum one of the manufacturers. Getting a US licence to import the rubber is near to impossible, but I helped him to get one. After making a really good profit, as thanks he built and gave me the house.*

Like the rest of Tokyo, even in the sought-after, postwar subdivision of

Takanawa, residents lived and worked cheek by jowl, in a hotchpotch of houses, factories and shops. The Furuya's 100-square metre, four-roomed home was one of the smaller houses but, coming from 30 square metres, it seemed like a palace. Residents were pleasant and polite, but their lives were distant, with community ties less important and anonymity pervasive.

> *Customer behaviour has completely changed, with people spending on larger items and more frivolous habits. In 1955 I bought a record player, with the finest tone I've ever heard. During the war with shellac so scarce, a cheap, unbreakable, vinyl resin was developed, and new records, spinning at 45 revolutions per minute, are replacing the old 78s.*
>
> *With the increased variety of local and imported products, retail distribution has been revolutionised. Shopping is less leisurely, and a new species of retailer has emerged – the self-service store. Frozen foods were introduced in 1952, and a year later the first supermarket, Kinokuniya, opened. Today supermarkets take trade away from the city centre. Two years back, we spent 20 000 yen per month on housekeeping, today 30 000.* Food purchases and eating habits are also different. Rice consumption has dropped. For breakfast I have toast and jam, and a glass of milk. At lunchtime and for work dinners, I eat Western style, often pasta or spaghetti. At home okasan maintains a traditional diet – much appreciating the revolutionary electric rice cooker I gave her for Christmas 1955.*
>
> *Tokyo's appearance has changed dramatically, recovery much easier than for London or Dresden, where brick remains slowed reconstruction. With everything flattened, it provided a clean slate. But the population swelled so rapidly there was no time to plan a new road system, so the old system remains. Smaller cities, like Nagoya, were similarly flattened, but have been able to better plan their rebuilding.*
>
> *By 1955, the population of Tokyo was back to six million. Four years*

---

* A bowl of noodles costing 20 yen in 1946 was now double the price. A cup of coffee had gone up 10 yen since 1946, now costing 50 yen per cup. If coffee wasn't wanted, there was now a choice of Coca-Cola, introduced in 1957, or a canned beer, launched in 1958.

> later, the population has reached nearly nine million. Reclamation has extended the shoreline and new suburbs appear on the edge of the city: a paddy field sprouts a factory, a suburban street becomes a subway track. But such disorganised development has resulted in dangerous roads, and we have no civic amenities: there's nowhere for children to play, or the elderly to socialise. Schools are overcrowded. There are not enough hospitals and maternity clinics, nor doctors, dentists, midwives and teachers. And land prices escalate daily. The city is like a 'toy box', buildings in a jumble, as if the toy box had been emptied out on the floor. Ginza Street has been democratised, polite society rubbing shoulders with workers, class barriers crumbling as incomes increase.

With time on his hands, Hisashi often went into central Tokyo for a coffee.

A distinctive car culture had emerged, with well-heeled citizens loving to make a show, and traffic was heavy. Public transport had improved, and the city was scored with roads, railway lines, tram tracks, and subways, jammed during rush hours. As quickly as air travel was becoming the norm, urban traffic was slowing as roads clogged with more and more vehicles.

In the Ginza, traditional style, two-storey shops were sandwiched between ten-storey, concrete department stores, life insurance offices and city banks. To Hisashi, banks in the Ginza spelled a poor Japan: banks should be one street back of the main thoroughfare. For him, the Ginza had been lowered in tone, but it was exciting, exotic, so un-Japanese and contemporary. Today he was heading for Shiseido wanting to see 'Foremen', their first range of cosmetics for men.

> Standing out amongst the darkness of new Japanese-made cars, and old-fashioned American Buicks, Chryslers and Chevys, are yellow Nissan taxis, older, red Italian Fiat convertibles and khaki-coloured jeeps. Heads turn as a Fleetwood Cadillac glides by, all shiny chrome and sleek rear fins. Men-horses pull perfumed *geisha*, as bicycle boys holding aloft trays of food weave through the throng.

Competing in a furore of sights, sounds and smells, a barrage of advertising attracts his attention to a multitude of goods. Billboards publicise movies, cigarettes and *pachinko* (a type of pinball). Advertisements on buses and trams promote department stores. Posters everywhere extol this or that brand of men's pomade, and with a suave smile Sammy Davis Junior endorses Suntory Whisky. A man in a brown bear suit peddles dried salmon. A tube of toothpaste hands out samples. A ski bunny in yellow pants and a pink parka shoves handbills at passersby. *Chin-don, chin-don*. Strapped into his wooden frame, a *chin-don-ya* (a 'ding-dong' musician who performs for publicity purposes) advertises a new noodle shop; *chin*, he beats a drum with his left hand, *don* with his right he strikes a tin plate.

All familiar to Hisashi, shops belt out the latest hits: 'cool jazz' from Miles Davis; the twanging guitars of 'Mac the Knife'; the elegant orchestration of Porgy and Bess; and currently top of the hit parade, the breathy, little Japanese tune 'Black Petals'. And, floating gracefully above, a new phenomenon no one can ignore, huge, helium-filled promotional balloons.

The smell of grilling eel mingles with that of dried fruit roasting, and steaming rice cakes brushed with sweet syrup. But it is the whiff of percolating coffee that draws him into his favourite coffee shop. Gleaming chromium machines throatily disgorge both Brazilian and Vienna blends and, feeling extravagant, he orders a Vienna. From his window seat, to the sound of Perez Prado's 'Quizas, Quizas, Quizas', he sips the velvety brew and observes the street. Along the pavement, well-turned-out pedestrians, mostly in Western dress, stride confidently. There are noticeably more women and, with fashions keenly followed, he sees skirts that are full circle, pleated, or flared, and others that are narrow and tight, in patterns and florals. Youngish, uniformed, working women are strolling arm-in-arm during their lunch break. Gum-chewing girls in tight pants gossip alongside *kimono*-clad seniors. Serious-faced '*sararii-men*' in suits stride proudly, bypassing groups of elderly, traditionally garbed farmers window-shopping.

Leaving the coffee shop, the throbbing engines of a dozen Harley Davidsons vie for his attention. Stopped at the lights, the *kaminari-zoku* (thunder tribes) rev their powerful throttles. Astride their guzzling beasts of chrome, the pioneering sons of the *narikin* are part of a pack, flaunting their wealth and thumbing their noses at tradition. With buzz-cut or slicked-backed hair, wearing the mandatory goggles, black leather jacket, jeans and work boots, they consider themselves the epitome of American youth. Watching their antics, more solid citizens appear startled, disapproving or appalled. After his initial disbelief, Hisashi cannot resist an amused smirk – Japanese riding bikes built for Americans look ridiculous.

To an extent, wealth, status and power had been reshuffled. Three new categories of rich had emerged as the lower classes moved up: first, those who profited on the *yami-ichi* during the occupation, and those who bought goods for resale from departing American and UN troops; next the *yakuza*, who helped themselves to what they wanted; and a third group, industrialists like the originators of Sony, Matsushita (now Panasonic) and Honda.

A huge gap has widened between us and Eiko. We merely exchange New Year greeting cards confirming all is well. While okasan, Yayoi and I are in Tokyo, she's moved around with her husband's promotions, enjoying a wealthy lifestyle inherited from his parents. However, in general the gap between farmers and urban dwellers has closed. The rebels of the 1936 coup would be pleased that one of their aims has been achieved. Synthetic fertilisers, mechanisation, diversification, and the return of labourers have increased output, though more and more are leaving the countryside for cities, with the agricultural sector beginning to shrink.

A new class of intelligentsia has emerged, their attitude being 'the war is over, so let's enjoy ourselves'. Like my family, many of the pre-war urban middle class lost everything, with their homes destroyed and forced to sell their assets. Today, the old-fashioned intelligentsia favouring the British style has disappeared, with the new class 100 per cent American. British tea has been replaced by American coffee, and classical music by jazz.

Sadly a moral malaise is spreading and the young spend extravagantly, valuing only what is 'new': new colours, new clothes, new food and new music. They chew gum walking in the street. They display affection in public. The older generation still mend and repair. Though, whatever their age, people only think about money. And there's money about. Most people have jobs and higher, steady incomes. Since 1955, with the merging of the Liberals and Democrats [Liberal Democratic Party], we have a stable majority in the Diet, which helps foster economic growth. Everyone got behind the war, and today, resolved to leave the past behind, everyone is united in wanting to improve our standard of living, to have Japan accepted by the super powers, and to eradicate the shame of defeat.

Barely a day goes by when the word 'war' does not still arise in conversation. Even today the postwar slogan, '100 million confessions' was used: still nothing but an egotistical attempt by the government to absolve itself from blame for the war. And people at large passively concur.

Undoubtedly the war was catastrophic: 2.5 million soldiers and 1.5 million civilians died; almost 10 per cent of the population lost their homes; 35 per cent of our national wealth was lost. Another 1.5 million city dwellers died of starvation and disease during the occupation. The government achieved their goal to reduce the population, but all in all, defeat was not to be grieved over. Thanks to America, Japan benefited from globalisation much sooner than Europe. Without the war we wouldn't be where we are now.

In October 1959, Hisashi was finally declared fit for work. He thought his career was over. Japanese employees, particularly those in senior positions, lost status after long-term sick leave, especially when TB was suspected. Returning to work, they were given 'a seat by the window'; that is, relegated to a lower position. After 15 months off, Hisashi was not surprised to hear he had been demoted to Assistant Manager, with his salary reduced accordingly.

Chapter 67
The Sun Rises Again

Hikari wa tsuneni kage wo tomonawu
Light always accompanies shadow

HISASHI'S LOWER INCOME was a problem. However, having observed the company frequently fielding requests from foreigners wanting accommodation, he decided to build a Western-style annex on to his house for homestay guests. Few Western-style hotels were available, and those that were were extremely costly.

The new room was always occupied, and for 20 years the Furuyas took in long-term guests, mainly Americans and Brits. And it was a good income. Initially advertising in the *Japan Times*, he charged a third the hotel rate, the price including meals, cleaning and laundry. After a time there was no need to advertise, some people returning several times or referring their friends.

One young Englishman came out to work for the Mormon Church. His wife, who followed a month later, much to the Furuya's surprise, arrived with three-week-old Tanya. Once they were accustomed to the idea, and had located a Western-style cot, they enjoyed the novelty of having a baby in the house. Hisashi took his role as godfather seriously, and was amazed to see how Tanya had grown when the family returned to stay two years later.

A Scotsman came out to teach English. Returning a second time, he fell in love with one of his students. Although her parents approved them marrying, her grandfather did not; however, Hisashi's letter reassuring the old man the *gaijin* was a serious-minded young man ensured the marriage went ahead. After living in England for a time, the couple and their baby son returned to Japan, and stayed in the annex again until they needed more space.

Hisashi was an eligible man, and each year Ryoko still received, and refused, two or three marriage proposals for him. One such proposal came via the homestay business. When briefly introduced at Hisashi's office, Kazuko, a wealthy real estate agent, decided Hisashi would make a suitable husband. On the pretext of enquiring how to run a Western-style homestay, her business partner approached Ryoko, actually wanting to broker a marriage between Kazuko and Hisashi. Ryoko refused but, unusually, she told Hisashi in case he found out about the proposal at work. Ten years earlier he would have resented his mother's meddling; now it barely registered.

The economic boom continued through the sixties. And growth was phenomenal. Modifying and improving overseas technology and procedures had brought huge gains to Japan. Inventions unexploited elsewhere were made to work by the Japanese: the world of communication changed forever with the use of the transistor to make portable radios. Japan led the world in the production of ships and cameras, was second in electronics and third in the chemical, steelmaking, and watch industries. Growth fuelled investment, which fuelled greater growth. Machines replaced age-old skills and emptied the factory floors. Workers exchanged blue collars for white, former white-collar clerks moving into management.

Foreign observers suggested low wages and a poor standard of living had fostered Japan's economic rise. That was true immediately after the war, but not by the early sixties. Though wage rates were lower than in Britain and America so, too, were consumer prices. Nor did long hours of work explain the Japanese success: Labour Law stipulated an eight-hour workday. Success came from a mixture of ingenuity, cooperation and compliance, dexterity and expertise, meticulousness and prudence, and economies of scale. And, while other nations nationalised their industries after the war, most in Japan remained in private hands.

At this time, most Japanese considered themselves middle class and the new dream seemed attainable: a house in the suburbs filled with gadgets to make life easy. A survey in 1963 showed that half the homes in Tokyo had refrigerators, 70 per cent had washing machines and 91 per cent televisions. But income differences persisted.

In 1960, under the American Anti-Trust Law, Standard Vacuum had been compulsorily split into two separate companies, Mobil and Esso; the former concentrating on land business, the latter on marine. Hisashi stayed with Mobil and less than a year after returning from sick leave he was back on the fast track. Promoted to Manager of Market Research and Sales, he travelled extensively around Asia.

The year 1960 was a particularly good year, and the Furuya family's sun was at its zenith.

Car production had increased, but private cars were still a luxury; although in Takanawa, most houses, including the Furuyas', had a car parked outside. Uncommonly for a woman, Yayoi had learned to drive, and not having to contribute to household expenses meant she was able to save enough to buy her own car, a new Nissan/Datsun Bluebird, a car she subsequently renewed every two years.

To celebrate his promotion and Yayoi's new car, Hisashi took his mother and sister to an *onsen* (hot spring) at Hakone for ten days over the New Year: a holiday that became an annual event. At the foothills of Mount Fuji, Hakone, one of the official barriers between Edo and Kyoto, had been a popular site since the Tokugawa period.

And, after 20 years of languishing in the closet, surviving war and adversity, out came Ryoko's grey cashmere coat. In no mood to wear it before now, it had lain inside its original carton, folded meticulously, wrapped in its thick, creamy coloured, rice-paper wrapper.

Cocooned in the warm, grey cashmere coat worn over one of her best *kimono*, Ryoko walked slowly down the path from the house, savouring the return to her former status. Her successful, immaculately suited son held open the front passenger door of her daughter's new car. The grey cashmere coat made her feel elegant and affluent. No longer feeling it necessary to hunch her shoulders, she held her head up high.

Travelling slowly for her convenience, they stopped every hour for fresh air and to enjoy the view. Arriving at the exclusive hotel, Ryoko was gracious in the extreme, her manner, attire, and old-fashioned hairstyle instantly distinguishing her as a conventional, well-to-do, elderly lady of good breeding. And the hotel staff reacted in kind.

By 1963 Hisashi was on the executive payroll, as Manager of Planning and Economics, and on 145 000 *yen* per month, double his previous salary. Two years later his salary increased to 184 000 *yen* per month. An average middle-aged, white-collar worker in a medium-sized company earned 40 000 *yen* a month, an older manager in a larger firm 70 000, and a young factory worker 25 000. But even on such a salary Hisashi was disciplined and prudent, though he was beginning to indulge, purchasing audio and visual equipment and rare books, attending concerts and holidaying overseas.

Like Yayoi, he still went to the movies about once a week. People packed the cinemas: American screen stars had become Japanese idols. But now in the corner of the Furuya living room there was a small black and white screen. Hisashi had bought a television when broadcasting began in Japan in 1953. Initially television was a luxury few could afford, but aspirations to own one spread rapidly. At the weekends the Furuya family sat glued to the wrestling, baseball and boxing, but Ryoko's favourites were the American quiz shows.

For Hisashi, television brought the world home. He watched in 1961 as Russian cosmonaut Yuri Gagarin became the first man to travel in space. He saw the Berlin Wall constructed. In 1963, he watched in horror when American President John F. Kennedy was assassinated. Then there was the thrill of seeing under the sea: amidst shoals of tropical fish, Jacques Cousteau swam through meadows of sea grass and reef corals.

In 1964 their black and white set was relegated to Ryoko's

bedroom, a colour television having arrived in time to watch the Tokyo Olympic Games. To Hisashi, the Games were the point when Japan finally retrieved her honour.

Tokyo was readied. Skyscrapers appeared on the skyline. Washington Heights, handed back to the Japanese government, was turned into accommodation for athletes. And the games brought the *Tokaido Shinkansen*, which, because of its speed and bullet shape, soon became known as the Bullet Train. A powerful symbol, the train was the image of the new Japan. There was nothing like it anywhere else in the world, and Hisashi was proud to have been a member of the top-level engineering committee responsible for its design and construction. Only the Americans had developed a lubricant with strong enough fibre to apply to high-speed power turbines and jet engines, and it was Hisashi who recommended and sourced the lubricant for the wheel axles.

Invited on the trial run, Hisashi felt great satisfaction to have contributed to such a unique project. Thundering between Tokyo and Osaka, the sleek air-conditioned train could reach a maximum speed of 220 kph, breaking all records for a passenger train service and reducing the six-and-a-half-hour trip to two-and-a-half hours.

The sixties was characterised by intense growth, Japan having become the world's second largest economy. And still it grew. Urbanisation had risen from 40 to over 70 per cent, and by the end of the decade Tokyo's population was over 11 million. Housing was in short supply and land prices skyrocketed. Blocks of high-density, high-rises were being built on the periphery of the city, with husbands commuting 60 to 90 minutes one way to and from their offices downtown.

Society had undergone subtle change. While educational background and money were still important, occupation was now the main measure of status. The average family was nuclear and small in size. And with more money to spend, the American habit of dining out had caught on, with once or twice a week people heading to the family oriented fast-food chains and enjoying the exotic new foods.

The Furuya mother, son and daughter were still living together, with Hisashi continuing to maintain the household. Shifting to Takanawa, Ryoko had become more affable. Hisashi had wanted her to renew contact with old friends and acquaintances, but she still preferred to keep to herself, and stayed mostly at home. Slowly things had begun to improve for her. After the JAL contract, Hisashi's salary had risen sharply, and since he was no longer a 'salesman', Ryoko had started to feel proud of him. The retailers delivering to the house had changed their attitudes – not only had the size of her orders increased, but she wanted the highest quality, and their reaction to her change in circumstances pleased her no end. Things were back on track, her status returned. When the annex had been built she had also been able to employ a housekeeper, though she still liked to do the cooking herself.

Life, too, with modern appliances, was much more convenient for Ryoko. When deep freezers and fridge-freezers had made their debut in 1961, the family's old GE fridge had still been going strong so there had been no need to replace it. But with a greater than ever variety of frozen goods available, the freezer was easier to fill. Four years later, Hisashi bought Ryoko one of the first microwave ovens. At an astronomical 198 000 *yen* and, even though she would never use it, for Ryoko it was an obvious status symbol.

Independent, educated women were still rare at this time and there were few high-salaried positions for those such as Yayoi. Even in 1960, only 5.5 per cent of all women had advanced to higher education as Yayoi had done ten years earlier. However, through Hisashi's connections she found a good job with a German company, her work including overseas travel and a new network of women friends. So Yayoi, too, was enjoying life.

While most Japanese women deemed marriage necessary for their fulfilment, Yayoi never considered remarrying. Observing her married schoolfriends, with couples separated into different social worlds – their husbands absorbed in their jobs, and her friends absorbed with mothering and rearing children to pass exams – she had decided that the new stereotype, the so-called *kyoiku-mama* (education mother, or wife of a well-paid *sararii-man*) was not for her. Yayoi did not want to slot into the accepted role. Her intellect needed to be challenged and her talents utilised: after all, she too was the daughter of the literary Jinjiro, and the granddaughter of a scholarly priest. However, she did enjoy the frivolous side of being a woman. Lipsticks, perfumes and tubes of this and that cluttered her dressing table. As for her clothes, one moment she twirled in a circular skirt, the next she presented a slim silhouette. The latest subtleties of fashion were not for Yayoi only, though. After a lifetime of standardised anonymity, Hisashi had become interested in fashion also, buying brighter ties and suits with longer lapels.

Then in 1969, after nearly 20 years with Mobil, Hisashi thought it was time for a change. Headhunted by Danfoss Japan* to become Sales Manager, he was the most senior Japanese employee in the company, and on a huge annual salary of 3.6 million yen. However, after a year of being caught up in a vicious wrangling for power, he decided the salary was not worth it, and left to take up a position with less responsibility, albeit less salary, as a section head at Chrysler Corporation.

Living through the era of high-speed growth had been exciting, but he was nearly 50 years old and wearying of the pace. Even on a lower income, Hisashi, his mother and sister still maintained a good lifestyle. His savings were substantial and, though they spent over 100 000 yen a month on household expenses, he had sufficient income left for small luxuries.

At the end of 1972, Ryoko fell and broke her hip. Hospitalised for several weeks she never regained her strength and, in March 1973, aged 75, she died peacefully in her sleep.

Hisashi felt ambivalent. Grieved at losing his only remaining

---

* Danfoss was a large Danish company manufacturing parts for cooling systems.

parent, at least this time there was no guilt, only satisfaction that he had almost fulfilled the obligation he had inherited from his father. There was also a sense of relief. His mother's demands and expectations had ruled and limited his life, but at last he was free; though regretfully he decided that at 53 he was too old to marry. So he and Yayoi continued their lives together.

Traditionally, the Japanese observe filial piety for generations, with ceremonies conducted on anniversary dates of parents' deaths. But for Hisashi and Yayoi, religion played little part in their lives. However, wanting to put things right, Hisashi had a new tomb-yard built at Taiso-*ji* at the foot of Mount Hiei. He also transferred the ashes of Jinjiro and the twins, from Tomoko's temple, to join Ryoko at Taiso-*ji*.

And once again, folded meticulously and wrapped in rice paper, with camphor balls added to keep the insects away, the grey cashmere coat lay unworn in its box on the middle shelf of the closet.

Chapter 68

Choking on Success

Ko-to shishite, so-ku niraru
When the cunning hares have been hunted down,
the hound is cooked
(People who outlive their usefulness are abandoned)

GLOBAL DEMAND FOR CONSUMER GOODS was starting to slow and worldwide commerce was becoming more competitive. Energy sources were becoming increasingly costly and complicated to access. Most developed countries were over-supplied with goods and population growth was levelling off. Consumers were spending less.

To protect themselves against exporters like Japan, many countries were developing protectionist policies. In 1971, America abandoned the gold standard system of currency that had operated since 1944,* and transferred to a floating exchange rate. They expected that an appreciated *yen* would make Japanese goods too expensive on the world market. However, it also meant it cost less for Japan to import resources, and as a result they continued to sell competitively.

Then in 1973, the oil crisis hit and everyone, including Japan, was obliged to modify their economic structure. Expensive resources and the sharp rise in oil costs sent inflation spiralling.

Rapid Japanese growth stopped. The economy had overheated and it slumped into a recession with severe industry cutbacks. But, even so, during the latter 1970s, Japan still managed to become the

---

* The gold standard was a system by which the value of a currency was defined in terms of gold, for which the currency might be exchanged.

world's top exporter of electronics, computer technology, investment, car production and robotics, which generated massive trade surpluses. A slower tempo provided time to absorb the postwar transformation.

By 1975, 25 per cent of people in Japan lived within the vicinity of Tokyo. However, the central city population was dropping. Real estate was expensive and commercial high-rise was taking over. Suburban growth was slightly more orderly, with improved public services, but each year, it seemed to Hisashi that crime, gambling and immorality increased. He was upset that traditional values were crumbling: 'The wild, postwar generation were growing up without filial piety' and everyone seemed preoccupied with themselves. Most people were more affluent, but their self-indulgence and unconstrained materialism had widened the gap between rich and poor.

The greater population brought more traffic, more noise, more confusion and more stress. Ballooning growth and reckless political decisions were fouling the city and causing serious pollution problems. 'Tokyo–Yokohama asthma' was affecting thousands. Every half hour, traffic police standing at busy intersections had to take oxygen breaks, and the education board was distributing face masks to schoolchildren. But it was not just polluted skies and water, industrial wastes, urban sprawl and traffic congestion that were a concern, now there were new forms of contamination. Radio and newspapers warned of mercury poisoning in local produce and flatfish, so people were more concerned about what they put in their mouths than what they inhaled; though the government did little.

Political standards were degenerating, and Hisashi's confidence in the government was at an all time low, as stories of corruption and scandal hit the headlines. Like many, he would have preferred another party in power, but the socialists or communists were too small to unseat the Liberal Democratic Party [LDP] and, in any case, he did not think they would be any better. The LDP had led the government since 1955, but its hold was slipping as internal squabbling and sleaze damaged its reputation. Former Prime Minister Tanaka was indicted over his involvement in financial scandals connected with Lockheed, the American aircraft company.

In April 1978, Hisashi left Chrysler,* his plan to build up a small import–export business that would see him through the next ten years.

When he was working at Mobil Oil, a lecture given by a visiting American had stimulated his interest in the company's distribution channel, from the oil fields in Saudi Arabia to their storage tanks in Japan. Postwar supplies came from the Middle East, where production costs were negligible in comparison to transportation and storage. He had noticed that as the supertankers transporting the oil got bigger and faster, trans-ocean costs decreased, but bigger wharves and storage facilities meant higher on-land costs.

Few Japanese had knowledge of the new distribution systems, and Hisashi saw an opportunity to act as a consultant in his semi-retirement. He could also act as middleman to source warehouse equipment. For a while, things went according to plan, then the 1980 world-wide recession hit Japan. Hisashi, like most others, thought it was just another business downturn. However, it was the deepest depression yet.

Hit hard by the oil crisis, industrial production declined. Many businesses failed, though some consolidated and some diversified. Many one-industry towns were ruined, but others, close to new industries, profited hugely: especially those who manufactured cars, electrical goods and their components, as well as the retail sector and service trades.

Most developed nations similarly affected faced high unemployment rates and fell into the trap of creating more low-waged jobs. However, Japan coped 'the Japanese way'. Sector stakeholders rallied around and compromised to keep industry going and people employed,

---

* The official age for retirement was in transition between 55 and 60, the government pension available at 60.

which enabled Japan to pull out of the recession less affected than most other nations. To assist, the banks extended easy credit, which was secured against inflated land prices.

The economy emerged stronger than ever. However, the popularity of Japanese goods overseas was causing friction, particularly in America. To avoid trade barriers, Japanese manufacturers began investing in overseas production, including in the United States. They also purchased foreign bonds, equities and prestigious properties. Throughout the 1980s, Japan led the world. Its standard of living was one of the highest in the world and unemployment was almost non-existent; but increasingly other nations were protesting about Japan's insular ways.

Restricted by the recession, Hisashi's clients downsized, with some going out of business. Consequently his income and standard of living plummeted. His pension helped cover basic household expenses, but by 1981 his business had dwindled away, and he realised his earning days were over. At a time when the average family was easily saving 25 per cent of their household income, he had to live off his savings.

Household expenses were 200 000 *yen* per month. Yayoi had a new car, and kept up to date with fashion, but still paid nothing towards the housekeeping. To save money Hisashi walked everywhere. He went without new clothes and small luxuries. His '*giri* to his name' meant he could never let others, even Yayoi, know his plans had failed and that his assets were being depleted. Over the next ten years, he felt as if he was stumbling in the dark. Financial worries, the incessant noise and congestion, increasing pollution, and the erosion of traditional values aggravated his anxiety and stress. Once again he felt he was a failure, and with it came the realisation of his mortality.

In 1985, at age 65, he was looking for a new life insurance policy. 'At your age, ours is the only policy available,' stated the insurance agent. Hisashi was aghast. The terse words of the salesman shocked him into believing his useful life was over. It was not just a matter of the insurance. He felt that the salesman's words were symptomatic of a general trend. His generation were being treated as 'forgotten people', their lifetime of skills and knowledge no longer of value to society.

The visit to the insurance office compounded his feelings of inadequacy, disillusionment and displacement. All his schoolfriends had wealth, power, status and heirs. Was he always to feel this sense of being 'out of specification' with his peers?

Then hope, unbidden but so welcome, sprang afresh. It would soon be time to travel to his final destination across the Sanzu-no-kawa, and by planning how best to live the remainder of his life, he could ensure it was a pleasant journey. He felt a 'new man' and took back control of his life.

However, there were two issues to resolve. First, a plan required a timeline. And second, where should he spend those final enjoyable days? He had no idea how long it would be before he would be called to cross the river. Shop after shop, he searched for a book on how to calculate his life expectancy. Finding nothing, he averaged the ages of when his parents had died. Goodness, he had only three years to go!

Chapter 69

Every Day a Sunday

Kokoro ni shiawase wo maneku niji wo,
itsudemo, itsuitsu mademo
A rainbow in your heart will bring happiness
always and forever

To MAKE THE BEST of his remaining three years, Hisashi decided to use a 'thousand-day calendar'. Every morning before getting out of bed, he would count the days to go. During the first year he would arrange his estate, assuming that Yayoi, ten years younger, would take over his household. Then for the final two years, his dream was to enjoy happy days with 'Every day a Sunday'.

His second problem was more difficult. Tokyo was dear to his heart, but it was no longer hospitable to the aged, him in particular. He could move upcountry, but he had no native place, so he would be 'cold-shouldered' wherever he went. Then the thought came: why not be cold shouldered in a different country altogether?

With higher incomes, better housing, improved diets and medical care, the Japanese people were living longer. For decades having maintained a level at five per cent of the population, the number of over 65s had now more than doubled. Healthy, well-to-do 'silver hairs', free of family ties, were being encouraged by the government to move overseas; so why not him?

Fifty-five-year-old Yayoi was still working for her German employer. But by chance the company was about to be taken over, so she decided she would shift with her brother.

Setting criteria for their choice of country was easy. It would be an English-speaking country, and one that was politically and economically stable. It would be a country welcoming to Asians and those of different religions. It would have a mild climate, and a good medical service. After canvassing friends and acquaintances overseas, they narrowed the choice to the west coast of America, Canada or New Zealand.

And why did they choose the little-known city of Dunedin in New Zealand? It was simply because they had more information about it. They knew little about New Zealand, but Hisashi had a business acquaintance who lived in Dunedin. While attending a World Trade Exhibition in Tokyo some years earlier, Hisashi had met a representative of the New Zealand Embassy who put him in touch with a Dunedin man wanting business contacts in Japan.

During 1985 and the following two years the Japanese brother and sister visited Dunedin, and confirmed their desire to live there.

Hisashi was pleased with his decision, but by the time he was ready to leave Japan, his calendar had less than 100 days to go. Wanting to postpone the date of his crossing for another 'thousand days', he prayed to the red and blue demons for an extension. The demons guard the checkpoint on the *Sanzu-no-kawa*, deciding who enters paradise and who enters hell. To reinforce his prayers, he tightened controls on his health, and even if reproached by others, did not go out at night.

Aside from his feeling of disillusionment with Japan, Hisashi could foresee the 'bubble economy' would soon burst, and he wanted to be away before then. Like the frog in Aesop's fable unable to swell to the size of a cow, he knew the bubble was bulging far beyond its real worth. But one good consequence was that the price of real estate had soared.

In 1986, his house in Takanawa had reached an exorbitant value, and his banker advised him to sell and buy an apartment. Even though it meant buying the apartment at the top of the market, with the leftover cash in his pocket Hisashi judged it was good timing to be leaving Japan. In 1988, he purchased an apartment in Dunedin. And the following April, 69-year-old Hisashi and 59-year-old Yayoi packed up their lives and crossed the globe.

> Sitting comfortably aboard their Air New Zealand flight, Hisashi has plenty of time to reflect. He feels no regret or sadness. He knows he has made the best decision. It is the start of the greatest adventure of his life, and he wonders whether his feelings are the same as those felt by British migrants travelling to New Zealand in the mid-nineteenth century. But what should he state on his arrival papers? If he says he is retired, the New Zealand government might worry he will want a benefit. If he says he is self-supporting, they might impose heavy income tax. Finally, he decides on the former, an honest reflection of his status in Japan.

Hisashi's second 'thousand-day-calendar' started in Dunedin, but in the twinkling of an eye, it too flew away without him realising his dream of 'Every day a Sunday'. On the contrary, he was overly busy, just like the wartime expression: 'Monday, Monday, Tuesday, Wednesday, Thursday, Friday and Friday; a week'.

He and Yayoi had arrived in New Zealand on visitor visas, which meant they had to renew their visas regularly. If Hisashi kept his Japanese passport, he would continue to receive his pension, so they decided that rather than applying for New Zealand citizenship they would apply for permanent residency with frequent visitor status. But with all the paperwork required, it took nearly four years to be approved for residency. Worried about illegal Asian immigrants, the New Zealand Immigration Service had introduced strict requirements for approval, and all documents submitted had to be verified, which lengthened the process. At one point, Hisashi had to prove he had been to university. Having lost his graduation certificate when their shelter had been burgled during the occupation, he had to wait three months for a copy to arrive from *Todai*, then, wait for that to be authenticated by Immigration.

Just after arriving in Dunedin, a souvenir shop in a hotel lobby had come up for sale. To prove his genuine desire to contribute to the New Zealand economy Hisashi bought it. Taking on sales staff meant Yayoi could focus on the accounting aspects of the business, while he was responsible for the inventory and purchasing. And they enjoyed the opportunities it afforded them as they travelled around the country to source stock. However, running a shop was more difficult than they had realised, and New Zealand business customs were completely different to those in Japan. Hisashi often felt like Alice in *Alice in Wonderland*. Other times he felt annoyed with himself that he did not know his 'proper place' in the new environment, and it took several years before he could relax. Finally, in 1994, after five years of business losses, Hisashi sold the shop.

Back in 1991 he had purchased a weekend house on a ten-acre block just outside Dunedin where, in return for maintaining the property, a neighbouring farmer grazed his sheep. Here, Hisashi could listen to the silence and smell 'the clean air'. He could hear the birds' merry notes, and then, such silence would reign that he wondered whether he had lost his hearing. But in the silence, a voice from the past would pester him: 'How can you be so easily satisfied? Do you have no backbone; no noble spirit? Why do you indulge in such simple peace and happiness? You should be challenging yourself for the betterment of Japan.'

His new life seemed to deride his past training, and for years that pesky voice embarrassed and bewildered him. But after selling the shop, he found it easier to ignore, and eventually realised it was 'the curse of his upbringing'. He already stood on the banks of the Sanzu-no-*kawa* so he no longer owed allegiance to Japan.

Precise calculations of time look good on paper, but his journey had its own span. At last, in 1997, commencing calendar number five, he achieved his 'Every day a Sunday' and he chuckled with delight. And ever since then Hisashi has enjoyed sweet sleep and a keen appetite; and he much appreciates the sound of silence.

Every morning before getting out of bed, he continued to count the days. As he confirmed that his limbs were working, he would smile to himself; and he was even happier if he had no appointments for the day. Now he had nothing to do but wait for the day to cross the river. Naturally, at times he felt nostalgic for Japan, but perhaps these were instinctive feelings, just as migratory birds instinctively return to their birth place. He had been imprisoned within the Japanese behavioural code, and now he had known freedom, he could never go back. He was pleased he had left.

And what he thought would happen had happened. The bubble had burst in 1990. Over-inflated land values and over-extended banks had collapsed. In 1993, after 38 years, the Liberal Democrats had been swept from power, the new coalition inheriting the largest national debt in the industrialised world. In January 1995, an earthquake ravaged the city of Kōbe, the cost of reconstruction another burden on the economy. Months later a millennial cult leaked deadly gas into the Tokyo subway. Hisashi was pleased he had found his safe haven.

Throughout the decade, as expected, the aging population in Japan had risen steadily. How would he have fared if he had stayed there? In New Zealand his Japanese pension gave him a most comfortable standard of living. In Japan he would have barely made ends meet.

Being the eldest, Hisashi had been preparing his estate so that everything would be in order for Yayoi after he crossed the river. This had included selling the Tokyo apartment and his weekend house, and buying a newly built townhouse in a retirement village in Mosgiel, 15 minutes from Dunedin.

But in July 1999, after a short illness, Yayoi died of cancer. She never got to see the townhouse completed, though she had chosen the curtains. Hisashi sold their Dunedin house and moved to Mosgiel.

He had fulfilled his exacting roles as son, brother and employee, faithfully and selflessly. He had repaid the final instalment of his *on*. His father had had to die to gain release from his burden. Hisashi's release was a gift that added many years to his life.

Epilogue

A Book is Born

Kenja no ichigen wa ju nen no bengaku ni masaru
A single conversation with a wise man
is better than ten years of study

* * *

Onaji kama no meshi wo kuwu
We unrelated persons, but on thee-and-thou-terms,
have been great friends, both in joy and in sorrow

I STILL MISS YAYOI. No matter our age difference, sometimes she was like a sister, other times my mother; but above all she was my friend.

It is sad that we never said goodbye. She was hospitalised with cancer while I was overseas for work. I visited her each day in the week that I was home, then went away on a week's holiday that had been booked for some time. Yayoi told me there was nothing to worry about and that I should go – the doctors thought she still had a couple more years. However, in the middle of the holiday my mother telephoned to say Yayoi had died.

Her funeral was a small affair with invited mourners only. I spoke briefly, describing Yayoi as my sister, mother and friend. Appropriate words indeed, as I was totally unaware that Yayoi, only the day before she died, had told my mother she considered me her sister, daughter and friend.

Yayoi and Hisashi had quickly become part of my family, and me part of theirs. In Dunedin they joined our family occasions, and on my work trips to Japan I stayed with them. Each year they went back to Tokyo for six weeks, staying in the Takanawa apartment, arranging their trips to coincide with mine. Having sold most of their belongings, they lived there simply, and I was the only one who ever stayed with them. I would arrive at Narita Airport a week after them, Hisashi taking the two-hour bus ride to meet my evening flight. Arriving at the apartment, Yayoi would welcome me with a hug and a cup of hot chocolate. My *futon* would have been laid out on the *tatami*, with chocolates Hisashi had brought from Dunedin on either side of the pillow.

We usually went out for our meals; and every spare minute we visited art galleries and museums, often going by taxi; on their own, Hisashi and Yayoi ate at home, only going out on business, and never by taxi. Hisashi would not let me go out on my own and escorted me to wherever I was working. But it was not until years later that Yayoi admitted how put out she had been that he would do these things for me and not for her.

I met their friends and neighbours, and visited their homes, attended a *kimono* school graduation, and participated in the *cha-no-yu*, experiencing a Japan I would never see when staying in a hotel. Staying at the apartment within the Japanese community gave me a gentle introduction to the hidden world of traditional Japan. Yayoi and Hisashi guided me, teaching me what I should and should not do in certain company and particular places.

For work, Hisashi was my 'guide dog' and interpreter, and undoubtedly his sponsorship gave me greater credibility than had I been on my own. But at other times, Yayoi was my accomplice for shopping and other fun, as we visited the best coffee shops in the Ginza and the best designer boutiques.

On one visit we went to the *onsen* at Hakone and stayed at the same hotel overlooking the lake where they had spent every New Year between 1960 and 1989; also the stage for Ryoko's regal arrival in her cashmere coat.

It is late afternoon in the autumn. The mountain is russet and gold. A narrow road shaded by lofty cryptomeria, part of the old *Tokaido*, runs around the lake. A rickshaw carrying two tourists races along.*

The staff remember Yayoi and Hisashi, and greet them warmly. Yayoi, eager for her bath, waits only long enough for a snack and a cup of *sencha*, which she explains will stop us feeling dizzy and weak in the hot water.

Modern *onsen* are segregated, but I am still embarrassed. I have never bathed naked in public before. Following Yayoi's lead I undress and join her in the wet area. Other women are leaving and luckily no one else arrives. I feel ridiculous, overflowing the plastic stool, but Yayoi is unruffled, and we are soon giggling like schoolgirls. We scrub vigorously, rinsing with basins of water, dousing with the hose, and then venturing outside to the pool.

The air is cool. The silhouette of Mount Fuji looms familiarly. A maple rustles its leaves. Ever so slowly sinking into the water, my body tingles with the heat. The water lapping over the edge, the breeze fanning my face, the sun dropping below Fuji's perfect cone, and the changing colours of the sky, soothe my soul.

My lobster-red body feels smooth and soft, muscles and nerves relaxed. Changing into freshly starched *yukata* and slippers, we shuffle red-cheeked and ravenous to the dining room, where Hisashi joins us. Sitting with other similarly clad guests, we sip *sake* and enjoy another elaborate meal.

Whenever I was with Hisashi and Yayoi, they made sure I sampled Japanese food. All had to be tasted, from *purasuchikku-foodo* (fast food replicated in plastic displays) to exquisite gourmet delicacies, and everything in between. It was sublime to eat haute cuisine at a *ryotei* (high class traditional restaurant). Then there was the *Sushi-ya* (*sushi*

---

* Rickshaws appeared in the 1870s. The wife of an American missionary in Tokyo was so upset seeing coolies carrying customers on their backs that her husband conceived the rickshaw.

restaurant; *ya* means restaurant) that serves *sushi* and *sashimi*, and the *Sukiyaki-ya* (*sukiyaki* restaurant) where beef and vegetables are cooked at the table. Of the various noodles sold at *Soba-ya*, my favourite was *udon* noodles in hot, spicy gravy. Eating noodles it is customary to suck them lustily into your mouth with *hashi*. I had great trouble, my mother having stressed to me that I should chew quietly with my mouth closed. Hisashi said it would be difficult for me to learn anyway – my mouth muscles have not been trained to slurp slippery noodles.

Yayoi and her friend Kyoko always took me to the *Yakitori-ya*. It felt so exotic, being the only foreigner, sitting at the counter watching the head-banded chef's rapid handiwork, then washing the grilled chicken down with *sake* drunk from wooden box-cups. I also loved the *Tonkatsu-ya* (pork cutlet restaurant), where deep-fried crumbed pork was served with shredded cabbage, and a Japanese version of Worcester sauce. And, Hisashi's favourite, the *Unagi-ya* (eel restaurant) serving grilled eel, an expensive dish long prized as a stamina-giving food in summer. And, not to be overlooked, Mos Burger, the local hamburger chain, which Hisashi had never visited until he met me. First sampled when he was 74, it is now a must whenever we visit, and it makes an amusing anecdote to tell his friends.

* * *

One day some months after Yayoi's funeral, I received my inheritance. This treasure had been buried underground during the war, and stowed away again after Ryoko's death. Now, nearly 30 years later I had the privilege of bringing it to light once more.

> Hisashi's lounge floor is almost hidden beneath stacks of faded rice-paper *kimono* bags, his passion for order portrayed in the perfect piles. I am excited, but control myself, and begin on the pile Hisashi suggests. Opening the first wrapper, I carefully undo the cotton tie, then fold back the paper flaps to expose a cream *kimono* sumptuously embroidered with bright flowers. Hisashi explains this is Yayoi's twenty-first *kimono*.

I hold it up, and released from its 50-year confinement, it ripples to the floor, shimmering under the lights, with not one crease. How beautiful she must have looked.

Soon the room looks like Aladdin's cave, with glorious *kimono* gleaming like jewels. Some are vibrant with multi-coloured embroidery, while others are pale and understated. Some are intricately patterned with chrysanthemums and camellias, while others are patterned in stripes, and even houndstooth. The pungent aroma of camphor permeates the room. I ask so many questions. Who wore that? Where would she have worn it? Why are these sleeves longer? Hisashi, as an 80-year-old male, is highly amused, but remembers when his mother or Yayoi wore this one or that, and which one was appropriate for what occasion. Ryoko never wore Western dress, so most of the *kimono* are hers, their subdued hues providing a foil for Yayoi's vivid adolescent *kimono*. Yayoi wore nothing but Western dress, her twenty-first *kimono* a concession to Ryoko.

There are different weaves for different seasons: most are silk, some are linen, with a few made of cotton. Some are heavy brocade, some are gossamer fine. Some are lined, while some are not. One is quilted for winter. There are formal *kimono*, others for everyday use, some for shopping, some for casual visiting or at home. But it is not just *kimono*, there are also *haori*, brightly coloured for day, ornate for formal wear, and black for funerals. There are undergarments, removable collars, *tabi*, *geta*, *zori*, small pouch bags and formal fans, cords and sashes, pads and stiffeners, and long opulent *obi*. Finally, I come to the last bag, which is thicker than the others. I see then feel the soft fabric, and there is Ryoko's grey cashmere coat.

I instantly fall in love with the grey coat. While I admire and treasure the 24 *kimono*, I know they will never be part of my wardrobe. Wearing a *kimono* I look what I am, a Westerner playing dress-up. But the grey cashmere coat is something else. Even before I try it on, I know it will suit me, and that I will wear it in my everyday life.

Wearing Ryoko's cashmere coat I feel connected to Japan. It gives me a Japanese identity that is unable to be bought off the rack. It is as if this gift confirms my honorary membership of the Furuya family. And the *kimono* have intensified my interest in the lives of the two women who wore them.

That interest had its roots in a weekly lunch date Hisashi and I had begun after Yayoi died. The week after the funeral, he talked about 'the rubbish' he had collected during his life. He wanted to burn it so his estate would be no burden to sort. However, as he described the photographs, newspaper articles, diaries and souvenirs of World War II, I was alarmed by the potential loss of such treasure, and saddened to think he believed no one would be interested. Naturally, I wanted to see it all, and from there my curiosity turned into a passion to collate everything and to write Hisashi's story.

That first Wednesday put our relationship on a completely different footing. In Japan he had felt repressed by his upbringing, obliged to meet society's expectations. He had felt oppressed by his *giri*, obliged to meet his father's expectations. In this new country, he could ignore others' expectations. And now, Yayoi's death had signalled the end of that oppressive *giri*. However, even though freed from the constraints of Japanese society, he still found it difficult to completely change his conditioning. But being 'out of specification' gave him the capacity to adapt well.

In the relaxed atmosphere of his favourite restaurant he opened up. He was still composed and courteous, but gone was his customary reticence and inscrutability. When we first met, he had let Yayoi do the talking, and I never expected him to become so forthright. He had found it a challenge adjusting to a new conversational style and interpreting the colloquial 'kiwi' vocabulary. Gradually his reserve melted away. He liked to chat and everyone commented on how much more gregarious he had become. It was as if a stopbank had burst, causing decades of unspoken words and feelings to pour forth. Initially I was surprised at how vulnerable he allowed himself to be, amazed at how much he trusted me. Such an outpouring would never have happened if he had been living in Japan, or if Yayoi had been alive: the shame would have been too great. But by a 'touch of sleeve' the time, place and relationship was right.

The second Wednesday, he produced the album. During 1946 he had collated wartime documents and newspaper articles, pasting them with comments on to naval charts, the only paper he could find. There were no photographs as they had all been stolen from the underground shelter. In 1959, when he was on sick leave, he had transferred everything to an album Miss Takenaka had given him ten years earlier, adding comments and photographs copied from Yoshiji's negatives.

The album gave me a basic structure. However, it soon became obvious that I needed to understand the history of Japan so I could place Hisashi and his life in context. As he toiled over the translation of the album, I researched Japanese history, each Wednesday asking questions about what I had read.

There were so many questions to answer, not just about his family, but about Japan and the war. Tangible artefacts revealed the poignant passage of his life: his school badges and prefect certificates, his naval identification card, his officer's sword and uniform buttons, wartime postage stamps and the family ration book, as well as Jinjiro's World War I officer's sword, his World War II gate pass, his priority train pass, and his honourable mention from Kawanishi when he retired. Having such memorabilia is rare. Old records, keepsakes and photographs are not valued or well maintained in Japan, and in addition, so much had been destroyed and lost during the war and occupation.

Translation of the album took months and translation of the diaries another two years. And as Hisashi retraced his life, he was surprised to realise how closely he had followed the trend of what had happened to Japan. Though reading his words of 60 years earlier, never far from his mind was the saying of the first Tokugawa *shogun*: 'Life is like travelling a long road with a heavy burden on the back.'

His diary gave me a glimpse into a momentous period of history. Although I had his permission and approval, at times I felt like a voyeur, seeing into his heart as I, too, lived through his dogged determination to survive. I would pore over the pages of his closely printed script, endeavouring to put myself in his place. What was he really thinking behind his casual words? Some things had been too hurtful to reveal in detail. His three cursory mentions of Miss Takenaka had not alerted me to her significance. Then, one day I had asked if he had ever been in love. Unfazed, he quietly explained their relationship, and showed me the tea cup she had given him.

As he re-read his diaries, he felt as if they had been written about someone else, and he would smile at the 'boy' he had been, feeling compassion for him, so young and serious. He was surprised at the memories that floated back: that dawn so long ago at the mill when he organised the collection of body parts is still clear in its detail; likewise the scene at the bridge over the Sumida-*gawa*. And I will never forget his expression as he described standing in his empty bedroom before he left for the navy. One day he found a list of classmates who had died in the war. Recalling their boyish faces, he 'lament[ed] their deaths, and the loss of their untapped talents', especially in relation to his own 'piling up of insignificant years'. And he was dismayed to find he still felt shame over his father's death.

Initially, I was baffled that Hisashi felt no bitterness about the war. He has none of the animosity that many Westerners still hold towards the Japanese. He retains an almost academic detachment, recalling events without rancour for what might have been. He says acceptance is the 'Japanese way'. Similarly, the Japanese did not expect the Chinese to resent Japan for winning in Manchuria. It was simply Japan's turn to win.

He had recently seen an Australia New Zealand Army Corps [ANZAC] Day service on television, impressed to see former New Zealand servicemen gathering at dawn services to remember fallen comrades. He empathised with the feelings that drove these old soldiers to participate. Hearing the *gunka* (military march) called *Sallying Forth on the Sea*, so popular in Japan during the war, created similar feelings in him.

In 1997 he had written an article for his middle school's sixtieth anniversary magazine, divulging a secret he had hugged to himself since the war. As a schoolboy, fearing a negative response to such an expression of emotion, he had resisted in saying how much the music of the *gunka* had meant to him. However, he felt confident his classmates would appreciate his feeling, and sharing his secret would lighten his load as he journeyed to the river.

I know little Japanese language, but that in many ways has been an advantage. In our interviews with other Japanese, with him as interpreter, I found out things I could never have done on my own. With me directing the questions, he found out things he would never have asked. Over the years I have become accustomed to his old-fashioned formality, his cryptic comments and his curious expressions. He has become used to my directness and informality. Our relationship, like Ryoko's grey cashmere coat, transcends age, culture, personality and gender.

Our Wednesday lunches became a ritual and remain so. Arriving at the pub, we seat ourselves at our usual booth, which Hisashi laughingly calls 'our office'. Trudy the waitress greets us with, 'Your usual?' While waiting for our 'usual' grilled blue cod, we discuss the past week: Hisashi's latest recipes, my mother's health, what he has seen on Japanese television. Linda, the restaurant manager, drops by for a chat.

It is amazing what unexpected gems have popped up over lunch. As Hisashi says: 'scraps of chattering words contain plenty of valuable particles of truth'.

Many of the finer details of his story turned up in this way, often sending us off on a new trail. One day as I added salt to my fries, out came the story of manufacturing salt at the Fisheries laboratory in 1946. He beamed as he recalled his secret pleasure at getting one over the government, and that snippet led me to explore rationing and the *yami-ichi*.

After lunch we go to the supermarket. Seeing a Magnolia Apollo in the garden section reminded him of the one that had grown in the garden of his childhood home, and impulsively he bought it.

Before Yayoi died he had never had to do the shopping, cooking or housework. Confucius said gentlemen should stay out of the kitchen and Hisashi, like most Japanese males, had always been happy to leave it first to his mother, then to Yayoi. A man living alone tends to eat out, or to buy a pre-cooked meal from a department store deli. Here in Dunedin, at 79 years old, he had to learn a new way of life. Today he enjoys ambling along the supermarket aisles, thinking of recipes, and comparing prices with Japan.

During the research for this book we often went back to his house, where we got straight down to business discussing my questions. One afternoon, I noticed the walls of the dining room were lined with containers filled with water. I looked blankly as he explained that snow was forecast. He pointed out the primus cooking stove and the candles. He was prepared for power cuts or broken water mains. Rooted in his childhood, it was an habitual reaction to an impending snowfall, heavy rain or a strong wind. This resulted in the story of the 1945 *taifu*.

Discussing material for the book created feelings of ambivalence for Hisashi: while he had found some entrenched restraints suffocating, tradition had provided certainty and comfort. And now he says the Japanese people should preserve their roots, as sometimes the old ways are the best. He regrets that developments in Japan have resulted in new types of citizens who have cast aside their traditions and history. Switching to a modern lifestyle makes it easier for them to indulge themselves, and detach from family obligations.

Without my impetus, Hisashi would never have re-read his diaries or re-visited his uncomfortable past. And, as our research developed into a book, he could see that it might be a healing book, not only for himself, but that it could form a bridge between Japan and the West. He was so energised by that idea that his feelings of being a failure disappeared. Contributing to the book affirmed his life and validated his experiences – his 'piling up of insignificant years' had significance after all. He believes his peers have a duty to hand down the story of Japan's defeat to the next generation, so that the chronicle of their mistakes can be used as a 'precious lesson'. So at 80 years old, with this new lease on life, he planned how best to give me as accurate a feel of his world as he could. He found me books to read, websites to explore and documentaries to watch on Japanese television. But pivotal to my understanding were our trips to Japan: making new friends, visiting historical sites, his old haunts and those of his ancestors, as well as meeting old friends, family and ghosts.

* * *

Hyakubun ikken ni shikazu
One hundred hearings are not as good as one viewing

Late one afternoon in May 2005 Hisashi and I stand on the top floor of the 36-storey Japan World Trade Centre, near Hamamatsu-cho-*eki*. Sweeping glass enables us to see a full 360 degrees. Heat and smog hang in a haze, with grey buildings and grey sky seemingly merging as one.

Spread out before us we see Tokyo and its satellite cities – Yokohama, Kawasaki, Funabashi and Chiba – as well as the hinterland and the Pacific Ocean. The skyline extends upwards and outwards, a vast, overbuilt vista of concrete and glass, neon and tangled wires. Tokyo has overpowered the land and lagoon, and there are only three pockets of green: Meiji-*jingu* and the neighbouring Imperial Annex Garden, Ueno Park, and the Shinagawa green belt. Elevated expressways and train tracks slash through the city. Hisashi marvels at its transformation as he points to places we have visited. The original structure of Tokyo radiating in rings around the Imperial Palace has long gone. Even in his lifetime, after an earthquake, fires, *taifu* and war, the city has been rebuilt several times.

Looking north to the palace it is hard to imagine that once the waters of Edo Bay extended almost to its perimeter. Using the palace as our marker, we walk anticlockwise, tracing the old Edo boundary, now the 29-station Yamanote loop line that encloses central Tokyo,* the subway crisscrossing the city below ground. From Hammatsu-cho we move towards Shimbashi-*eki*, from where Hajime travelled to Yokohama 100 years before.

Hisashi points out the Ginza, its three boulevards enclosed between the expressway and railway line, clearly seen on the eastern side of the loop line, and closest to the sea. The original Ginza grid has stretched south to merge with Shim-*bashi*, and north to Kanda, on its way engulfing Nihom-*bashi*, once the heart of Shitamachi. He points towards the Kimuraya Bakery at the Shim-*bashi* end, a must for Tatsuko on their family outings; in Nihom-*bashi*, Fugetsudo ice-cream parlour, Hajime's favourite shop. Further along, he can see Kanda, where he loved to browse in the second-hand bookshops.

Northeast of the Ginza, extending from Kanda to the Sumida-*gawa*, we can just make out the narrower streets and smaller buildings of old Shitamachi, in their midst Asakusa and Senso-*ji*. We follow the bridges over the Sumida-*gawa*, where Hisashi watched the fireworks as a child; ignominiously crewed as cox; and five years later saw the aftermath of the 10 March air raid.

On the western side of the railway line, within the loop, all the way to Kanda, we have an uninterrupted view of high-rises, all concrete, glass and steel. Past Shim-*bashi* is Hibiya, where a new Imperial Hotel stands on the site of Frank Lloyd Wright's creation; and not far away is the naval headquarters where Jinjiro worked. Next is Nagatacho, the location of the *Diet*; and Hisashi's middle school, where the coup took place that snowy winter in 1936; and not far from there, the

---

* Its most important stations are Tokyo, Ueno, Shinjuku and Shibuya.

Imperial Palace. Directly east of the palace is the 19-platform Tokyo-*eki*, business-focussed Marunouchi, and behind the rows of corporate glass, pockets of upmarket housing. Carrying on, Hisashi spies what he thinks is *Todai*'s campus.

Continuing in a northeasterly direction from Kanda, outside the loop line, we see the hills between Tokyo and Chiba, and tucked unseen behind the hill, Narita International Airport. Hisashi reminds me that back when he boarded at Nakamura's farm, the two cities had still been separate. Back within the loop line, opposite Asakusa, we focus on the green of Ueno Park, where near here, at *Ameyoko* beside Ueno-*eki*, Hisashi treated himself to a dried Hokkaido herring and a satsuma orange during the occupation.

Halfway around the perimeter of the thirty-sixth floor, we look west of the palace to Shinjuku-*eki*: said to be the world's busiest station. Mid-way between us and the station is Aoyama, where Jinjiro lived as a boy.

South of Shinjuku, with our backs to the palace, we look southwest to the distant Hakone, where Ryoko, Yayoi and Hisashi spent their New Year holidays; on a good day we could have seen Mount Fuji. What we can see closer in is Shibuya and the green swathe of Meiji-*jingu*, where Hisashi went for the Seven-Five-Three festival, and where he and Ryoko prayed for success in his high school exams. Hisashi draws my attention to the shrine's outer garden, the site of the former Washington Heights, where he bought his fridge. The swirling roof of the National Stadium built for the 1964 Olympics indicates where he stood in the rain to watch the parade of drafted students in 1943.

We move further around to get a clearer view of Shibuya-*eki*, where he transferred lines to primary and middle school. Outside of the loop line, looking southwest of the station, we find Sangenjaya, where the family lived until the air raid. Due south within the loop is Takanawa, where Hisashi tries to identify his old apartment. Next door is Shinagawa-*eki*, the start of the old *Tokaido*, and where he changed trains to the naval institute on Miura Peninsula. Looking down, Hisashi shows me where the lagoon once lapped the edge of the track.

Now back full circle, swinging up from Shinagawa to Hamamatsu-cho, we look out over the remains of Tokyo Bay into which the *kurofune* steamed in 1853. The bay has shrunk, more than two kilometres of the lagoon in front of the loop line having been reclaimed. Still reminiscing, Hisashi describes how a vast industrial maze built on fill had mushroomed after the war. Today, ultra-modern, multi-storey developments glittering in the setting sun encroach on the smokestacks, storage tanks and warehouses. Dockyards loom against the darkening sky: cranes, ships and massive concrete storage tanks, even a replica of the Statue of Liberty, competing for space. A giant technicolour Ferris wheel circles against the sky. The illuminated Rainbow Bridge arcs over the lagoon, linking Shim-*bashi* to the island of Odaiba, where orphans were caged during the occupation. He points to where four Edo forts stood on artifical islands along the sea side of the lagoon. Today, the forts are part of the foundation for the monorail connecting Tokyo Bay with Narita Airport.

We watch as the orange sun sinks into the sea. From on high it is magical. Twinkling below, windows light up in rows. The western hills glitter like gold. Street lamps are sprinkled like stars. Car headlights become comets, leaving luminous trails of light. The *Shinkansen* whooshes past.

Outside on the pavement, the lights seem garish and gaudy and our eardrums are under instant attack by the constant background roar. Engines rumble, exhausts belch, brakes screech and car doors slam. Couriers whizz by on bicycles. A traffic policeman blows his whistle. A beeping delivery truck backs down an alley. Sirens wail. Music blasts from bars. Pneumatic jackhammers judder. Mobile phones and jet planes join in. Something fast and heavy rattles above us, electric rails spark and a commuter train screeches around the curve. Beneath us, the subway leads downtown. Among the messy overhead cables, high-wattage ideograms vie with a five-storey television screen.

We are to dine at the Imperial Hotel tonight. From Hamamamatsu-cho to Shim-*bashi*, to the Ginza and across to the hotel in Hibiya is only a short walk. Work is over. People are swarming out of offices. Bars are opening for business. We plunge into the hordes.

Hisashi finds it difficult to reconcile today's Ginza with the Ginza of his youth. He misses the *karan~koron, karan~koron*, the pre-war harmony of *geta* on the pavement. Today, well-suited young men hold hands with girlfriends wearing the latest designs. A monk texts on his mobile phone. A woman waits at the traffic lights with a Dalmatian dog wearing miniature boots to match her own.

I know well what to expect when I visit Tokyo, but it still takes a day or two to adjust. Pulsating with relentless energy and commercialism, its wealth beyond the imagination of most New Zealanders, Tokyo intoxicates me. But its wall-to-wall people and traffic, pollution, neon and noise can become too much. Hisashi, after living in Dunedin for 16 years, finds it the same. For me, the city appears more affluent and active than ever, though Hisashi thinks it is a façade, a breeding ground for disillusionment. For him, Tokyo has lost its heart: like a doughnut, empty in the centre. Real estate prices have driven the middle class to the outskirts, creating a city of commuter congestion. Of Japan's 140 million people, 30 million live in the Tokyo metropolitan area on less than two per cent of the total landmass, nine million of those living within the loop line, its population swelling on weekdays by three million commuters.

When we travel on the loop line we try to avoid rush hour. Taking our tickets from a vending machine we weave our way to the barrier gate. As we insert our tickets in the slot, the machine grabs them, and spits them out at the end of the gate. Facing an onslaught of dark-suited *sararii-men* at rush hour requires equal determination and focus, but doing as they do, heads down, avoiding eye contact, we beeline our way through. On board, for me, such crowding feels claustrophobic and offensive, and Hisashi now sees rush-hour carriages as 'cattle carriers'. He comments on the plethora of posters pasted above windows and flapping from the ceiling. Little is in English, but he says they are nothing but celebrity gossip and junk.

People are neatly dressed: smart young office workers rub shoulders with young mothers and toddlers in designer wear. Some unsmiling, middle-aged women sit on their own, while others chat cheerfully, clutching their department store carrybags. Deadpanned *sararii-men* sit with heads lowered: one wears a surgical mask over his mouth and nose, while several sleep. Tertiary students slouch in corners, their heads in books or with phones glued to their ears. Pasty faced adolescents, girls in dark sailor suits, boys in dark military style tunics have taken over the exits; others text madly on their cell phones. Hisashi, a head shorter, cannot see past them as they converse rowdily over his head. Before the war, at 1.64 metres, he was taller than average and could see over the heads of most people standing in the train. Inscrutable, he observes. Over dinner he will share his thoughts.

He comments that many Japanese people seem at a loss, and compares them to deep-sea fish, which look only in the short distance, with some even losing their eyes. Take for instance, the now downtrodden *sararii-man* worried about losing his job and finding his family less respectful: he has no idea there is another world full of light. Some women are also oppressed, expected to work, bring up a family, and care for elderly parents, while others value their husband only for his salary as they have fun with their women friends. On reflection, Hisashi believes middle-class women of his mother's generation were more fortunate than their counterparts today. Today's toddlers bicker and moan in public, shout and jump about. How his mother would have frowned. And as for today's youth, to him they appear a spoiled generation with over-indulgent parents.

In this environment of shifting values and conduct, people appear to have lost their way, unsure what it is to be Japanese. While he admires the independence of the new generation, he thinks they have taken things too far, tending to be over-confident, especially in rejecting the family system.

On our travels together, we have journeyed all over Japan to Aomori, Chiba, Fukiya, Fukuoka, Gifu, Hakata, Hakone, Himeji, Hirosaki, Hiroshima, Kamakura, Kanazawa, Kochi, Kurashiki, Kurume, Kyoto, Matsushima, Miyajima, Nara, Nikko, Okayama, Otaru, Sapporo, Takahashi, Wakayama, Yokohama, Yokosuka, and Zushi. We have visited many of his old haunts in Tokyo.

We also visited Kototoi-*bashi* over the Sumida-*gawa*. What I did not expect was dozens of Tokyo's homeless scurrying in and out of makeshift homes on the embankment. I find it hard to imagine how beautiful the river must have been when Sakuzaemon the physician strolled along its tree-lined banks. Hisashi says little, his mind full of wartime images of civilian casualties.

My friend Kyoko, one of Yayoi's closest friends, lives nearby. Kyoko's 98-year-old mother, Tsuru, tells me how it was during the 10 March air raid. Although she and her eight children had already been evacuated some 20 kilometres away, she could see the bombers arrive. There were so many they blocked out the sky, red flames contrasting against the darkest green, and the bombs fell so fast they looked like they were falling in slow motion. The day after the raid, her husband had gone to see what had happened to their home. She can still remember the scenes he described.

At Senso-*ji* in nearby Asakusa, like three-year-old Hisashi, I place a smouldering joss stick in the mound of ash in the giant censer, wafting the smoke over myself for good luck.

We visit the *Mikasa*, the flagship on which Jinjiro served in World War I. Decommissioned after the war, it has been permanently berthed at Yokosuka Naval Base. Hisashi has a photograph taken in 1935 showing the extended family standing on the *Mikasa*'s deck. Seventy years later, as I photograph him with Eiko standing on the very same spot, he feels proud of his father.

It is the first time I have met Eiko and her daughters. Eiko's *otto* has died and Eiko, disabled by a stroke, is in a wheelchair. Hisashi is sad her daughters are 'paying for their heritage, both expected to serve their mother', especially since Eiko fought against having to care for her in-laws. One daughter has not married because she must look after Eiko; the other is married, but living close by. Theoretically, Eiko's eldest child, the only son, should have taken care of her but, on his marriage, he renounced his family and inheritance.

We visit numerous Shinto shrines. Most are dedicated to a single profession, though a few, such as the *hachiman-sama* for abundant water supply, are like chainstores, popping up everywhere. While the locations of shrines have not changed, their place in people's lives has. Prayers are still said for success at work, healthy childbirth, help in passing exams, and even in finding a husband. But Hisashi thinks that perhaps prayer is a socially accepted habit rather than a search for spiritual guidance.

One November trip, we visit Meiji-*jingu*, enjoying the colourful parade of children, parents and grandparents in traditional, often rented, dress at the Seven-Five-Three festival. We also visit the controversial Yasukuni-*jinja*. Here the spirits of soldiers who have died in the Emperor's name since 1868 are enshrined; among them are convicted war criminals.

At the ablution trough we wash our hands and rinse our mouths. A towering *torii* leads us along the avenue lined with cherry and gingko trees, white cooing doves roosting in their lush foliage. For appearances' sake, Hisashi stands to attention in front of the shrine, joins his hands in prayer, bows slightly, claps twice and withdraws. Afterwards he tells me that this is his first visit since he was a schoolboy. Influenced by his father, he disapproves that it glorifies aggression. He sees 'an archive' of the Meiji regime, its significance obsolete, except as an educational resource to help young people realise the futility of war. He thinks the lesson of World War II is still to be learnt. Japan has never faced its role as an aggressor.

Visiting *Todai* is entirely different. We take photographs of each other standing at the splendid, double-doored red *daimyo* gate, through which generations of Furuyas walked during the Tokugawa period. We find Maeda's crest on a fence tile. Giant gingkoes provide cover down the entire length of the pavement, green, fan-shaped leaves with their colour slipping to gold. Fallen leaves dance in the wind. A white-gloved street cleaner moves up and down with his handcart and broom.

An old man and the ghost of a young man wander along the pavement. I take a photograph.

Gazing into the campus, Hisashi sees the same brick and wrought-iron fence. Many of the buildings are the same. The red gate is unchanged. But gone is the male bastion of privileged youth in black, high-buttoned tunics. The students are completely contemporary in dress, speech and their expressions, though it is not just the students that are different. He is 'obliged to admit' he, too, has changed. He does not fit in. He expected to be 'dipped in nostalgia'. But so much time has elapsed he thinks of himself as a stranger in a strange street, and feels shaken.

The ghost of the young man, and the ghosts of other young men who died in the war, make him feel lonely and sad. His memories seem irrelevant to anyone but himself, or those who were there.

A fortnight later we look at the photograph of the back view of the solitary man wandering under the gingko trees. Hisashi sees a man betrayed by a 'sweet memory', his figure 'an empty container'. He recalls the story of 'Urashima Taro' the fairy tale fisherman welcomed under the sea by the fish and mermaids. Returning to the human world, Urashima at first thinks everything is the same. But he soon realises he is an old man, and it is no longer his world. Hisashi feels just like Urashima.

Touring further afield, we visit the temples where Jitsuzen lived, Sato and Tomoko's small temple, Tomoko's son's temple, and Hiroshima. Using Kyoto as a base for overnight visits, we travel by the *Shinkansen* and local lines. When Hisashi was a boy, the trip from Tokyo to Kyoto took nine hours, now on the express *Shinkansen* it takes only two. He is proud of his part in its introduction, and remembers the first meeting when all present wondered whether the new train would be able to compete with air travel.

The long, bullet-shaped train stands motionless at the platform, pristine in its blue and white livery. A voice crackles over the loud speaker announcing its imminent departure. From our seats inside we watch as a white-gloved official glances at the platform clock. Moving purposefully to the control panel studded with switches and flashing lights, he pauses, checks with the clock on the wall, twists a knob, and waves to someone unseen. Soon, on schedule and with scarcely a tremor, we slither forward, faster and faster, nearly reaching today's maximum speed of 300 kph.* The middle-aged conductor, immaculate in navy uniform, white gloves, and gold-braided cap, bows as he enters and leaves the carriage. Fast on his heels the waitress trundles up and down with her trolley selling refreshments.

Heading out of Tokyo, on the raised iron track sitting above the urban sprawl, we are pleased to be avoiding the gridlock of vehicles below. Quick as a flash, narrow winding lanes disappear from view, twisting and turning, for all the world like 'a sheep's intestines'. I laugh at Hisashi's description, but it is apt.

The track hums beneath the wheels. Block upon block of apartments speed past. Market gardens and the occasional rice paddy are hemmed in by buildings. High-rises and factories loom over low-rises, and every so often, graveyards of car hulks, bicycle parking lots, and golf practice ranges. Haphazardly plonked pylons straddle gardens and fences. Huge billboards, ventilation flues, smoke stacks, oil tanks, ball-shaped natural gas containers, and a spider's web of wires obscure the view. Predominantly a dull landscape, colour comes from bushes clipped into orbs, plants tumbling from window boxes, bedding aired over balcony rails and washing hung on the line. The train sweeps across a bridge, struts flashing past as down below the Tama-*gawa* flows. And still the scenery is the same.

Twice we visit Eizan-*ji* at Mount Hiei to see where Jitsuzen lived. Taking the cable car up the precipitous, tree-covered slope is far easier

---

* An increase of 80 kph over the 40 years since it first ran.

than the trudge in Jitsuzen's day. Hisashi explains that each temple has its own special features, but if seen from the air, each compound conforms to a common cosmic pattern.

To me, Eizan retains a hint of its power and lofty purpose of bygone days. Old and new stand side by side, in an eclectic blend of religious architecture. Every path hugs to itself echoes of the past. And now and again, I catch glimpses of priests in flowing robes. On the top of the Mount stands the temple's most sacred hall, where the present-day, stockinged-feet faithful prostrate themselves before the Buddha, then one by one, they stand to light candles and incense.

On our second visit to Eizan, we call at the temple library, where Hisashi is fascinated to read his grandfather's words. The bulletins written between 1882 and 1892, some of which Hisashi translates, give a window into what was happening in Japan at that time. Jitsuzen's articles, and the copy of his 1893 lecture in Chicago, are tangible evidence of the erudite and respected man he was.

Eigen-*ji* by comparison is a complete contrast. Travelling out of Kyoto in the opposite direction to most others, our taxi noses through the early morning snarl. Slowly, we leave the traffic behind. Along the steely waters of Lake Biwa, small fishing towns hug the shore. As we go inland, sleepy villages line the road; behind them, patchworks of paddies and vegetable plots. In a timeless, Japanese scene, a farmer wades knee-deep in a flooded field. Utilising every piece of available land, he has terraced the sides of the hill, and planted flowers along the dykes.

It is the aftermath of a rainy spring day. A mist partially shrouds the mountains. Drizzle blankets everything, us included. The compound is possessed of a holy silence. Tall trees hover over the ancient buildings, and it is so quiet you can almost hear your heart beat. On approach, only a narrow wing is visible, trees crowding in as if to conceal the buildings. It is decidedly a modest temple given its importance but, Hisashi reminds me, this is the Zen tradition. Wandering closer, we see the subtle beauty of the humble wooden and plaster buildings. There is a rightness about their size and proportions. The temple does not amaze or overwhelm with its magnificence. It just is! The essence of the temple has been preserved and I breathe in its age and wisdom.

We walk under a tunnel of trees, which gives me the feeling of entering a secret place, and I hover between dream and reality. A priest appears to float in the mist. And nothing in this classic cameo suggests it would have been any different 100 years ago. The peace and tranquillity, the echo of the temple bell, and the aroma of incense all serve as reminders of the Abbot priest Jitsuzen.

No temple has ever charmed me as much as Eigen-*ji*. You do not have to be Buddhist to appreciate Zen. This is Hisashi's first visit. He is pleased for his grandfather, for finding such a pleasant and simple place to live out his days. He can understand the current trend towards esoteric Zen, but is annoyed it confuses what is Japanese with what is Zen and with what is Buddhism. Zen has long been associated with both, but they are not one and the same.

Fortunately, a scroll written by Jitsuzen, the poem quoted on pages 59 and 60 of this book, survived to be handed down to his grandson. After our visit the scroll became more meaningful for Hisashi. The ideograms of the ancient script had been difficult for him to translate, but he understood his grandfather's mood, tinged as it was with sadness and regret, and the relief he felt to be returning to his place of rest. The scroll holds pride of place in Hisashi's entrance hall, a reminder of how the world was.

Nikko was instantly recognisable from the faded sepia images taken by Yoshiji in 1939, but they bore little resemblance to those we took. As we wandered among hundreds of milling tourists, it was impossible to take a photograph without someone being in the way. It was early afternoon when we reached Tosho-*gu*.

> The mountains have thrown the area into shadow and the air is heavy with *sugi* pollen. Amidst the dark forest, the buildings are ostentatious. Intricate carvings and riotous colour have been meticulously preserved,

with animals, birds, flowers, fruit and children emblazoned on every manmade surface. It is like being in an enchanted folk tale. What secrets are concealed behind those brightly coloured *fusuma*? Whose ghost lives behind that black window opening? I half expect to meet a *samurai* dressed in battle regalia.

Hisashi brings me back to reality, when he comments that such pretension is neither useful to man nor beast. Nevertheless, he admits the holiday spent here with Yoshiji was one of the happiest periods of his life.

Hiroshima was also a must. He thought my education would not have been complete without a visit. It is a totally different city to what it was prior to 8.15 a.m. on 6 August 1945.

The resounding boom of the Peace Bell rings out over the wooded park as visitors strike the huge bronze bell. Others stand in prayer before the cenotaph, through which you can see the distant A-bomb dome.* In the museum we see a wristwatch frozen at 8.15 a.m. and a 13-year-old boy's charred lunch box, complete with its carbonised remains.†

Hisashi does not condemn the Americans for their choice, agreeing it was the only way to force Japan to cease fire. What upsets him was the Japanese government's lack of action as regards the 'voiceless victims'. He wonders why medical measures were not initiated for 20 years, by which time many victims had died. Assistance for Korean and Taiwanese victims took even longer.

Not all of our trips were directly related to Hisashi's history. Some were planned to give me a historical context. Two such places, Fukiya and Kurashiki, gave me a picture of old Japan. Fukiya is a picturesque, time-warp of a Tokugawa hamlet, its mines a rich source of copper for the *shogun*.

The weather is perfect. We stop frequently to take photographs.

---

* The skeletal shell and dome of the Industrial Promotion Hall built in 1914.
† Hiroshima is important, but must be put into context. Many more people were killed during the Battle of Okinawa and in the air raids on Tokyo.

Everything is green. The soil is rich. Cosmos, in shades of pink, float along the narrow roadside above the paddies. Windows down, we enjoy the warmth and birdsong as the black taxi drives leisurely past undulating fields of greeny golden grain. Farmers wave as we pass. Trees close in as the road zigzags upwards. Among the verdant landscape and gentle hills, the entirely original cluster of lattice-windowed houses and shops are stained in the local red-brown 'bengarra' (iron oxide) colour. Hisashi has never been here before, and is intrigued this isolated pocket has survived.

Over the years we have visited numerous traditional houses intended to resemble Japanese life in the nineteenth century. But the most special experience is staying in one. We stayed twice in a classic *ryokan* converted from rice storehouses in Kurashiki. During the Edo era, Kurashiki was a storage centre for the *shogun*'s rice taxes.

Little has altered since the *shogun*'s day: the compact precinct of two-storeyed shops and houses flanks a willow-fringed canal. It is picture-perfect: buildings clad in white mortar with black tiles; two gently arching bridges; golden carp gliding through the water; white swans drifting on the current; stone paved streets; ivy clambering around windows; tubs overflowing with flowers. There is no rushing here. Hisashi and I meander, savouring the history and elegance. I can hear the ghostly clatter of *geta* along the cobbled street beside the canal. I can see barges piled with rice. I can see shadowy figures as black-haired, *kimono*-clad women merge with the night, their white-painted faces illuminated in the light of their lanterns.

The *ryokan* we stay in faces the canal. In a perfect line at the entrance, matching beige slippers await arrivals, shoes shelved by the *ban-toh-san* (a kind of concierge) who screens visitors. The blue *kimono*-uniformed *nakai-san* (maid) glides on slippered feet. Smiling, bowing politely, she guides us to the small tearoom for the requisite cup of *matcha*, served while we register. We become friendly with the gracious, old *okami-san* (exact translation 'lady general') who owns the *ryokan*. The *okami-san* loves *kimono* and has never worn Western dress.

Up the narrow twisting staircase, *tatami*-matted suites are separated by *fusuma*. You can hear them glide in their tracks as guests enter and leave. Soft sunlight diffused through grid-like *shoji* gives a gentle start to the day. Come evening, moonlight works its magic.

We visited Wakayama to meet Hisashi's 93-year-old half-aunt, Tomoko. Tomoko is still living at the temple she inherited from her mother, Sato. She should be living with her eldest son at the temple he inherited from his father, but, not wanting to be a burden, she has chosen to live independently off her government annuity. She has been a good priest and a good mother, her four sons all highly successful.

I think she is wonderful, a relic of old Japan; and so stooped she does not even reach my shoulder. Her bright brown eyes never leave me, and she keeps hold of my hand, even through lunch. It makes me feel special, and that she approves of me. She and Hisashi talk at length. Tomoko is worrying about the temple's future. With only a few supporters, its income is meagre and she has no successor. Hisashi has no suggestions. She gets out her photograph albums and we talk about the family. As we leave, she tells him how happy she had been living with his family and studying to be a teacher. If she could have continued her studies, she may have walked a different path.

Hisashi is glad we have seen Tomoko. A couple of months after our visit, she died. The temple would 'die a quiet death', deleted from the 'temple register'. Her death prompted me to ask Hisashi whether he wanted to visit Japan again to say goodbye to his old friends. He replied simply that 'old men should leave quietly'.

* * *

Au wa wakare no hajime
To meet is the beginning of the parting

Hisashi showed me everything he could to help me understand Japan. But, even though he was my key that opened many doors, Japan remains shrouded in mystery.

Seated in 'our office' at the pub, my friend looks at me from across the generations, from across the oceans, and asks me who he is.

I look into his face. I see his refined features. But above all I sense his spirit and exceptional intellect. At his core, though, is an elemental *on* so great he would still sacrifice his own happiness to do what he considers right. It is clichéd to talk about the clash of old and new, the disparity between east and west, but that is Hisashi, just as it is Japan. He has seen the impact of war, occupation, Westernisation, industrialisation and growth. He has moved with dignity between two cultures. He has an awareness of mankind and a capacity to recognise what is relevant.

Hisashi does not want to live out his days in a '*Kintaro-ame* society'. *Kintaro*, a plump boy doll attached to a milky sweet, is 'lucky' confectionery sold for the 'boys' festival'. The sweet is divided into identical portions, just as Japanese people are made to the 'same specification'. But neither does he want to be a Kiwi. He is somewhere suspended between the two. Yet whatever happens, he wants to leave this life from Dunedin.

Hisashi's inherent Buddhist and *samurai* ancestry has provided him with a fatalistic perspective on death, his own included. Theoretically, he aspires to attain the detachment of a warrior, but he is 'not so pure in thought', still fearful of facing his death, though he has begun the process. His tombstone and funeral have been organised for some time.

During Christmas dinner in 1996 my mother had asked Yayoi what she got for Christmas. Yayoi had smirked behind her hand, replying Hisashi had bought them a plot in the Dunedin cemetery. Her tombstone is now written in white. Hisashi's name is in red, to be changed when he crosses the river.

He can still hear the *furin* ringing across the decades, but the boy he was then would not recognise the man of today. He is like a work of *origami*, the creases and folds of paper similar to the creases and folds of his life. Even the most complicated folds look simple from the outside but, like him, they hide old flaws and uncover new shapes.

Since being in New Zealand he has had time and a clear head to rethink his understanding of what it means to be a human, what it means to belong to a culture, and what he has learnt and gained through contact with people whose experiences and values differ from his own. Books and music, peace and contentment have become his constant companions. He listens to the early morning birdsong and the rustling of autumn leaves. He sniffs the scent of the golden roses at his front door, and appreciates the salmon-coloured azalea next door but one. He watches the weather on the horizon, the formation of clouds, the soft light of dawn and rosy sunsets. He takes time to enjoy his food and savour a good cup of coffee.

* * *

> *Kawa wa todomaru koto wo shirazu*
> Ceaselessly the river flows
> (The river flows without ceasing,
> yet its waters are never the same)

Now that I am nearing the end of the book, I can feel Hisashi slipping away. It is as if he has finished his job. I think he has taken to paddling at the edge of the Sanzu-no-*kawa*, watching the current, checking the temperature, assessing his options as he looks towards the other side of the river.

I know he is 87. I know death is inevitable. I just never associated it with him. There is a timelessness about him. He is so curious, continually seeking to learn and understand, which makes him seem much younger. But suddenly, it occurs to me he is preparing to cross the river. His face is sometimes ashen. His eyes do not twinkle as often. He does not always hear what I say. He is much slower in his movements and thoughts. He lapses into Japanese more and more, and often I have to repeat a question. For months I have noticed how frail he was becoming, but have not wanted to face facts.

For eight years we have devoted much of our lives to this book. We have spent weeks together on our trips, with never a harsh word between us. Given our differences, there have been many times when each of us has been puzzled or confused by the other's words or actions. But through it all, we have had this extraordinary, enduring connection of minds.

The last few weeks I have lacked my usual energy and enthusiasm. I am tired, too. I suspect deep down I know that once I am finished everything will change. I know it is time to finish the book and let it go. But it is not just the book; it is also time to let my friend go.

Sixty years ago, Yanagida gifted Hisashi with a new perspective and techniques with which to cope with the ebb and flow of his life. Hisashi has done the same for me. I am truly honoured to be guardian of his wisdom. And in time, my turn will come to pass on the gift he has bequeathed to me.

As I unfolded the seasons of Hisashi's life, my life was also undergoing seasonal change. Coping with my father's death, then with my mother's deterioration, also with cancer, it felt like the winter of my life. But, now I see it was spring, with glimmers of growth and new beginnings among the season's characteristic unsettled pattern.

Hisashi says that, irrespective of what happens to him or me, or to Japan or New Zealand, irrespective of war, poverty or unhappiness, the earth will continue to rotate 365 times a year. While people may suffer, the earth feels nothing. The human race is miniscule, nothing but a frail 'microcyte' in the universe. Life is but a passage through time. And like the cherry blossom, time and opportunity run out for each of us.

This old man will leave silently. And my blue eyes will mourn.

GLOSSARY OF JAPANESE WORDS

Amaterasu-Omikami   the Heavenly-Shining-Sun-Goddess
Ameyoko   Confectioner's Alley
bakufu or *shogunate*   military government
bancha   low grade coarse tea for home use
ban-toh-san   a type of concierge
bashi   bridge
bintsuke abura   a pomade used for keeping an elaborate hairstyle in place
Bodhisattvas   Buddhas-to-be
bonsai   the growing of miniature trees
Buddha   'the enlightened one', the name given to Gotama who founded Buddhism
Buddhism   a widespread Asian religion based on Buddha's teachings
bunkin takashimada   wedding hairstyle
bunraku   traditional puppet theatre
Bushido   'The Way of the Warrior'
cha-no-yu   tea ceremony – ritual tea drinking raised to an art form
cha-shitsu   teahouse
chasen   bamboo tea-whisk used when making *matcha*
chashaku   bamboo tea-scoop
chawan   tea-bowl
chippu   a tip for service
chonin   tradesmen class – craftsmen and merchants
Confucianism   Ancient Chinese philosophy calling for strict social order
daikon   radish
daimyo   a feudal lord
Diet   Japanese Parliament

dola   a homeless person or an orphan
Edo   literally 'river town', the Tokugawa era name for today's Tokyo
eki   railway station
engawa   a veranda-like wooden porch
eta   literally 'full of filth', a pariah class in pre-*Meiji* times
furin   a hanging wind chime
furoshiki   large square cloths, like scarves, used to wrap and carry things
fusuma   a paper covered sliding door used to partition a room
futon   a traditional Japanese bed
gaijin   foreigner
gawa   river, such as Tama-*gawa*, the Tama River
geisha   a traditional highly trained female practitioner of the arts
genkan   entrance hall of a house
geta   traditional wooden sandals with high supports
gimu   the full, unconditional repayment of *on*
Ginza   *Gin* meaning silver and *za* place, the original site of the *shogun*'s mint
giri   'right reason' implying the obligation to repay *on*
gishi   rectitude
go~go~go   a Japanese sound effect, booming
gonin-gumi   five family associations directly responsible for each other
gunka   military march
gura~gura~gura   a Japanese sound effect, shaking
hachimaki   *samurai* headband

haiku 17 syllable poem arranged in three lines of 5–7–5 syllables
haisen defeat
haji shame
hakama pleated loose-fitting trousers for men, like culottes, worn over a *kimono*
Hanabi-taikai the annual firework exhibition on the Sumida-*gawa*
hanshi special use paper
haori half-coat or jacket
happi loose informal jacket
hara-kiri the informal word used instead of *seppuku*, *samurai* style suicide
hashi chopsticks
hibachi charcoal brazier of ceramic or metal
Hinamatsuri Girls' Day, 3 March
hinin the so-called non-human class in pre-*Meiji* times
hinoki Japanese white cedar or cypress
hiragana the cursive form of Japanese syllabic writing
hishaku wooden ladle used in the tea ceremony
hondo the main hall at a temple
Honshu the main island of Japan
igusa-rush grass from which *tatami* is woven
ikebana the traditional art of flower arranging
inro a tiny storage box for holding medicines worn dangling from the *obi*
Ittoen an organisation whose members live frugally in the spirit of penitence
ji a Buddhist temple, such as Eizan-*ji* or Eizan Temple
jingu a high status Shinto shrine, such as Meiji-*jingu*
jinja a Shinto shrine for people at large, such as Yasukuni-*jinja*
juzu rosary beads
ka-tori-senko mosquito-repelling incense

kabuki a popular form of theatre in the *Edo* era
kaido highway
kaiten literally 'return to heaven', the suicide midget-submarine in World War II
kako-cho the book containing past family records
kami the Shinto term for a deity
kamikaze 'divine wind', the name given to suicide bombers in World War II
kan equivalent to 8.267 pounds
kana a simpler script than *kanji*, made up of *katakana* and *hiragana*
kanji the Japanese way of reading the Chinese system of ideographs
kannushi a Shinto priest
katakana an angular form of Japanese syllables
Kempeitai Military Police
kesa the mantle worn by a Buddhist priest on special occasions
kimono a Japanese gown with wide sleeves worn by men and women
kingyo goldfish
koan a non-rational conundrum used as a tool in meditation
koden the monetary offering to a departed spirit
Kodomo-no-hi Children's Day, 5 May – a national holiday
kofuku surrender
koi carp
koku equivalent to 5.11 bushels or 186 litres
konro a small portable cement stove which burns wood chips and paper
koryan a kind of corn produced in Manchuria
kosaku tenant farming
kotatsu a low, heated table or foot well
koto Japanese harp
kotsutsubo earthenware urn
kun christian name then -*kun*, denotes a close friend of one's own age

kuro-fune the American Black Ships that sailed into Edo Bay in 1853
kyoiku-mama 'education mother', or 'wife of a well-paid *sararii-man*'
kyu~kyu squeak, squeak
machii pre-*Meiji* city enclaves with people grouped by their profession
manju a steamed Japanese muffin
Marunouchi within the castle walls
matcha powdered green tea used in the tea ceremony
Meiji 'enlightened rule', the name given to the reign of the Emperor 1868–1912
Meiji-jingu the Shinto shrine which deifies the Emperor *Meiji*
miso paste made from fermented soybeans
mompe women's work pants
mon crest
mu nothingness
nakai-san maid
nakodo middleman who arranges marriages
nanakamado mountain ash or rowan tree
narikin new rich
nasu eggplant
natto fermented boiled soybeans mixed with soy sauce and *negi*
negi spring onion
NHK Nippon Hoso Kyokai, the government-run broadcaster
Nihom-bashi (Nippon Bridge) the hub of the five main *kaido*
niisan elder brother
Nippon (Japan) the source of the sun
nisei an American of Japanese ancestry born in the US
noh classical theatre in which actors wear masks
noren a split curtain in a shop or restaurant doorway indicating they're open
nori seaweed
obasan legal aunty
obi a wide sash worn with a *kimono*

Oishii how delicious
ojisan legal uncle
oka joki 'land steamer', the name jokingly given to the first train
okami-san exact translation 'lady general'
okasan mother
omozukai principal puppeteer in *bunraku*
on hierarchy of obligations
onsen hot spring
otomo male secretary
otosan father
otto referring to someone's husband, for example Eiko's *otto*
pachinko a type of pinball
palanquin portable litter
prefecture the unit of local administration used post the *Meiji* Revolution
purasuchikku-foodo fast-food replicated in plastic displays
ringi process of circulating a draft plan for collective approval
Rinzai Zen Zen sect popular with elite *samurai*, which concentrated on *koan*
roji dew ground or the water sprinkled garden
ryokan traditional Japanese inn
ryotei a traditional high-class restaurant serving haute-cuisine
sake rice wine
samurai a mediaeval warrior
san family name then -*san*, refers to a same or older generation male or female, relation or friend, used like Mr, Mrs or Miss
san-hachi the 38, a military rifle used in the Russo–Japanese War 1904–05
sanskrit sacred Indian script
Sanzu-no-kawa Sanzu River, the Buddhist Styx, the border between this world and the next
sararii-man a man from the educated, urban, middle class

sashimi   raw seafood
Sectarian Shinto   perpetuated family and ancestor worship post-*Meiji* Revolution up to the time of occupation
sencha   green tea made in a pot and given to guests or the elderly
senpai-kohai   senior–junior relationship existing between men of the same background
senryo-gun   occupation forces
sento   public bath-house
seppuku   suicide by piercing the abdomen, used exclusively by *samurai*
shamisen   traditional three-stringed instrument shaped like a banjo
shi   family name then *-shi* is used when addressing a senior male
shinchu-gun   stationary troops
Shinkansen   the Bullet train
shinso   a closeted maiden brought up with the utmost care
Shinto   the indigenous Japanese religion, meaning 'The Way of the Gods'
shiso   a herb
Shitamachi   literally Downtown, the working class district of Edo
sho   0.477 of a gallon, or a little less than a litre
shochu   low-class spirit
Shogun   literally the 'barbarian-subduing Great General', the pre-*Meiji* military ruler of Japan
shogunate or *bakufu*   military government
shoji   wooden latticed, paper screens used to divide rooms or cover windows
shusen   the termination of war
shushin   moral training
soba   thin noodles made from buckwheat and wheat flour
soba-ya   a noodle restaurant
Sodo Zen   Zen sect popular with warriors, which emphasised *zazen*

somen   delicate noodles made from wheat flour
State Shinto   perpetuated national loyalty and obedience by inculcating loyalty and obedience to the Emperor during the *Meiji* era, up until occupation
sugi   Japanese cedar
sukiyaki-ya   a restaurant where beef and vegetables are cooked at the table
sumo   a type of wrestling popular in Japan
Susanowo   the common name for *Takehaya-Susanowo*, the storm god
sushi-ya   a restaurant which serves *sushi* and *sashimi*
sutra   texts derived from the Buddha and other enlightened beings
tabi   two-toed Japanese socks worn with a *kimono*
Takehaya-Susanowo   the Valiant-Impetuous-Storm-God
taifu   typhoon
tansu   portable wooden storage chest
tatami   aromatic woven matting edged with fabric, roughly one by two metres
tayu   chanter in *bunraku* puppet theatre
Tendai   the Buddhist school that acted as guardian for the Imperial Family
Todai   the common name for Tokyo Imperial University
tofu   bean curd made from pulped soybeans
Tokaido   the 600-kilometre highway between Edo and Kyoto
Tokko   civilian Special Higher Police or 'Thought Police'
tokkotai   Special Attack Force, namely *kamikaze* bombers and *kaiten*
tokonoma   an alcove in a room where flowers or a scroll are displayed
Tokyo   Eastern capital, the new name for Edo after the *Meiji* Revolution

Tokugawa the family name of the dynasty that ruled Japan between 1603 and 1867
tonari-gumi compulsory, self-governing, wartime neighbourhood associations
tonkatsu-ya a pork cutlet restaurant
Tora! Tora! Tora! Tiger! Tiger! Tiger!
torii traditional gateway to a Shinto shrine
tsubo one *tsubo* is equivalent to two *tatami* mats
tsukemono pickled vegetables
udon thick noodles made with wheat flour
ukiyoe woodblock prints of life in Edo
unagi eel
unagi-ya a restaurant serving grilled eel
wabi the state of being quietly clear and calm
wagashi confectionary made from sweet bean paste
wasabi Japanese horseradish made from grated *wasabi* root
ya restaurant

yakitori Japanese style shish-kebab
yakitori-ya a restaurant selling *yakitori*
yakuza a gangster, member of an organised crime syndicate
Yamanote Uptown
yami-ichi black market
Yasukuni-jinja the shrine dedicated to fallen soldiers
yatai mobile, open-air stalls
yen Japanese currency
yukata light cotton summer *kimono*
yuzu Chinese lemons
zaibatsu family-owned financial clique comprising interconnected businesses
zazen sitting in religious contemplation
Zen its literal meaning, meditation, a Buddhist school which is split into two sects – *Rinzai* and *Sodo*
zori formal Japanese sandals worn with *kimono*
zukku canvas duck-shoes
zushin a Japanese sound effect, thumping

Bibliography

A Look into Japan – Japan Travel Bureau Inc, 1986

Aihara Kyoko, *Geisha: A Living Tradition* – Carlton Books Ltd, London 2000

Allinson Gary D, *Japan's Postwar History* (Second Edition) – Cornell University Press, New York 2004

Batty David, *Japan's War in Colour* – Carlton Books Ltd, London 2004

Benedict Ruth, *The Chrysanthemum and the Sword* – Secker & Warburg, London 1947

Bunce Dr William K, *Religions in Japan* – Charles E Tuttle Co, Tokyo 1955 (for the Civilian Information and Education Services, General Headquarters, Supreme Commander for the Allied Powers)

Christopher Robert C, *The Goliath Explained* – Charles E Tuttle Co, Tokyo 1983

Chronology of Japanese History – Bilingual Books, Kodansha International Ltd, Tokyo 1999

Dunn Charles J, *Everyday Life in Traditional Japan* – Tuttle Publishing, Boston 1972

Eating in Japan, Japan Travel Bureau Inc, 1991

Fahr-Becker Gabriele, *The Art of East Asia* (English Edition) – Konemann Verlagsgesellschaft mbH, Cologne 1999

Forrer Matthi, *Hiroshige* – Translated from the Dutch by Peter Mason, Prestel Publishing Ltd, London 2004

Gillespie Oliver A, *Official History of New Zealand in the Second World War 1939–45: The Pacific* – R E Owen, Government Printer 1952 (for the War History Branch, Department of Internal Affairs, Wellington New Zealand)

Golden Arthur, *Memoirs of a Geisha* – Vintage UK Random House, 1998

Hearn Lafcadio 1899, *In Ghostly Japan* – Tuttle Publishing, Tokyo 1971

Hearn Lafcadio 1890, *Writings from Japan* – Penguin Books Ltd, UK 1984

Insight Guides, *Japan* – APA Publications GmbH & Co Verlag K G (Singapore Branch) 2003

Insight Guides, *Tokyo* – APA Publications GmbH & Co Verlag K G (Singapore Branch) 2003

Ishida Takeshi, *Japanese Society* – University Press of America Inc, Washington 1971 (reprinted by arrangement with Random House Inc)

Japan: Profile of a Nation – Kodansha International Ltd, Tokyo 1995

Kamakura Keiko, *Guide Book for 50 Kabuki Masterpieces* – Seibido Shuppan K K, Tokyo 2004

Kawasaki Ichiro, *Japan Unmasked* – Charles E Tuttle Co, Tokyo 1969

Keene Donald, *Essays in Idleness* – Translation of essays written by the priest Kenko around 1330, Columbia University Press, New York 1998

Lafayette De Mente Boye, *Samurai Strategies: 42 Martial Secrets from Musashi's Book of Five Rings* – Tuttle Publishing, Singapore 2005

Lamont-Brown Raymond, *Kamikaze: Japan's Suicide Samurai* – Cassell Military Paperbacks, Cassell & Co, London 1997

Living Japanese Style – Japan Travel Bureau Inc, 1986

Man-tu Lee Anthony, *Zen* – Barron's Educational Series Inc, The Ivy Press Ltd, New York 2000

Maraini Fosco, *Meeting with Japan* – Hutchinson & Co Ltd, London 1959

Milton Giles, *Samurai William* – Hodder & Stoughton, London 2002

Munro David, *The Oxford Dictionary of the World* – Oxford University Press, Oxford 1995

Nakane Chie, *Japanese Society* (third printing) – Charles E Tuttle Co, Tokyo 1986

Nishi Kazuo and Hozumi Kazuo, *What is Japanese Architecture?* – English-language copyright, Kodansha International Ltd, Tokyo 1985

Notobe Inazo 1900, *Bushido: The Soul of Japan* – Kodansha International Ltd, Tokyo 2002

Okuzumi Yoshishige and Saotome Katsumoto, *Air-raid Tokyo (US Tactical Mission Report)* – K K Sanseido, Tokyo 1990

Ozawa Takeshi, *Kanto Big Earthquake Photographed* – K K Chikuma Shobo, Tokyo 2003

Pilgrim Ruri, *Fish of the Seto Inland Sea* – HarperCollins Publishers, London 2000

Richmond Simon and Dodd Jan, *The Rough Guide to Japan* (Third Edition) – Rough Guides Ltd, New York 2005

Sen Soshitsu, *Chado: The Japanese Way of Tea* – Weatherhill, New York 1979

Soseki Natsume 1905, *I am a Cat* – Translated by Aiko Ito and Graeme Wilson, Tuttle Publishing, North Clarendon USA 2002

Spector Ronald H, *Eagle Against the Sun: The American War with Japan* – First published in Great Britain by Viking, 1985

Spry-Leverton Peter and Kornicki Peter, *JAPAN* – Book Club Associates, by arrangement with Michael O'Mara Books, London 1987 (based on the television series 'JAPAN', produced for Channel Four by Central Independent Television plc)

Takashima Taiji, *Fountain of Japanese Proverbs* – K K Hokuseido Shoten, Tokyo 1981

The Collins Atlas of World History – William Collins Sons & Co Ltd, London 1987

The Constitution of Japan – Kashiwashobo Publishing Co Ltd, Japan 1993

Toson Shimazaki 1872, *Before the Dawn* – Translated by William E Naff, University of Hawaii Press, Honolulu 1987

Tsuchiya Yoshio, *The Fine Art of Japanese Food Arrangement* – Translated by Juliet Winters Carpenter, Kodansha International Ltd, Tokyo 1985

Tsuji Masanobu, *Singapore the Japanese Version* – Ure Smith Pty Ltd, Sydney 1960

Tsunetomo Yamamoto, *Hagakure The Book of the Samurai* – Translated by William Scott Wilson, Kodansha International Ltd, Tokyo 2002

Wells H G, *The Outline of History, Being a Plain History of Life and Mankind* – Cassell & Company Ltd, London 1920

Yoshihito Takada and Vardaman Jr James M, *Talking About Buddhism Q & A* – Bilingual Books, Kodansha International Ltd, Tokyo 1997

Yoshimura Akira, *Kanto Big Earthquake* – K K Bungei Shunjyu, Tokyo 1977

Tokyo Metropolitan Government Wartime Regulations

Acknowledgements

Numerous people have helped me give birth to this book. Over the years, their steadfast encouragement and support has fuelled and sustained my passion to write Hisashi's story.

To my friends in Japan, Seiichi Kobayakawa, Susumu Kojima, Kyoko and Tsuru Konishi, Matsuko Okamoto, Tomoko and Fumio Okita, Nobuhiko Sato, Chieko and Yoshio Tagaya, I give heartfelt thanks for their patience in answering my questions and searching for obscure information.

To my friends in Dunedin who read and re-read my words, my parents Margaret and the late Len Bell, Chrissy B Anderson, Lala Frazer, Sylvia and the late Douglas Girvan, Anna Marsich, Ella Shirley, Martin Stewart, Stuart Walker, and Chikako Van Koten, I am eternally grateful for their suggestions and their much needed listening skills. I am particularly indebted to Alison Adams who helped me edit the text as the story grew and grew, and who was always there when she was needed; to Lynley Hood for her wise words; to the late Reg Graham for his assistance in preserving Hisashi's photographs; and to Toni Plant, whose massage skills helped me survive the years of sitting at the computer.

Thank you also to everyone at Longacre Press who brought my book safely and skilfully through its labour, in particular my editor Barbara Larson.